Kitchen Technique

Kitchen

Technique

A Complete Guide to Practical Cooking

Wendy James, Gill Edden & Grizelda Lorford

Consultant editor: Norma MacMillan

Crescent Books · New York

This 1982 edition is published by Crescent Books
Distributed by Crown Publishers, Inc.

Printed in Italy

h g f e d c b a

Library of Congress Cataloging in Publication Data
Main entry under title:

Kitchen technique.

   1. Cookery.   I. James, Wendy.
TX651.K58   641.5   82-5028
ISBN 0-517-37741-1   AACR2

Photographs were supplied by: Editions Atlas, Editions
Atlas/Cedus, Editions Atlas/Masson, Edition Atlas/Zadora,
Breville, Electrolux, Mary Evans Picture Library, Flour
Advisory Board, Archivio IGDA, Lavina Press Agency,
Mansell Collection, Orbis GmbH, Ronan Picture Library,
Tate & Lyle Refineries, Thermador.

Line illustrations by Kate Simunek
Home economist – Jilly Cubitt

Photographs on pages 2–9 show techniques in the making
of filet de boeuf en croûte (recipe on page 185)

Photography by Paul Williams
Home economist, Jane Suthering

Contents

Introduction

Where do you start when you're choosing equipment for your kitchen, stocking up your pantry, filling your freezer or cooking a meal? With this excellent guide to cooking techniques on your bookshelf, you have the answer immediately in front of you.

With this practical book you can learn the complete art of kitchencraft. It's perfect for beginners yet a must for the more experienced cook. It begins with the art of food preparation – you can learn, for instance, how to chop and dice vegetables, cut up a chicken, scale a fish and segment an orange.

The book then guides you through the maze of equipment available for all the different methods of cooking and explains the advantages and disadvantages of each. There's also information on blenders and grinders, knives, beaters and bowls, food processors and microwave ovens. All the facts are there to help you make those important decisions about what to buy that's best for you.

From here *Kitchen Technique* goes on to help you cook the most delicious meals for your family and friends. Whether you're making simple family suppers or cooking for a company dinner you'll find all the recipes and hints you'll need.

Each method of cooking is dealt with in a separate chapter, beginning with the techniques you'll need to master to produce the best results. Alongside these techniques you'll find a glossary of world-wide terms associated with that method. These are followed by easy-to-read charts that show, at a glance, how long it takes to, say, boil an egg, steam a globe artichoke, fry onions rings or roast beef.

Each chapter includes a selection of recipes that are cooked by that method. In the chapter on boiling, for example, the opening recipes teach you how to make basic stock and progress from there to soups — minestrone, consommé, Normandy shellfish soup, to name but a few. Recipes then follow for spaghetti, honey-glazed ham and poached salmon, finishing with oranges à la turque and apricot mousse.

Other chapters are just as diverse; in baking you'll learn how to make bread, cookies, cakes, filet de boeuf en croûte, pizza, cheese soufflé and coffee caramel ring.

Color pictures throughout *Kitchen Technique* show you what the finished dishes will look like. Each recipe includes how long it takes to prepare, how many it serves and what equipment you'll need. Where a recipe is suitable for freezing, instructions are given for packaging, storage and thawing. Ingredients are listed in cup and spoon measures, in the order in which they're used. Clear step-by-step instructions mean that every time you cook a recipe the results will be perfect, and throughout the book you'll find clever tips for saving time and effort in the kitchen, little items of cook's know-how to help you make the most of your food.

There's also a chapter on preserving, which covers smoking and drying, making jams, jellies and marmalades, canning fruit and freezing. The freezing section includes charts detailing preparation, packaging, storage time and uses for meat, fish, poultry, vegetables, fruit and problem foods: all designed to help you get the most from your freezer. It then shows you how to 'chain cook' foods such as apples, ground meat and simple pie pastry to their best advantage.

The final chapter in *Kitchen Technique* deals with garnishes. Concise, easy-to-read instructions with clear illustrations show you how to give your food a professional finish. Learn how to make butter roses, carrot flowers, radish waterlilies and fluted mushrooms. Know when to use herbs and greenery for decorating and what to coat in nuts, poppy seeds, sesame seeds and peppercorns. There's also a section on cooked garnishes – bacon rolls, carrot balls, croûtons and celery bundles – each to lend appeal to soups and main courses. A chapter on garnishing and presentation would not be complete without cake and dessert decoration; all the tricks of the trade are here for you to follow.

From start to finish *Kitchen Technique* is the book you'll turn to for clear, easy-to-follow and complete information. It's more than a recipe book and it's more than a reference book. With *Kitchen Technique* by your side you'll quickly master the arts of the kitchen yourself.

Food preparation and equipment

The preparation of food is perhaps the least glamorous of all the different aspects of cooking, yet despite this it is still one of the most important. A dish that contains improperly prepared ingredients, for example, can be totally spoiled – in exactly the same way as it can by the use of poor quality ingredients or an incorrect cooking method. Many cooks gloss over the preparation part of cooking, hastily throwing unprepared ingredients into the pot in the vain hope that this will go unnoticed in the finished dish. Yet a few extra minutes spent at the preparation stage always pays dividends with the end result. Take peeling oranges. It is a simple enough job with the right equipment and the right technique, yet dishes like Pommes Bristol (apples and oranges in vanilla-flavored syrup) or Turkish oranges (whole sliced oranges in caramel), in which the fruit is the main ingredient, can so easily be ruined by unsightly and inedible pieces of white membrane.

Food preparation is unglamorous because it is the behind-the-scenes work for which the cook takes very little credit. Family and guests might remark on the perfect piping or the pretty garnish, but they are unlikely to comment about how well the carrots have been sliced!

Don't be discouraged by this, but take comfort in knowing that the standard of your cooking will be much higher if you spend more time and trouble on preparation. And remember when entertaining that the more time spent beforehand on preparation means more time with your guests.

Part and parcel of the whole preparation scene is careful organization. Food should be prepared at the right time for the finished dish, both to ensure it is used in prime condition and to avoid panics and rushes at the end. If it is not to be used immediately, it should be stored correctly – or all the valuable preparation will obviously be lost. Therefore before embarking on a recipe, especially an unfamiliar one, read it through from beginning to end at least once, to be aware of the different preparation processes that will be needed. There is nothing more infuriating than coming across an ingredient in a recipe that needs previous soaking.

Modern discoveries about loss of vitamins in cooking have led to a variety of views about cutting food into small or large pieces and about peeling (most nutrients lie just below the skin). Choosing the correct kind of preparation for the ingredient in hand is vitally important – if the food is to be cooked properly. Simple though this may sound, it is not always so easy in practice. Many good examples of clever preparation can be learned from the Chinese and Japanese, because the whole art of oriental cooking relies completely on preparation. Most oriental dishes are cooked over extremely high heat for a very short time; for this reason the actual cooking is one of the simplest of all cooking methods. What the diner does not usually see is the amount of time, skill and effort that has gone into the preparation of the various ingredients. Fast cooking over high heat necessitates the food being prepared in special ways: meat is most often sliced very thinly *across* the grain, for example, which allows the heat to reach the meat fibers quickly and tenderize them at a faster rate than if the meat were cut into chunks. Shredding is another example of special preparation, and a common form of preparing vegetables in oriental cooking. Carrots that are shredded can be stir fried in a minute or two for example, rather than in the 10–20 minutes they take by the more conventional method of slicing and boiling. So when preparing food, think ahead to the cooking method and coordinate this with the method of preparation.

Correct preparation is not only vital if the food is to be cooked properly, it is also essential to ensure that food tastes good and is easy to digest. Salting is a good example of this: salt is sprinkled onto certain watery foods which are then left to stand until the moisture is drawn out. Salting is used with eggplants to draw out their moisture for two reasons: eggplant juices taste bitter when cooked, and undrained eggplant flesh absorbs so much oil when fried that it can be indigestible.

Cucumbers and zucchini that are to be fried should be salted, otherwise their water will be released into the cooking fat and prevent them from cooking properly. Tomato shells and cucumber boats that are hollowed out to be stuffed must also be salted, otherwise their fillings or stuffings will become watery and therefore insipid or even tasteless.

Fish is another ingredient that needs careful and correct preparation if it is to be easy to digest and, no less important, to avoid wastage. This is true of any food that contains bones, particularly poultry, since incorrect boning can lead to large quantities of flesh being lost. Bones (and scales in the case of fish) are also unpleasant, just as pits and seeds are in fruit, especially in composite dishes such as pies and puddings.

It may take a little time and plenty of practice before you can chop vegetables in swift, even slices, or cut up a chicken in a matter of minutes. But providing you follow the correct techniques, speed and proficiency will follow naturally.

In the following pages the do's and dont's, the whys and wherefores of food preparation are explained in alphabetical order. The art of good cooking is in the preparation – so what better place to start?

Food techniques

barding

Covering food, usually meat or poultry, with a protective layer of fat before roasting, to compensate for a lack of natural fat (see also page 122). The fat melts and bastes the meat during roasting.

beating

To incorporate air into a food or foods or to combine ingredients, using a spoon, whisk or electric mixer.

binding

To combine ingredients by adding a beaten egg or a thick roux sauce so the food will hold its shape during cooking. Used for croquettes, meatballs, salads.

blanching

Food is plunged into boiling water quickly to make skins of tomatoes, onions, nuts etc, easy to remove.

boning

Removing part or all of the skeleton from meat, poultry or fish to allow for the next stage of preparation (eg, stuffing or rolling), or for easier serving and eating (see also pages 118, 121).

breading

To coat food with flour and beaten egg, then with fine dry bread, cracker or other crumbs to provide a crust when cooked.

bruising

To crush an ingredient without breaking it into pieces, in order to release its flavor. Mostly done to fresh ginger root, garlic or herbs like mint.

chilling

Reducing the temperature of an ingredient or mixture by leaving it in a cold place, to make it easier to shape or to set it.

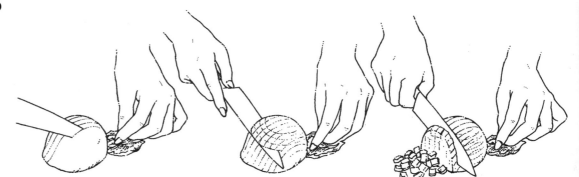

Fold back skin, cut along length   *Holding root, cut horizontally*   *Cut downwards to separate bits*

chopping

Chopping should produce pieces of even size but of a random shape (see also dicing). Firm-textured foods are often halved, cut lengthwise into strips or slices, then piled up and cut across lengths into pieces. The food is halved to create a flat surface so it can't slip. To chop small foods (parsley or nuts): place on a board. Hold a heavy knife at the tip to keep it down on the board and with other hand raise the blade and lower it sharply onto the food. By holding the tip down and raising and lowering the knife while moving it in an arc on the board, the food can be kept together in a thin layer as it is being chopped into even smaller pieces. Meat with bones is chopped with a cleaver into small pieces for stews and casseroles.

Hold tip of knife down, raise and lower blade onto the nuts, traveling in an arc

To chop an onion: cut in half lengthwise from top to root end, peel the loose skin back over the root but do not remove. With cut side on board, hold skin firmly near root to steady onion while keeping fingers away from the knife. Cut downwards at $\frac{1}{4}$ inch intervals, beginning cut at root end. Now make horizontal cuts into the onion, working towards root. Chop down at right angles to first cuts – this releases root and skin and divides onion evenly.

coating

Done to protect food from heat, to prevent liquid seeping out, to stop fragile foods disintegrating, or to give contrasting outer texture. Coatings – most applied before frying – can be egg and breadcrumbs, seasoned flour, oatmeal or batter. Sauces are also used to coat foods before baking or serving. Also called breading.

coring

Removing core from fruit or vegetables. Use a special corer for fruit, rotating it so it reaches core and seeds. Use vegetable peeler to dig out woody stems of vegetables.

cracking

To break shells to extract kernels from nuts, or to remove flesh from crustaceans

(crab, lobster). Pits of peaches, apricots are cracked to remove flavorful kernels.

crushing

Breaking an ingredient into small particles with a knife (use flat part of the blade), pestle or rolling pin, or in a blender, juicer or food processor. Garlic can be crushed in a special garlic press or, if using a knife, a board. Cookies, crackers and nuts can be crushed between sheets of waxed paper or in a plastic bag with a rolling pin.

cutting

Dividing food vertically, horizontally or diagonally into portions, sections, slices, strips, dice, pieces, chunks and cubes to decrease cooking time or break up connective tissue. In pastry and cookie making, special cutters are used for shapes.

cutting in

To mix fat (shortening, butter, margarine, lard, etc.) into flour for making pastry. The mixture is reduced to tiny flour-coated particles of fat using two knives or a pastry blender.

cutting up

To divide meat or poultry into manageable pieces before cooking. To cut chicken into

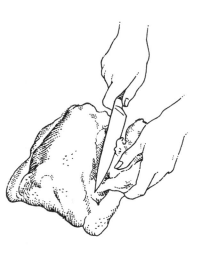

1 To cut up a chicken, push legs out and away from the body and with a sharp knife sever the joint where leg is attached to carcass

2 Remove the other leg in the same way. Now change to poultry shears which are needed to cut through the wishbone and part of ribs

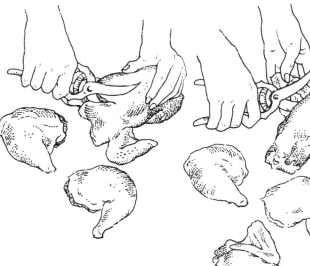

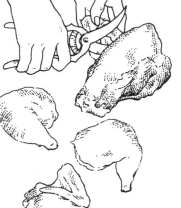

3 Carefully remove one wing, cutting into the carcass so that the wing is surrounded with some breast making it more substantial

4 Remove the second wing in the same way, leaving the carcass in a compact shape

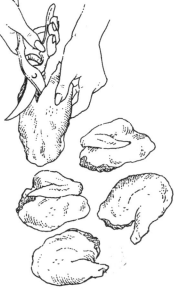

5 Still using shears, cut away the ribs and backbone in one piece — they form the base of the carcass
6 Divide the breast into two equal parts to give 6 pieces. To make 8 pieces, divide each leg at the joint to separate thigh and drumstick

6 pieces, push the legs away from the body and cut through the joint where the leg is attached to the carcass to remove the legs. Cut through the breast just above the place where the wing is attached to the carcass to remove the wing with a small portion of breast attached. Repeat with the other wing. Using poultry shears cut the base of the carcass (the ribs and backbone) away from the breast section. Cut through the breastbone to divide the breast into two. By dividing the leg portions at the joint the chicken is cut into 8 even-sized pieces.

degorger

French culinary term meaning to drain out impurities. Draining, salting, soaking are the most common ways to "*dégorge*" food.

desalting

To remove excess salt from foods. Soaking in water is the best way — salt fish should be covered with cold water and left for a minimum of 12 hours. The food is then drained, covered with fresh cold water, brought to a boil and drained again before further cooking. Anchovies (canned and fresh) should be soaked in milk or water for about 20 minutes.

dicing

To cut into tiny cubes. First cut the food into thin slices lengthwise to make very thin matchstick strips. Stack the strips together in a neat pile and cut across the strips to make tiny dice. An excellent example of dicing can be found in a mirepoix.

dissolving

To mix a dry ingredient such as cornstarch, sugar or gelatin into a liquid until the dry ingredient has completely disappeared.

draining

To drain off juices from food, either because they taste unpleasant, or because they will interfere with the cooking.

drawing

A term which applies to feathered poultry and game and fish. It means to remove the innards (see page 120). For poultry and game, it is done simply by inserting your hand into the body cavity and quite literally "drawing" out everything you find! Ready-to-cook poultry and game has already been drawn. Round fish can be drawn through the belly which is slit open with a knife or scissors. Place the flat of the blade behind the entrails and slide them out. (Do this on a sheet of paper which can be wrapped around the waste to dispose of it neatly.)

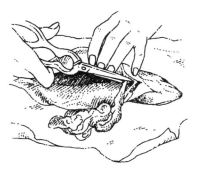

Round fish to be served whole are drawn through the gills. Grasp the fish in one hand and twist its head to one side. Push a finger inside the gills and hook it under the entrails; draw them out and snip off. Rinse fish and pat dry.

dressing

This is a loose term to describe plucking, singeing, drawing and trussing of poultry and feathered game (see page 120). The preparation of fish, also referred to as dressing, embraces trimming, scaling, and drawing. Dressing a crab includes both the cleaning and the final presentation of the meat in the shell.

filleting

The term that describes dividing fish lengthwise into boneless sections. The method used depends on whether the fish is round or flat.
To fillet round fish: scale, cut off head, tail and fins, and gut through the belly. Place opened fish flesh down on board and press firmly along backbone with thumbs to loosen it. Turn fish over, release bone with knife and lift out carefully so rib bones are also removed. Cut along center to divide into 2 fillets.
To fillet small round fish: cut off heads and gut through belly. Hold fish open under running water so the force of the water separates fish into 2 fillets and washes out the backbone.
To fillet flat fish: cut off head, trim fins off with kitchen scissors. Cut through fish along backbone. Slip knife blade under flesh on one side of the backbone. Using back and forth sawing motion with flat blade always scraping against the rib bones, gradually work the fillet away from the bones and detach. Remove the second fillet in the same way. Turn fish over and repeat on other side to divide into 4 fillets.
To divide a flat fish into 2 fillets: cut off head. Hold tail, make cut into flesh inserting knife at a 45° angle so cutting edge is away from you and pressed against the bones. Make a sweeping cut towards the head to remove the whole side of the fish. Repeat on the other side, but do not remove skin or the halves will divide in two.

folding in

The term used to describe the gentle process of combining two ingredients or mixtures — at least one of which has been aerated by whipping or beating — losing little air. It is done either by a figure of eight action or under and over till ingredients are well combined.

grating

Rubbing food in an up and down motion against different sized holes with cutting edges which reduce it to fine pieces or granules. Rotary graters are most often used for cheese or chocolate which would soften if hand held. The colored part of orange and lemon rind is grated on a fine grating surface and a brush is needed to remove bits that cling.

grinding

To reduce food by tiny particles or even to a powder, by using either a hand or an electric grinder. Most types of grinder are adjustable so the size of the grounds can be varied according to taste or individual recipes. Meat is ground by being pushed through holes of varying size and chopped off in lengths by revolving blades. This breaks up connective tissue, tenderizing the meat and shortening cooking time.

hulling

To remove leaves and stems from berries before serving or cooking. Use your fingertips or a small pincer-like device called a huller.

husking

To remove the outside leaves and silk from an ear of corn before cooking.

infusing

To season a liquid by soaking a flavoring agent in it. Also called steeping, this is how tea and coffee are made. When the liquid is heated, this process is called mulling.

juicing

To extract juice from fruits, usually oranges, lemons, pineapple, grapefruit, by crushing flesh, then straining. Vegetable juices are purées, obtained by processing.

larding

To thread meats that have little or no natural fat with strips of fat or *lardoons*, using a special larding tool (*lardoire*) or larding needle. The fat is literally "sewn" in at regular intervals, either on the surface or through the meat parallel with the grain of the meat (see also page 114).

liquidizing

Reducing a solid to a liquid in a liquidizer, also called an electric blender or vitamizer, or food processor with a special attachment.

macerating

To soften by steeping. Usually applied to sweet foods (marinating is used for savory) like fresh fruits steeped in sugar before jam making, or in spirits or liqueurs for desserts. Dried fruit for cakes, desserts is often macerated in alcohol to give flavor and plumpness.

marinating

To soak food in a liquid or pickle. called a marinade. Originally a fisherman's technique for fish (hence the name), meat too is marinated to make it tender or add flavor. A marinade should contain an acid such as wine, vinegar or lemon juice which acts on the muscle fibers in the meat or poultry, breaking them down and helping to make meat or poultry more tender. Most marinades also contain oil, spices, herbs and other flavoring ingredients. Marinating times vary, but the usual rule is up to 6 hours for small items, up to 24 hours for large. If a marinade is to be used longer than this, it should be strained and reboiled every two days. Cool before using again.

mashing

To break down food by pressing it to pulp. An electric blender or food processor will also mash food. Soft fruit like bananas and vegetables like avocados can be mashed with a fork. Other foods have to be at least partially cooked before mashing is possible, using a potato masher or ricer, or a vegetable masher which is similar to a pestle.

measuring

The first stage of preparation when following a recipe in order to achieve intended results. Standard measuring cups and spoons are used

for both liquid and dry ingredients. Spoons and cups of dry ingredients should be leveled by running the back of a knife across the top. Liquids have a convex shape, so measure required amount at eye level.

milling

Using a machine to grind ingredients by crushing them between two hard, rough surfaces. The term is used for peppercorns, coarse salt and wheat, whether ground commercially or at home.

mincing

To reduce to very fine pieces.

paring

Cutting a fine, top layer of skin or rind from fruit or vegetables without removing the white membrane. Parings, especially from citrus fruits, are often used as a flavoring before being discarded.

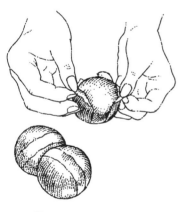

peeling

To remove the protective outer layer from fruits or vegetables. Some fruits are easily peeled with the fingers but others, and most vegetables, need a short-bladed knife or special peeler. After cooking, vegetable skins are removed more easily.

piercing

To make a hole, usually with the tip of a knife or a fine skewer. Lobsters are killed when the nerve behind the head is severed by piercing (see also pricking).

pitting

Removing the elongated or round hard pit from center of fruits to make them easier to eat, or for stuffing. Remove pit with a special gadget which punches it out, or by slitting fruit and prising it out. Fruits can be cooked whole and the pits removed later. Sometimes, especially in jam-making, peach, apricot and plum pits are cracked so the kernels can be used to add almond flavor to other fruit.

podding

To remove peas and beans from their cases — squeeze the sides of the pods gently so they pop open and the seeds can be detached. Young tender pods are sliced, or trimmed and eaten whole (eg, snap beans, sugar peas); good quality pods can be used for soup.

pounding (1)

To flatten meat by beating with a meat mallet, rolling pin or the side of a cleaver, to tenderize it and to shorten cooking time (see also page 88). Effective with veal and thin steaks.

pounding (2)

To divide an ingredient into small pieces or even a paste by pressing it, usually in a mortar with a pestle. Fish that has been dried is often pounded to break down fibers; octopus is beaten to tenderize them. Nuts, garlic or anchovies are reduced to a paste to release flavors and give a smooth consistency.

pricking

Puncturing foods with a fork or fine skewer. Fruits and vegetables for baking are pricked to allow steam to escape, preventing bursting. Pie crusts are pricked to release air trapped under-neath and prevent doming. Pricking duck before roasting allows fat to escape and baste the bird [see also piercing].

proving

A term used in bread making to describe the rekindling of life in compressed or active dry yeast. This is done by dissolving the yeast in lukewarm liquid, sometimes with a little sugar added to help the yeast "work". If the yeast liquid froths after 5 to 20 minutes, it "proves" that the yeast is alive and will raise the bread dough.

puréeing

To reduce cooked foods to a smooth pulp. Rubbing food through a sieve gives an even consistency: food mills have several sieving plates to vary textures. Electric blenders and food processors with blades revolving at high speeds purée foods fast.

rendering

To separate liquid fat from its surrounding, as drawing the fat from bacon over gentle heat. This is done either to get rid of the fat or to make it usable for frying, etc.

ricing

Forcing cooked potatoes through a mechanical sieve called a ricer. The sieve holes cause the potatoes to come out in shreds resembling rice — hence the name.

rinsing

To wash food under cold running water to remove dirt, peelings or salt (see salting). Unless foods are to be cooked in water, dry them before cooking.

salting

As well as emphasizing the flavor of foods, salt draws out water by osmosis. This is especially important when preparing watery vegetables like cucumber or tomatoes for frying or stuffing. Any bitter juices can be removed from eggplants by sprinkling with salt. Because salt has this effect, tender meats should not be salted before broiling

or frying or the result will be dry; tougher cuts like brisket of beef are "corned" to tenderize fibers.

sawing

To cut with a serrated-edged blade in a to and fro motion. Hard foods such as bones can only be cut with a kitchen saw. Frozen blocks of food are sawn into required sizes with a frozen-food knife with an especially tough serrated edge.

scalding

To heat within a few degrees of boiling point. A technique used in distinct ways in cooking — to sterilize equipment and jars when preserving; to heat liquids till almost boiling to infuse flavorings.

scaling

To remove scales from fish before cooking if fish is to be served in its skin which may be eaten. Scrape skin with the back of a knife or a fish scaler against the direction in which scales lie. Work from tail to head on paper to collect the scales, then rinse fish and pat dry.

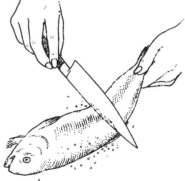

scoring

Incising or making a shallow cut in the surface of a food such as a skin or rind, to prevent bursting (baked apples) or to encourage the food to cook thoroughly (broiled whole fish). Bases of some vegetables are scored with a cross to reduce cooking time. The fat on meat may be scored to prevent the edges curling during cooking.

scraping

Scratching away the surface of fruit or vegetables with a knife. Foods with a very thin skin, such as new carrots or potatoes, or asparagus stalks, are scraped rather than peeled so fewer nutrients are lost.

scrubbing

Washing by rubbing with a stiff, wet brush to remove dirt from skin of vegetables, especially those with ridged or wrinkled surfaces (celery, jerusalem artichokes). Shell-fish should be scrubbed.

seasoning

Enhancing the taste of foods by the addition of salt, pepper or other spices which not only add, but also emphasize flavors. Salt is added to meats after cooking as it tends to draw out the juices, delaying browning.

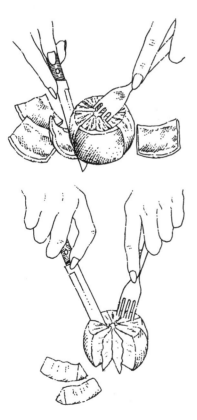

segmenting

To divide citrus fruits into their natural divisions. Cut slice off top and bottom. Hold the fruit by spearing on a fork, then, using a serrated knife, cut away the rind and white membrane from the flesh. Cut on either side of each membrane to release segments. Often grapefruits are halved and a cut made between the flesh and rind with a curved knife, then segments are loosened as above. The membrane network can then be lifted out and discarded and the fleshy segments can be left in the shell for serving.

shelling

Removing shells or hard outer layers of nuts, eggs or shell-fish. Crack nuts by squeezing between hinged metal nut-crackers. Hard shelled crustaceans are cracked open with a hammer to remove flesh. Other shellfish and hard-cooked eggs have thin brittle shells which can be peeled away with fingers. Some vegetables are said to be shelled (see podding).

shredding

Cutting food into fine strips with a large knife or an electric shredder to shorten cooking times and make foods easier to eat. Cabbage is cut into quarters so the core is removed, then the wedges are sliced thinly. Turn wedges as you shred so strips are not too long. Lettuce leaves and other delicate greens are loosely rolled and shredded with a very sharp knife to prevent bruising. Cheese is shredded on a grater with fairly large openings.

shucking

To remove the edible parts of a fish from a shell or vegetable from a pod (see also podding). The term, however, is used mainly for oysters. To shuck an oyster, hold firmly in a cloth and insert a short thick bladed knife into the "eye" at the hinged end. Twist the blade to prise open the shell, break off top shell. Loosen the flesh but leave it in the shell to serve.

sieving

To rub or push cooked foods through a mesh to remove any seeds, core or tough fibers and make a smooth purée (see also puréeing).

sifting

Shaking dry ingredients through a fine-meshed sieve to remove any lumps; or to mix ingredients such as spices and leavening agents into flour, and to aerate the mixture. This is essential to add extra air to cakes, cookies made by the creaming method.

skinning

Removing the outer membrane from some fruits, vegetables, furred game and fish. Skins of fruits and vegetables are often loosened by dipping them into boiling water (see blanching), then stripping the skin away with the fingers. Whole flat fish can be skinned by cutting through the skin just above the tail and tearing the skin towards the head. To skin an eel, make a cut behind the head, grip the skin and tear if off towards the tail. Fish fillets are placed skin down on a board and a knife is slipped between the flesh and skin so the blade is held at an angle of 45° (see filleting). See also page 114 for skinning furred game.

slashing

To cut open with a knife in a single, random movement. Slashes are made in the sides of fish to allow the heat of a broiler or oven to penetrate, or in pastry lids before cooking so the filling can be seen.

slicing

Dividing food into flat pieces of desired thickness with a knife or a fixed or revolving blade. When slicing with a knife, regulate the thickness of the slices (and slice more safely) by positioning the fingers and cutting vertically

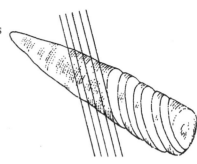

through the food. Move the fingers back along the food to give the desired thickness, position the knife as before and remove the next slice. With practice, this can be done at high speeds. The food can also be divided into diagonal slices which have a much larger surface area. Tender meat is cut into fine slices and strips across the grain for stir frying.

snipping

Cutting fresh herbs into tiny bits straight into mixtures with kitchen scissors reduces time and dish washing.

soaking

To immerse food in a liquid to soften it or reduce strong flavors or colors, or to make it more digestible. Dried legumes are soaked overnight in cold water (or brought to the boil, boiled for 2 minutes, and left to stand, covered, for 2 hours) to soften them, and reduce the cooking time. Some variety meat is soaked to remove impurities and odor. Sometimes potatoes are soaked to draw out excess starch – generally, however, vegetables should not be left to soak as they lose crispness and valuable nutrients.

sponging

To soak a setting agent in liquid till it softens and absorbs the liquid. It is not necessary with gelatin, but isinglass, and the vegetarian agar-agar and carrageen which are both from seaweeds, are all sponged before being dissolved.

squeezing

The same as juicing in terms of fruit. The word can also be applied to foods which are wrapped in cloth and squeezed dry — duxelles, for example, made with finely chopped mushrooms, onion and shallot, are placed in a dish towel and it is twisted tightly to extract moisture before frying.

straining

To pour liquids through a fine-meshed sieve in order to remove unwanted particles.

stretching

To make bacon slices longer and thinner before lining a terrine, making bacon rolls or barding chicken. Place the bacon slice on a board and, as you press down and away with the back of a large knife, pull the slice towards you.

stringing

To remove the coarse filament from the seams of edible pods or celery. Cut through the tip of the pod but don't cut through the "string". Pull it along the length of the vegetable and discard it. Repeat at the other end of

the pod to remove string from the other side. Celery strings can be removed together by pulling trimmed top of stalk downwards.

stuffing

To fill a cavity in meat, poultry, game, fish, fruit or vegetables. Stuffing, also called dressing, improves flavor, corrects fattiness or dryness and extends serving portions.

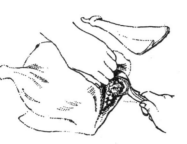

temperature

In food preparation the temperature of the kitchen and ingredients is sometimes very important. Eggs to be beaten need to be at room temperature (they'll take 30–40 minutes to reach 65° from the refrigerator). In pastry making, ingredients and equipment (including hands) need to be as cool as possible; in bread making, everything needs to be warm so while yeast is proving, warm flour and the bowl too. In jam making, warm the sugar so that it doesn't reduce the temperature of the fruit too much and will dissolve much more quickly, stopping scum. Chocolate won't melt well, and egg whites won't thicken well if there's too much humidity in the kitchen.

tossing

A method of coating food in a dressing or sauce by lifting and mixing ingredients together lightly with two spoons or salad servers. Foods are coated with seasoned flour or breadcrumbs by tossing them in a plastic bag.

trimming

To neaten the shape and general appearance of food by cutting away inedible parts (skin on meat, fins, heads and tails of fish, stalks and stems of fruit and vegetables). Meat can also be trimmed of fat. Edges of pastry are trimmed before baking.

trussing

To fasten poultry, game or boned meat into a compact shape with string and/or skewers before cooking to give a neat appearance, ensure even heat distribution and make carving easier. (See also page 121.)

vandyking

Term used to describe zigzag cuts in skin or rind of fruit (usually lemons, oranges, melons and tomatoes) to give a "pointed beard" shape (after Van Dyck the painter). Fish tails left on for serving are "vandyked" when trimmed to a V shape.

warming

An important part of yeast cooking — room, ingredients and equipment should be warm (76–82°) or the yeast will not be activated. In preserving, sugar should be placed in the oven to warm before adding to fruit — cold sugar dissolves slowly and thus lengthens boiling time. Wheatgerm and wholewheat flour which are often stored in the refrigerator to prevent them going rancid should be brought to room temperature or warmed in the oven before use.

washing

To agitate vegetables and fruit in cold water to clean them before cooking. To avoid loss of nutrients, never wash them in warm water and don't leave vegetables to soak.

whipping

To beat cream with a rotary or electric beater or whisk

till aerated and of required consistency. The trick is to have a bowl deep enough so that the cream is always over the beaters; everything must be cold.

whisking

A mechanical method of incorporating air into egg whites and egg-based mixtures or cream with a special tool called a whisk.

wiping

Cleaning meats, fish or vegetables with paper towels or damp cloth (see also page 115).

wrapping

To protect food from air, heat or water by enclosing it in foil, plastic wrap, wax paper, cheesecloth, or a different food (such as pastry or vine or lettuce leaves).

zesting

The zest of citrus fruit is the oil in the rind, the part that gives the fruit its color, aroma and flavor. Zest can be extracted with a special tool called a zester, which scrapes the outer part of the skin, or the finest side of the grater. If zest is required for sweet dishes, rub a sugar cube against the skin till impregnated, then crush before use.

Knives

1 *Small vegetable knife* 2 *Grapefruit knife* 3 *Boning knife* 4 *Chopping/general knife* 5 *Cook's knife* 6 *Bread knife* 7 *Carving knife* 8 *Narrow metal spatula* 9 *Smoked salmon/ ham slice* 10 *Sharpening steel* 11 *Wooden knife rack* 12 *Electric carving knife* 13 *Meat cleaver* 14 *Frozen-food knife* 15 *Double-edged carving knife* 16 *Large cook's knife* 17 *Filleting knife* 18 *Fruit knife* 19 *Double-crescent chopper or mezzaluna* 20 *Crossed steel sharpener for serrated knives*

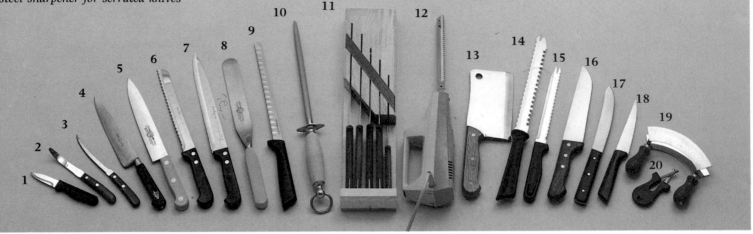

A good knife must have a sharp blade. Carbon steel is highly regarded because of its hard finish and sharp cutting edge, but it does blunt quickly. It also stains and rusts, so it needs a lot of care or it will discolor and give food a metallic flavor. After use, rub with a soft cloth or damp cork dipped in scouring powder, then rinse in warm water. Dry immediately and keep in a dry place. If you are not going to use the knife for a while, smear the blade with a little olive oil.

The alternative blade material is stainless steel, which has a less sharp cutting edge but it keeps sharp longer and never rusts. Edges can be flat ground (the sides of the blade are smooth), or hollow ground (the length of the blade has a marked bevel which gives it a thinner cutting edge that stays sharper longer).

Knives with serrated edges saw gently through soft foods such as tomatoes. Serrated edges are also found on bread and carving knives, though some have scalloped edges — the gaps between the teeth are wider and more curved. Double-edged knives have two edges, one straight and one with curved or square indentations. They should be stored in a guard for safety.

Always use a wooden chopping board (laminated or marble surfaces will blunt blades) and scrub frequently to prevent bacteria gathering. Straight-edged knives can be sharpened on a knife steel or a dampened Carborundum stone. Hold knife, with blade pointing away from you at a 45° angle to the steel, and with a light stroking movement, draw the knife toward you from base to tip, first on one side, then the other. The move-

ment is the same if you use a Carborundum stone. Sharpen serrated, scalloped or double blades with a small, crossed steel, drawing the blade through where it crosses. Home sharpening will eventually wear down the teeth of serrated knives, so it is advisable to have them professionally reground and sharpened. Store sharp knives separately from other kitchen utensils for safety's sake; a knife rack, magnetized bar or wooden case is best. When buying a knife make sure that: the blade is well riveted into the handle, not just glued on; it is well-balanced with a comfortable handle; and that it is the right length. A good knife will last for years and prove to be a sound investment if you choose wisely to begin with.

Vegetable knives need to be straight-edged with a blade of about 4 inches in length for chopping small vegetables (onions, carrots, celery) and paring and scraping. Longer blades — 10–12 inches — are best for chopping heftier vegetables (cabbage, turnip). They can also be used for chopping raw meat. Swivel-headed or rigid peelers are useful for paring fruit, coring apples, as well as peeling vegetables. Knives with small, thin blades, a fine serrated edge and a pointed tip are essential for slicing soft, squidgy or juicy fruits (tomatoes, oranges). They can also be used for segmenting grapefruit, although a more flexible curved knife has been invented for this. For finely chopping fresh herbs, garlic and onions, mezzaluna (curved-bladed "rocking" choppers with a handle at each end), and the automatic choppers that bounce up and down like kangaroos, are useful.

Meat knives come in a variety of shapes. A meat cleaver makes quick work of bones and the flat side can also be used for pounding meat. A boning knife is very sharp to cut through tough sinews. It is long and curved and should be held like a dagger. A carving knife should also be very sharp to cut cleanly without tearing the meat. The blades need to be about 1 inch wide with either a straight or scalloped edge. An electric carving knife is the most efficient. Double-edged knives, with heavy and fine toothed sides, will cut through dense blocks of frozen food.

Poultry shears are used for cutting up raw or roasted poultry — heavier ones are more likely to cut through bones. Sharp kitchen scissors with serrated edges make a lot of preparation easier (cutting bacon, snipping chives or parsley).

Fish filleting knives have a flexible, straight-edged blade with a pointed end, and should be between 6 and 10 inches long. The 10 inch size knife can also be used for carving whole cooked fish such as salmon.

Bread knives should be long-bladed and serrated or scalloped. A scalloped meat carving knife can be used for bread too.

Palette knives have a long flexible blade with a rounded end and are used for lifting cakes and cookies off baking sheets and spreading frosting on cakes.

Graters and slicers

Graters and slicers are designed to do what knives cannot do so well. Graters are able to reduce food to very fine slices or strands and slicers can slice thinly and evenly with the least amount of effort.

Most graters have two types of grating surface: small round holes which have a sharp jagged edge that tend to tear the food and produce compacted gratings without a distinct form. This surface is good for making breadcrumbs, but some foods clog up between the sharp points, so as you work you have to brush off the gratings.

The second type of surface is made up of holes shaped like fingernails, which have a protruding sharp, smooth-edged lip on which food is grated downwards into well-defined slivers. The larger holes will shred carrots, onions and potatoes; but don't use them for shredding cheese and suet as, roughly prepared, they will give you indigestion – shred them on medium-sized holes. The finest grating surfaces should be used for citrus fruit rinds and nutmeg.

Traditional graters are box or conical-shaped with a choice of three or four cutting surfaces and at least one slicing blade. You can stand them upright on a plate or dish, so they remain stable as you use them. For foods that only need shredding, grater bowls made of rigid plastic or metal are useful. The tight-fitting lids consist of a slicing blade and two sharp grating surfaces. Food is grated through the lid and into the bowl.

Rotary graters consist of a cylindrical cutting surface to which a handle is attached and it is housed in an outer casing with a top opening into which food is inserted and pressed against the cylinder. As the handle is turned, the food is shredded through the rotating grating surface. The cylinder must be close enough to the outer casing to prevent food becoming packed in between. Rotary graters come in metal or plastic, but the latter does tend to break. Some types also come with three cylinders with different grating sizes and they are ideal for grating small quantities of chocolate, suet, nuts and cheese directly into sauces. A food mill shreds, grates and slices raw vegetables, fruit, cheese and nuts, with special cutting disks in different sizes. The interchangeable disks slot into a bowl made of either plastic or metal and are rotated by a handle.

Slicers are generally made of stainless steel. There are two types – one with a circular blade, the other with a flat cutting edge.

Circular slicers have one or more circular slicing plates, which can be adjusted for different thicknesses of food and are able to slice food like ham and cheese into paper thin slices. These rotary slicers can usually be clamped on to a flat surface or held by a suction pad. The cast-iron rotary bean slicer has a clamp. Beans are fed through a small groove in the top edge of the plate and, as you turn the hand-crank, they emerge sliced at the bottom.

Flat slicers have either strong, thin wires which give a knife-like edge, or blades set into a wooden, plastic or metal form. Mandolines, invented by the French, look rather like a guillotine (but are used flat). They have two or three plain and fluted blades set into a narrow frame and are used for slicing vegetables, solid cheeses and other firm foods.

The simplest form of bean slicer has a plastic rectangular casing in which several slicing wires are set – each bean is pushed through the wires and is pulled out of the other side sliced.

1 Rotary grater 2 Stainless steel grater and shredder 3 Plastic cheese grater 4 Food mill 5 Mandoline 6 Grater and shredder bowl 7 Rotary bean slicer 8 Simple bean slicer

Beaters and bowls

Beaters are basic to creating more volume in an ingredient. They are also needed for making sauces and combining ingredients to given an even consistency. Beating increases volume by 7–8 times the original amount in egg whites and stretches the proteins to incorporate air bubbles. If you over-beat, air bubbles burst and the mixture collapses. With cream the combination of high butterfat and beaten-in air creates the desired thickness. Over-whipping will cause the cream to separate. Egg whites, even after being frozen, make much better foam if brought to room temperature before beating begins. Cream, on the other hand should be chilled, as should the bowl and beaters.

Both the shape and material of the bowl are important in beating. Top width is essential for egg whites where beating is done in the round, raising and lowering the beaters to incorporate air. Deepness is needed for cream so that the beaters are always covered. All bowls for beating either of these ingredients should have rounded bottoms as a flat bottom obstructs the action of the beaters.

Unlined copper bowls are ideal for egg whites for the slight acidity of the copper strengthens the walls of the air bubbles making a more stable foam of a greater volume. Aluminum and stainless steel discolor egg whites, and volume will not be as much in glass and stoneware as the eggs will not cling to the sides. Glass and stoneware, however, are perfect for cake batters. Plastic bowls are difficult to keep entirely grease-free (complete anathema to egg whites).

Wire whisks are made of loops of wire attached to a handle. Although quite a bit of muscle power is needed, they are the best to use as they can be moved around more freely, thus incorporating more air. The balloon whisk is the most efficient out of this group as the loops are wider at the bottom enabling air to be quickly forced in. A balloon whisk and a copper bowl are the best combination for eggs. Eggs should be one to three days old and at room temperature. Separate the yolks from the whites, making sure that no yolk whatsoever gets into the whites, then start beating the white slowly, working from the bottom of the bowl and lifting the whisk high in a circle in order to incorporate as much air as possible. When whites start foaming, increase the size of the circles so that you are using the whole bowl, and increase the speed until you are beating as fast as you can. When whites are stiff, continue beating fast, but with whisk down in the whites and in contact with the bowl to stiffen and "tighten" the whites rather than beating more air into them. Continue until a shallow peak which holds its shape is formed when you lift the whisk.

Wire whisks (either a coil shape or balloon) are also necessary for making sauces, especially those that are flour based, as the granules of starch present in flour burst when they reach boiling point becoming

1 *Round-bottomed glass bowl* **2** *Twig whisk* **3** *Glazed ceramic gripstand bowl* **4** *Copper bowl* **5** *Flat-bottomed mixing bowl* **6** *Plastic mixing bowls* **7** *Hand-held electric mixer* **8** *Rotary beater* **9** *Flat wire spiral whisk* **10** *Balloon whisk*

gelatinous; beating distributes this throughout the sauce, thickening it and breaking up lumps.

Rotary beaters have two beaters that are intertwined and operated by a handle on the side which you turn. There's another handle at the top where the beaters join so you can hold the beater steady. These beaters will beat eggs and cream successfully although not to the same volume as that given by balloon whisks. A rotary beater cannot incorporate as much air because it must be supported by the bottom of the bowl. They are much less tiring to use but they do tend to skid about and will only whip amounts of over 1 cup.

Twig whisks are a bunch of twigs, usually birch, tied at the top to form a handle. Great for small amounts of cream, or sauces on the stove, they are held upright between your palms and twirled by rubbing your hands together. Their disadvantage is that they do not leave a hand free to steady the bowl or pan.

Hand electric mixers beat quickly and effortlessly but, where egg whites are concerned, do not give the best results. The whites expand less because the machine's blades do not pass continuously through the whole body of the whites; its also more difficult to judge the change of consistency and over-beating can result. Electric mixers, however, are ideal for combining ingredients together which would otherwise take a long time and a lot of muscle power – egg yolks and sugar for example, or for creaming butter and sugar, or for making all-in-one cake batters. With both rotary beaters and electric hand mixers, flat-bottomed bowls are easiest to use as their straight sides keep the ingredients together rather than splashing them about. There is also less chance of the beaters skidding too much.

Bowls need to be in different sizes to be used for varying quantities. It is much easier to get good results if you mix a small quantity in a small bowl and vice versa. A bowl with a pouring lip is also useful for more liquid mixtures. Three sizes of glazed ceramic bowls are an asset, for not only can they be used for mixing but also for delicate mixtures like custard sauce and when ingredients like egg yolks have to be cooked by indirect heat.

Food processors

Food processors are neat and compact machines that take up little space on a countertop and, at the change of a blade and press of a button will chop, shred, slice, purée, blend or mix, doing a number of jobs that a variety of large and small gadgets are designed for. Once you have a food processor, a sharp knife and a whisk are probably the only other implements you'll need to carry out most food preparation. It is invaluable to a busy cook who is often cooking for large numbers, or one who has little time in which to get a meal together – it solves the dish washing problem as well!

The processors are easy to assemble. They have a powerful motor base, operated by an on/off switch – some have two speeds or a pulse button enabling you to stop the machine quickly without having to turn it off – a bowl, cover made of clear plastic so that you can see that the food isn't over-processed, and a feed tube, through which you drop or push the food with the pusher provided (don't use your fingers or a spatula as they might become entangled with the blades). Most come with interchangeable stainless steel blades and disks for slicing, chopping, shredding, grating, and puréeing and a plastic blade and disk for kneading ingredients for bread and cakes. The stainless steel knife blade is the master tool and it can also make good, light pastry in a matter of seconds. One make of food processor has just one knife blade and one reversible stainless steel disk, instead of several, to deal with everything.

The knife blade used in conjunction with the disk produces finely ground ingredients – one side of the disk is used for slicing, the other for shredding. Another type has two speeds – 1200 rpm for mixing, kneading and processing fruit and vegetables; 4200 rpm for chopping. Most machines have a maximum level marked on the bowl so as not to strain the motor or, with liquids, to prevent any spills. It is always best to process food in small batches rather than over-fill the bowl.

To use a food processor, you lock the bowl in place on the base, fit the appropriate disk or blade, cover tightly with the lid and it is ready for the food to be dropped in down the feed tube. When the machine is set in motion you continue to drop pieces of food in. Most processors can hold up to 1 pound of meat, so it is necessary to empty the bowl of the processed meat from time to time. When slicing, the thickness of slices depends on how much pressure you apply to the pusher when helping the food down the feed tube.

While you are getting used to your food processor, you will probably find that it is very easy to over-process food, and that the carrots you only wanted chopped are puréed before you know it. This is where a pulse button comes in handy as you can keep stopping the machine to check how it is doing. Hard foods, such as tough root vegetables like turnip, should be peeled and cut into smallish pieces so as not to strain the motor, and then processed in short bursts. When processing vegetables with different consistencies for the same dish, like carrots which are hard and onions which have a high water content, put all the carrots in first, followed by the onions.

With a processor, the possibilities are limitless where labor-saving is concerned, but good organization is essential to get the best out of your machine. If you are cooking a large amount, work out first how much needs to be sliced and do all the slicing at once, so that you change the blades the least number of times. Or if you need to process only a small amount of breadcrumbs, do a large amount and store the surplus for another dish.

When preparing vegetables for a casserole, process more than you need and use what's left over in soups. Larger quantities of meat can be processed, packed into usable portions and frozen. Pastry can also be made and frozen.

If you only need a small amount of mayonnaise, for example, you might as well

Food processors all set for action

make a large amount. This is no longer an arm-tiring, time-consuming job — a few bursts on the processor and you have a perfect emulsion.

Another way of getting the best out of your food processor is to make multiple meals in one cooking session. You can do this when there is a glut of seasonal produce and some time to spare. If, for example, you have a large amount of mushrooms, you can process them all at once, make several meals out of them and freeze. You could do the same with raspberries and strawberries in a very short but abundant season.

Leftovers can be processed to make interesting new dishes; making preserves, where large amounts of ingredients have to be sliced or chopped, is no longer a chore. And, as a processor is so speedy, salads — using ingredients such as cabbage, carrot and cucumber — can be prepared at the last minute, thus keeping in maximum goodness.

However, the food processor cannot incorporate air into ingredients, so egg whites cannot be beaten into a froth and cream cannot be whipped, although some models are now being made with beater attachments. Processors cannot extract juice (they liquidize instead), but a juice extractor can often be bought separately. As processors vary in performance and safety measures it is always advisable to see one demonstrated before buying. Check for noise, ease of cleaning, size, efficiency and if it has a comprehensive instruction and recipe booklet with it. Follow the instructions carefully, especially where safety is concerned and never keep the machine within reach of children — the metal blade and disks are very sharp and should be treated with respect. Never put your hand into the bowl when it is attached to the motor, even when it is switched off and, when cleaning the blade and disks, wash them separately rather than in a bowl of sudsy water in which you have to feel around to find them. Some machines will only operate when the lid is firmly on and you cannot take off the lid until it is switched off. Nevertheless, the rotating blades do take a while to slow down and at the slowest rate can give you a very nasty cut.

Before cleaning your food processor, unplug it. Wash the different parts in warm water with a little detergent and rinse and dry thoroughly. Some plastic bowls and lids are dishwasher proof but check with the instructions first. Never immerse the motor body in water, just wipe clean with a damp cloth and dry. When you first use a food processor, it is important to work with specially devised recipes, as you will have to rethink certain cooking processes — for example, you will need less water when making pastry. But you'll find that the more you use your processor, the more ways you will discover of making it work for you.

Microwave ovens

A microwave oven uses electro-magnetic waves to cook food. These high-frequency waves agitate the moisture molecules in food, producing heat which cooks the food. The waves bounce off all sides of the oven back into the food, cooking it from the inside outwards. The container that holds the food does not contain moisture so while the food cooks away it will stay quite cold.

A microwave oven can be used on its own or in conjunction with a traditional oven. It can thaw frozen food, cook certain raw foods and reheat pre-cooked dishes. The last factor is invaluable for organizing and preparing dinner parties. All microwave ovens come with instruction booklets and these vary according to the make and model. Below are some guidelines that apply to microwave cooking in general.

Starting temperature of the food will affect the cooking time — generally, the warmer the food at the start, the shorter the cooking time.

Density of food is important. A roast of meat with tightly packed molecules will not be penetrated by the waves as fast as a more porous food like bread which will cook more quickly.

Volume refers to the amount of food being cooked. Because of the energy pattern in the ovens the more space that's taken up by dishes or foods, the less room there is for the waves to bounce and cooking time will be longer. Three potatoes for example take longer than one, though not three times as long. A large number of potatoes would be better being cooked by conventional means.

Arrangement of foods is done to ensure the maximum concentration of the waves. Corn on the cob is best placed like the spokes of a wheel; when a mixed group of ingredients is being cooked or reheated, place the denser ones around the outer edge of the container with porous ones in the middle.

Delicate ingredients such as high protein dairy foods (eggs, milk, cheese, cream) will toughen, separate or curdle at too high a temperature. This is also true of mayonnaise, and kidney beans and mushrooms which will burst. Dried beans should always be soaked before being cooked by microwaves.

Container size and shape are recommended in microwave recipes to give the best results. A tall narrow container increases cooking time, a shallow broad container will reduce it for there is more surface available for the waves to penetrate. Puddings and sauces need large containers to prevent the mixture boiling over as it gets hot. When making jam, confectionery or chutney, the container needs to be able to withstand the high sugar temperatures and be large enough to keep the contents from spilling over into the oven when they boil. Never use metal dishes or foil containers in the oven: they prevent the microwaves from reaching the food and can even reflect the waves, seriously damaging the oven.

Coverings are needed for foods which should be kept moist (fish, steamed puddings) and vegetables which rely on steam to cook. Sauces or gravy might evaporate so they need a cover, as do foods which are likely to splash or splutter, but cover only lightly. Be careful when taking covers off after cooking as the rush of steam can be quite unexpected. Boil-in-bags should be punctured as should baked potatoes as the steam build up could cause the bag or food to split open or burst.

Stirring is necessary for some foods — puddings for example — where the outside edge has cooked first and the center needs to be redistributed to ensure even cooking. Always stir from the outside in so the uncooked part is brought to the outside. But stirring only needs to be done occasionally. Soups and stews need to be stirred once or twice during cooking to give a more even distribution of heat.

Turning is needed for dense foods, such as roasts or poultry, to expose the undersides to the microwaves. Turn halfway through recommended cooking time; very large roasts should be turned three or four times. If the energy pattern in the oven is uneven, and there isn't a turntable to rotate foods automatically, dishes must be turned by hand several times during the cooking period.

Browning of some foods occurs naturally (meats and poultry brown after about 10 minutes), but for small pieces of meat such as hamburgers, chops, steak, a browning skillet will be necessary or the food can be completed under the broiler. Cakes do not brown in most ovens and it is easy to overcook them — once they are risen and springy to the touch, still moist on top, they are ready. Cookies and breads also do not brown to the same extent as they do in conventional baking.

Standing time is like carry-over cooking time and with foods cooked by microwaves, the standing time recommended is really a part of the cooking time for food continues to cook after it has been removed from the oven. The more dense the food, the longer the standing time, for it gives the juices a chance to redistribute themselves and to make carving easier. If thawing foods in a microwave oven, the food will be exposed to the waves for a recommended number of minutes per

pound and standing time must be allowed before going on to cook the food.

Meal planning with microwaves is easy if you remember that the foods that need to be cooked longest should be cooked first. As reheating is such a dramatic and prized part of cooking by this method, all the foods could be prepared at another time and placed in the oven for seconds, or at the most, minutes.

Adapting recipes is not difficult so long as you have a microwave cookbook which has a similar list of ingredients to the recipe you have. It will give you guidelines for cooking time, container size, power setting; or you can cook the dish for a quarter of the conventional cooking time, then cook in short bursts until the food is to your liking.

Cakes, quick and yeast breads, cookies need to have their baking powder and/or soda reduced by a quarter or one-third. Cake batters need to be very slack (the microwaves are attracted to moisture) and in most cases, ingredient proportions are different from conventional recipes. Never flour the container as the cake will have an unpalatable cooked flour crust, but do grease lightly.

Sauces or fillings thickened by flour or cornstarch need slightly less liquid than conventional recipes, and the thickening agent should be blended in well before cooking.

Rice and pasta might just as well be cooked conventionally for very little time is saved.

Appetizers and sandwiches need bread that's already toasted. Pastry appetizers stay pale, do not microwave well.

Pies with an upper and lower crust are a problem for the filling will heat up more quickly than the denser pastry which will not brown. Tarts in which the pastry has been baked unfilled first are successful in microwaves.

Check your microwave cookbook to see what wattage the recipes were tested at. If at 700, for 500 watt ovens increase times by about 15 seconds to the minute, for 600 watt increase by about 10 seconds to the minute. Times should be decreased for more powerful ovens. Always underestimate rather than overestimate cooking times as the residual heat will make the food carry on cooking — even the internal temperature of the food can rise when it is out of the oven!

Stewing less tender cuts of meat can be a problem in a microwave oven that doesn't have a slow-down control. Quick cooking will not tenderize tougher fibers, and meat is perhaps better cooked by conventional means, then reheated in the microwave oven.

Deep-frying is not possible in a microwave and shallow frying is not advised, because as there's no temperature control it is possible to overheat fat. Foods that have

been deep or shallow fried by conventional means can be reheated with good results in a microwave oven. Most foods can be cooked in a little butter or margarine (baked potatoes can be rubbed with it to improve the taste).

Boiling and steaming can be carried out in a fraction of the normal time and with vegetables and fish especially result in excellent flavor and color. Both cook virtually in their own liquid which means they retain water soluble vitamins and other nutrients. Cooking time is so swift that liquid has almost no time to evaporate — denser root vegetables need a little more than greens, but neither needs very much to cook to perfect tenderness.

Eggs cannot be cooked whole in their shells as the heat build-up inside will cause the shells to burst. They can be quickly scrambled or poached, however, in the dish in which they are to be served, saving dish washing.

Preserves, jams, jellies and marmalades are very quick to make and there's no risk of boiling over if the right sized container is used.

Melting and dissolving ingredients such as chocolate, fat and gelatin can be done perfectly in a fraction of the usual times, as can making a hot drink in a cup — stir and it's ready.

Puddings take between 6 and 9 minutes (depending on the wattage and the size of the puddings — the times above are for a 4 cup pudding) which is the most dramatic comparison between conventional and microwave possible.

Bakes and roasts are also cooked very quickly compared with conventional means and the look of the end result becomes acceptable with practice. Chocolate and other dark batters are, for example, recommended for cakes (there's no browning) or they can be frosted which will cover the top. Pastries and breads can be flashed under the broiler after cooking and glazed to give them an appetizing look before serving.

Blenders and mills

Blenders and mills can either be bought together with the same base, or as separate units. They are both useful pieces of electrical equipment: a blender (also called a liquidizer) will chop and purée vegetables, meats, sauces, soups and baby foods; and a mill will process or grind small amounts of dried foods, coffee, nuts and spices.

Blenders consist of a tall jug or goblet made out of plastic or thick glass which fits on to a motorized base which can have one speed (used in bursts of seconds) through to the more versatile 14 (allowing greater amounts to be blended at different speeds).

The goblet has sharp blades – usually 4 – on the bottom and one or two of these should point downwards to lift up any food that goes beneath the blades. As the blades revolve at high speeds, they break down the food drawn on to them in a downward spiralling action. Sometimes if the ingre-dients are too thick, the blades create an air pocket into which nothing will flow. If this happens, turn off the machine and push the food down with a spatula, but if it persists more liquid will need to be added. Small goblets hold about 5 cups and the large about 1 gallon.

A plastic goblet can scratch or stain, so always use a rubber spatula to scrape out food. Glass ones tend to break easily. Some goblets cannot take boiling liquids so this is something to check before buying. In use, as a safety precaution, always warm the goblet before pouring hot liquids in. All blenders should have a lid that screws or can be pressed firmly into position (*before* the motor is started) to keep the food inside. A goblet shouldn't be more than half filled with liquids because the spiralling action causes them to rise and fall. Lids should have a small cap in the center which can be removed while the motor is going to add an ingredient slowly (eg, oil when making mayonnaise). When making breadcrumbs add the cubed bread little by little through the hole so as not to overstrain the motor – cover the hole with your hand immediately you let go of the food, though, as the crumbs will jump back out of it.

The most sophisticated blender around is like a food processor, but it can heat too. Quite a breakthrough in making sauces, for the ingredients can go in in any order and become smooth and blended and brought to serving heat without any supervision. It has a powerful motor which can reduce even bones to paste, and is able to keep going without any strain.

Always follow the manufacturer's instructions to get the best out of your blender. Check the upper time limit for continuous use and stick to it or you'll injure the motor. If it seems to be laboring, stop immediately. Never insert large hard lumps of food, as they can damage the blades or burn out the motor.

To clean the goblet, half fill with mild soapy water and whizz, then rinse and dry. Never submerge the motor part in water, and always make sure that the base of the goblet is clean and dry. If your blender has a rubber washer check that it is flat before screwing on the top and replace it as soon as it shows signs of perishing. Do not put a plastic goblet in a dishwasher – the extreme heat of the drying element may melt it!

Electric or coffee mills are much smaller versions of blenders, but have stronger blades. The longer the coffee beans are processed the finer the grains – the same goes for any other ingredients that you grind such as whole spices or bread. Mills cannot be washed, only wiped out with paper towels, so if you do grind a lot of coffee it will tend to flavor anything else.

1 *Free-standing electric blender* **2** *Electric blender with accessories* **3** *All-purpose electric mill*

Boiling battery

Saucepans are made in a variety of materials. Copper is the most effective conductor, followed by aluminum, cast iron and stainless steel. A sandwich of copper in the base of pans will make them heavier and more efficient — a layer of copper painted on will not. Linings will not improve conductivity if the pan material itself is not efficient. Enamel is used with cast iron to prevent it rusting, and tin with copper (the exception is a sugar boiler) to stop verdigris developing. Best quality stainless steel keeps a "new" look about it for years. Aluminum is prone to staining in hard water areas, but this cleans off easily. Copper needs effort to keep it shiny. Enameled cast iron is hard wearing and can be very heavy — because it holds heat well it is the material recommended for induction hobs (these can only be activated by ferrous metal) and many ceramic ones.

Non-metallic saucepans are made of toughened heat resistant glass or French porcelain, both of which are most attractive but need attention in use to prevent breakage (you can only drop them once). With electric hot plates, they have to be placed on a heat diffuser or asbestos pad. Glass ceramic is mostly used for casseroles which can become saucepans as needed. **Saucepans** should have fairly heavy and very even bases. Any roughness will scratch ceramic hobs for example, and thin bottoms will distort with heat causing "hot spots" where food can stick and burn. Lids should fit tightly and knobs and handles be made of a non-conductive material and be fixed to the lids and pans securely. Poor fittings may work loose with time, and can lead to a serious accident.

Stockpots are tall, narrow pans. They have two short handles rather than one long one because they are very heavy when full.

Milk pans and small pans for sauces usually have a pouring lip, and often have a non-stick or enamel coating. Always use non-metal implements to prevent marking the lining. These pans should be hung rather than stacked or linings will be damaged.

Double boilers have a top pan which fits inside the bottom so boiling water in the bottom pan will give the gentle heat needed to thicken or melt whatever's in the top pan (sauces, chocolate, scrambled eggs). Some double boilers have an accessory steamer section.

The Dutch oven was a covered stewing or baking pot that was hung over an open fire or set among the coals. Today, a Dutch oven is usually thought of as a heavy, round, short-handled or top-handled pot to be used for cooking on top of the stove, although in the Midwest the Dutch oven is an oval, domed roaster. A Dutch oven when made of metal and with a wire loop handle is often called a **kettle**.

Fish poachers are rectangular, oval or square pans with a rack so the food can be lifted in and out easily when poaching.

1 *Metal colander* 2 *Stainless steel saucepan* 3 *Enameled casserole* 4 *Heat-resistant glass double boiler* 5 *Non-stick milk pan* 6 *Heat diffuser* 7 *Porcelain enameled saucepan* 8 *Steamer* 9 *Glass spoon rest* 10 *Skimmer and perforated spoon* 11 *Pan rest*

Frying battery

1 *Porcelain enamel sauté pan with lid* 2 *Cast iron crêpe and omelette pans* 3 *Metal sauté pan* 4 *Sauté pan with non-stick coating* 5 *Flameproof ceramic sauté pan* 6 *Oval frypan for whole fish* 7 *Square griddle* 8 *Aluminum skillet* 9 *Cast iron all-purpose pan* 10 *Decoratively enameled skillet*

The traditional shallow flat-bottomed frying pan used to be made with three or four legs so the pan could be placed on the hearth close to the fire. These original long-handled pans, also called skillets, were always made of heavy iron; imported brass and copper utensils were only for the wealthy. Today's skillet comes in a multiplicity of sizes and materials but is still instantly recognizable by its shape. **Shallow** skillets should be made of a material capable of withstanding high temperatures without buckling and one which conducts heat quickly and evenly. Thin pans of any description will not last the pace. The base should be absolutely level (as, of course, should the burner) or liquid fat will collect in pools, hot spots will develop and the food will scorch.

Aluminum and coated or uncoated cast iron are excellent holders of heat and, with flameproof ceramic, the most warp-resistant; steel and stainless steel are not good conductors of heat, but can be found with copper-clad bases to overcome this disadvantage. Copper skillets are usually tinned inside, need great care if they are to stay bright, and the protective lacquer

1 *Deep-fat fryer with basket and lid* 2 *Electric deep-fat fryer* 3 *Electric deep-fat fryer with lid to filter smells* 4 *Electric frypan* 5 *Electric crêpe maker*

must be removed from both inside and out before using. Enamel-coated pans are easy to clean, but do not take kindly to being scraped with metal kitchen tools, and the cheaper ones may chip easily.

All handles must be firmly set and easy to grip, and the pan itself must be well balanced. Give the end of the handle a sharp tap — if the pan promptly resumes a flat position, it is well balanced. Any lid must fit snugly. Oval frying pans are specially produced for fish and can be used for poaching too.

Omelette and crêpe pans should have thicker bases than skillets and should be rounded where sides meet the base to help in removing the finished food. They should always be used only for making omelettes and crêpes. Use a 6 inch diameter pan for a 2–3 egg omelette, a 7–8 inch pan for a 4–5 egg one. Wipe out with paper towels after each use instead of washing: there is no health risk in this as seasoned pans are sterilized by high heat before any food is added. Store the pans in a place where air circulates freely or the oil may turn rancid.

Non-stick coatings, made of a fluoro-carbon resin that is sprayed on and then heat-treated, are a great advantage when frying. Not only do they help to stop food sticking, but very little fat need be used. There are even special pans available for non-fat frying. Non-stick pans must not be overheated — "non-stick" does not mean "non-burn" — a medium heat is recommended as maximum even for crêpes. Burnt-on food particles may be removed by thorough washing and scouring with a nylon scourer, followed by a film of oil for protection. Metal utensils will damage these surfaces.

Electric frypans are, in fact, mini ovens for you to boil, bake and steam in them as well as frying. They are a lot more economical to use than an oven when cooking for 2 or 3 people.

Deep-fat fryers must also have thick bases which conduct heat evenly and well. The basket should clip and rest securely on the pan when lifted for draining and the mesh

close so food cannot slip through it. Electric deep-fat fryers are economical and versatile. Their average range is from small (2-cup capacity for 1 or 2 servings) to large (2½-quart capacity for 4 servings). They come in aluminum or stainless steel, and some have a non-stick coating; all have an electric base unit, a fitted frying basket and a lid (unless it has a filter, remove it when frying). In some, the lids are integral to keep the cooking smells down to a minimum — always a problem with deep frying. Most have variable heat settings.

Although a very thick frying pan could double as a griddle, it would be worth investing in a cast iron one for cooking bacon, flapjacks and "griddle breads" such as scones. If you also have a deep-frying thermometer, a capacious skimmer (non-stick ones are useful) or slotted spoon, a pair of kitchen tongs and a fine mesh strainer lined for straining the fat — your frying equipment is complete.

Fondue battery

Tabletop cooking ranges from the formal to the informal throughout the world. In the Far East, where braziers and hibachis originated, the cooking is almost a ceremony. In France, since the turn of the century, fashionable restaurants have vied with each other to create ever more astonishing dishes which could be finished with a flourish at the table before their admiring clientèle. But chafing dish (named after the thrifty French *réchauffée* — reheated) cooking also had its practical side. The ingredients were always of the finest quality, thinly cut, were assembled and ready for quick frying. While the customers were admiring the skill of the chef, he had the satisfaction of knowing that their after-theater suppers had not taken hours to prepare.

Thin strips of tender beef, veal, chicken or shellfish, shallow fried with the minimum of fuss, a little chopped shallot, a scattering of sliced mushrooms, a dash of piquant sauce or perhaps a little garlic, are briskly flamed and finished in a little sauce and the dish is ready. For Boeuf Stroganoff, sour cream is used; the Australian Steak Diane is flamed with brandy; Lobster Newburg is reheated gently and served with a sauce of egg yolks, butter and cream; shrimp can be similarly treated and kidneys are skewered, fried in a chafing dish and spread with piquant mustard to finish cooking.

On the sweet side, there are famous Crêpes Suzette (crêpes rich with orange-flavored butter and liqueur, page 108), apple crêpes flamed with Calvados (from Normandy), dark morello cherries warmed with Kirsch (invented in the US to celebrate Queen Victoria's jubilee) and bananas flamed in rum and sprinkled with brown sugar (a Caribbean special).

Flaming is almost a prerequisite of this type of tabletop frying and some sleight of hand is required on the part of the cook. It helps if the liqueur or spirit is first warmed in a metal spoon or ladle, then set alight and poured over the food in the pan. Shake the pan to distribute the flames among the contents and burn off all the alcohol. Whatever you do, keep hold of the match. It is neither dignified nor convenient to try and fish splinters of carbonized wood out of an expensive preparation! Never be tempted to pour alcohol straight from the bottle into a heated pan or the contents of the bottle could also catch fire. If the food is too wet or not hot enough, the alcohol will be diluted, lose its strength and refuse to flame.

The older chafing dishes were made of silver plate and came in three parts: a shallow frying pan with a wooden handle (the "blazer"), a handleless pan fitted below it to contain water, and the stand fitted around an adjustable spirit lamp. Today, copper gratin pans or flambé pans are often used over spirit burners in restaurants, whereas the electric frypan — thermostatically controlled and easy to use — will serve the same purpose at home. Always use top quality ingredients, have them on hand, do not have more fat in the pan than is strictly necessary and, if cooking over a spirit burner, watch for drafts.

The Swiss contribution to the tabletop feast is *Fondue bourguignonne* (page 105) in which cubes of prime steak (6–8oz per person) are speared on special long forks, placed in sizzling hot fat until fried to the individual taste, and then dipped in a variety of savory and piquant sauces. A fondue party can be fun, but do not be tempted to invite more guests than there is room for forks in the pot, or you will have a war game on your hands! Do supply a second fork for the cooked food to be transferred on to before it is eaten. No one who, in the heat of the moment, has eaten the food straight off the blistering hot cooking fork will wish to repeat the experience. As well as beef, pieces of chicken and even crusty dry bread can be used to stretch the meat.

Fondue pots must be able to withstand high temperatures and metal (stainless steel, tinned copper or enameled cast iron) pots are best. Fondue pots for oil should have inward-sloping sides to stop splashes and help retain heat. A lid should cover the pot while the oil is heating, although it is better to heat the oil on the stove before transferring it to keep warm on the trivet over the table burner. For safety, the pot should not be more than half full of oil; one with a 1–1½ quart capacity should hold enough to cater for 6–8 people.

Fondues which use boiling broth aren't frying, of course, but are worth mentioning. The Italians have *Bagna cauda*, in which raw vegetables are dipped in a hot garlic and anchovy-flavored sauce. This is similar to the oriental fondue where beef and vegetables are cooked at the table in boiling bouillon. The Chinese cook pieces of meat, chicken and vegetables in a chicken broth flavored with soy sauce

and ginger, kept hot in a steamboat or hot pot. When the food has been eaten, the stock is drunk as soup. Frying is used in the Japanese *Tempura* (page 104), freshest, finest fish and vegetables are dipped in batter before being tabletop fried, drained, dipped in a sauce and eaten. *Sukiyaki* is similar, but uses meat and chicken rather than fish, and no batter. We have developed sweet fondues served for dessert. Marshmallows and pieces of firm, sliced fruit are dipped in melted chocolate enriched with cream and honey, or in fudgy toffee sauces laced with rum.

In Switzerland, the fondness for cheese fondue persists (the word comes from

1

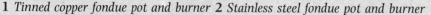

1 *Tinned copper fondue pot and burner* 2 *Stainless steel fondue pot and burner*
3 *Enameled cast iron pot with burner* 4 *Pottery fondue pot for cheese and sweet fondues*

fondre, to melt). The traditional recipe uses only Swiss Gruyère and Emmenthal cheeses and light, white wine for melting them slowly in the now familiar *caquelon* or earthenware pot. Kirsch is added to the fondue, which is eaten with cubes of crusty French bread speared on the fondue forks and dipped into the melted cheese. The bouillon, cheese, oil or sauce can of course be brought to the right heat on the stove, then placed over the burner. Whatever you cook on your tabletop, place heatproof mats and trays underneath, and take care to control the table burner. The food will be a talking point as well as being something different.

4

3

2

Roasting battery

Roasting pans are oblong or square and come in a variety of sizes — one may be supplied with your oven. They should fit your oven comfortably, with room at either side. Juices will burn on the bottom if the pan is too large; if too small for the roast, the lower half braises in the moisture trapped by the sides — heat should circulate freely. Generally speaking, roasting pans are 2–4 inches deep with straight or slightly sloping sides.

Roasting pans are made in different materials — from thick-gauge to lighter aluminum, stainless steel, enameled steel, enameled cast iron, ovenproof porcelain, ceramic glass, clear heatproof glass and glazed earthenware. Those which can be used on top of the stove as well, to make gravy, are the most useful.

Any handles should be securely riveted and wide enough to be gripped with oven-gloved hands. Pans with a rolled top edge or a generous rim are easy to lift (roasts of meat and large birds can weigh heavy on wrists!). Roasting pans should be smooth and have no seams or crevices in which fat can collect or germs breed. Non-stick roasting pans need care as scratches affect the non-stick properties.

Covered roasting pans are good for meats which might give out too much moisture in the dry heat and be dry to eat. It's a sort of steam roasting, for although liquid isn't used (fat doesn't create steam) some moisture is drawn from the meat. The same effect is achieved by the use of clear roasting bags and foil. With foil, the roast should be loosely wrapped, shiny side inside and the joins firmly sealed. In covered roasting the oven temperature needs to be slightly higher and the meat may take a little longer to cook, but the inside of the oven stays clean and free from fat splashes. Most bags or foil should be opened for the last 35 minutes of roasting time to brown the meat. In a microwave oven, remember to puncture a roasting bag and don't use a metal tie.

A roasting rack keeps meat or poultry from frying in the fat. The rack should have widely spaced parallel bars to allow the fat to drip through without collecting and to make the rack itself easy to clean.

Metal spoons or a bulb baster, which is like a syringe with a rubber bulb at the end, are used for basting. The bulb is pressed to suck up the fat from the pan, then pressed again to release it over the meat. It is a most efficient way of basting roasted or barbecued meats.

A meat thermometer is the best way of ensuring that the meat is cooked to your liking. The spike is pressed into the thickest part of the meat, avoiding any bone and keeping the head of the thermometer away from the source of heat to

prevent it misting up. The dial should be marked with a temperature scale (either Celsius or Fahrenheit) which gives the internal heat and thus indicates the stages of doneness (eg, "rare", "well done").

An oven thermometer can be used to check the oven's heat and thermostat. Place it on the middle shelf, or the shelf you intend cooking on. The thermometers are rectangular in shape and should sit evenly on the shelf to give a proper reading. Leave in place for 20 minutes before checking the temperature and adjusting the dial on the oven.

Larding needles are used for interlarding lean meats. Those with ridged spring-clip tops are easy to thread with thin strips of fat. After the strip has been placed in the meat along the grain, the clip can be released and the needle removed and rethreaded. The needles are made of stainless steel and should be washed in hot soapy water and dried well before being stored.

Butcher's needles need to have a large enough eye to take the string (use a fine cotton thread for poultry, a thicker one for meat). Curved ones are often easier to use than straight ones. To truss chicken, fold flap of skin over neck end and hold in position by folding ends of wings backwards and under. Turn bird on to its back and press legs into the sides to plump breast. Insert needle through nearest wing leaving a few inches of thread hanging out, into thigh on same side, through body and bring it out through thigh on other side. Now push needle through second wing, then the body and bring it out in center of wing on other side near to thread hanging out. Cut thread, tie both ends in secure bow. Place more thread in needle and truss vent end to hold in stuffing. Push through skin on one drumstick (leaving short length protruding), into gristle on both sides of the tail, and bring it out through skin of the other drumstick. Push needle back through

carcass under drumsticks, cut thread and tie ends securely at the side.

A simple method of trussing without using a needle can be found on page 121.

Poultry lacers are small metal skewers used for trussing birds and holding a layer of barding fat in place without string. Large metal skewers keep boned, rolled roasts in shape, and are used for the "skewer test" for doneness (see page 112). With microwaves, only wooden skewers must be used.

1 *Heavy-gauge aluminum pan with handles* 2 *Light aluminum roasting pan* 3 *Roasting pan with rack* 4 *Meat thermometer* 5 *Oven thermometer* 6 *Wooden skewers for using in a microwave oven* 7 *Metal skewers* 8 *Butcher's needle* 9 *Larding needle* 10 *Bulb baster*

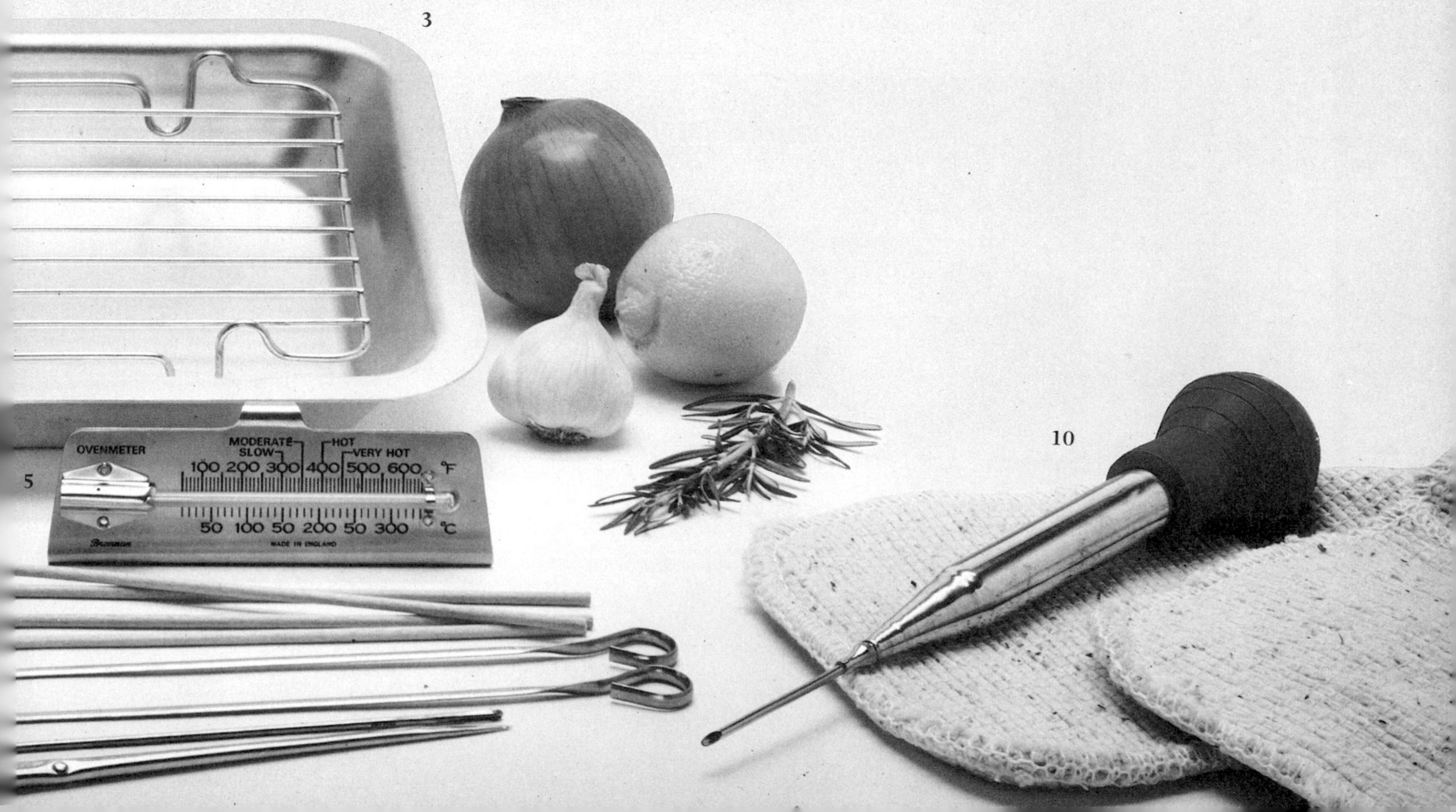

3

5

10

OVENMETER
MODERATE SLOW HOT VERY HOT
100 200 300 400 500 600 °F
50 100 50 200 50 300 °C
MADE IN ENGLAND

Broiling battery

Conventional broilers are incorporated in the oven, usually at the top. Many double ovens have the broiler element in the smaller oven, which saves heating up a bigger oven. An automatic rotisserie is sometimes fitted into the oven, or it can be bought as an extra.

The most sophisticated of the built-in electric oven/broilers have evenly distributed heat without a radiant element (called thermo-broiling) so that food can be broiled in hot air on all the shelves at the same time.

In fuel saving terms, the best broilers are those which have two elements, so that if you're cooking something small, only one element need be turned on. In cooking terms, all broilers should have at least two positions: high, close to the heat source for very tender foods, and lower, for foods which need less fierce heat. The third and lowest position is often achieved by removing the rack and placing the food on the bottom of the broiler pan. In broiling the more positions there are the better the results.

The broiler pan when pulled out should stay firmly horizontal so the food and fat can't fall on the floor, or on you. A handy feature of some broiler pans is a "basting corner", a cut-away section of the rack which enables you to spoon over the juices during cooking, especially useful with meat.

After cooking, don't pour hot fat down the sink, or you'll end up with a blocked drain. Wait until the fat has solidified and then remove it with a spatula. Wrapped in paper towels it can then be thrown away with your normal kitchen waste. If you want to keep the fat for cooking, pour off and strain while it is still liquid.

Electric contact or infra-red grills are ideal when cooking facilities are limited. The simplest models toast sandwiches well.

1 *Electric sandwich toaster* 2 *Portable rotisserie broiler* 3 *Electric toaster* 4 *Electric contact grill* 5 *Round sandwich toaster* 6 *Waffle iron*

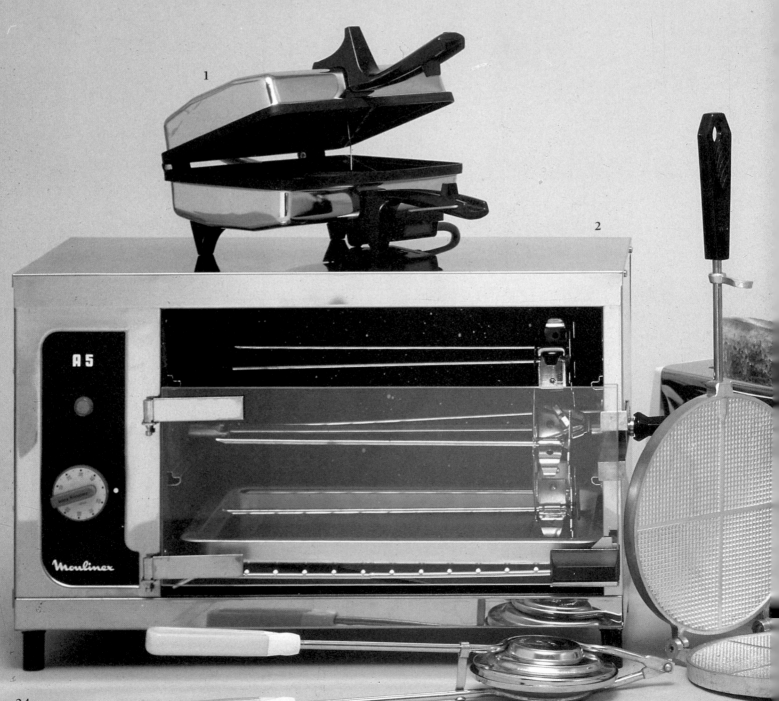

but are not so good for chops and steaks. (Unless the grill has a rising hinge, the top won't lie flat on top of the food and cooking will be uneven.) A number of sizes are available, the largest taking, for example, six chops. Some models have an automatic thermostat, others have a variable temperature control. With all types, adequate ventilation is necessary as cooking fumes escape.

In comparison with conventional broilers, contact grills are economical to run, as cooking times are very short indeed and some even double up as small ovens. You can also use this type of grill for cooking frozen foods, provided you wrap them in oiled foil first. Even though the plates are non-stick, a little oil should be brushed over the surface before preheating. Cleaning must be scrupulous, or any food particles remaining on the plates will smoke. All in all, this is probably the best alternative to the conventional broiler, as most models will act as grills, toasted sandwich makers and, opened out flat, a satisfactory griddle.

Portable broiler/ovens have several variations. Toaster-ovens will bake, as well as broil and toast. A rotisserie may double up as a broiler if the element is at the top, or simply roast on a revolving spit if it uses indirect, radiated heat. The latter type normally has a kabob cooking facility as well. Again, these are useful when kitchen space is at a premium. Some rotisserie models incorporate an automatic timer, while the more advanced designs are self-cleaning. The free-standing broiler/oven type of appliance usually has a smaller capacity than its fixed counterpart.

Electric toasters Probably the first of the purpose-made electric broiling appliances, toasters come in a wide variety of styles. Most have an automatic timer which regulates the browning of the toast (dry bread takes less time than freshly baked). Some toasters will accommodate thick slices of bread, frozen waffles and even English muffins. The "pop-up", or even "pop-out" mechanism must be easy to operate. Some cut off the heat if the bread gets stuck because it's too thick, or have an alarm which sounds so that you can work the removal by hand. Two and four slice toasters are the most common and the larger ones will toast one or two slices instead of four if need be. A crumb tray is a useful feature, but should be cleaned when the toaster is disconnected from the power supply.

Electric snack and sandwich toasters cook food in less time than a normal broiler although preheating of about 10 minutes is necessary. They efficiently heat through sandwich fillings at the same time as toasting the bread (both sides at once). Enclosed between the two heating plates, the filling gets sealed in; some models even have inbuilt cutters to seal the edges of each sandwich.

The heating plates are non-stick, making them easy to clean. The unit itself is quite large and weighs 3–4½lb. For this reason, you may find it takes up rather a lot of room in a small kitchen, though of course it can be stored when not needed. **Non-electric sandwich toasters** are designed for use on a normal stove burner, but not all suit an electric stove. They have two circular plates about 4 inches in diameter, ending in two long handles. A little more complicated to use than electric sandwich toasters, this type naturally requires less initial outlay. You butter the outside of the sandwich, put the filling in the middle and trim off the edges. (As the device has circular plates, you end up with, literally, a round sandwich!) Then you simply put the toaster over a gentle heat, allow about 5 minutes each side, and remove sandwich.

Waffle irons usually need no fat and use direct heat in cooking. Although you should preheat non-electric waffle irons, the cooking technique is similar to the non-electric sandwich toaster. You simply place the iron over a low heat, turn it when steam appears and check that the cooked side is golden brown. The iron will stop steaming when the waffle is cooked. Electric waffle irons take 5 minutes to warm up, cook evenly and do not need turning.

Two points to remember: do not leave fat in the drip tray of any broiling device while the heating element is switched on; it may either catch fire or start to smoke. Under no circumstances place any electrical appliance in water, and always unplug the appliance before cleaning or wiping over the outside casing.

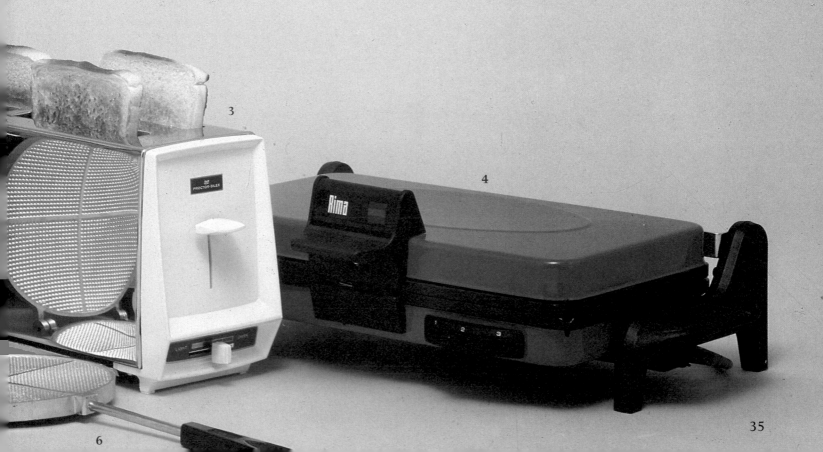

Barbecue battery

Purpose-built barbecues range from a small, disposable single-use set that comes complete with a ration of fuel, to the large, elaborate variety, either with wheels or stationary. The Japanese hibachi which literally means fire-bowl has become the simplest form of barbecue to buy, providing an ideal introduction to barbecuing. Consisting of a solid cast iron fire box fitted with one or several grills, the hibachi can either be round or rectangular, with or without a fold-away stand or detachable legs with wheels. The charcoal fire is contained in the bottom of the fire box and simple draft controls help to regulate the fire and cooking temperature. As the hibachi is small and extremely portable, it is popular for use in a small backyard or patio, or on picnic and camp sites. However, one disadvantage of the single grill hibachi is that the center of the grill tends to reach a higher temperature than the perimeter, requiring food either to be placed in the middle or to be moved around the grill to ensure even cooking. Larger grills can be elaborate versions of the hibachi, with the fire box – probably a shallow tray – mounted on legs. These are often called brazier barbecues and may sport revolving grills, so the chef does not need to lean over the heat in order to turn the food. Braziers can range in size from a foldaway picnic model, which has cooking space for about four people, to a large grill providing cooking room for 20 on a table-height grill.

These larger, more elaborate grills may offer luxurious extras, like a hand or battery-operated spit, useful for turning whole chickens and similar foods, or a shelf beneath the grill. Of the accessories available, a hood which covers the food is

1 *Two-rack hibachi tabletop barbecue* 2 *Hinged wire broiler for hamburgers, steaks, etc.*
3 *A brazier barbecue with revolving grill, windshield and battery-operated spit*
4 *Charcoal briquets* 5 *Portable picnic barbecue* 6 *Metal skewers for kabobs* 7 *Mitts*
8 *Long-handled spatula* 9 *Long-handled tongs* 10 *Fish frame for turning whole fish*

probably the most advantageous, as it allows the cooking time to be regulated more precisely and eliminates the need for basting. Vents in the grill base may be opened or closed to control the heat and, when opened, the cover acts as a windshield. When cooking is finished, extinguishing the fire becomes a simple matter of closing the cover and the vents, thereby cutting off the oxygen supply to the fire. The most sophisticated type of grill is that powered by bottled gas or an electric element which heats a bed of lava rock, providing a charcoal effect, but with heat controls similar to a conventional oven — very good where barbecuing is done in a confined space (a balcony or roof top) where smoke might be an irritant to neighbors.

But, for some, there is no substitute for searing over ash-crusted charcoal, which adds its special flavor to food.

When barbecuing, place the charcoal — which comes in either wood charcoal pieces or briquets (wood alone burns too fast and gives off a great deal of smoke) — to give a bed of embers about 3 inches thick. Make sure the grills are nickel or chrome-plated steel with bars close enough to prevent food slipping between them when turned.

Special barbecue firelighters, briquets or jellied alcohol should be used for lighting the fire; ordinary firelighters smell of paraffin which lingers and infects the food, and gasoline should never be used, as they can easily lead to an out-of-control fire. Have the food ready for cooking before lighting the fire, even though this will take 45–60 minutes to reach the correct temperature (a lot less for gas barbecues). If the charcoal flares a lot at the merest drop of melted fat, it is too hot — raise the grill position and close the draft regulator. To keep the fire going, place new charcoal around the perimeter of the fire to be warming ready for ignition.

A number of tools are required for successful barbecuing. As it is essential to baste all foods with melted fat or oil during barbecuing, a 1 inch natural bristle brush is useful (man-made fibers melt or burn). At least one pair of long-handled tongs for turning both food and charcoal is a must, and a long-handled fork for testing and removing food is useful. Long skewers for kabobs should be flat to prevent food skidding around on them and preferably should have metal handles — wood will burn. Other useful accessories include a long-handled spoon; a bulb baster; a fish holder, which is a fish-shaped grid designed to ease turning and prevent bits falling into the fire; a meat grid ideal for cooking several steaks at once or flat vegetables like mushrooms. Kitchen foil is useful for lining the grill base, facilitating cleaning, and also to wrap small foods which need slower cooking. Oven mitts which extend well over the wrist and a generous apron in flameproof material are essentials for the cook— and a fire extinguisher or bucket of sand should be within reach, just in case: nothing could ruin a barbecue faster than too much fire!

Braising battery

Prime consideration in the making of any type of braise or casserole is the choice of pot in which it is to be cooked. Basically casseroles are heatproof dishes in which you cook and from which you can serve.

Pots for braising and casseroling must have a tight-fitting lid to prevent excessive evaporation so that the steam can be used in the cooking. Weight, too, is important. If you find a pot heavy to lift when it is empty, try and imagine what it would be like lifting it out of an oven when full. The very large casseroles can hold about 5½ quarts and require a two-handed grip and strong arms. Not all pots can be used to brown meat at the beginning of cooking;

make sure you select the right one for the recipe.

Earthenware is probably the universal favorite for casseroles. The rustic hand-thrown pots are full of imperfections, even at their best; the glaze is often crazed, the material is porous but foods which are slow-cooked in them always taste good. No two seem to be alike in the rough earthenware category, but if glazed inside and if outside the glaze doesn't extend to the base, and if the lid fits snugly, it will meet the requirements. To cure the pot before using, fill it with salted water and potato peelings and bring to simmering heat in the oven. Cool and dry thoroughly, and always store on an open shelf with the

lid off. Most of the pots aren't suitable for top-of-the-stove cooking; if you must always use a heat-diffuser. Pots made of the better, and more expensive, class of earthenware will chip with rough treatment but are a little tougher than the rustic ones. They don't usually need curing.

Stoneware is an advance on earthenware in terms of toughness and is considered the best pottery available. It's resistant to thermal shock (change in temperatures) and can go from freezer to oven. It cannot, however, be used on top of the stove, so initial frying and reduction will have to be carried out in other pans.

Heatproof glass casseroles retain heat well but will not take sudden changes in temperature. They are inexpensive, can be plain or decorated, but cannot be used on direct heat. The same qualities occur in

expensive china and porcelain casseroles.

Glass-ceramic casseroles are good all-rounders and can go from freezer or refrigerator to oven or microwave without any waiting. They are light to handle.

Stainless steel casseroles should have a core of copper or similar conductor of heat in the base to ensure there are no "hot spots" — places where food will stick or burn because of uneven distribution of heat. Watch handles on these — they should be securely anchored so they won't loosen in use and should be able to be gripped securely when wearing oven mitts. These pots double as saucepans.

Aluminum casseroles need a thick base for the material is such an excellent conductor of heat that long-cooked food, especially if thickened, is likely to stick and burn. Heavy-based ones can be used as saucepans as well as casseroles.

Copper makes the best casserole for it fulfills all the requirements and looks wonderful when well cared for. The pots are expensive, and the tinned inside needs regular cleaning to remove discoloration (use a half lemon dipped in salt, or vinegar and salt, then wash in warm soapy water). The outside too needs impeccable care to keep its shine.

Cast iron is still a top favorite and has a set future with induction hobs which need ferrous metal to activate. The casseroles conduct and retain heat well over minimal heat which makes them excellent on fuel. They are, however, heavy, and when hot don't take kindly to cold liquids. They can also rust, especially on the base, so always read accompanying literature to see if they have been given a protective coating.

Enameled or porcelainized casseroles can be light or heavy depending on the metal underneath. The coating is used to give a non-scratch, easy clean surface to cast iron, steel and aluminum. If the conductor itself is not good (and steel isn't) the coating will not make the pot better.

The choice of casseroles is wide, and while cost is a major guide to quality, countries all over the world have survived with inexpensive earthenware for centuries and cooks in high and low places swear by its reliability. Casseroles that double as saucepans lessen the need for more equipment, and those that resist the change of temperatures are obviously excellent for anyone who relies on quick meals from the freezer. Sizing is something to consider, for apart from anything else extra large pots take up a lot of space.

1 *Cast-iron casserole* 2, 3, 5 *Various bean pots* 4 *Earthenware casserole with handle* 6 *Porcelainized aluminum casserole* 7 *Porcelainized steel rectangular casserole* 8 *Stainless steel casserole* 9 *Glass-ceramic dish, suitable for freezer or oven* 10 *China casserole; make sure they are flameproof* 11 *Small porcelainized cast-iron casserole*

Baking battery

1 *Non-stick baking sheet* 2 *Langue de chat pan* 3 *Shallow non-stick baking pan* 4 *Figure '2'-shaped pan* 5 *Deep round cake pan* 6 *Layer cake pan with ease-out lever* 7 *Heart-shaped cake pan* 8 *Deep* *square cake pan* 9 *Horseshoe-shaped pan* 10 *Non-stick loaf pan* 11 *Deep heart-shaped cake pan* 12 *Wire cake rack* 13 *Plastic spatula* 14 *Plain and decorated muffin tins* 15 *Non-stick layer cake pan*

Choosing a baking battery really depends on the type of cooking you do most. You could have a whole range of layer cake pans in different diameters but this is unnecessary unless you make cakes very frequently. If space for storage is at a premium it makes even more sense to choose the shapes that have more than one use — springform cake pans, for example, can be used for pies and tarts. Baking pans are usually made of tinned steel or aluminum. If the tinned coating is too thin, it may wear off and the steel will rust. Aluminum is a good heat conductor, but for best results it should be sturdy — very light bakeware dents easily and can get too hot. All metal bakeware should be smooth inside with no crevices where food can get trapped; rolled edges make pans easier and safer to handle. Non-stick coatings vary in quality, but their presence enables food to be unmolded easily. The best ones will stand up to quite rough treatment but metal scourers or implements can mark the surface. Even non-stick pans should be greased before use (the trick is to use a different fat from the one in the recipe, shortening and oil being the best for they are bland and won't flavor the cake) and bottoms should be lined when making cakes with a high proportion of egg whites or nuts. After use, wipe rather than wash and store in a plastic bag. Metal bakeware without non-stick linings should be washed immediately after use, dried in a warm oven and brushed with a light coating of cooking oil before storing. As the atmosphere in most kitchens tends to be damp, anything likely to rust should be stored where air can circulate.

1 *British raised pie mold* 2 *Tinned steel pudding mold* 3 *Pâté en croûte mold* 4 *Fluted tart pan* 5 *Fluted flan ring* 6 *Brioche mold* 7 *Hinged pâté mold with patterned sides* 8 *Springform pan* 9 *Glass savarin mold* 10 *Springform tube pan*

Ovenproof glass and ceramic bakeware has the advantage of being smooth inside. Heat is conducted slowly and evenly, but these types of dishes need to be placed on a heated baking sheet in the oven to prevent any sogginess in the base of cakes or pastries. Their resistance to thermal shock (sudden change in temperature) is not very great so take care when transferring from oven to worktop. This type of bakeware is easy clean and doesn't need to be oiled before storing.

Cake pans can have loose bases or spring clips at the side. When using springform pans place base rim side up on worktop, place round above it and then close the clips – this will ensure that the base fits the groove in the side and won't move or allow batter to escape. Bases can then be greased and floured, or greased and baselined for making cakes; for pastries, run knife around edge before releasing clips. Remember that round pans take less batter than square – a 7 inch round is equal to a 6 inch square.

Round pans with sloping sides are called by the French name *moule à manqué*. Individual molds for small or large cakes can be bought in a variety of shapes; muffin tins are plain or patterned to achieve different ends (madeleines, éclairs, cupcakes, barquettes etc).

Ring molds and tube pans are used for making savarins, brioches, kugelhopfs and come in a variety of sizes and traditional patterns.

Tart pans can be used for sponge cakes or pies – some have raised centers for fillings, some have fluted edges and a choice between removable or fixed bases, some are deep, some shallow. They range from tiny to party-size and offer great versatility. Fluted flan rings with or without bases can be difficult to clean so always soak after use.

Loaf pans and pâté molds are plain or patterned, come in a wide range of sizes and shapes, and some have hinged sides making for easy removal of hot water crust pies, pâtés and breads. Wash immediately after use, coat with light brushing of oil and store in plastic bags.

Baking sheets (or cookie sheets) are usually oblong with shallow sides and are mostly used for cookies, and as a base for plain or fluted flan rings when making pastry cases. Jelly roll pans are similar but have deeper sides.

Wire racks, essential for cooling cakes, cookies and some pastries, are meshed to allow good circulation of air. If leaving food (especially cakes) overnight, cover with a towel to prevent it becoming crusty.

Other equipment useful in baking includes a rolling pin which can be wood, with or without handles, or ceramic with a facility for filling with cold water when pastry making (everything cold with pastry, everything warm with bread). A wooden board is best for bread making, a marble slab for pastry making. A rubber headed spatula is the next best thing to children for getting mixing bowls absolutely clean; a flexible wide metal spatula aids the parting of a cake or pastry from a pan.

Preserving battery

The equipment you need for preserving depends on the type of preserving you are going to do. A preserving kettle makes sense for a jam-maker, but as it doesn't have a cover, it isn't any use for canning. With jars, the same again is true.

Preserving kettles used for making jams, jellies, marmalades and chutneys should be made of aluminum or stainless steel, with or without enamel linings, and should have a wide top for maximum evaporation (the driving off of the liquid ensures a good set). Copper can be used for jams, but it must *not* be lined with tin as this melts at a lower temperature than the boiling point of sugar. Copper, iron or brass must not be used when making chutneys as they react with the vinegar to give an unpleasant taste.

The ideal preserving kettle should be deep so that a sweet preserve mixture will only fill it halfway, for after the sugar is added and a rolling boil is established, the mixture will rise. If you don't have a preserving kettle, it's best to divide the mix between saucepans, or use an open pressure cooker. To help prevent the preserve from burning on the bottom or

1 *Stainless steel preserving kettle* 2 *Jelly bag* 3 *Jelly thermometer* 4 *Wide-mouth funnel for filling containers* 5 *Mason canning jar* 6 *Bailed canning jars with glass lids* 7 *Metal ladle* 8 *Trivet*

forming a scum, rub inside the pan base with glycerine or butter.

Bowls for brining vegetables to be pickled should be made of glass, pottery or stone because of the effect of salt on metal.

A good sharp knife is needed for preparing the fruit and vegetables.

A jelly thermometer will indicate setting point in jams, but there are other ways of discovering when setting point has been reached (see page 23).

Spoons for stirring can be made of wood or stainless steel and should have long handles. A skimmer or slotted spoon is needed for skimming off pits and scum as they rise to the surface of jam. A wooden spoon can also be used for the flake test (see page 196).

Muslin is always useful for containing seeds and pith to help extract the pectin in jam making, or for wrapping whole herbs and spices in pickling.

Jelly bags are large seamless bags specially designed for making jelly, and you can make your own from any closely woven material, such as unbleached muslin, flannel or even a dish towel as long as the weave will allow the fruit to separate

from the liquid that is to become jelly. First the jelly bag is scalded with boiling water, then each corner is secured so the bag is suspended, and a bowl placed below the bag. The cooked fruit is poured into the bag and left until the juice has dripped through into the bowl — this takes at least two hours but don't leave for longer than 24 hours or it will have to be reboiled to kill bacteria. Don't be tempted to press the fruit as this will cloud the jelly.

Jars for jams, jellies, chutneys and marmalades can be any shape or size, as long as they have no cracks or chips and can take the boiling mixture and processing. Wash well in warm, soapy water, scald with boiling water and place upside down to dry. Heat in a 225° oven. Fill while hot. Jars used for canning should have lids that

Above: smoking equipment to use at home in an airy place such as a fireplace, shed or conservatory where the fumes can disperse easily. Made of aluminium, smokers have a box to hold the sawdust, a rack for the food, a lid to keep the heat in and a windshield for the fuel container

allow air and steam to escape during processing, so that they will form a vacuum when cooling (see page 198). Jellies may be sealed with paraffin wax.

A boiling water bath is the finishing touch for jams, to insure against spoilage. Process at 212° for 10 minutes in a canner. A boiling-water bath is also suitable for strong-acid foods (fruits and vinegared mixtures, including most tomato products), but all other vegetables, etc. must be processed in a pressure canner.

A funnel with a wide mouth is specially designed to sit in a canning jar so that mixtures can easily be transferred from pan to jar without any spills. Alternatively, you can use a metal ladle the same size as the jar tops or a heat-resistant jug.

Label all preserves clearly with the name and date when they were made.

Smoke boxes for home smoking consist of a metal box lined with sawdust, a grid to hold food and a tight-fitting lid. The box is placed over a container of fuel — usually wood alcohol — which causes the sawdust to smolder. The smoke builds up in the box and cooks the food at the same time. The food is usually left till the box is cold before serving.

Boiling

Boiling is a method of cooking by "moist heat" in liquid at a temperature of 212° at sea level. Once the liquid – and it can be stock, acidulated water, salted water or water flavored with wine, herbs or spices – has reached its boiling point, it can get no hotter and if kept at that temperature will evaporate into the atmosphere. The longer the cooking, the more nutrients are lost with the steam created in the process.

In most cooking, after the boiling point has been reached, the heat is reduced to 185–190°, known as the simmering temperature. The water can swirl around the food destroying any bacteria and cooking food thoroughly without causing it to disintegrate which it would do if left at a full fast boil.

Moreover, a rolling boil soon raises the vapor pressure of the liquid to a point where it is greater than the atmospheric pressure outside the pan, and it will boil over. Atmospheric pressure has a great effect on the boiling point of liquids. The less dense the atmosphere, the lower the pressure exerted on the surface of the liquid – this results in a lowered boiling point. If you live in Denver, Colorado, at a height of 6,000 feet above sea level, water boils at 201° and because the simmering temperature is correspondingly lower, the food takes longer to cook. If you happened to be cooking at the bottom of a mine shaft which is below sea level, the reverse would be the case. Salt added to water raises the boiling point to 224° and food will cook more quickly. This, apart from taste reasons, is why it is added at the start to vegetables which have a short cooking time, and at the end to stocks and stews which have a slower cooking time. Salt also draws out natural juices in food, and in long cooking you want these to be sealed in. Simmering tenderizes tough cuts of medium-quality meat such as brisket of beef, and renders elderly poultry more succulent.

Simmering in water extracts strong flavor from foods – salted meats such as ham, and vegetables such as onions, peppers and thick-stalked greens. Stocks and soups are simmered to get the maximum flavor from the bones, vegetables and other ingredients. Long simmering, unfortunately, extracts water soluble, heat-affected nutrients (vitamins B1 and C, for example) which is why it is important to keep the pan covered to lessen the rate of evaporation.

The amount of liquid used when boiling foods is subject to argument. The "conservation" method favors little water in a tightly closed pan so that all the nutrients are contained. This can cause green vegetables to turn gray because of a chemical reaction between the vegetable chlorophyll and the steam. You also have to take care that the food doesn't burn! Using a lot of water, especially in short cooking required particularly with green vegetables, is considered by others to be best so long as the cooking liquid is not thrown away but is used as a base for soups, sauces and gravies. A lot of water keeps its heat longer than a little water, and quickly heats greens through. Root vegetables require a lot of water and longer cooking at a simmering temperature with the lid on.

simmer

Most food is simmered not boiled in liquid. Small bubbles of dissolved air float upwards to break just below the surface. The temperature of 185–190° can be maintained over low heat

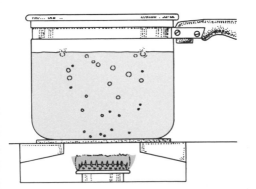

medium boil

Here, the surface is quite turbulent and the temperature of the water is 212°. Evaporation happens fastest at boiling point and will take with it volatile acids from foods

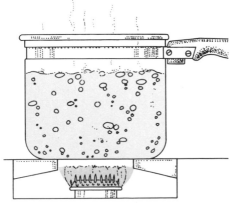

rolling boil

The temperature is no higher – unless sugar or salt is added – but the water boils faster as heat is higher. Used in jam making, cooking pasta, or to reduce liquid, most other foods will break up

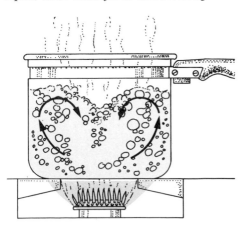

Boiling techniques

absorption

A measured amount of rice will be cooked to perfection in twice its volume of water only if no evaporation takes place. The pot must be covered as soon as rice and water are in, brought to a boil, then reduced to simmer.

additions

Various things are added to foods which are boiled.
Acids such as vinegar, lemon or cream of tartar help to counteract alkalinity in hard water, and preserve red color in vegetables and fruit. They will also keep white foods white especially if freezing.
Butter is added during jam making to prevent it boiling over, and to lessen scum.
Oil is added to fast boiling water when cooking pasta to prevent it sticking together.
Salt flavors as well as helping foods cook quicker as it raises boiling point. Add after water comes to a boil, or at end of cooking of beans and meats (it toughens otherwise).
Sugar is added in pinches to enhance natural sweetness of vegetables, or to glaze them. Added to fruit and cereals for sweetness – but generally at the end of cooking.

blanching

Has a variety of meanings. It can mean placing foods in boiling water to loosen skins (almonds, tomatoes, onions), or it can be applied to the whitening of variety meats (sweetbreads) and vegetables (salsify) in vinegared water before cooking. The French term for a flour paste used for whitening is *un blanc*. In freezing, foods are blanched to prevent enzyme action causing deterioration in color and flavor even while frozen. The food is put into boiling water for a set time, then into ice-cold water for the same time.

blood heat

This is the temperature at which rennet works to set junket – 98.4° on a thermometer, or when a little finger dipped into the milk feels neither hot nor cold. The term "hand hot" applies to water and is used with yeast and yogurt. For yeast the temperature should be 105° for fresh, 110° for dried; for yogurt, 110–120°.

clarifying

Method used to filter and clear stocks and broths. Egg whites and sometimes shells and ground meat are put into the boiling liquid. As the eggs coagulate specks of meat and vegetables are trapped and come to the top of the pot as a crust which should be lightly cracked in the middle so simmering can be seen. Liquid is strained when clear.

conductivity

The way heat passes through pots is important in cooking. Conductors of heat in order of effectiveness are: copper, aluminum, cast iron, stainless steel. Stainless steel pans often have a copper-coated base to improve conductivity, but a "sandwich" of copper in the base is much more effective. Copper pans are lined with tin to prevent formation of verdigris, a poisonous green coating. Preserving kettles aren't lined because the melting point of tin is lower than the boiling point of sugar. Plain steel is liable to become hot in places – called hot spotting – which can cause food to burn and stick. Even when coated with enamel inside and out, if the steel is not of good quality the pan's performance will not be improved. Enamel coatings are added to pans to make them easy to clean, but they will scratch or chip if treated harshly. Big pans need medium to heavy-ground bases so they won't distort and become uneven – aluminum cast in a mold will not distort.

covering

A lid helps keep steam and any nutrients dissolved in it in the pan or pot – this is important when little water is used with vegetables (called the conservation method). With stocks or stews which have a long cooking time and a lot of liquid, partial covering is best. Pasta, however, should not be covered; nor should most green vegetables as a chemical reaction of their chlorophyll and the steam will make them turn an unattractive gray color.

double boiling

Safeguard for delicate sauces, egg custards or chocolate which will spoil if over-heated. The food is kept at a distance above simmering water during cooking, either in a bowl over a pan, or in a double boiler made specially for the purpose.

infusing

Also called steeping, this means bringing a liquid to the boil, then pouring it over flavoring (herbs, spices, tea) and leaving it to stand so the flavors are drawn out. When milk is infused, it is brought almost to boiling point with flavorings (onions, cloves, blade of mace, bay leaf, peppercorns for sauces; vanilla bean or cinnamon stick for custards), covered and left to stand.

par-boiling

Boiling foods for a short time to partly cook them. Usually applied to root vegetables and tubers which will then be sautéed, roasted or baked.

percolating

A method of brewing coffee in which coming-to-a-boil water is cycled through coffee grounds to extract the flavor.

poaching

Ideal for delicate food, it is cooked in liquid at a temperature of 180–185°.

reducing

Method used when a large amount of liquid needs to be lessened, eg with stocks, sauces. The liquid is boiled uncovered over a high heat in pan with large surface area – as liquid evaporates, the flavors are concentrated. Any alcohol included disappears in the steam, but the taste remains. Meat or fish stock boiled down to one-tenth or less of its original volume is syrupy when warm, and jellied when cool – this is the best method of freezing stocks for the concentrate takes little space. Do not add too much seasoning before reducing liquids as they will increase in taste. Generally speaking, only unthickened liquids are reduced; oil and milk are not reduced.

refreshing

When boiled foods are cooked ahead of eating, rinse under cold water to stop the cooking. Before serving place in fast boiling water for 2–3 minutes, then drain.

replenishing

Keep a kettle of boiling water ready to replenish liquid in pan after evaporation. It must be boiling or the temperature will be reduced and cooking time lengthened.

scalding

Has several applications. In general it means pouring boiling water through material to sterilize it, making it easier for liquid to drain through when making jellies, or straining clarified stocks. Butter muslin is also scalded

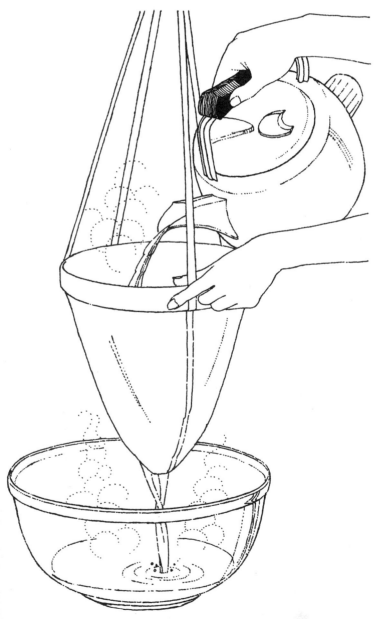

before being used to drain coagulated milk to make curd cheese. The term is used too for milk brought almost to boiling point either for infusing, or for custards.

skimming

Technique used to clear stocks and stews of fat and scum which rise to the surface. It can be done during boiling with a skimmer or strips of paper towels; if left to cool, the fat will set and can be lifted off with a skimmer. Jam at a rolling boil is skimmed once or twice to remove any frothy scum, pits and seeds which would spoil look when set.

sterilization

Method of destroying harmful bacteria. Essential in preserving and canning, jam and yogurt making, and in preparing muslin and jelly bags used for straining. Most milks are heat treated to extend keeping qualities – pasteurized milk is heated

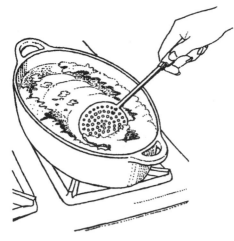

for the least amount of time. Fresh untreated milk should be sterilized before making yogurt – bring to just below boiling point (190°), maintain temperature for 10 minutes. Strain, then cool.

timing

Vitally important in boiling if foods are to look and taste their best. Foods should be boiled as close as possible to eating although some are left to stand in their cooking water. Over-cooking destroys food value, flavor and texture.

thickening

This can be done at various stages during boiling – the term for it is liaison, which means a combination of ingredients which bind and thicken. Sauces are thickened by a roux, a mixture of melted fat and flour, heated to expand the starch and cook the flour before liquid is added. Flour or cornstarch can be blended with water or mixed with cream and stirred into a soup or stew (after reduction of liquid if there's too much) while simmering. The starch grains burst and collapse at 200° and become gelatinous – keep stirring for 3–5 minutes so the liquid thickens evenly. Arrowroot works more quickly: it is blended with hot water, stirred in off the heat, and thickens liquid in time it takes to return it to boiling point. Grated potatoes, semolina and tapioca take 15–20 minutes to break down or become transparent and thicken soups and stews. Beaten eggs, often mixed with cream, enrich as well – place in tureen, pour in boiling liquid and whisk all the time till thick. Heavy cream and yogurt are also good thickeners.
Beurre manié is made by mashing equal amounts of butter and flour together. Whisk small pieces into sauces and soups at the end of cooking time, and bring to a boil whisking.

Sugar boiling techniques

Successful sugar boiling relies on care and attention — it certainly can't be rushed. Cover the required amount of sugar with water and bring very slowly to a boil (the sugar must be dissolved before the water boils or the syrup will be grainy). Weather and altitude are also important — dry, cool weather is perfect for sugar boiling. On humid days, you'll need to add a few degrees to each stage, because of the way sugar absorbs moisture; the higher you are above sea level, the more the temperature at each stage will be reduced (at 6000 feet syrup will reach soft ball at 220°).

The stages of sugar boiling are critical in making confectionery for each gives a different texture. While the sugar is boiling wash down the pan sides above the level of the liquid with bristle brush (nylon will melt) dipped into cold water, or you can cover the pan for 2–3 minutes so steam will condense on the lid and wash the crystals back into the liquid. A pinch of cream of tartar or a squeeze of lemon juice will also stop graining.

After the sugar has dissolved, never stir the syrup. When using a thermometer make sure it is heated in hot water first (so it won't break). In between testings put it back into hot water to remove any crystals.

In jam making, sugar should be 60% of the final weight of the jam — too much and it will crystallize, too little and it will grow mold. Jam is made at a full rolling boil to evaporate the liquid and extract the pectin to thicken the jam.

Syrups for poaching fruit or for soaking cakes made from yeast dough have different densities (that is, the amount of sugar to water); they usually reach the right concentration after a set boiling time. They should never reach soft ball stage.

To clean pans in which sugar has been boiled, fill with water and bring to a boil uncovered (put in sugar-coated spoons as well). Jam and toffee will melt into the water and can be poured away.

Left: making caramel to coat candy apples. A brush is needed to wash down the crystals before sugar dissolves, and a thermometer to indicate the stage at which syrup is ready (345°). If a copper pan is used it shouldn't be tin lined for tin melts at a lower temperature than the boiling point of sugar

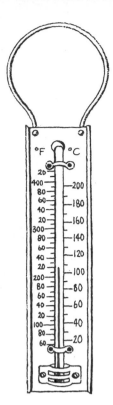

sugar thermometer

A sugar thermometer should register up to 400° and has the various boiling stages marked. Check its accuracy frequently by bringing it to a boil in water (212°). Always warm it in very hot water before sliding it into the center of the boiling mixture. Hold it firmly and don't let it touch the pan base or you'll get a reading of the metal's heat, not what is being cooked. Bend down so your eye is level with the rim of the pan. When the required temperature is reached, remove pan from heat, then take out thermometer and place it back in jug to cool.

220°

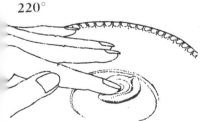

jam setting point

Remove pan from heat and drop a little jam from a spoon on to a chilled saucer. A skin should form on the surface in less than 5 minutes and should wrinkle when pushed gently with a finger. If it doesn't, cook the jam more.

225°

thread

Don't continue to stir once the sugar has dissolved in the water. Always have a bowl of cold water on hand when testing the various stages of sugar boiling. For thread stage, use a spoon to lift a little syrup out of the pan and pour it slowly into the bowl – it will thicken before it reaches the water. Alternatively, dip fingers in cold water, quickly into the syrup, then back into cold water. The syrup should pull into a soft thread as the fingers are separated. At this stage, it's ready to be made into butter cream.

230–234°

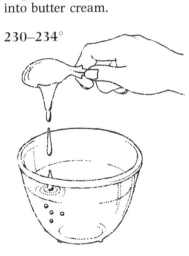

large thread

Boil the syrup for a little longer then test again for the thread stage. This time, the thread formed should be shorter and thicker and will snap rather than stretch when pulled. If a little of the syrup is dropped into cold water from a spoon, it should form small, pearl-like balls in the water. The syrup is ready to be used for adding fruits and boiling them until crystallized.

234–240°

soft ball

Drop a little syrup into the cold water, leave for 1 minute; when rolled between finger and thumb it should form a soft malleable ball. Use for fondant, fudge, some frosting and cooked almond paste.

270–290°

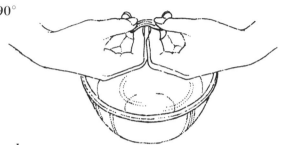

soft crack

Pour a little of the sugar into cold water. This time threads should form that bend but do not break; they are brittle, but stick to teeth. Use for hard caramels, marshmallow, nougat.

300–310°

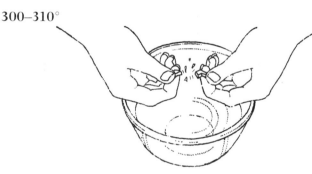

hard crack

Tested again in the cold water, the sugar forms brittle threads that crack like glass, do not stick to the teeth. Use for making nut brittles, spun sugar and candied fruits.

250–266°

hard ball

Test once again as for the soft ball stage. This time, the ball that is formed should be harder, firmer and cannot be squashed by the fingers. This is the stage at which it is used for Italian meringue and the softer caramels.

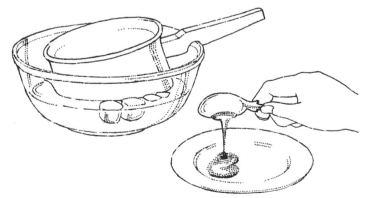

caramel

As the sugar continues to boil, it turns a golden brown, then darkens rapidly. Watch it carefully as it quickly burns. Use it for crème caramel, oranges in caramel, some cake toppings.

Poaching techniques

Poaching, in cooking terms, means capturing the heat of the liquid at the lowest possible termperature for the shortest possible time. At around 180–185°, which is just below simmering point, there are no bubbles and the liquid merely trembles a little. Though poaching is usually carried out on top of the stove, it can be done in the oven but, in this case, less liquid is used, the pan is always covered and the liquid is brought to poaching point before it is transferred to the oven.

Poaching is gentle — soft-fleshed foods such as fish, eggs, and fresh or dried fruits do not break up, and shrinkage is reduced to a minimum because of the lower temperature. It is not a suitable method for tenderizing tough tissue. Delicate food should be poached just long enough for it to develop its maximum flavor and be cooked through. If a thermometer is used during the process, it is only to check that the temperature is right — for if the water boils, the food will break up.

Chickens up to 12 weeks old are poached to retain their delicacy of taste and texture. Chicken breasts are similarly cooked in water with an acid — wine or lemon juice — which keeps them white. A boned, stuffed, rolled gelantine is wrapped in cheesecloth and poached before being cooled, untied and coated with a chaudfroid sauce. Delicate dumpling mixtures of chicken or fish which are bound together with beaten egg whites are poached rather than simmered.

Whole fish — usually the larger ones like salmon, bass and rainbow trout — are placed in a fish kettle or poaching pan containing simmering salted water, wine, fish stock or court-bouillon which comes up to within 1 inch of the top of the fish. The liquid must be brought back to a simmer — to firm the skin a little and destroy bacteria — before the heat is lowered to poaching point. If the fish is to be served cold, let it cool in the poaching liquid so the fish stays plump and moist. Smaller fish or shellfish are usually placed in simmering water and then the heat is turned down. Fruit is poached in syrup which because of the sugar content is at a slightly higher temperature than water. The principle is, however, the same: the fruit cooks till tender without disintegrating. Another way is to cook halved fruit gently in a little water in a covered pan and then mix in the sugar when the fruit is tender. Cook just a little longer so sugar dissolves and thickens the cooking liquid, but watch it so it doesn't burn. Poaching can be done off the heat with quick-cooked foods like eggs, kippers.

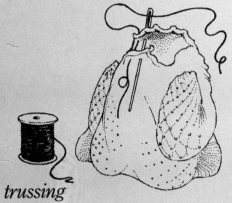

trussing
Compactness is essential during poaching which is why stuffed poultry should be sewn across vent to keep stuffing inside

en colère
Simple trick for poaching fish in round pan — remove backbone, put tail in teeth

cupping eggs
If not using an egg-poacher, give eggs good shape by breaking into a cup before adding to the shivering water

Poaching around the world

à la cancalaise French garnish for fish comprising poached oysters and shrimp in sauce.

au bleu French term for freshly caught freshwater fish which when covered in boiling vinegar turn blue before being poached.

boller Danish egg-enriched small dumplings poached in soup.

bunter hans Large German dumpling made with breadcrumbs, wrapped in cloth and poached.

butternockerl Austrian dumplings poached in salted water and served in clear beef soup.

coddler British porcelain or china pot with a lid in which an egg is poached (the process can also be called boiling and steaming!)

compote French cold dessert of fresh or dried fruits poached in sugar syrup.

en colère French term used for fish (it literally means "in anger"). The backbone is removed and the fish's tail is pushed into its mouth — an easy shape for poaching in a round pan.

oeufs à la neige French dessert in which "eggs" of whisked egg white are poached, drained and served on sweet egg custard.

quenelles Delicate French dumplings of fish or white meats bound with thick sauce, lightened with egg white and poached.

FOOD	0	5	10	15	20	25	30	35	40	45	50
apples, whole				SY							
rings			SY								
apricots, whole			SY								
halves			SY								
bass			per lb				CB				
chicken, stewing, whole							W	CB	per lb		
quarters						W	CB				
chicken, broiler, whole					per lb		CB				
quarters							CB				
cod, steaks				CB	ST						
fillets			M	CB	ST						
dumplings						W	ST				
eggs (3½ mins)				WM							
flounder, whole				CB	M						
fillets			CB		M						
haddock, fillets			CB		M						
smoked, fillets			W		CB	M					
kippers, whole			W								
fillets			W								
mackerel, whole					per lb			W	CB	ST	
peaches, whole				SY							
halves			SY								
pears, whole				SY							
halves, quarters			SY								
quenelles			W	ST							
salmon, up to 6lb				per lb			CB				
7lb and over				per lb			CB				
steaks/cutlets			CB								
sole, whole				CB	M						
fillets			CB		M						
trout, small whole				CB							
whiting, whole				CB	M						
fillets			CB		M						

Alternative poaching liquids: W water; CB court-bouillon; SY syrup; ST stock; M milk

Boiling

Foods which need only short cooking time are placed in boiling water, and the timing begins when the water returns to a boil. When cooking green vegetables, a lot of water will cook them faster so that they retain their color, texture and flavor. If little water is used on the grounds that fewer nutrients (minerals and vitamins) will be lost, the vegetables are more likely to alter in appearance and taste because they take longer to become tender. Covering the pan (with green vegetables) will hasten cooking but will cause the vegetables to discolor — remember that adding alkaline baking soda will preserve the green but will destroy vitamin C. Pasta should be cooked uncovered from start to finish in a large pan full of plenty of swiftly boiling water to prevent strands or shapes sticking together — if you don't have a very big pan, keep adding more boiling water during cooking (the same applies for rice by the "into boiled" method).

FOOD	TIME IN MINUTES
almonds, soak to skin	
apricots, halved	
artichokes, globe	
beans, lima	
green	
boiling rings (sausage)	
broccoli spears	
brussels sprouts	
cabbage, wedges	
shredded	
calamares (squid)	
carrots, old, sliced	
cauliflower, florets	
celeriac, quartered	
celery, hearts	
chestnuts, to skin	
choko, sliced	
corn, on the cob	
kernels	
cornmeal	
eggs, to soft cook	
medium	
large (3¼ mins)	
extra large (3¾ mins)	
eggs, to medium cook	
medium	
large	
extra large	
eggs, to hard cook	
medium	
large (4½ mins)	
extra large	
eggplants, whole	
(to prepare for stuffing)	
figs, to skin	
frankfurters	
greens, shredded	

Time scale: 0, 5, 10, 15, 20, 25, 30, 35, 40

FOOD	TIME IN MINUTES
kippers	
kohlrabi, small whole	
leeks, sliced	
small whole	
lobsters	
spiny (crayfish)	
oatmeal	
oats, rolled	
okra	
onions, pickling, to peel	
medium, to parboil	
pasta, cannelloni, lasagne	
macaroni	
broad noodles	
shells, spaghetti	
vermicelli, thin noodles	
stuffed	
peaches, to skin	
pears, whole	
peas, fresh	
peppers, to blanch	
plums, halved	
rice, ground	
flaked	
long grain	
short grain, pudding	
semolina	
snow peas	
summer squash, chunks	
tapioca	
tomatoes, to skin	(½ min)
vegetables, frozen	
vine leaves, to blanch	
winter squash, chunks	
whole, to stuff	
zucchini, sliced	
small whole	

Time scale (minutes): 0, 5, 10, 15, 20, 25, 30, 35, 40

cook's know-how

All vegetables should be prepared so they are equal in size and will cook at the same speed – but do remember that the more cut surfaces there are, the greater the leeching (the drawing out into the liquid of water soluble vitamins and minerals). Add a little vinegar or a slice of lemon to the pan when cooking eggs in boiling water – if they do crack in the movement of the water, the whites won't ooze out. Reduce heat so eggs cook at a simmer.

Boiling from cold

Food from which a nutritious and rich broth is required should be put into cold water and brought to a boil. It extracts the juices and flavor so that they mingle in the liquid during long, slow cooking. Added vegetables and herbs flavor both the broth and the food being boiled, especially in stocks and stews. The method is also used to remove an undesirable taste — oversaltiness in ham, for example — and anything that will spoil the look of a finished dish like, for instance, scum from meats such as veal; the liquid is discarded and the process begun again. Dried vegetables are brought slowly to a boil, boiled for a short time then left to soak, thus reducing soaking time from 12 hours to two. It is also the way to reconstitute dried food. Gradual absorption plumps them whereas boiling water will "set" the outside before the inside cooks. Root vegetables which are more dense than those grown above the ground cook more evenly when placed in cold water which is brought to a boil.

FOOD	TIME IN MINUTES	TIME IN HOURS
	0 5 10 20 30 40 50	1 2 3 4
apples, sliced		
artichokes, jerusalem		
barley		
beans, dried, to hot soak		
dried, soaked		
dried soy, soaked		
beef (brisket)		
up to 3lb	per lb +30 mins	
3½lb and over		per lb +45 mins
beets, small whole		
bones/trimmings for stock		
beef		
fish		
poultry		
brains*		
carp, steaks		
carrots, old sliced		
cherries		
chestnuts, to purée		
chicken, whole, stewing		
clams		
crabs, whole		
cranberries		
currants, fresh		
eel, chunks		
eggs, to soft cook		
medium (2½ mins)		
large (2¾ mins)		
extra large		
eggs, to medium cook		
medium (3½ mins)		
large		
extra large (4½ mins)		
eggs, to hard cook		
medium		
large		
extra large		

*Just bring to boil

FOOD	TIME IN MINUTES								TIME IN HOURS			
	0	5	10	20	30	40	50	1	2	3	4

fish, dried*
gooseberries
haddock, smoked*
ham
  1–3lb   per lb+25 mins
  4–9lb   per lb+20 mins
  10lb and over   per lb+15 mins
lentils, to soak*
marrow bone
oranges, whole
  shredded
parsnips, quartered
periwinkles
plums
pork, head
  fresh pork sides
  pig's feet
potatoes, whole, new
  quartered, old
rhubarb
rice, long/medium grain
  brown
  wild
rutabaga, chunks
salsify
scallops
spinach
sweetbreads, lamb
sweet potatoes, small
tongue, beef, whole, fresh
  beef, pickled
  lamb
tripe
turnips, quartered
yams, chunks

*Just bring to boil

An onion or bouquet garni can be added when boiling dried legumes, but leave salt to the end or it will make the skins tough.

With fruits such as currants, cranberries and gooseberries, sugar should not be added till the fruit has softened otherwise the skins will toughen.

When cooking meat cuts or bones for stock, skim as water comes to a boil or scum will sour and spoil the cooking liquid.

Brown stock

This is a rich, meaty stock with excellent color and flavor. It can be clarified to make consommé (page 58). Use it in hearty soups and stews and for braising red meat and vegetables. Don't throw the meat away after straining; grind it, season well and use to stuff peppers or pasta or to make a hash

Makes about 1½ quarts

Overall timing 4¾ hours plus cooling

Equipment Stockpot, skimmer, butter muslin, sieve

Freezing Boil strained stock rapidly to reduce to 2–3 cups. Pour into ice-cube tray and freeze. Pack cubes into freezer bags, seal and label. Freezer life: 6 months. To use: add to soups, gravies, casseroles, diluting as required

INGREDIENTS

1	Marrow bone or veal shank
1lb	Beef shank
1	Carrot
1	Onion
1	Stalk of celery
2 quarts	Cold water
	Bouquet garni
6	Black peppercorns

METHOD
1 Wipe the bone and saw into pieces (if using veal shank, split it in half). Wipe and trim the beef and cut into large pieces.
2 Place in a stockpot and cook, stirring, over a high heat till browned.
3 Scrape and halve the carrot. Remove any papery or damaged skin from the onion, leaving the inner brown skin on, then cut the onion in half. Wash the celery and cut in half.
4 Add to the meat with the water, bouquet garni and peppercorns. Bring slowly to a boil.
5 Skim off any scum. Reduce the heat, almost cover the pan with a lid, then simmer for at least 4 hours without boiling.
6 Wring muslin out in hot water and use to line sieve. Strain stock and discard the flavorings. Leave the stock to cool completely.
7 Skim off any fat, then use the stock as required. Cover and refrigerate if not using immediately.

White stock

White stock, made entirely from veal, has a gelatinous quality and delicate flavor, making it superb for use in fine sauces or soups. Raw veal releases a great deal of gray scum, so it needs to be blanched in boiling water and then rinsed thoroughly under cold water. Rather than waste the meat, remove it from the pan after about 2 hours and serve it separately

Makes about 1½ quarts

Overall timing 4¾ hours plus cooling

Equipment Stockpot, skimmer, butter muslin, sieve

Freezing Boil strained stock rapidly to reduce to 2–3 cups. Pour into ice-cube tray and freeze. Pack cubes into freezer bags, seal and label. Freezer life: 6 months. To use: add to soups, gravies, casseroles, diluting as required

INGREDIENTS

1 lb	Boneless veal shoulder roast
1	Veal shank
1lb	Breast of veal
1	Carrot
1	Onion
1	Stalk of celery
	Bouquet garni
6	White peppercorns
2 quarts	Cold water

METHOD
1 Wipe the meat and chop the shank and breast into pieces. Place in a pan, cover with cold water, bring to a boil and simmer for 5 minutes. Drain and rinse thoroughly under cold water, then return to rinsed pan.
2 Scrape and slice the carrot; peel and quarter the onion. Wash and chop the celery. Add vegetables to the pan with the bouquet garni, peppercorns and water.
3 Bring slowly to a boil. Skim off any scum, then reduce the heat, partially cover with the lid and simmer for at least 4 hours.
4 Wring muslin out in hot water and use to line sieve. Strain the stock and discard the flavorings. Leave the stock to cool completely.
5 Skim off any fat, then use the stock as required. Cover and refrigerate if not using immediately.

Poultry stock

Uncooked bones and giblets give the best results — when these are not available use a whole stewing chicken instead. Prepare the stock as below and simmer till the chicken is tender. Remove from the heat and leave to cool, then lift the bird out, carve the meat neatly and use as required. Crack the bones and carcass, then return to the pan with the skin and complete cooking, straining and skimming. For game stock, replace chicken trimmings with those from game birds

Makes about 1½ quarts

Overall timing 3½ hours plus cooling

Equipment Rolling pin, stockpot, skimmer, butter muslin, sieve

Freezing Boil strained stock rapidly to reduce to 2–3 cups. Pour into ice-cube tray and freeze. Pack cubes into freezer bags, seal and label. Freezer life: 6 months. To use: add to soups, gravies, casseroles, diluting as required

INGREDIENTS

1lb	Uncooked poultry carcass, bones, giblets
1	Carrot
1	Onion
1	Stalk of celery
	Blade of mace
	Bay leaf
6	White peppercorns
2 quarts	Cold water

METHOD
1 Wash the carcass and bones and crush with a rolling pin. Place in the stockpot. Wash the giblets and add to the pan.
2 Scrape and halve the carrot. Peel and halve the onion. Wash, trim and halve the celery. Add to the pan with the mace, bay leaf, peppercorns and water.
3 Bring slowly to a boil, then skim off any scum. Reduce the heat and partially cover with a lid, then simmer for at least 3 hours.
4 Wring muslin out in hot water and use to line sieve. Strain stock and discard the flavorings. Leave the stock to cool completely.
5 Skim off any fat and use as required. Cover and refrigerate if not using the stock immediately.

Fish stock

Home-made fish stock is cheap and quick to prepare. The strong, concentrated type, known in France as *fumet de poisson*, is best for making fish sauces, while a lighter stock is sufficient for soups and poaching liquids. Ask the fish merchant for white fish trimmings. You shouldn't use strong, oily fish like herring or mackerel, but you can utilize shells from lobsters and shrimp. Fish stock doesn't keep well so don't use if it's more than 2 days old

Makes about 1½ quarts

Overall timing 55 minutes

Equipment Stockpot, skimmer, butter muslin, sieve

Freezing Boil strained stock rapidly to reduce to 2–3 cups. Pour into ice-cube trays and freeze. Pack cubes into freezer bags, seal and label. Freezer life: 1 month. To use: add to soups, sauces, casseroles, diluting as required

INGREDIENTS

1 lb	White fish trimmings including a head from cod, turbot or halibut
1	Carrot
1	Onion
1	Stalk of celery
	Bay leaf
3 tablespoons	Lemon juice
	Parsley stalks
6	White peppercorns
2 quarts	Cold water

METHOD

1 Wash the fish trimmings and place in the stockpot. Scrape and slice the carrot; peel and slice the onion. Wash, trim and slice the celery. Add to the pan with the bay leaf, lemon juice, parsley stalks, peppercorns and water.
2 Bring slowly to a boil. Skim off any scum, then reduce the heat. Partially cover and simmer for 30 minutes.
3 Wring out muslin in hot water and use to line sieve. Strain stock and discard the flavorings. Cover and chill if not using immediately. Otherwise use within 2 days of making.

Right: Bouillon — good clear stock served as a broth. Garnish with baked choux balls, shredded crêpes, or an egg yolk and chives

Thin soups

Thin soups rely for their flavor on a good strong basic stock made by the long simmering of either vegetables or meat. Although not thickened with flour, puréed vegetables or egg yolk and cream, they need not necessarily be clear. Often the stock is strained to remove the original flavorings, then an endless variety of ingredients can be added. Cheese, egg, noodles, or shredded or chopped meat or vegetables can make the soups quite substantial, but on the whole, they are served as appetizers rather than as main dish soups

Consommé

Consommé, the classic thin soup, is made from meat stock and carefully clarified. It can be served hot with various garnishes, or chilled and jellied. Try it cold with cream and a sprinkling of salmon caviar

APPETIZER   Serves 6

Overall timing 6 hours

Equipment Roasting pan, large saucepan, grinder, jelly bag

Freezing Complete to end of Step 7. Pour into a rigid container leaving 1 inch headroom. Cover, label and freeze. Freezer life: 3 months. To use: thaw at room temperature if serving cold, or place block in pan and reheat gently. Add sherry and salt just before serving

INGREDIENTS

	Brown stock
1lb	Marrow bone, sawn into pieces
1	Veal shank
1lb	Beef shank
2	Onions
2	Carrots
1	Stalk of celery
	Bouquet garni
6	Black peppercorns
2 quarts	Water
	Other ingredients
½lb	Lean beef for stew
1	Egg white
2 tablespoons	Dry sherry
	Salt

METHOD

1 Preheat the oven to 425°. Wipe the marrow bone, and veal and beef shank and place in a roasting pan. Cook near the top of the oven for about 30 minutes, turning occasionally, till browned.
2 Transfer to a large saucepan. Wash the onions, scrub the carrots, wash and trim the celery. Add to the pan with the bouquet garni and peppercorns.
3 Add the water and bring to a boil. Skim off any scum, cover and simmer for 3 hours. Strain and leave to cool.
4 Grind the beef for stew into a large saucepan and add the cold stock and the egg white.
5 Heat gently, whisking, till the egg white forms a thick froth on the soup. Stop whisking and bring slowly to just below boiling point.
6 Reduce heat to a gentle simmer so the foam is not disturbed. Simmer for 1½ hours.
7 Pour boiling water through a jelly bag hung over a bowl. Wring out the bag and discard the water. Pour the soup carefully into the jelly bag, letting the foam fall gently into the bag after the soup has run through. Pour the soup through again – it should be very clear and glossy by this time.
8 Add the sherry and salt to taste. Either reheat gently and serve hot, or chill and spoon the jellied consommé into chilled bowls to serve.

Below: Swiss consommé – plain consommé is accompanied by tasty pieces of marrow bone on toast and chopped parsley. Provide small spoons for scooping out and eating marrow

Swedish vegetable soup

A light, but delightfully refreshing thin soup which is flavored by a variety of vegetables which also provide some crunch and lots of color

APPETIZER Serves 6

Overall timing 1 hour

Equipment Saucepan

Freezing Pour into a rigid container, leaving 1 inch headroom. Cover, label and freeze. Freezer life: 3 months.
To use: place block in pan, heat gently till thawed, bring to a boil and adjust seasoning

Below: Swedish vegetable soup – a hot soup to serve on the cooler days in spring

INGREDIENTS

2	Large onions
1	Large leek
$\frac{1}{4}$ cup	Butter
1	Garlic clove
$\frac{1}{2}$ lb	Ripe tomatoes
$1\frac{1}{2}$ lb	White cabbage
$1\frac{1}{2}$ quarts	Water
1	Bay leaf
	Salt
	Freshly-ground black pepper
1	Red pepper
1 tablespoon	Chopped fresh dill

METHOD

1 Peel and chop the onions. Wash and trim the leek, cut into 1 inch lengths, then into quarters.
2 Heat the butter in a large saucepan, add the onions and leek and fry, stirring, for about 10 minutes till golden.
3 Peel and crush the garlic, add to pan. Blanch, peel and finely chop tomatoes; wash and shred the cabbage. Add to the pan and fry for 3 minutes, stirring well to release any sediment.
4 Stir in the water, add bay leaf and bring to a boil. Season, cover and simmer for 20 minutes.
5 Meanwhile, wash, deseed and thinly slice the pepper. Add to the soup and simmer for a further 10 minutes.
6 Remove from the heat, stir in the dill and adjust the seasoning. Serve immediately with buttered wholewheat or rye bread.

Thickened soups

Thickened soups are generally richer and more substantial than thin ones. They fall into two basic categories – those which thicken naturally by dissolving the starch in their ingredients (potatoes, beans, rice), and those which are thickened by the addition of some agent such as cornstarch, semolina, a roux, starchy vegetable purée, eggs or cream. The consistency required will dictate what thickener is used. For instance, mashed or grated potato makes for a grainy texture, while cornstarch imparts a clear, glossy finish, and the egg yolk/cream liaison, which binds as well as thickens, gives a fine, delicate smoothness. Thickeners can be added at the beginning of a dish, or be put in at the last minute.

Chicken and corn soup

Corn is a staple food in almost every country in South America and avocados are among the most popular of all fruits so it is hardly surprising that they are combined in this Latin American dish. Nourishing chicken stock is thickened with mashed potato, slices of corn are added and the soup is poured over cream, capers and sliced avocado

APPETIZER   Serves 6

Overall timing 1½ hours

Equipment Saucepan, potato masher

Freezing Not recommended

INGREDIENTS

2lb	Chicken portions
1	Large onion
2 tablespoons	Butter
¼ teaspoon	Ground cumin
1½ quarts	Chicken stock or broth
1lb	Floury potatoes
	Salt
	Freshly-ground black pepper
2	Ears of corn
1	Ripe avocado
¾ cup	Light cream or half-and-half
1 tablespoon	Drained capers

METHOD

1 Wipe and trim the chicken. Peel and chop the onion. Heat the butter in a large saucepan, add chicken and onion and fry for 5 minutes, turning chicken occasionally.
2 Add cumin and fry for 2 minutes. Add stock and bring to a boil. Cover and simmer for about 35 minutes till chicken is tender. Meanwhile, peel and dice the potatoes.
3 Lift chicken out of the pan. Add the potatoes to the stock, season and simmer for 10 minutes till tender.
4 Meanwhile, remove skin and bones from chicken and cut meat into strips. Husk the corn, discarding the silk. Cut into 1 inch thick slices, slicing across the cob.
5 Mash the potatoes in the soup to thicken it. Bring to a boil and add corn slices and chicken meat. Simmer for 10 minutes.
6 Peel and halve the avocado, removing the seed, and slice the flesh thinly. Place in a tureen with the cream and capers.
7 Taste the soup and adjust seasoning. Pour into the tureen and serve immediately with fresh bread.

Below: Chicken and corn soup – sweet, young ears of corn are best for this dish

Normandy shellfish soup

Normandy is famed for its shellfish and with dishes like this luscious soup one can see why. The liaison of egg yolks and cream gives a wonderfully smooth, rich texture

LUNCH OR SUPPER   Serves 4

Overall timing 1 hour

Equipment 2 saucepans, sieve, butter muslin

Freezing Not recommended

INGREDIENTS

1lb	Cockles or clams
2lb	Mussels
2½ cups	Water
¼ cup	Butter
½ cup	Flour
2½ cups	Milk
1 tablespoon	Lemon juice
¾ cup	Dry white wine
	Cayenne
2	Egg yolks
¾ cup	Light cream
1 tablespoon	Chopped parsley
	Salt
	Freshly-ground white pepper

METHOD

1 Scrub the cockles or clams and mussels. Put into a saucepan with the water and cook over a high heat for about 5 minutes till the shells open.
2 Strain the liquid through a sieve lined with butter muslin, and reserve. Remove cockles or clams and mussels from their shells, discarding any that remain closed, and reserve.
3 Heat the butter in a large saucepan, add the flour and cook for 1 minute. Gradually add the shellfish cooking liquid and milk and bring to a boil, stirring constantly. Cover and simmer for 10 minutes.
4 Add the lemon juice, wine and a pinch of cayenne with the reserved cockles or clams and mussels. Heat through for 5 minutes.
5 Put the egg yolks, cream and parsley into a warmed soup tureen and beat lightly with a fork. Pour the hot soup into the tureen, stirring constantly. Taste and adjust the seasoning and serve immediately with hot croûtons.

Spinach and pumpkin soup

An Italian-style soup made with a variety of vegetables which are cooked, then puréed and quickly fried with garlic and onion. The spinach turns the soup an attractive deep green color. If pumpkin is not available, use a summer squash instead – it will give the same kind of texture

APPETIZER   Serves 6

Overall timing 30 minutes

Equipment 2 saucepans, bowl, food mill or blender

Freezing Not recommended

INGREDIENTS

2	Medium-size turnips
2	Large potatoes
½lb	Pumpkin
4 cups	Chicken stock or broth
2lb	Spinach
	Salt
1	Large onion
1	Garlic clove
¼ cup	Butter
	Freshly-ground black pepper

METHOD

1 Wash and peel the turnips and potatoes. Peel the pumpkin and discard fibrous center and seeds.
2 Dice the vegetables and put into a saucepan. Add the stock and bring to a boil. Cover and simmer for 10 minutes till tender.
3 Meanwhile, wash spinach thoroughly. Discard any withered leaves or coarse stalks. Put the spinach into a large saucepan with only the water that clings to it, and a little salt. Cover the pan and bring to a boil. Simmer for 5 minutes, shaking the pan frequently. Drain, reserving the liquid. Spread the spinach on a board and shred finely.
4 Drain the vegetables, reserving the liquid. Purée the vegetables in a food mill or blender.
5 Peel and finely chop the onion. Peel the garlic. Heat the butter in a clean saucepan, add the onion and fry till transparent. Add the crushed garlic and the puréed vegetables and fry, stirring, for 5 minutes. Stir in the reserved cooking liquids and bring to a boil. Season to taste, then serve hot, with plenty of croûtons.

Wash and peel turnips and potatoes and prepare pumpkin. Dice all vegetables and simmer in stock for 10 minutes till tender

Wash spinach and put into pan with water that clings to it, and salt. Simmer for 5 minutes. Drain, reserving cooking liquid. Spread spinach on board and shred finely

Drain vegetables, reserving cooking liquid. Purée vegetables in food mill or blender. Peel and chop onion and fry in butter, till transparent

Add peeled, crushed garlic and puréed vegetables to pan and fry for 5 minutes. Stir in reserved cooking liquids and bring to a boil. Season. Serve with croûtons

Thick soups

Rich, hearty and full of warming nourishment, thick soups make a delicious meal in themselves. You will need a spoon and a fork to eat them as they usually contain chunks of some form of protein and vegetables, and may include pasta or rice to make them even more substantial. It's often not necessary to add a thickening agent as starch in the ingredients used dissolves in the liquid during cooking and thickens it naturally

Friuli minestrone

One of the many regional variations of Italy's famous soup. The vegetables can be varied according to what's in season, but beans and barley are a must for authenticity

LUNCH OR SUPPER   Serves 4—6

Overall timing 2 hours plus soaking

Equipment 2 bowls, 2 saucepans

Freezing Not recommended

INGREDIENTS

$1\frac{1}{2}$ cups	Dried pinto beans
1 cup	Pearl barley
2 quarts	Water
$\frac{3}{4}$lb	Lean boneless pork
4	Bacon slices
1	Onion
1	Stalk of celery
1	Carrot
1	Potato
1lb	White cabbage
3	Sage leaves
3 tablespoons	Olive oil
1	Garlic clove
	Bay leaf
	Salt
	Freshly-ground black pepper
$\frac{1}{2}$ cup	Grated Parmesan cheese
1 tablespoon	Chopped parsley

METHOD

1 Put the beans into a bowl, cover with cold water and leave to soak overnight. Soak the pearl barley in a bowl of warm water for 4 hours, changing water once.

2 Drain the beans and rinse. Put into a saucepan with the measured water and bring to a boil over a moderate heat. Drain the pearl barley, rinse and add to the beans. Cover and cook gently for 15 minutes.

3 Meanwhile, dice the pork, and chop the bacon. Peel and finely chop the onion; wash, trim and chop the celery; scrape and dice the carrot. Peel, wash and dice the potato; shred the cabbage. Chop the sage.

4 Heat the oil in another saucepan, add prepared pork, bacon, onion and the peeled and crushed garlic and fry till meat is browned. Add prepared vegetables, sage, bay leaf and seasoning, cover and cook for 10 minutes.

5 Add beans and barley mixture to pan and bring to a boil. Cover and simmer for $1\frac{1}{2}$ hours or till beans and barley are tender. Taste and adjust seasoning and serve with Parmesan and parsley.

Minestrone napoletana

A specialty of Naples, this is a superb soup which is full of the flavor of fresh vegetables and herbs. Rice adds substance as well as thickening the liquid, and Caciocavallo, a firm slightly salty cow's milk cheese made in several parts of Italy, lends its distinctive flavor. If this cheese is not available, you can use Parmesan, Pecorino or a sharp Cheddar

LUNCH OR SUPPER   Serves 8

Overall timing 2¼ hours

Equipment 2 large saucepans

Freezing Pour into a rigid container, leaving ¾ inch headroom, cover, label and freeze. Freezer life: 3 months. To use: place block in pan, and reheat gently till thawed

INGREDIENTS

1 lb	Green cabbage
¾ lb	Broccoli
¼ lb	Belgian endive
1	Onion
1	Red pepper
3	Zucchini
¾ lb	Pumpkin
¼ lb	Whole green beans
¼ lb	Bacon
2 tablespoons	Olive oil
1	Garlic clove
1 teaspoon	Dried oregano
1 tablespoon	Chopped parsley
1 tablespoon	Chopped fresh chervil
1 tablespoon	Chopped chives
1 tablespoon	Chopped fresh tarragon
2 quarts	Chicken stock or broth
2 tablespoons	Tomato paste
¾ cup	Long grain rice
	Salt
	Freshly-ground black pepper
¼ lb	Caciocavallo cheese

METHOD

1 Trim, wash and shred the cabbage. Trim broccoli and cut into spears. Chop endive; peel and chop onion. Deseed pepper and cut into strips; trim zucchini and cut into matchsticks. Peel pumpkin, remove seeds and fibers and chop. Trim and dice the beans. Cut bacon into strips.

2 Place bacon in saucepan and fry till fat starts to run. Add olive oil, onion, peeled and crushed garlic, pumpkin, cabbage, endive, oregano and half the remaining herbs. Cover and cook for 10 minutes.

3 Gradually pour in stock, stirring to release sediment. As each addition comes to a boil, add more. Stir in tomato paste, cover and simmer for 30 minutes.

4 Add broccoli, pepper, zucchini and beans and cook for 30 minutes more. Add rice, salt and pepper and cook for a further 30 minutes.

5 Sprinkle with remaining herbs and serve immediately with grated or diced Caciocavallo to add to individual servings, and crusty bread.

Left: Minestrone — regarded as one of Italy's greatest dishes. Three of the many variations are Friuli minestrone and Minestrone di pasta (both in foreground) and Minestrone napoletana (at the back)

Minestrone di pasta

While restaurants offer minestrone as an appetizer, in Italian homes it's generally regarded as a meal in itself. This is a fairly simple, but full-bodied version of the soup and the calf's foot gives it a special texture. It needs only fresh bread and lots of Parmesan cheese to make it complete. Broken spaghetti can be substituted for pastina — pasta shaped to look like rice — if preferred

LUNCH OR SUPPER   Serves 4–6

Overall timing 2¾ hours plus soaking and overnight standing

Equipment Saucepan

Freezing Pour into rigid container, leaving ¾ inch headroom, cover, label and freeze. Freezer life: 3 months. To use: place block in pan and reheat gently till thawed

INGREDIENTS

¼ cup	Dried cannellini beans
2 quarts	Water
2	Ripe tomatoes
1	Onion
1 teaspoon	Salt
	Freshly-ground black pepper
¼ cup	Tomato paste
1 teaspoon	Dried oregano
¼ teaspoon	Cayenne
1	Calf's foot
6 oz	Pastina

METHOD

1 Wash beans, then place in saucepan with the water. Bring to a boil and boil for 2 minutes. Remove from heat, cover and leave to soak for 2 hours.

2 Blanch, peel and chop tomatoes; peel and chop the onion. Add to beans with seasoning, tomato paste, oregano and cayenne. Split the calf's foot and add to pan. Bring to a boil slowly, cover and simmer for 2 hours or till meat and beans are just tender.

3 Remove from heat, skim surface and leave overnight.

4 The next day, skim off any excess fat. Remove calf's foot with a slotted spoon. Cut off meat and chop into small pieces, discarding any skin and bones.

5 Place meat in soup. Bring to a boil, add pastina and cook till al dente. Taste and adjust seasoning. Pour into warmed tureen and serve with crusty bread.

Sicilian spaghetti with eggplant

This mouthwatering pasta dish, which makes a filling lunch or supper, is sometimes known as *Spaghetti alla Norma* after Bellini's most famous opera. The spaghetti is cooked in boiling salted water until it is al dente — tender but firm to the bite. This is the perfect way to serve spaghetti; test it during cooking until you are quite sure it is right

LUNCH OR SUPPER Serves 4

Overall timing 45 minutes plus draining

Equipment Colander, 2 saucepans, skillet

Freezing Not recommended

INGREDIENTS

1	Large eggplant
	Salt
1lb	Ripe tomatoes
1	Garlic clove
3 tablespoons	Oil
2 teaspoons	Chopped fresh basil
	Freshly-ground black pepper
¾lb	Spaghetti
	Oil for frying
½ cup	Grated Pecorino or Parmesan cheese
	Sprig of fresh basil

METHOD

1 Wash and thinly slice the eggplant. Put into a colander and sprinkle with salt. Leave to drain for 1 hour.

2 Blanch, peel and chop the tomatoes. Peel the garlic. Heat the oil in a saucepan, add the crushed garlic and fry for 1 minute. Add tomatoes, basil, salt and pepper, stir well and cook over a low heat for 15 minutes.

3 Put spaghetti into a saucepan of boiling salted water and cook till al dente. Meanwhile, rinse eggplant slices under running water and gently squeeze dry. Heat ½ inch oil in a skillet and fry eggplant slices on both sides, a few at a time, till crisp. Drain on paper towels and keep hot.

4 Drain spaghetti thoroughly. Put into a warmed serving dish and pour tomato sauce over. Add eggplant slices, sprinkle with Pecorino or Parmesan, garnish with sprig of basil and serve immediately with extra grated cheese.

Left: Sicilian spaghetti with eggplant

Above: Shrimp pilaf — rice, fish and vegetables combined in one flavorful dish

Shrimp pilaf

Dry and spicy pilafs are popular in the Middle East and the Balkans. The rice absorbs the tomato stock as it cooks and then juicy shrimp are stirred in for additional texture. The pilaf is topped with cheese and parsley

MAIN DISH Serves 4

Overall timing 1 hour plus 1 hour thawing time if using frozen shrimp

Equipment Heavy-based casserole with tight-fitting lid or chicken fryer

Freezing Not recommended

INGREDIENTS

1lb	Small peeled shrimp
2	Large onions
2	Fresh green chili peppers
2	Garlic cloves
1 tablespoon	Oil
½lb	Bacon
1 cup	Long-grain rice
16oz	Can of tomatoes
	Salt
2 cups	Chicken stock or broth
2 tablespoons	Chopped parsley
2 tablespoons	Grated Parmesan cheese

METHOD

1 If using frozen shrimp, thaw. Peel and slice onions. Wash, deseed and slice chili peppers. Peel and crush garlic.

2 Heat the oil in the casserole. Chop the bacon and fry in the oil until well browned and crisp. Add the onion, chili peppers and garlic to the casserole. Cook over a medium heat for a few minutes until onion is soft and transparent but not brown, stirring occasionally.

3 Add the rice and stir for 2–3 minutes until grains are coated with oil. Add the canned tomatoes with their juice, salt and chicken stock. Bring rapidly to a boil, then reduce heat, cover and simmer for 15 minutes on a very low heat. Stir and add the shrimp. Cover and cook for a further 5 minutes.

4 Spoon mixture into deep serving dish, and mix well. Sprinkle with chopped parsley and grated Parmesan and serve immediately.

Poule-au-pot

MAIN DISH   Serves 6

Overall timing 4 hours

Equipment Trussing needle, thread, 2 large saucepans

Freezing Not recommended

INGREDIENTS

3½lb	Stewing chicken with giblets
4	Bacon slices
½ cup	Pork sausagemeat
1 cup	Soft breadcrumbs
2 tablespoons	Chopped parsley
	Salt
	Freshly-ground black pepper
2	Eggs
4	Medium-size onions
4	Small turnips
6	Large carrots
2	Leeks
4	Stalks of celery
¼ cup	Butter
	Bouquet garni
1½ cups	Long grain rice

METHOD

1 Wipe and trim the chicken and cut off the tail. Reserve the giblets. Finely chop the bacon. Mix the sausagemeat, bacon, breadcrumbs, parsley and plenty of seasoning together and bind with the eggs. Spoon inside the chicken and sew up the vent with a trussing needle and thread. Truss into a neat shape.

2 Peel the onions and turnips; scrape the carrots. Wash and trim the leeks and celery. Heat the butter in a large pan and fry the chicken over a moderate heat till browned all over. Add 1 of the onions, 2 carrots, 1 turnip, 1 leek and 1 stalk of celery and fry for 3 minutes. Pour off any excess fat.

3 Add the bouquet garni, chicken giblets and cold water to cover the chicken (about 3 quarts) and bring to a boil. Skim off any scum, reduce the heat and cover the pan. Simmer gently for about 2¼ hours.

4 Use a slotted spoon to remove vegetables and bouquet garni and discard. Add the remaining fresh vegetables and seasoning to pan. Cover and simmer for a further 45 minutes till the chicken is tender.

5 Remove the pan from the heat and strain 6 cups of the cooking liquid into another saucepan. Cover pan containing chicken to keep hot.

6 Add salt to the liquid to taste, stir in the rice and cover tightly. Bring to a

Honey-glazed ham is served with apple rings fried in butter

boil, simmer for 15–20 minutes, till rice is tender and has absorbed liquid.

7 Taste rice and adjust seasoning. Put on serving dish. Remove chicken from the pan, place on rice and discard the trussing strings. Arrange the vegetables around the chicken and serve.

Honey-glazed ham

MAIN DISH   6–8 servings

Overall timing 2¼ hours plus overnight soaking (if necessary)

Equipment Large saucepan, small saucepan, roasting pan, skillet

Freezing Not recommended

INGREDIENTS

4lb	Country-style ham
	Whole cloves
2 tablespoons	Clear honey
3 tablespoons	Brown sugar
2	Crisp apples
¼ cup	Butter

METHOD

1 If soaking is required, put ham into large bowl, cover with water and let soak overnight.

2 The next day, drain the ham. Place it in a large saucepan and cover with fresh water. Bring to a boil. Remove any scum. Reduce heat, cover and simmer for 1½ hours.

3 Preheat the oven to 350°. Remove ham from pan, allow to cool slightly, then cut off any rind. Score fat in a lattice pattern and put a clove in the center of each "diamond".

4 Gently heat honey and sugar in a small saucepan until melted. Brush over the surface of the ham. Put ham in a roasting pan and cook in the oven for 20 minutes, basting from time to time. Take care not to let the glaze burn.

5 Five minutes before the ham is ready, peel, core and slice apples into ¼ inch thick rings. Melt butter in a skillet and fry the apple rings on both sides until lightly golden and tender.

6 Serve the ham on a platter surrounded by the apple rings.

Pois à la paysanne

VEGETABLE   Serves 6

Overall timing 45 minutes

Equipment Saucepan

Freezing Not recommended

INGREDIENTS

¼ lb	Pearl onions
2 lb	Fresh peas
3	Medium-size carrots
½ lb	Small new potatoes
1	Head of Bibb lettuce
1	Thick slice of bacon
¼ cup	Butter
	Sprig of thyme
	Sprig of tarragon
	Bay leaf
	Salt
	Freshly-ground black pepper
¾ cup	Cold water

METHOD

1 Blanch the onions in boiling water for 5 minutes to loosen the skins. Shell the peas; scrape and dice the carrots. Scrub the potatoes; wash the lettuce and tear into pieces or cut into fine wedges. Cut the bacon into strips and peel the onions.

2 Heat the butter in a saucepan and fry the bacon and onions for 3 minutes, or till bacon fat begins to run. Add the remaining vegetables, herbs tied together, salt and pepper.

3 Stir in the measured cold water and bring to a boil, stirring occasionally to release sediment from bottom of pan. Cover and simmer for 25 minutes till the vegetables are tender.

4 Remove the bouquet garni, and serve immediately.

Pois à la paysanne — a vegetable dish from the heart of the French countryside

Puréed green beans

An unusual vegetable dish that's almost a meal in itself

Trim green beans, removing strings as necessary. Cook in boiling water

When beans are cooked — about 10 minutes — drain well and purée them in a food mill

Put purée into a clean saucepan and blend in mashed potatoes with a spoon

Add butter to vegetable mixture, then stir in grated cheese and heat through gently

Poached salmon and vegetables

An Indo-Chinese dish in which salmon and mixed vegetables are simmered in stock, white wine and soy sauce, and grated ginger adds an exotic flavor

MAIN DISH   Serves 4

Overall timing 35 minutes

Equipment Shallow flameproof casserole

Freezing Not recommended

INGREDIENTS

1	Stalk of celery
1	Small cauliflower
1	Shallot
4	Salmon steaks
2 cups	Fish or chicken stock or broth
4 teaspoons	Soy sauce
2 tablespoons	Dry white wine
1 teaspoon	Finely grated ginger root
2 teaspoons	Sugar
	Salt
1 cup	Frozen peas
2 teaspoons	Cornstarch
2 tablespoons	Water

Below: Salmon mayonnaise – careful garnish turns the fish into a splendid work of art

METHOD

1 Trim and wash the celery and cauliflower. Divide the cauliflower into small florets; thinly slice the celery. Peel and thinly slice the shallot. Wipe the salmon steaks.

2 Put the stock, soy sauce, wine, ginger and sugar into the casserole and bring to a boil. Taste and add salt if necessary. Reduce to a gentle simmer and carefully add the salmon steaks. Cover and simmer for 5 minutes.

3 Add the celery, cauliflower, shallot and peas. Cover and simmer for a further 5 minutes till the salmon and vegetables are just tender.

4 Lift the salmon steaks out of the liquid and arrange on a warmed serving platter. Lift out the vegetables and arrange around the salmon. Keep hot.

5 Blend the cornstarch with the water, add to the cooking liquid and bring to a boil, stirring constantly. Cook for 2 minutes, then remove from the heat. Taste and adjust seasoning.

6 Spoon over the vegetables and serve immediately with boiled rice or potatoes.

SALMON MAYONNAISE

Poach a 3–3½lb cleaned whole salmon in court-bouillon, allowing 10 minutes per lb. Leave to cool completely. Chill 1½ cups aspic (made with gelatin if necessary) till syrupy. Wash half a cucumber, cut in half lengthwise; then slice very thinly. Carefully remove skin from fish; place fish on serving plate. Arrange cucumber slices on head and tail end of salmon to look like scales. Thinly slice 6 stuffed green olives. Place a slice on the eye; arrange the rest on the middle of the salmon. Spoon the aspic over salmon till evenly covered. Leave to set. Put 2 tablespoons thick mayonnaise in pastry bag fitted with small plain tube and pipe zigzag lines around the "eye" and edge of "scales". Chill for 1 hour. Garnish with washed and dried leaves from a Bibb lettuce, sprigs of watercress, radish roses and 1–2 lemons cut lengthwise into wedges. To serve, cut 4 portions from each side of the backbone, then turn salmon over and repeat on the other side. Serve with mayonnaise and boiled potatoes or potato salad. **Serves 16**

Poached kippers

A simple but nourishing family meal served with parsleyed new potatoes. As an alternative to the butter sauce, try it with sour cream

MAIN DISH   Serves 4

Overall timing 20 minutes

Equipment Large saucepan

Freezing Not recommended

INGREDIENTS

8	Kipper fillets
	Fresh parsley
6 tablespoons	Butter
2 teaspoons	Lemon juice
½ teaspoon	Freshly-ground black pepper

1 Bring a large pan of water to a boil, add the kippers and poach for 5 minutes.
2 When the kippers are cooked remove from heat, drain well and place on a warm serving dish with the skin side down. Garnish with parsley.
3 Melt the butter and stir in the lemon juice and pepper. Pour over kippers at the table and serve with boiled new potatoes and lemon wedges.

cook's know-how

For a good Sunday supper that's economical and a little different, try Kipper croquettes. Cook ½lb of kipper fillets by just covering with water, then bringing to a boil. Remove the skin and flake the flesh finely. Mix with 1 cup of mashed potatoes (leftovers will do) and a beaten egg. Season generously. Divide the mixture into 8 equal portions and shape into oblongs or balls, using floured hands.
Using palette knives to handle the croquettes, first coat them with seasoned flour, then roll them in beaten egg and finally coat them again with breadcrumbs, patting crumbs on to the ends of oblong croquettes with the fingers. Fry the croquettes quickly in deep fat until golden brown, drain on paper towels and serve at once accompanied by broiled tomatoes and tartare sauce and a green salad.   **Serves 4**

Above: Poached kippers — a different approach to serving a traditional British fish

Oranges à la turque

The Turks are well known for their sweet tooth, and the sugary syrup used here is a traditional feature of their pastries and desserts. Caramelized and spiked with Cointreau, it's used to macerate the oranges and gives them an exquisite flavor with a light kick

DESSERT   Serves 4

Overall timing 30 minutes plus maceration

Equipment Lemon zester or vegetable peeler, saucepan, flat-bottom dish

Freezing Not recommended

INGREDIENTS

4	Large oranges
1 cup	Sugar
2	Cloves
1½ cups	Water
3 tablespoons	Cointreau
4	Crystallized violets

METHOD

1 Wash the oranges and pare the rind from 2 of them with a zester or peeler. Shred rind into fine long strands and then blanch in boiling water for 5 minutes. Drain and rinse in cold water, then dry on paper towels.

2 Put the sugar into a saucepan with the cloves and water and heat, stirring, till sugar dissolves. Bring to a boil and boil rapidly, without stirring, till a golden caramel color.

3 Meanwhile, cut away the peel and white membrane from the remaining oranges, collecting any juice. Place oranges in flat bottom dish with shredded rind.

4 Remove caramel from the heat. Carefully add the Cointreau and any orange juice, and stir over a low heat to dissolve the caramel. Pour over the oranges and rind and leave to macerate for 3 hours, turning the oranges and rind in the caramel occasionally.

TO SERVE

Arrange the oranges on individual serving plates and spoon the caramel over. Pile the shredded rind on to the oranges and decorate each with a crystallized violet, and an orange leaf, if liked. Serve with cream if liked.

One way of preparing oranges is to cut a slice from top and bottom. Place one cut end down and cut peel from sides with a serrated knife, holding the orange steady with a fork

To make the oranges easier to eat, slice across segments with a serrated knife, holding orange steady with a fork, and serve in slices. Or reassemble the sliced orange on a toothpick

Left: Oranges à la turque — an impressive dish that's a delight to serve and to eat

Apricot mousse

A smooth and creamy cold dessert that can be made well in advance. For one, use dried apricots (choose light-colored ones so that the dessert will have a pleasant golden look) and for the other, canned fruit. The canned fruit version is also adaptable for making a mousse with fresh apricots when they are in season

MADE WITH DRIED FRUIT

Overall timing 4 hours including soaking and chilling

Equipment 2 bowls, 2 saucepans, blender or food processor, individual glasses or 1 serving bowl

Freezing Pour into container, cover, label and freeze. Freezer life: 1 year. To use: thaw for 4–6 hours at room temperature or 6–8 hours in refrigerator

INGREDIENTS

1½ cups	Dried apricots
½ cup	Sugar
2 teaspoons	Grated orange rind
1 teaspoon	Grated lemon rind
6 tablespoons	Orange juice
2 tablespoons	Lemon juice
1 envelope	Unflavored gelatin
1½ cups	Whipping cream
	Fresh or toffee-coated* walnuts

METHOD

1 Place apricots in a bowl and cover with water. Leave apricots to soak for 2 hours.

2 Set aside 4 apricots for decoration. Put rest in saucepan with ¾ cup of the soaking water; stir in the sugar. Bring to a boil, then cover and simmer for 20 minutes. Plunge pan into cold water to cool apricots quickly.

3 Purée apricots and juice; stir in grated rinds. Warm the fruit juices, then stir in the gelatin until completely dissolved. Stir into purée and leave to thicken slightly.

4 Whip cream until thick, then fold most of it into apricot mixture. Place in individual glasses or 1 large bowl and decorate with nuts, remaining cream and reserved apricots. Chill for 1 hour before serving.

*Melt ¼ cup of sugar over heat till brown caramel forms. Off heat, skewer walnuts, dip in caramel and let set on a sheet of aluminum foil.

Above: Apricot mousse – made from dried fruit, cream and citrus juices

MADE WITH CANNED FRUIT

Overall timing 1¼ hours including refrigeration

Equipment Blender or food processor, 2 bowls, 4 individual serving dishes

Freezing Not recommended

INGREDIENTS

16oz	Can of apricots
3	Eggs
2	Petit suisse cheeses
2 tablespoons	Heavy cream
2 tablespoons	Sugar

METHOD

1 Drain apricots. Take out 4 halves, chop them and set aside. Purée the remaining apricots in a blender or food processor until smooth.

2 Separate the eggs. Add yolks, Petits suisses cheeses, cream and sugar to the apricot purée in the blender, and mix till smooth and creamy. Otherwise, beat them all together in a bowl until they are well combined.

3 Beat the egg whites till very stiff, then gently fold into the creamed mixture with a metal spoon, also adding the reserved chopped apricots.

4 Divide the mixture between four individual serving dishes and chill for at least 1 hour.

TO MAKE A MOUSSE FROM FRESH APRICOTS

Choose fruit that is very ripe – you will need about ¾lb. Remove the pits and poach the fruit gently in a sugar syrup made with ½ cup sugar and 6 tablespoons water, then proceed as in the recipe left.

Steaming

Steaming is another method of cooking by "moist heat". The steam itself is a transparent gas and it occurs once water has reached its boiling point. (If you look at the tip of the spout of the tea kettle next time the water is boiling you will "see" – or rather, not see – the steam. What we tend to think of as "steam" is in fact the vapor changing itself back into droplets of water as it cools.

There are two basic techniques of steaming. Direct steaming is the term used when the steam comes into contact with the food itself – in a traditional tiered steamer, on a "flower" trivet (which also acts as a container for the food), in a saucepan with a colander inside (not perched on top), or in a pressure cooker.

Indirect steaming happens when the food is put into another container, such as a steaming mold which is covered, then set in a pan of boiling water which comes no higher than halfway up the side of the container. A lid is placed on the pan and the steam circulates around the food.

When food is placed on a covered plate which acts as a lid over a pan containing boiling water, this is also called indirect steaming. It is a very efficient way of warming through previously cooked food – especially meat or vegetables. Steaming also plays a part in braising and stewing, since any tightly covered container holding liquid becomes to some extent a steamer. Meat baked or roasted in a covered pan is also partly steamed as is poultry in a clay schlemmertopf. As a cooking method, its great advantage is that it retains more of the flavor and the nutrients in the food than almost any other. Usually no fat is added, so the food stays light, moist and easy to digest; "boil in the bag" foods are in fact steamed – the sealed bag goes into boiling water which heats fat or liquid in the bag and this produces steam.

Unlike water, steam *can* get hotter and hotter if the heat is not turned down, or if extra pressure is applied (as in pressure cooking); so once the steam has reached a compatible cooking temperature, the heat should be adjusted. Though the lid on the pan should be tight fitting, it should not be so tight that excess steam cannot escape if necessary, and the water must be kept on the boil, or steam will cease to be produced – in long cooking, it needs to be replenished. As the steam rises in the steamer and circulates around the food, it transfers some of its heat to the food by conduction; it also comes into contact with the surface of the food and the sides of the pan, both of which are cooler. This causes the steam to condense and turn back into water but, as it does so, it releases the same amount of heat (energy) that was needed to turn water into steam in the first place – and this all helps the cooking process. Though steam is hotter than water, it does not cook more quickly – you should allow up to 10 minutes more than boiling time when steaming vegetables, for example. However, much depends on the size and thickness of the food.

Steaming carried out on top of the stove is economic on fuel if the pan is used to cook several things at the same time. Meat in lots of liquid can be in the bottom pan, and different vegetables, wrapped separately in foil, can be in the top pan. Wrap loosely and leave space between the packages so steam can circulate – include a pat of butter or a little water in the packages if you like. Leafy green vegetables and peas should be very fresh and young or they won't steam well. Large, whole vegetables such as cauliflower or a crisp white cabbage steam well and keep their shape.

steaming with a little water

Food is kept out of the water on a trivet (the collapsible type made specifically for vegetables fits most pans) and the water should be boiling so that steam is created, but flame height is medium so steam doesn't lift lid off pan

steaming with a lot of water

In a double steamer both pans can be used, the bottom one containing a food that is cooked by boiling, and the steam given off cooks the food above. The base of top pan is perforated to let steam through

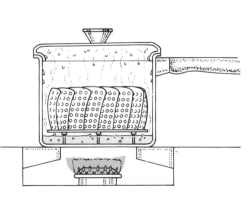

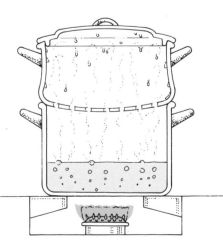

Steaming techniques

asparagus steamer

Made in aluminum or stainless steel, tall ones hold bundles upright; flat ones can also be used to poach fish, boil ham.

bamboo steamers

Chinese bamboo baskets that stack so that several ingredients can be steamed at the same time, the one that takes longest (usually rice) going in the bottom closest to the boiling water – line base with muslin to prevent rice slipping through bamboo. Can be used in a wok, or in deep stewpot with baskets placed on a rack; the top basket must be covered with a lid or closely-fitting foil. The baskets are made in a range of sizes, the larger ones being able to hold whole dishes.

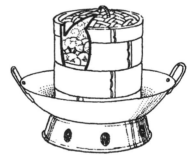

cereal steamers

Rice steaming balls are made of aluminum with spring-clip to close two halves securely, and chain to keep ball above boiling water. Can be used to steam round plum pudding as well. Rice comes out molded into a round.

Couscous steamer (couscousier) is aluminum; has large bottom half to hold stew, soup, the steam from which cooks the prepared couscous (semolina) in covered pan above.

colander

Useful for converting saucepan into steamer. It should fit inside pan without its base touching the water. It must be metal and top should be covered with foil so steam cannot escape. Covering is important whichever steaming method is being used.

direct steaming

Term used to describe the technique of placing food in a pan so it comes into direct contact with the circulating steam from boiling water.

double steamers

Tiered system based on the Chinese bamboo steamers, but made of metal. They fit on top of each other so more food can be cooked at the same time. Remember to put food requiring most cooking in bottom, food requiring less above – some steamers have vent which can be adjusted to control the amount of steam, thus slowing down cooking. Individual steamers can be bought to fit standard-size pans and can be stacked to give same result.

flavorings

Foods being steamed rely on their own natural flavors being retained and are not usually pepped up. However, steaming can be done over a well flavored bouillon or stock, or an onion or bouquet garni can be added to the water. Stuff whole fish with fresh herbs, or sprinkle ground spices over vegetables. Seasoning is done at the table as salt draws out juices which defeats the point of steaming.

indirect steaming

The term used to describe the technique of placing food in a covered heatproof mold or similar container which stands in boiling water in a covered pan. It's a cross between a water bath (bain-marie) and double boiling, but is classed as steaming for the cooking is done in the steam from the water.
This method is suitable for soft mixtures like sweet and savory suet puddings, sponge puddings and fruity plum puddings which need to be kept in shape.
Molds can be stainless steel, heatproof glass, ceramic, aluminum or heatproof plastic which have their own lids (don't use lids in pressure cookers).
Lining is essential if rich fruit puddings are steamed in metal (use foil or doubled parchment paper) and are going to be stored. Also applies to suet pastry which must be shaped to fit mold.
Expansion must be allowed for when cooking savory and sweet suet or sponge puddings. The mixture will rise in the mold so never fill more than a generous two-thirds.
Covering the mold is necessary and the trick here is pleating, which helps the greased paper and foil covers to open out as the food rises. The covering must be tightly tied to keep out water.

Take a triangular piece out of the dough. Cover and reserve

Place large piece of dough in mold, pressing joins to seal

Roll out reserved dough. Wet pastry rim, press lid in place

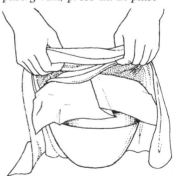

Cover with pleated greased paper or foil. Place cloth over

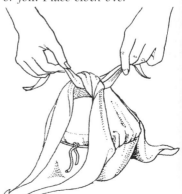

Secure cloth beneath rim with string, tie opposite ends on top

plate steaming

A form of indirect steaming particularly suited to cooking small fish fillets. Two matching heatproof plates (ceramic or enameled steel) enclose the fish and are placed over a pan of boiling water. It's energy saving if the bottom pan is cooking food to serve with fish. Covering a plate with another, or with a saucepan lid or foil, is a good way of keeping a whole meal or cooked foods hot, or of reheating cold cooked foods.

pudding molds

Can be made of stainless steel, aluminum, heatproof glass, ceramic or boilable plastic. Aluminum and steel molds have their own lids which saves covering and tying but remember to allow for expansion. Sizes range from about 5 inches (1 quart capacity) to 8 inches ($2\frac{1}{2}$ quart capacity). Darioles are mini molds which hold $\frac{1}{2}$–$\frac{3}{4}$ cup.

replenishing

Vitally important in direct and indirect steaming. As water evaporates, add boiling water from tea kettle to required level (no more than halfway up sides of mold). A metal jar lid or down-turned saucer placed in the water will have more space to rattle in as the water level sinks — good warning of time to add more. Work quickly so there's little interruption to the steam flow.

staining

Occurs especially during long steaming (eg, with puddings). Can be avoided by acidulation — adding a little vinegar or slice of lemon to boiling water. Stained pans can be brightened by cooking rhubarb in them.

steamers

Made of aluminum, stainless steel or enameled steel. Can be bought in variety of sizes as saucepan plus steamer, or as steamer with lid to fit your existing saucepans or stewpot. All lids should fit snugly and the heavier (ie, thicker gauge) the pan base, the more stable the unit. Aluminum can dent and will also stain unless water in bottom pan is acidulated. Collapsible steamers are usually "flower" shaped,

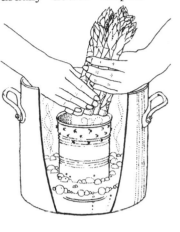

made of aluminum or steel with hinged flaps that open out like petals. On legs so it remains above water; shape fits many sizes of pan.

steam boiling

This method of cooking is used with vegetables where tough stalks need to be boiled and delicate tops need to be steamed (eg, asparagus, broccoli). In a deepish pan, bundles can be propped up with crumpled foil or can be stood in an empty can with holes punched in bottom and sides.

The term steam boiling can also be applied to puddings which are wrapped in a cloth, the ends of which are held by the pan lid and keep most of the pudding out of the boiling water.

trivet or rack

A three-cornered platform made of wood or metal that keeps containers off the base of the pan during indirect steaming. In pressure cookers it raises separators from the metal. Collapsible vegetable steamers are sometimes called trivets as they have three legs.

wrapping

Very fresh, even-sized vegetables wrapped in separate foil packages can all be steamed in the one pan of boiling water — saves fuel and

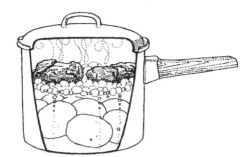

dish washing. The vegetables will cook in their own steam from the heat created by the boiling water, and their flavors won't mingle. The packages float and shouldn't be too close together for the steam needs to circulate. Remember to cover the pan.

Pressure cooking techniques

In a pressure cooker, the steam is sealed in and, being increased in temperature by pressure, makes food tender in one-third or less of the usual cooking time. The two major points in cooking this way are: it saves fuel, and foods retain more flavor and nutritive value. By cutting down on time so dramatically it also means that meals can be prepared and served much more quickly.

Pressure cookers are a sort of "cinderella" of cooking. They were very popular in the 50s and 60s but gradually were put aside in favor of the vast numbers of pots and pans arriving on the scene. They have emerged again and their new streamlined shapes are taking their place alongside cookware designed with fuel and time saving qualities in mind. They can only go from strength to strength with clearer instructions and more imaginative suggestions for exploiting their versatility.

Completely automatic cookers are available which make the process easier, and with most of the others the weight is put on *before* the cooker's placed over the heat so that all you have to do is reduce the heat so the hiss of steam is steady and gentle sounding. The exception to this is when cooking steamed puddings.

Pressure cookers can be used on gas (both mains and bottled), electricity (rings and flat surface) and solid fuel stoves. The open cooker (that is, without the lid) can be used to brown meat and sweat vegetables before pressure cooking, and also provides a large heavy-based pan for cooking a lot of rice or pasta, or for making jam. Large amounts cannot be cooked under pressure for there would not be sufficient space left for the steam to circulate. Soups or stews must never come higher than halfway up the cooker; with vegetables the pan should be no more than two-thirds full.

Liquid, which forms the steam, is the essence of pressure cooking. It should be water, stock, wine or milk, but not melted fat or oil. The minimum quantity required is 1 cup for the first 15 minutes of cooking plus $\frac{1}{2}$ cup for each further 15 minutes of cooking time, or part thereof. Thickening agents aren't added till the end of cooking time as they will retard the steam and can cause the food to burn.

Timing is established by the size and density of the foods. Because the trapped steam is forced through the food under pressure it cooks 1lb or 3lb of cut-up potatoes in the same time, 4–6 minutes. Similarly $\frac{1}{2}$lb of beef chuck steak cut in chunks will take the same time as $1\frac{1}{2}$lb – 20 minutes.

A cut of meat on the other hand is denser and is cooked by weight — 1lb will take 15 minutes, 3lb will take 45. When foods containing leavening agents are cooked in containers (eg, puddings in molds), a short steaming time is necessary before pressure cooking (without it the pudding would be heavy). Usually 1 quart of boiling water is placed in the cooker with the rack and covered pudding, the lid is placed on top, then the pudding is steamed gently for 15 minutes with little steam coming from the vent. After this the weight is added and the cooker brought to pressure.

Plastic boilable bowls can be used and they give quicker results (5 minutes less), but the lids can buckle and prevent steam from penetrating the mixture so cover with greased pleated paper and cloth. Some manufacturers recommend adding a few minutes to the cooking time if foil is used to cover.

In long steaming such as with puddings, vinegar or a slice of lemon should be added to the water to prevent the cooker from discoloring.

When cooking custards don't use metal containers which hold the heat and spoil the texture of the custard.

After cooking the pressure must be reduced before the lid can be removed. Risen mixtures or those contained in a breakable container are reduced slowly: left off the heat for 10–15 minutes. Other foods: stand cooker in bowl of cold water or place under cold running water. Pressure has been reduced if, when you gently tip the weight, no hissing occurs. Always follow the manufacturer's advice about caring for your cooker.

The amount of liquid is based on the time needed for cooking — the formula is 1 cup water, stock, wine or milk plus ½ cup for every further 15 minutes

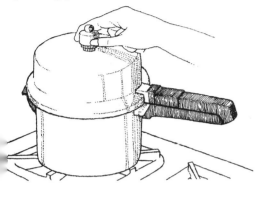

After the food goes in, the top's put on with arrows on cover and base lining up. The correct weight is placed on the center vent and pressed down till a click is heard. The cooker is then put on high heat

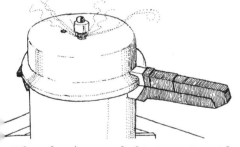

When there's a steady hissing noise with a flow of steam from around weight, reduce heat till a gentle hissing sound is heard. Start the timing from this point

At the end of cooking pressure must be reduced before the cover can be removed. Quickly: run cold water over sides, not top. Slowly: leave at room temperature

FOOD	TIME IN MINUTES								
	0	5	10	15	20	25	30	35	40
artichokes, globe			H CW						
artichokes, jerusalem			H CW						
beans, lima			H CW						
green			H CW						
beef, boned brisket					per lb			H CW	
for stew, cubes				H CW					
beets				H CW					
broccoli			H CW						
brussels sprouts			H CW						
cabbage, wedges			H CW						
carrots, old quarters			H CW						
new whole			H CW						
cauliflower, whole			H CW						
florets			H CW						
celery, hearts			H CW						
chicken, whole			per lb		H CW				
quarters			H CW						
chickpeas, soaked					H RT				
corn on the cob			H CW						
custards, 1 quart			H WR	RT					
individual			H WR	RT					
fava beans, soaked								H RT	
fish, oily, fillets			H CW						
medium whole			H CW						
fish, white, fillets (3½ mins)			H CW						
steaks/cutlets (4½ mins)			H CW						
fruits, to stew			H RT						
ham			per lb	H CW					
lamb, boneless rolled breast					per lb	H CW			
lamb hearts							H CW		
leeks, small whole			H CW						
lentils, soaked				H RT					
navy beans, small soaked					H RT				
onions, medium whole			H CW						
pickling			H CW						
oxtail								H CW	
parsnips, quartered			H CW						
peas, fresh			H CW						
dried split				H RT					
dried whole					H RT				
pheasant, browned							H CW		
pork, boned and rolled					per lb	H CW			
potatoes, old halves			H CW						
new whole			H CW						
puddings, 1 quart									
sponge steam 15 mins, then							L WR	RT	
sponge with fruit steam 15 mins, then								L WR	RT
suet crust with filling steam 15 mins, then								L WR	RT
Christmas (plum) steam 15 mins, then					H WR RT	per lb			1¾ hours
rabbit portions					H CW				
rutabaga, quartered			H CW						
soybeans, soaked							H RT		
stocks, brown									H CW
fish			H CW						
poultry						H CW			
tripe, blanched				H CW					
turnips, small whole			H CW						

Pressure cooking abbreviations: H high, M medium, L low pressure; WR with rack; RT reduce pressure at room temperature; CW reduce pressure under cold water

Steaming

Foods that are steamed range from the delicate (fish, whole or in fillets, veal cutlets), through the sturdy (root vegetables, whole cauliflowers) to the hard (couscous, processed wheat with a coating of moistened flour). The denser and harder the foods the longer the steaming time, of course, but in all cases the food should be light and tender, moist and succulent when served. If using a steamer rather than a basket, the water boiling in the bottom can be cooking potatoes or rice — but in the top part put foods which will steam in the time it takes for the potatoes or rice to be tender. Make sure there's enough water in the bottom pan to last the time suggested in the charts. If you have to remove the lid to replenish, it will take some minutes for the steaming level to be re-established, so take that into account. And remember always to replenish with boiling water.

FOOD	TIME IN MINUTES	TIME IN HOURS
	0 5 10 20 30 40 50	1 2 3 4
artichokes, small jerusalem	████ to ~30	
asparagus	███ to ~15	
beans, green, whole	███ to ~15	
sliced	██ to ~12	
beets, small whole	█████ to ~40	
brains	███ to ~20	
broccoli spears	███ to ~20	
brussels sprouts	███ to ~15	
cabbage, green, wedges	███ to ~15	
white, wedges	████ to ~30	
carrots, new, whole	███ to ~20	
cauliflower, whole	█████ to ~40	
florets	███ to ~15	
celeriac, sliced	███ to ~20	
celery, hearts	████ to ~30	
chicken, breasts	████ to ~30	
quarters	█████ to ~40	
whole (3lb)	██████ to ~1 hour 15	
Christmas pudding, to cook		
2–3 cup		5 hours
1 quart		7 hours
1½ quart		9 hours
Christmas pudding, reheat		
2–3 cup		~2 hours
1 quart		~2 hours
1½ quart		~3 hours
corn, kernels	██ to ~12	
couscous, prepared	███ to ~20	
cracked wheat, precooked	██████ to ~45	
dumplings, savory	████ to ~30	
sweet	███ to ~20	
egg custards, savory	█████ to ~40	
sweet	██████ to ~45	
fish, oily, fillets	███ to ~15	
steaks/cutlets	████ to ~30	
fish, white, fillets	██ to ~12	
steaks/cutlets	███ to ~20	
greens, tops	██ to ~10	
kohlrabi, slices	███ to ~20	
lamb chops, thin cut	███ to ~20	
leeks, small whole	████ to ~25	
onions, medium whole	██████ to ~45	

FOOD	TIME IN MINUTES						TIME IN HOURS			
	0	5	10	20	30	40	50	1	2	3	4
peas, fresh											
pork chops, thin cut											
potatoes, new whole											
waxy quartered											
pumpkin, chunks											
rice, brown											
rice, white											
rutabaga, chunks											
scallops											
snow peas											
sponge puddings											
2–3 cup											
1 quart											
1½ quart											
squash, chunks											
suet puddings, savory											
2–3 cup											
precooked filling											
1 quart											
precooked filling											
1½ quart											
cooked filling											
suet puddings, sweet											
2–3 cup											
precooked filling											
1 quart											
precooked filling											
1½ quart											
precooked filling											
sweetbreads											
sweet potato, chunks											
turnips, small whole											
slices											
veal, cutlets											
zucchini, small whole											

flavorings know-how

As steaming is used to cook foods so that natural flavors are kept in, salt should not be added as its will draw out the juices. It is much better to add after cooking. Spices like mace can be sprinkled over parsnips for extra flavor; herbs like savory over green beans; caraway seeds over cabbage. It is however usual to serve steamed foods with sauces made from some of the water into which some nutrients will have been drawn. Cereals can be steamed over stews or soups so that their flavor will enhance the cereal's.

How to prepare and cook asparagus

To prepare asparagus for steaming begin just below the tips and scrape downwards to remove the coarse scales or fibrous coat. Use either a swivel-blade potato peeler or the back of a knife. Be careful not to damage the tips as you scrape. The woody ends of the stems must be removed. If you're confident enough, break them off; otherwise use a sharp knife. The "woodiness" is usually only about an inch in length.

Divide the spears into bundles – about 2 inches in diameter. Tie each bundle securely around the center with string, keeping the tips as close together as possible.

To cook asparagus use either an upright steamer made for asparagus (see right, bottom picture) or a rectangular steamer which has an adjustable platform so that the tips are kept above the boiling salted water. Save the cooking water – it makes a delicious basis for soups. If you don't have a tall pan, wrap asparagus in foil (close the parcel so water can't get in) and place in boiling salted water. Cooking time is between 10 and 20 minutes – it will depend on the length and thickness of the asparagus – but never more or the spears will break up. Lift out bundles, untie string and drain asparagus well.

TO SERVE

As freshly cooked asparagus is very tender and could break up if disturbed too much, it's easier to divide the spears between the individual serving plates rather than serve them all on one help-yourself plate. Serve the accompaniment separately if you prefer. It helps to have small fingerbowls handy – use warmish water and float a slice of lemon in each one. Paper napkins will also be useful.

Scrape the fibrous scales from stems

Trim off the woody ends at the bottom

Tie the bundles securely in the middle

Cook in pan over boiling, salted water so that asparagus cooks in the steam

Asparagus maltaise

Sauce maltaise is a classic French sauce with a Hollandaise base and it takes its name from the blood (or Maltese) oranges which are used to flavor and color it. When blood oranges are not available use ordinary ones, and add a little red food coloring a drop at a time till you achieve the color you want

APPETIZER   Serves 6

Overall timing 1 hour

Equipment 2 saucepans, steamer, sauce whisk, bowl

Freezing Not recommended

INGREDIENTS

2lb	Asparagus
3 tablespoons	White wine vinegar
1 teaspoon	White pepper
1½ cups	Unsalted butter
5	Egg yolks
1 teaspoon	Salt
2 tablespoons	Fresh orange juice
4 teaspoons	Grated orange rind
	Red food coloring (optional)

METHOD

1 Prepare and steam fresh asparagus in salted water for 10–20 minutes or till just tender. Chill quickly under cold water, drain and set aside.

2 Boil the vinegar and white pepper in a saucepan until reduced by half. Allow to cool. Cut the butter into 6–8 pieces.

3 Whisk the yolks with salt in a bowl till thick and creamy. Whisk into the vinegar as it reheats over a pan of gently boiling water. Drop the butter in, piece by piece, whisking rapidly until each piece is absorbed before adding more butter. If the sauce begins to curdle, remove pan from heat, stir in a drop of cold water and another piece of butter before returning to the heat.

4 When all the butter has been absorbed add the orange juice, orange rind or food coloring if using – add it drop by drop till sauce reaches the shade you want.

5 Reheat the asparagus by putting it back in hot water for 1 minute, remove, drain and place on a serving dish. Pour sauce over and serve immediately.

Raie aux câpres

Plate-steamed skate with a piquant caper sauce

MAIN DISH   Serves 4

Overall timing 25 minutes

Equipment 2 saucepans, 2 large plates

Freezing Not recommended

INGREDIENTS

4 ½-lb	Pieces of skate
	Salt
1 tablespoon	Vinegar
6 tablespoons	Butter
2 tablespoons	Capers
2 tablespoons	Chopped parsley
3 tablespoons	Lemon juice
¼ cup	Light cream
	White pepper

METHOD

1 Wash the skate, place on one of the plates, sprinkle with a little salt and a few drops of vinegar and cover with the other plate. Place the plates over a large pan of boiling water and steam for 15–20 minutes, turning the fish once.
2 Remove the skin and keep the skate warm on a serving dish while making the sauce.
3 Melt the butter in a small saucepan, but do not brown. Add remaining vinegar, capers, parsley and lemon juice. Add the cream and seasoning to taste, then cook for 2–3 minutes, without boiling, till heated through. Pour over the skate. Serve with boiled or steamed potatoes and a tossed green salad.

Below: Raie aux câpres — a French-style dish that's delightfully simple to prepare

Salade Béatrice

This colorful salad of green beans, tomatoes and watercress makes a refreshing dish for winter days. The beans are steamed to retain their crispness and nutrients. The watercress, too, is a rich source of vitamin C

SALAD   Serves 4

Overall timing 30 minutes plus chilling time

Equipment Saucepan, colander, lid, salad bowl

Freezing Not recommended

INGREDIENTS

1lb	Green beans
	Salt and pepper
3 tablespoons	Oil
1 tablespoon	White wine vinegar
2	Tomatoes
1	Bunch of watercress
1	Hard-cooked egg yolk

METHOD

1 Wash and trim the beans. Place them in a colander or steaming basket with a close-fitting lid. Put the colander over a saucepan of boiling water and steam the beans until they are cooked through but still crisp. Cool.
2 Break or cut the beans into short lengths and put into a salad bowl. Season, add oil and vinegar and mix together well. Chill for 15 minutes.
3 Wash tomatoes and wipe them dry. Cut into quarters and arrange around the edge of the salad bowl with the washed and drained watercress.
4 Just before serving, garnish with sieved or finely chopped egg yolk. Toss salad at the table.

Put rice in colander (or top part of double steamer), then lower into cold salted water which must cover the rice

Place over a moderate heat and bring to a boil, then use two corks to raise the colander out of the water

Cover the pan, using a dish towel under the lid if it is not a good fit, and lower heat so water is just simmering

Steam the rice for about 20 minutes till tender, remove colander from pan. Stir rice and tip onto a warmed dish

Cantonese rice

Use chopped leftover vegetables or meat for economy in this tasty dish

LUNCH OR SUPPER   Serves 4

Overall timing 50 minutes

Equipment 2 bowls, wok or deep skillet, omelette pan

Freezing Not recommended

INGREDIENTS

6	Dried Chinese mushrooms
2	Small onions
½ lb	Bacon
½ lb	Roast pork or chicken
3 tablespoons	Oil
3 cups	Steamed long grain rice
¼ lb	Peeled cooked shrimp
1 tablespoon	Chopped chives
	Salt
¼ teaspoon	Cayenne
2	Eggs
	Freshly-ground black pepper

METHOD

1 Put the mushrooms into a bowl, cover with warm water and leave to soak for 30 minutes.

2 Peel the onions and cut each through stalk into 8 wedges. Dice the bacon and finely shred the pork or chicken. Drain and chop the mushrooms, discarding the stalks.

3 Heat the oil in the wok or skillet and stir-fry the onions, mushrooms, bacon and meat over a high heat for 3–4 minutes.

4 Add the rice and stir-fry for 1 minute. Stir in the shrimp, chopped chives, salt and cayenne and cook over a low heat for 3 minutes.

5 Meanwhile, beat the eggs with salt, pepper and 1 tablespoon cold water. Make a thin omelette, roll up and shred finely.

6 Pile the rice mixture on a warmed serving dish, scatter the shredded omelette over and serve immediately.

Fish tightly wrapped in foil will steam gently in its own juices and result in a moist, nutritious dish. Whole small white fish and steaks are generally cooked for 30 minutes per pound, oily fish for 35 minutes per pound. The usual oven temperature is 375°. The foil should be buttered or oiled, and you can add any flavorings you like, plus salt, pepper and 2 tablespoons of dry white wine, making sure the foil is sealed.

Finely chop flavorings of choice — herbs, anchovy fillets, onions, tomatoes

Place fish on buttered or oiled foil, and sprinkle top with flavoring mix

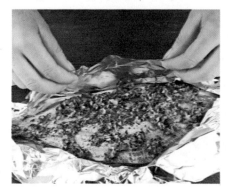

After adding liquid, bring foil ends to top. Pinch together to make package

Christmas pudding with Guinness

This recipe comes from Guinness, world-famous makers of stout, and it makes a large and a medium-sized pudding. Use fresh suet if you can get it — it does make a difference.

HOT DESSERT Serves 10–12

Overall timing 7¾ hours plus overnight standing time

Equipment Bowl, 1 quart and 1½ quart steaming molds, 2 saucepans

Freezing Not recommended

INGREDIENTS

1½ cups	Raisins
⅓ cup	Mixed candied peel
5 cups	Soft breadcrumbs
1½ cups	Brown sugar
1⅓ cups	Currants
1⅓ cups	Golden raisins
1¼ cups	Shredded suet
½ teaspoon	Salt
1 teaspoon	Apple pie spice
	Grated rind of 1 lemon
2 teaspoons	Lemon juice
2	Large eggs
¾ cup	Milk
1¼ cups	Guinness or other dark beer

Below: Christmas pudding with Guinness — festive flavors of fruit and spices

METHOD

1 Chop raisins and candied peel. Put into a bowl with all the dry ingredients and mix together well. Mix in lemon juice, beaten eggs, milk and Guinness.

2 Divide mixture between the 2 well greased steaming molds. Cover with the lids or foil tied on with string. Leave to stand overnight

3 Next day, place puddings in pans with boiling water to just below brims. Steam for 3 hours.

cook's know-how

Puddings can be stored, when cool, by re-covering and leaving in a cool place. To use, steam for a further 2–3 hours. One kept for next year will mature beautifully.

Basic sponge pudding

This recipe can be adapted to make almost any steamed sponge pudding

DESSERT   Serves 4–6

Overall timing 10 minutes (not including cooking time)

Equipment Bowl, 1 quart steaming mold, foil and saucepan or 8 inch square cake pan

Freezing Make pudding in foil container, cover, label and freeze. Freezer life: 3 months. To use: thaw at room temperature for 2 hours, then heat in preheated 375° oven for 30 minutes minutes

INGREDIENTS

½ cup	Butter or margarine
½ cup	Sugar
2	Eggs
1½ cups	Self-rising flour
¼ cup	Milk

METHOD

1 Cream the fat and sugar in a bowl till pale and fluffy. Gradually beat in the eggs one at a time.
2 Fold in the sifted flour with a metal spoon, adding milk to give a soft consistency.
3 Place in greased mold and cover with lid or foil. Put mold into a pan and fill up to rim of mold with boiling water. Cover and steam for 1½ hours. Unmold and serve immediately with cream or ice cream.

Orange upside down pudding

A warming oven-baked sponge dessert that's perfect for a wintry day

DESSERT   Serves 4–6

Overall timing 1 hour 10 minutes

Equipment 8 inch square cake pan, bowl

Freezing As for basic sponge pudding (see above)

Left: a selection of puddings all made from one basic sponge batter. Top, Orange upside down pudding; bottom left, Cherry pudding with jam sauce and left, Chocolate castles

INGREDIENTS

	Basic sponge pudding batter
3	Large thin-skinned oranges
¼ cup	Finely shredded marmalade

METHOD

1 Preheat the oven to 375°. Generously grease cake pan and line the bottom with parchment paper.
2 Make up basic sponge pudding according to instructions on this page, adding the finely grated rind of one of the oranges to the mixture.
3 Spread marmalade over bottom of prepared pan. Cut the peel and pith away from the oranges with a serrated-edge knife, then thinly slice flesh across the segments. Arrange slices, overlapping, over the bottom of pan. Spread sponge mixture over oranges with a spoon and smooth down the surface with a wet palette knife.
4 Bake for about 45 minutes or until firm to the touch. Invert onto serving dish and serve with custard sauce or cream.

Chocolate castles

Individual chocolate sponge puddings that taste as good as they look

DESSERT   Serves 4

Overall timing 45 minutes

Equipment 8 dariole molds or 8 inch square cake pan, bowl, saucepan

Freezing As for basic sponge pudding. Do not freeze sauce

INGREDIENTS

	Basic sponge pudding batter
¼ cup	Cocoa
1 cup	Chocolate chips
	Sauce
1 tablespoon	Cornstarch
1¼ cups	Milk
1 tablespoon	Butter
2 tablespoons	Sugar

METHOD

1 Preheat the oven to 375°. Grease the individual dariole molds or square cake pan.
2 Make the basic sponge pudding, substituting the cocoa for ¼ cup of the flour. Fold in half the chocolate chips.
3 Divide batter between dariole molds or cake pan. Bake for 20–25 minutes (35 minutes if using cake pan).
4 To make the sauce, blend the cornstarch with 2 tablespoons of the milk. Melt the remaining chocolate chips with the butter and sugar in the rest of the milk. Add cornstarch mixture and bring to a boil, stirring. Cook, stirring, until thick and smooth.

TO SERVE

Invert puddings out of molds and serve with a little of the sauce poured over, or cut into squares and serve cold with ice cream and the hot sauce.

Cherry pudding with jam sauce

A variation on the basic steamed pudding with a red jam sauce

DESSERT   Serves 4–6

Overall timing 1¾ hours

Equipment 1 quart steaming mold, bowl, foil, 2 saucepans

Freezing As for basic sponge pudding. Not recommended for sauce

INGREDIENTS

	Basic sponge pudding batter
⅔ cup	Glacé cherries
½ teaspoon	Almond extract
	Sauce
¼ cup	Red jam
⅔ cup	Water
1 teaspoon	Arrowroot
1 tablespoon	Lemon juice

METHOD

1 Grease steaming mold. Follow step 1 of basic sponge pudding method. Wash and dry cherries and toss in the flour. Complete Step 2 of the pudding method, adding the almond extract.
2 Spoon batter into prepared mold and cover with lid or foil. Place mold in large saucepan and fill with boiling water up to mold rim. Cover and steam for 1½ hours.
3 To make the sauce, melt the jam with the water in a small pan, then sieve. Blend arrowroot with lemon juice and stir into sauce. Bring to a boil, stirring.

TO SERVE

Unmold pudding and serve immediately with the hot jam sauce.

Frying

Frying is usually defined as the cooking or browning of food in hot fat or oil. It is quick because of the high temperatures that many fats and oils can reach before "smoking", boiling or decomposing.

Fat must be hot enough to seal the food and flavor it without burning the outside before the inside is cooked. If its temperature is too low, the fat seeps into the food, making it greasy and allowing soluble nutrients to escape.

Foods contain varying amounts of water and as they are put into hot fat, steam is formed inside. This works its way to the surface, helping in the cooking process and producing a mass of little bubbles which seethe and break on the surface of the food. This natural "barrier" keeps fat absorption to a minimum, but once all the steam has evaporated, the bubbles subside and the fat is able to rush into the food. To prevent this, most foods which are to be fried are coated. This insulation slows down the rate of heat penetration and fat saturation.

The more refined the fat, the more suitable it is for deep frying for it has greater stability, a higher smoke point and the ability to resist chemical breakdown in the presence of heat and moisture. The pan should never be more than one-third to half full to allow the level to rise when food is added. After use, deep fat must be strained and filtered as particles of cooked food will stick and burn the next time the fat is used.

Highly flavored foods should be fried last of all, and fat which has been used for deep frying fish must be kept for that purpose.

In shallow frying, the level of the fat can be anywhere from halfway up the side of a hamburger or chop, to the merest swirl over the bottom of the pan for cooking omelettes, pancakes or crêpes. The pan should not be crowded or covered otherwise the food will steam or braise instead of frying. It is important, too, that the fat is heated to a sizzle before adding the food so it seals instantly. Butter burns at a low temperature and it should be mixed with oil for shallow frying, or clarified.

Sautéing is now usually taken to mean the same as shallow frying, but little fat is used and the foods must be kept on the move in case they stick and burn. The pan is constantly agitated over the heat to prevent this. Stir frying is one of the basic methods of Chinese cooking. More time is spent in slicing, dicing and shredding the various meats and vegetables than in the frying itself (10 minutes at the *most*). Food must be kept constantly moving so it comes into contact with the small amount of oil and the hottest part of the wok, the best type of pan to use. Its rounded base and sloping sides make it easier to slide a spoon or spatula down and into the food in the "digging and tossing" motion that is required.

shallow frying

Also called sautéing, shallow frying is carried out on top of the stove over a medium heat. Though unsalted butter gives the best flavor, it browns very quickly — it's better to use equal amounts of butter and oil or oil alone. Clarified butter which has milk solids removed (it's these that burn) can be used, as can lard or block margarine

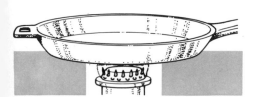

deep frying

Fat needs to be able to withstand high temperatures in deep frying, so oil is the only choice. The fat's heat (you should use a thermometer to check that it's right) seals the outside of the food, prevents moisture escaping and fat soaking in

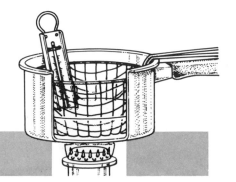

stir frying

Famous Chinese method of cooking is quick and easy. It uses little oil which is heated in the rounded bottom of the wok, the sloping sided pan used for stir frying. The cooked foods can be pushed to the side while fresh additions are being tossed and turned in the oil

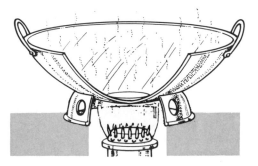

Frying techniques

absorption

This occurs when the temperature of the fat is too low, or the food is not well coated and absorbs fat.

basting

Eggs, for example, need to be basted with the hot fat during shallow frying if they are not turned.

blanching

Also called pre-frying, this technique is used with foods such as French fries and chicken pieces. The first frying partially cooks (useful when a large amount is being prepared), and the second frying completes the cooking and crisps the outside.

browning

This occurs on meats and other flesh foods when sugars/starches (carbohydrates) on the surface are caramelized by the hot fat. Brown a whole chicken, breast side down first, then on each side and finally on its back before braising. Some of the water in the food will evaporate and cause some shrinkage. If the fat isn't hot enough the water will seep out into the pan.

clarifying

Fat which contains milk solids or salt is not suitable for deep frying and will burn at low temperatures when used for shallow frying. Clarified butter can be bought as ghee or samna, or can be made at home. Gently melt in pan over low heat, or in low to moderate oven (up to 325°). The fat will separate into sediment topped by clear yellow oil. Skim off any foam and strain clear liquid into jar – covered it will keep for weeks in the refrigerator. Use milk sediment to enrich soups, stews, pastry. See also rendering.

coating or breading

Foods which are to be deep or shallow fried are usually coated to protect them from the fat's fierce heat, and also to prevent liquid from the food seeping into the fat. Raw foods are coated once, cooked foods twice with a short rest between. All food must be dry before any coating is done. Batters, except those containing beaten egg whites, should be left to stand for at least 30 minutes to allow starch grains to swell. Use tongs to dip foods into batter. Never overcrowd a basket when frying battered foods – the batter will stick to the sides. The most usual coatings are:

Seasoned flour Flour which has been mixed with salt, pepper, sometimes powdered mustard, ground mace. can be mixed on a board, plate or in plastic bag to which food can be added and tipped about till evenly coated. Used for whole white fish or fish fillets, liver, meat for casseroles, braising. Also first stage of breading.

Oatmeal Use coarse oatmeal, oat flour or rolled oats with oily fish (herrings, mackerel).

Egg and crumb Lightly beaten egg and fine, slightly stale breadcrumbs are used in sequence after flour. Egg can be brushed on large pieces, or food can be dipped into egg on flat plate. Crumbs can be on plate (use palette knife to flick them on) or on piece of waxed paper which can be pressed around food.

Fritter batters Main ingredients are flour, egg (sometimes beaten to make puffy coating), liquid (milk, cider, beer, water). Added yeast makes crisp batter; sugar is added to sweet batters. Chinese batter for shallow frying is made with forked egg white and arrowroot. It is not as thick as other batters which should cover the back of a spoon thickly.

Add recommended seasonings to flour on plate, mix together, then use to coat food lightly

Shake off excess flour then dip the food into beaten egg to cover both sides evenly

Fine, slightly stale breadcrumbs can be pressed on both sides of food with aid of waxed paper

Another method of securing the breadcrumbs on the egg is to flick them on with palette knife, then press down gently

Food can be placed in bag with seasoned flour and lightly shaken till coated all over

deep fat

This is the term for fat used in deep frying. It should never come more than halfway up the pan or it will overflow when food is added. After using, fat should be strained and stored either in a covered container or in the clean pan with lid in place. Always keep the fryer and basket clean. When fat smokes at 360° or foams when heated it should be discarded as it has broken down. Using any fat not at its best can be a health hazard – in taste terms it gives foods a bitter, nasty flavor.

deglazing

The basis of making gravy and some sauces. A small amount of wine, water or stock is added to a skillet or roasting pan and brought to a boil to dissolve pan juices and drippings. This is a sort of combination of boiling and frying, and during the process you should scrape the sides of the pan so that any drippings that cling are drawn into the liquid giving it flavor.

flash point

The stage at which fat will combust causing fire. It has been heated beyond its smoke point (that is, well above its correct frying temperature).

draining

After fried foods are cooked, remove from skillet or deep-fat fryer with slotted spoon (or a long handled skewer if cooking something like doughnuts or fritters which have a hole in the middle) and place immediately on paper towels to remove excess fat or oil before serving them.

After coating the food in batter, hold over the bowl so excess can drain off

flambé

Finishing touch for foods that have been pan fried. To be successful the food should be hot and the liquor or spirit warmed in a metal ladle before being ignited. In braising, after frying stage, meat is often flambéed to remove grease, concentrate flavors. The most popular spirit used for meat dishes such as *coq au vin*, or *boeuf en daube* is brandy.

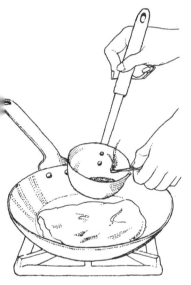

Never attempt to move the pan or douse it with water. Turn off heat, cover with lid or fire blanket. Fires in shallow skillet can be smothered with a lid or by a generous amount of baking soda.

foaming

Also called frothing, this is best indication that fat has broken down and is not able to be used again. The foam is yellowish and is made up of small bubbles which creep up the sides of the fryer.

frozen foods

Foods like potatoes that have been blanched should not be thawed before frying for as the water evaporates in the heat, the potatoes will absorb fat. Frozen foods require 25% longer frying than foods at room temperature, and a lower temperature is often recommended for the fat. Steak and chops over 1½ inches thick should be thawed before frying.

hazing

Description of the air above a pan which moves as wavy lines (like something in the distance on a very hot summer day) when fat reaches a temperature just below smoke point. Used in shallow frying only, never in deep frying for this is the stage before flash point.

non-stick

Pans are either treated with a special coating which cooks food without fat (though water sometimes needs to be added to prevent sticking) or a film of vegetable oil can be sprayed on to give the effect of dry frying.
You need special non-scratch

implements when frying in these pans to preserve surface.

overcrowding

Bad mistake to make when frying even if you are in a hurry. Too much in the pan reduces the temperature of the fat and causes much more absorption than there should be. Better to fry a little or few at a time and keep those hot while you fry the rest. Overcrowding also draws liquid from foods and this can help cause the fat to break down (called denaturing).

oxidation

This occurs in fats which have been exposed to the air — water is drawn in and affects fat used for frying. It also gives it an "off" flavor.

panade

Not the usual coating but one used in certain French dishes. It's a thick white sauce made of a high proportion of flour and fat (½ cup flour and ¼ cup fat) to 1¼ cups milk. It is also used to bind foods like croquettes before frying.

pan-frying

Similar method of cooking to sautéing and shallow frying. Sauces are often made in the pan after the meat or poultry has been cooked. The pan is deglazed with alcohol or stock and the sauce thickened by reduction.

pounding

Technique of tenderizing meats, and flattening them so that the frying time is kept to a minimum. Most usually done to veal cutlets, slices of chicken or turkey breast, and fine slices of beef (eg, top round) to make "minute" steak. For delicate meats place between sheets of moistened waxed paper and press evenly with rolling pin. For meats with more connective tissue use specially designed mallet with grooved edges which break through

the fibers and create characteristic indents.

rendering

Fat from beef, pork or chicken can be slowly melted, then strained and used for frying. Cut fat into smallish cubes and place in roasting pan with ½ cup of water for every lb of fat. Render in oven (200°) — as fat melts, impurities fall to bottom of pan and water evaporates. Well strained beef fat (drippings) can be mixed with pork (lard) and used to deep fry fish. Chicken fat is much used in Jewish cooking.

sauté

French word now used generally for shallow frying. The same rule applies about the heat of the fat (equal parts of clarified butter and oil, the classic sauté mixture, but not much of it), so the absolutely dry food can be seared and sealed. The pan must not be crowded and should be shaken, not stirred, to prevent food sticking. Sauté pans, invented by the French for this type of frying, are deeper than normal frying

To flatten delicate meats roll gently between sheets of moistened waxed paper

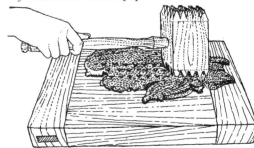

Frying or minute steaks need their fibers broken with a special meat mallet

pans, have straight sides and a lid which is used when steam frying. After the food is shallow fried, a little liquid is added, the pan covered and the food finishes its cooking in steam. Used mainly with chicken and veal, the technique also works well with eggs. High heat toughens protein, so if you like eggs tender but not crisp with the yolk lightly veiled, after they have fried till lightly set add 1 tablespoon water for each egg, cover, cook for 2 minutes.

searing and sealing

Foods whether shallow or deep fried, coated or uncoated, are added to fat at the right temperature so that it will seal in the juices and nutrients and brown it at the same time. If the food is wet or fat not hot enough, a layer of steam prevents sealing, the juices escape and food will absorb fat. Once sealed, the heat can be safely lowered till food is cooked through.

seasoning

Can mean either preparing a pan for frying by heating it with oil and salt, or adding flavoring agents. In the latter case, resist adding salt and pepper to fried foods until the foods are cooked (otherwise salt will contribute to the fat's breakdown).

shrinkage

When foods meet hot fat, the protein and starch "set" and the water content turns to steam. The heat also causes any fat in the food to run, and both of these cause the food to shrink. This is why sausages are pricked when added to a hot pan (there's no need if cold sausages go into a cold pan for the gradual heat draws out fat and prevents cases bursting), why fat on bacon and ham slices should be snipped so slices stay flat during frying (they can also be arranged in the pan so the fat part of one is over the lean part of the next). Foods which curl up in the heat should be held flat in the first few minutes of frying.

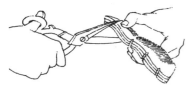

skimming

Deep hot fat should be skimmed with a special spoon between fryings to remove burnt specks or bits and pieces from the coating — if left in they give food an unpleasant flavor.

smoke point

Oils and fats can be heated to varying temperatures before they start to smoke which is the point before they "denature" or break down. Refining raises the smoke point of fats and oils.

soaking

Soaking French fries before frying removes excess starch and helps prevent the fries from sticking together. Matchstick-thin potatoes used for nests and grated potatoes for *rösti* aren't soaked for it is the starch which combines with the steam which causes them to stick together.

spattering

This happens when any water comes in contact with hot fat — which is why foods should be dry when fried. The water shoots out of the pan and takes hot fat with it so care is essential. Specially designed spatter guards are useful for covering pans during frying.

stir frying

Probably the best known of the "conservation" methods of cooking. It's a simple but stylish Chinese method of frying quickly in a little oil in a round-bottomed pan called a wok. The food (meat and vegetables) is cut into small, equal-sized pieces so they all cook in the oil at the same speed.

straining

Necessary with all fats after cooking — any debris left in can encourage the fat's breakdown. Store, covered, in a cool dark place.

sweating

Method of drawing flavor from diced vegetables by cooking them in a little butter over a low heat in a covered pan — a combination of frying and steaming. Essential first stage of braising and soup making.

temperature

The most important part of all frying is the temperature of the fat. A deep fat frying thermometer is the only real way of making sure that the fat is at the right temperature for the food you are cooking. Recommended temperatures are:

coated chops or vegetables, large chicken pieces 320°
battered or breaded fish, fritters, small chicken pieces 340°
doughnuts, battered onions, French fries 360°

If a thermometer is not available, you can use a small cube of day-old bread as a guide: if it becomes crisp and golden in 30 seconds, the temperature is about 360°.

tossing and turning

Food fried in little fat is turned once only and the side cooked first looks best for serving (it is also usually cooked longer). Fish fillets are an exception — fry skin side down first, then turn to serving side to brown. Uncoated meat should be turned as soon as blood or juices appear on the surface. Omelettes are rolled and not cooked on the second side,

except for thick omelettes (Spanish, Italian frittata) which can be inverted onto a plate, then slid back into the pan uncooked side down. Crêpes can be tossed, or turned with a wide-bladed spatula.

Deep-fried foods often need several turnings to ensure even cooking. Foods that float (doughnuts, fritters, choux) should be turned once halfway through cooking time.

to turn a thick omelette

After the base of omelette has cooked well and is set, place a flattish plate on top of the frying pan, then flip it so plate is right side up. Melt some more fat in the frying pan and when it is hot slide the omelette back in using knife with thick blade to push

to roll an omelette

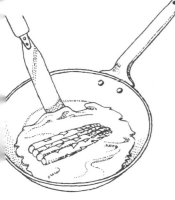

When omelette has set around the edges, run palette knife around to loosen it from pan

Hold the pan at an angle, then quickly flick it so one part of omelette folds in

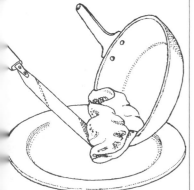

Simultaneously flick other side over, roll omelette out

to toss a crêpe

Use a crêpe pan and tilt it so batter runs over bottom and covers it in an even thin layer

Hold pan in front of you as though you were serving at badminton, then jerk it upwards

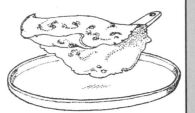

If the pan's been properly greased, the crêpe is well cooked underneath and the angle right, the crêpe should turn and land flat on the pan

Frying around the world

à la polonaise French term for soft breadcrumbs fried in butter and used for topping.

Aberdeen crulla A Scottish braided cake similar to a doughnut, probably forerunner of American **cruller. Koesisters** are the South African version.

aigrette French fried pastry.

albondigas Spanish meatballs.

alla milanese Italian term for egg, crumbed and fried foods. **A la milanaise** is French term.

alumettes Matchstick-thin French fried potatoes. **Mignonettes** are thicker, **Pont-neuf** are thickest.

bannock Griddle-fried oatcake from Scotland and North England.

beignet French, Swiss and Dutch word for fritter.

beurre frit Butter pats crumbed and fried to serve with fish.

blintzes Jewish crêpes, filled then rolled and re-fried.

blondir French term for light cooking in butter, oil or other fat.

boxty pancakes Griddle cakes of Ireland made from grated raw and mashed potatoes mixed with flour.

bubble and squeak English leftovers dish of fried mashed potatoes and cooked cabbage.

chapati Unleavened Indian bread cooked on a griddle. **Puris** are the deep-fried version.

churros Deep-fried choux pastry fritters popular in Spain, Mexico.

crème frite Crème pâtissière squares, egg and crumbed and fried as a French dessert.

crempog Welsh pancake.

crêpe French word for sweet and savory large, thin pancake.

croquettes Mixtures of cooked foods, egg and crumbed and fried.

croûtons French term for small cubes of fried bread used as garnish for soups, salads.

epigrammes French for tender "eye" of lamb, or sole, egg and crumbed and fried.

flapjack American pancakes or English griddle scones.

frikadeller Scandinavian meatballs. French and Belgian ones are **fricandelles.**

fritter Meat, fish or vegetable coated in batter. In Spain called **fritas,** in Italy **frittelle.**

fritto misto Italian deep-fried dish of meat, fish or vegetable mixtures.

goujon and **goujonettes** French terms for small strips of batter-coated fried fish.

hush puppies Fried cornbread from southern USA.

keftedes Greek meatballs.

kotlety po kievski Chicken in the Kiev style — boned, filled with butter, herbs and/or garlic, egg, crumbed and deep fried.

latkes Jewish potato pancakes.

leche frita Spanish/Portuguese dessert of thick custard, egg and crumbed and fried in oil.

loukoumades/loukoumathes Greek yeasted honey fritters.

nasi goreng Indonesian fried rice with meats and vegetables.

pain perdue French name for bread soaked in eggs and milk, then fried. The Danes have **arme riddere,** the Germans **arme ritter,** the British "poor knights of Windsor", and we have French toast!

pommes dauphine French fries of mashed potatoes and choux pastry.

rösti National Swiss dish of grated potatoes fried in lard.

Scotch eggs Hard-cooked eggs covered in sausagemeat, egg and crumbed and deep fried.

singin' hinny English griddle cake.

suppli Italian rice croquettes. If Mozzarella is included, they are called **telefonos.**

tortilla Mexican pancake, used as base for variety of dishes.

Wiener schnitzel Viennese veal cutlet egg and crumbed, then fried. Chicken and pork are also treated the same way.

Shallow frying

Shallow frying is a fast process, perfect for any foods which do not have tough connective tissue. Fewer vitamins of the B group are lost by frying than any other method, and as fried foods take longer to digest they have satiety value (you take longer to become hungry again). Oils and fats flavor and color bland but tender veal, white fish and young poultry. All vegetable oils are good for shallow frying, though olive is best for foods that will be used as a sauce (onions, tomatoes, etc).

FOOD	TIME IN MINUTES	Coatings
almonds		
bacon		
banana, whole		
slices		
bean sprouts, to stir fry		
blood sausage, slices		
brains, blanched		E&C SF
bread, croûtons		
crumbs		
slices		
chicken, breasts		E&C SF
small portions, to sauté		
cod, steaks/cutlets		SF
fillets		E&C SF
crêpes/pancakes	(1½ mins)	
croquettes, chicken		E&C
fish		E&C
meat		E&C
eggs		
eggplant, slices		SF
fish cakes		E&C
flounder, halved		E&C SF
fillets		E&C SF
hamburgers		
herrings, fillets		O
kidneys, veal, sliced		
lamb, halved		
pork, halved		
lamb, sirloin chops		
rib chops		
loin chops		
liver, lamb, sliced		
veal, sliced		
chicken, whole		
mackerel, whole		SF
fillets		SF
meatballs		SF

Time scale: 0, 5, 10, 15, 20, 25, 30, 35

Alternative coatings for shallow-fried foods: E&C egg and crumb; SF seasoned flour; O oatmeal

FOOD	TIME IN MINUTES								
	0	5	10	15	20	25	30	35	40
mullet, red, whole			SF						
mushrooms									
omelettes									
onions, pearl									
sliced									
plantain, slices									
pork, sirloin chops									
tenderloin									
loin chops									
spareribs									
potatoes, to sauté									
rice, cooked									
sandwiches									
sausages, large									
link									
skinless									
smelts, whole			SF						
sole, whole			SF						
fillets			SF						
steaks, minute									
$\frac{1}{2}$ inch rare									
medium									
well done									
1 inch rare									
medium									
well done									
sweetbreads, lamb									
blanched, whole			SF						
veal, blanched, slices			SF						
trout, whole									
turkey, breasts, slices			E&C						
veal, sirloin chops									
rib chops									
cutlets									
stuffed									
loin chops									
whiting, fillets			SF						

Deep-frying

Correct frying temperature is the key to success and this is influenced by: the size and shape of the food; how much is being fried; and, most important of all, the water content of the food — the more it contains the longer the food will take to fry (also, at high altitudes, the lower boiling point of water in moist foods will need lower fat temperatures). As a general guide, the highest temperature should be 380°.
Never leave pan of fat unattended over heat — the fire risk is too great.

FOOD	TEMPERATURE	TIME IN MINUTES	Coating
anchovies	340F		B SF
apple, slices	340F		B
banana, slices	360F		B
brussels sprouts	360F		B
calamares/squid, pieces	360F		B
carrots	360F		B
cauliflower, florets	320F		E&C
cheeses, soft	320F		E&C
chicken, bite-size pieces	320F		E&C
breasts, stuffed	340F		E&C
drumsticks	340F		E&C
legs	320F		E&C
choux, savory	360F		
sweet	360F		
cod, boneless steaks	340F		E&C B
fillets	340F		E&C B
corn, kernels	340F		B
doughnuts, ring	360F		
apple	360F		
jam	360F		
eggs (1½ mins)	360F		
eggplant, slices	320F		SF
endive, whole blanched	320F		E&C
figs, dried, stuffed	340F		B
flounder, halved	340F		E&C B
fillets	340F		E&C B
frankfurters	340F		B
goujonettes (any fish)	360F		E&C B
grayfish, steaks	340F		E&C B
haddock, fillets	340F		E&C B

Alternative coatings for deep-fried foods: B batter; E&C egg and crumb; SF seasoned flour

FOOD	TEMPERATURE			TIME IN MINUTES					
	320F	340F	360F	0	5	10	15	20	
kohlrabi, slices									B
leeks, pieces									B
mushrooms, whole									B
mussels									B
onion, rings									B SF
Pacific prawns, peeled									B
parsley, washed and dried (30 secs)									
parsnip, slices									B
pilchards, small, whole									B
pineapple, rings									B
pork, cooked cubes									B
potatoes, fries to blanch									
to brown									
chips									
croquettes									E&C
nests									
scallops									B
roes, soft, whole (shad)									B
sausages									B
spicy									
shrimp, peeled									E&C B
smelts, whole									SF B
soybeans, soaked and patted dry (2½ mins)									
sweetbreads									E&C
turkey, breast, sliced									E&C B
whiting, whole									SF
zucchini, sticks									B SF
slices									B SF
flowers									B

Carpetbag steak

A popular Australian dish in which thick juicy steaks are stuffed with oysters and gently fried in butter

MAIN DISH   Serves 4

Overall timing 30 minutes

Equipment Skewers, skillet

Freezing Not recommended

INGREDIENTS

4 × ½lb	Thick boneless sirloin steaks
	Salt
	Freshly-ground pepper
12	Oysters
2 tablespoons	Lemon juice
6 tablespoons	Butter

METHOD

1 Using a sharp knife, make a deep horizontal cut along one side of each of the steaks to make a pocket. Generously season the steak inside and out.
2 Remove the oysters from their shells and sprinkle the lemon juice over. Stuff 3 into each steak and close the steaks with a skewer.
3 Melt 4 tablespoons of the butter in the skillet. Add steaks and cook quickly for 1 minute on each side. Reduce heat and cook gently for 15–20 minutes, turning twice. Cook longer if you prefer steak well done.
4 Arrange on a warmed serving platter; top each with a pat of the remaining butter. Serve immediately with French fries and whole green beans.

Below: Carpetbag steak – a splendid dish named after the 19th century salesmen in Australia who carried a bag full of goodies

cook's know-how

Angels on horseback are small morsels traditionally served as an after-dinner savory, but perfect as appetizers too.

Preheat the broiler. Remove 12 oysters from their shells and sprinkle with lemon juice and a little cayenne. Use the blunt side of a knife to stretch 6 bacon slices. Halve the slices and wrap one around each oyster, securing with a toothpick. Arrange on foil-lined rack and broil for about 10 minutes, turning occasionally. Meanwhile, cut 12 bread triangles and fry in butter till lightly browned. Arrange on individual serving plates and place "angel" on top of each. Serve immediately.

Serves 6

Lemon fried veal cutlets

Veal is a tender meat and usually is not marinated but it's done in this case to add a lemony piquancy

MAIN DISH   Serves 4

Overall timing 40 minutes plus marination

Equipment Shallow dish, skillet

Freezing Not recommended

INGREDIENTS

4 × 6oz	Veal cutlets
	Salt and pepper
2	Lemons
5 tablespoons	Oil
1	Egg
⅓ cup	Flour
¼ cup	Butter
	Sprigs of parsley

METHOD

1 Wipe and trim cutlets. Place in dish and season. Wash lemons and grate rind from 1 over the veal.
2 Squeeze out the juice from the grated lemon, mix with 2 tablespoons oil and pour over the veal. Turn the cutlets till coated, cover and leave to marinate in a cool place for 1 hour.
3 Lift the cutlets out of the marinade and dry on paper towels. Beat the egg on a plate and season the flour on another plate. Dip the veal into the egg, then the flour, till evenly coated.
4 Heat the butter and the remaining oil in a large skillet, add the cutlets and fry for about 3 minutes each side till the juices run clear.
5 Arrange the cutlets on a warmed serving platter. Garnish with remaining lemon cut into slices, and parsley. Serve with green salad, minted peas.

Côtelettes d'agneau à la niçoise

If you have the fresh herbs, use them so as to taste this simple but effective dish at its best

MAIN DISH   Serves 4

Overall timing 1 hour

Equipment Skillet, saucepan

Freezing Not recommended

INGREDIENTS

1lb	Potatoes
¼ cup	Butter
2 tablespoons	Olive oil
	Salt and pepper
4	Large lamb chops
1 teaspoon	Dried rosemary
1 teaspoon	Dried thyme
1 teaspoon	Dried sage
¾ lb	Green beans
2	Large tomatoes
1 tablespoon	Chopped parsley
6 tablespoons	Dry white wine
1 tablespoon	Tomato paste
1	Small garlic clove

METHOD

1 Peel potatoes and cut into dice. Place in saucepan and cover with cold water. Bring to a boil, then remove from heat. Drain.
2 Heat half of the butter and half of the oil in a skillet, add potatoes and cook over medium heat for 10 minutes or until golden on all sides. Season. Remove from pan and keep hot.
3 Wipe meat and remove excess fat. Mix rosemary, thyme and sage and sprinkle over chops.
4 Heat remaining oil in skillet, add chops and cook for 5 minutes on each side or until tender.
5 Meanwhile, wash and trim green beans, removing strings if necessary. Plunge into boiling salted water and cook for 10 minutes or until tender. Drain thoroughly. Toss in remaining butter and season. Keep hot.
6 Arrange chops, potatoes and green beans on warmed serving platter. Halve and fry tomatoes in the fat left from chops and arrange on the platter. Garnish with parsley. Keep hot.
7 Remove any excess fat from skillet, leaving juices. Add the wine with the tomato paste and peeled and crushed garlic. Bring to a boil and cook for 3 minutes, stirring. Season and serve separately.

Below: Côtelettes d'agneau à la niçoise — dried or fresh herbs complement the flavor of the tender lamb chops

Fried eggs

Because it takes so little time, frying is always top choice when a quick meal is needed. The quicker an egg fries, the better it is. You can prevent a crispy underneath forming by piercing the white with the corner of the spatula, allowing the white to run into the holes. Sunny side up means the yolk's on top; eggs in the shade means a fine film of white covers the yolks (you baste as they fry). For a well-cooked yolk, turn the egg over and cook for 1–2 minutes more

To fry eggs, break them first into a bowl so they can be poured into pan

Heat the butter, fat or oil in pan over moderate to low heat. Add eggs

During frying, spoon over extra butter; pierce whites to ensure even cooking

Above: Oeufs Bercy — good breakfast or brunch dish of eggs, sausages and tomato catsup

Oeufs Bercy

A classic French dish which anywhere else would be called eggs with sausages and catsup — for that's all there is to it!

BREAKFAST OR BRUNCH   Serves 2–4

Overall timing 15 minutes

Equipment Skillet

Freezing Not recommended

INGREDIENTS

1 tablespoon	Oil
12	Pork link sausages
2 tablespoons	Butter
4	Eggs
3 tablespoons	Catsup
	Freshly-ground black pepper

METHOD

1 Heat the oil in the skillet. Cook the sausages till golden all over, then remove from the pan.

2 Melt butter in the pan, break in the eggs and place sausages over whites. Fry for 2–3 minutes, then spoon catsup around the edge of the pan. Sprinkle with pepper and serve with toast and fried tomatoes.

VARIATION

To make Oeufs Bercy sur le plat, you'll need individual heatproof dishes. Cook as above, and after the catsup has been added, place dishes under broiler for a couple of minutes to finish setting the surface. Grated cheese can also be sprinkled over, or tiny crisp croûtons.

Fried mackerel with creamy apple sauce

A splendid combination of textures and tastes lifts mackerel into the gourmet class. The apple in the accompanying sauce is fried in butter

Coat mackerel steaks with flour seasoned with salt, pepper and mild curry powder

Add apple to melted butter, cover and sweat over low heat till pulpy

To make sauce, sieve apple, cook with sugar, cream and egg yolks till thick

MAIN DISH   Serves 4

Overall timing 45 minutes

Equipment Plastic bag, 2 saucepans, large skillet

Freezing Not recommended

INGREDIENTS

$2 \times 1\frac{1}{2}$ lb	Mackerel
6 tablespoons	Flour
1 teaspoon	Mild curry powder
	Salt
	Freshly-ground white pepper
1	Large tart apple
$\frac{1}{2}$ cup	Butter
3 tablespoons	Oil
1 teaspoon	Sugar
$\frac{3}{4}$ cup	Heavy cream
2	Egg yolks

METHOD

1 Wash the mackerel and pat dry on paper towels. Cut into 2 inch thick steaks crosswise, discarding the heads and tails.

2 Mix the flour, curry powder, salt and pepper together in a plastic bag. Add the fish and toss lightly till evenly coated.

3 Peel, core and chop the apple. Heat $\frac{1}{4}$ cup of the butter in the saucepan, add the apple and stir till coated. Cover and cook over a low heat for 5–10 minutes till pulpy.

4 Heat the remaining butter and the oil in the skillet. Add the mackerel steaks and fry over a moderate heat for about 15 minutes, turning frequently, till the flesh is tender and the skin is crisp and golden.

5 Meanwhile, rub the apple through a sieve into a clean pan. Add the sugar and stir till dissolved. Gradually beat the cream into the egg yolks, then add to the apple purée.

6 Stir constantly over a low heat for 3 minutes without boiling till the mixture is smooth and thick. Add salt and pepper to taste.

7 Pour the sauce into a warmed sauceboat and serve immediately with the fried fish, new potatoes and buttered carrots or minted peas.

Right: Fried mackerel with creamy apple sauce — steaks with flavorful coating

Scrape carrots and cut into small chunks. Peel and chop the onions and the cucumber

Add prepared vegetables to the skillet with the garlic and stir-fry for 5 minutes

Above: Sweet and sour pork with cucumber, an Indonesian-style dish full of flavor

Sweet and sour pork and cucumber

Pieces of pork marinated in sherry or Marsala, lightly coated with egg and flour, then cooked and served with vegetables and a rich sauce

MAIN DISH   Serves 4

Overall timing 40 minutes plus marination

Equipment 2 bowls, plate, large skillet

Freezing Pack into rigid container, cover, label and freeze. Freezer life: 3 months. To use: reheat slowly from frozen

INGREDIENTS

1lb	Lean boneless pork
2 tablespoons	Dry sherry or Marsala
	Salt
	Freshly-ground pepper
1	Egg
3 tablespoons	Flour
3 tablespoons	Oil
2	Carrots
2	Onions
1	Large cucumber
1	Garlic clove
$\frac{1}{4}$ cup	Catsup
2 teaspoons	Soy sauce
2 tablespoons	Vinegar
1 tablespoon	Brown sugar
$1\frac{1}{4}$ cups	Water
1 tablespoon	Cornstarch

METHOD

1 Cut meat into $\frac{1}{2}$ inch cubes or into wafer-thin slices. Put into a bowl with the sherry or Marsala, season with salt and pepper and leave to marinate for 30 minutes.

2 Lightly beat egg in a bowl. Put the flour on a plate.

3 Heat the oil in a large skillet. Dip the pork pieces in the egg, then coat with flour. Add to skillet and cook for 8 minutes till golden brown on all sides. Remove from pan.

4 Scrape and chop the carrots. Peel and chop the onions and cucumber. Add to the skillet with peeled and crushed garlic and stir-fry for 5 minutes over fairly high heat.

5 Reduce heat to moderate. Add catsup, soy sauce, vinegar, sugar, water and reserved marinade to the pan. Blend the cornstarch with a little cold water and stir into sauce. Bring to a boil and cook for 3 minutes, stirring.

6 Return pork to pan and cook for 3 minutes more till heated through.

TO SERVE

Serve with plain boiled rice and side dishes of tomato wedges, chunks of cucumber and a little shredded coconut for sprinkling over the finished dish.

Above: Stir-fried liver and cabbage — a full-of-goodness Chinese dish

Squid with ginger and vegetable rice

Chinese-style stir-fried squid is served in a spicy, gingery sauce

MAIN DISH Serves 4

Overall timing 30 minutes

Equipment Saucepan, bowl, wok or deep skillet

Freezing Not recommended

INGREDIENTS

2	Large carrots
¼ cup	Oil
5 cups	Water
	Salt
1½ cups	Long grain rice
1½lb	Cleaned squid
1	Bunch of scallions
1 inch	Piece of green ginger root
2 teaspoons	Cornstarch
5 tablespoons	Dry sherry
2 tablespoons	Soy sauce
	Freshly-ground black pepper

METHOD

1 Scrape the carrots and cut lengthwise into ¼ inch slices, then into matchsticks.
2 Heat 2 tablespoons oil in a saucepan, add the carrots and fry, stirring, for 2 minutes. Add the water and bring to a boil, then add a little salt and the rice. Bring back to a boil, stirring, cover tightly and simmer for 15 minutes till the liquid is absorbed.
3 Meanwhile, wash and dry the squid and slice into thin rings. Cut the tentacles into 1 inch pieces. Wash and trim the scallions and cut into quarters lengthwise, then into 3 inch lengths. Finely grate or chop the ginger. Blend the cornstarch with the sherry in a bowl.
4 Heat the remaining oil in the wok or skillet. Add the squid and ginger and stir-fry for 3 minutes.
5 Add the scallions and soy sauce and stir-fry for further 2 minutes. Stir in the blended cornstarch and bring to a boil, stirring constantly. Cook for 2 minutes.
6 Fluff the rice with a fork and spread on a warmed serving dish. Season the squid mixture to taste, then arrange on the rice. Serve immediately.

Stir-fried liver and cabbage

The crinkly texture and good color of the savoy cabbage are used to advantage in this Chinese dish. It's a marvelous way of serving greens and liver to those who are not enthusiastic about either

MAIN DISH Serves 4

Overall timing 40 minutes

Equipment Bowl, heavy-based pan

Freezing Not recommended

INGREDIENTS

1lb	Lamb liver
	Salt
	Freshly-ground black pepper
½ cup	Flour
5 tablespoons	Sunflower oil
1	Large onion
1	Red pepper
1	Green pepper
1 tablespoon	Soy sauce
2 tablespoons	Chinese rice wine or medium sherry
½ cup	Stock or broth
½lb	Savoy cabbage
½lb	Fresh bean sprouts
4oz	Can of bamboo shoots

METHOD

1 Cut liver into thin slices. Season flour with salt and pepper and use to coat liver. Heat oil in pan, add liver pieces and fry quickly, for about 10 minutes. Remove from pan and keep warm.
2 Peel and slice onion, add to pan and fry for 5 minutes.
3 Deseed and slice peppers. Add to pan with soy sauce, rice wine or sherry and stock. Cook for 5 minutes. Wash cabbage and cut into fine strips. Add to pan with bean sprouts and drained bamboo shoots. Bring to a boil and cook, stirring, for 5 minutes. Add the cooked liver and cook for a further 1–2 minutes until heated through. Serve immediately.

Chicken Maryland

This dish of fried chicken with corn fritters, bacon and bananas, features on menus around the world as typical of the cuisine of the southern states of the US. There are many versions but basically it's a sweet-savory combination that looks good garnished with tomato wedges

MAIN DISH   Serves 8

Overall timing 1¾ hours

Equipment 2 bowls, 3 shallow dishes, deep-fat fryer, toothpicks, skillet

Freezing Not recommended

Below: Chicken Maryland – a delicious mixture of savory and sweet

INGREDIENTS

Corn fritters
1 cup	Flour
	Pinch of salt
1	Whole egg
¾ cup	Milk
12oz	Can of whole kernel corn
1	Egg white

Other ingredients
8	Boneless chicken breasts
	Salt
	Cayenne
½ cup	Flour
2	Eggs
2 cups	Soft white breadcrumbs
	Oil for frying
4	Bananas
12	Bacon slices
1	Lettuce
1	Tomato

METHOD

1 To make the fritter batter, put flour and salt in a bowl and make a well in the center. Break in the whole egg and gradually beat in the milk. Drain corn and add. Leave batter to stand.

2 Cut each chicken breast in half. Season with salt and cayenne. Dip into the flour, then into the beaten eggs, then into the breadcrumbs.

3 Heat the oil in a deep-fat fryer until hot or till a cube of bread browns in 1 minute. Fry the chicken pieces a few at a time for about 5–10 minutes, depending on thickness. Remove from pan, drain on paper towels and keep warm. Skim oil. Add spoonfuls of fritter batter. Cook for 3 minutes till golden. Drain on paper towels.

4 Peel bananas and cut into 3, then halve each one lengthwise. Stretch bacon slices and cut in half. Wrap a piece of bacon around each piece of banana and secure with a toothpick. Shallow fry in hot oil.

5 Arrange fritters, chicken and bacon-wrapped bananas on plate and serve.

Italian fried vegetables

Apart from pasta, the mixed fried food dishes are perhaps the most famous Italian specialties. The *fritto misto di mare* which uses a range of seafood is the best known and the same idea is used very effectively with a collection of vegetables, Zucchini flowers and apples provide a surprise element

LUNCH OR SUPPER   Serves 6

Overall timing 1 hour

Equipment Saucepan, shallow dish, deep-fat fryer

Freezing Not recommended

INGREDIENTS

1	Large eggplant
	Salt
$\frac{1}{2}$lb	Zucchini
$\frac{1}{2}$	Cauliflower
6	Zucchini flowers (optional)
$\frac{1}{2}$lb	Large flat mushrooms
2	Large apples
4	Eggs
3 cups	Fine dry breadcrumbs
	Freshly-ground black pepper
$\frac{3}{4}$ cup	Flour
	Oil for deep frying
	Sprigs of parsley

METHOD

1 Trim the eggplant and cut into $\frac{1}{4}$ inch thick slices. Spread on a plate and sprinkle with salt. Leave to drain for 15 minutes.

2 Meanwhile, trim the zucchini, cut in half lengthwise, then into 2 inch lengths. Wash the cauliflower and divide into florets. Blanch in lightly salted boiling water for 3 minutes, drain and rinse under cold water.

3 Wash and dry the zuchini flowers. Wipe, trim and quarter the mushrooms. Peel and core the apples and cut into thick rings. Rinse the eggplants and pat dry with paper towels.

4 Beat the eggs in the shallow dish and spread the breadcrumbs on a board. Toss the vegetables in seasoned flour, then dip into the egg and breadcrumbs, pressing the crumbs on to make an even coating. Shake off any excess.

5 Heat the oil in a deep-fat fryer to 340°. Add the eggplant slices and fry for about 4 minutes, turning occasionally, till crisp and golden. Drain on paper towels and keep hot.

6 Fry the zucchini and cauliflower florets for 5–6 minutes, and the zucchini flowers, mushrooms and apples for 3–4 minutes. Drain on paper towels and keep hot.

7 Arrange all the fried vegetables on a serving platter and garnish with parsley. Serve immediately with Tartare sauce and a green salad dressed with vinaigrette.

The vegetables should be cut into thin slices. The eggplants should be salted and drained, and cauliflower florets blanched

Below: Italian fried vegetables — egg and breadcrumbed, then deep fried till crisp and golden and served piping hot

Tempura

This is a Japanese dish in which each person fries a piece of fish or vegetable in batter.* Ready within seconds, the bits and pieces need to be drained on paper towels before being dipped in sauce and eaten

SUPPER Serves 6–8

Overall timing 25 minutes

Equipment Saucepan, bowl, metal fondue pot with burner, chopsticks

Freezing Not recommended

INGREDIENTS

	Tentsuyu sauce
¾ cup	Strong chicken stock or broth
¼ cup	Sweetened rice wine (sake) or sherry
2 tablespoons	Soy sauce
	Pinch of monosodium glutamate (optional)
6 inch	Piece of Japanese radish

	Other ingredients
1¼ lb	Firm white fish fillets
½ lb	Shrimp
½ cup	Mushrooms
1	Green pepper
2	Carrots
1	Small onion
1	Eggplant
8 oz	Can of bamboo shoots *or*
½ lb	Green beans
1	Egg
¾ cup	Cold water
¾ cup	Flour
¼ cup	Cornstarch
	Oil for deep frying

METHOD

1 To make the sauce, mix the stock, rice wine, soy sauce and monosodium glutamate in a pan. Bring to a boil, then pour into individual bowls and keep warm.

2 Remove any skin and bones from fish, then cut into 1 inch wide strips. Peel shrimp.

3 Wipe mushrooms. Wipe, deseed and slice pepper. Scrape carrots and cut into fine matchsticks. Peel onion and cut into thick rings.

4 Wipe and chop eggplant. Drain bamboo shoots and cut into bite-size pieces; or trim green beans and cut into lengths. Make sure all the prepared vegetables are thoroughly dry.

5 To make the batter, beat the egg with a fork, then gradually beat in the cold water to give a light, frothy mixture. Sift flour and cornstarch and add a little at a time, mixing lightly with the fork. Do not over beat – the batter should be quite thin and lightly coat the fork.

6 Heat the oil in a saucepan to about 350°. Transfer to metal fondue pot and place over a medium flame in the center of the table.

TO SERVE

Each person picks up a piece of fish or vegetable with chopsticks, dips it into the batter, then lowers it carefully into the oil. The pieces should be added a few at a time so the temperature of the oil is maintained. When the food is lightly browned, remove from the pan and drain on paper towels. Mix grated radish into sauce and use for dipping.

*In Sukiyaki, a similar Japanese dish, beef or chicken and vegetables are cooked in lard. Each person has a bowl of raw egg, helps himself to meat and vegetables with his chopsticks and dips into the egg.

Below: Tempura – crisp vegetables, fish and shellfish ready to be battered and fried

Fondue bourguignonne

A traditional meat fondue originally from Switzerland this is an impressive dish to serve at a dinner party. Cubes of steak are cooked at the table in hot oil and then dipped into a selection of tasty sauces. Results depend on using only the highest quality meat. If you're in any doubt about the tenderness of the steak, try marinating it for a few hours in a mixture of $\frac{3}{4}$ cup red wine and 3 tablespoons oil to break down the fibers (see page 114). Remember, though, to dry the meat thoroughly on paper towels before cooking or the oil will spit

SUPPER   Serves 4—6

Overall timing 15 minutes

Equipment Saucepan, metal fondue pot with burner, forks

Freezing Not recommended

INGREDIENTS

2lb	Fillet of beef
2—3 cups	Oil

METHOD
1 Using a sharp knife, trim steak and cut into small cubes.
2 Heat the oil to 375° in a saucepan. Carefully transfer to fondue pot and place over table burner.

TO SERVE
Give each guest a fork to spear the meat which they then cook in the hot oil. Serve with a selection of dips, pickles, side salads and crusty French bread or hot garlic bread.

Right: Fondue bourguignonne — put the fondue pot over the burner in the middle of the table and surround with condiments, dips and dishes of bits and pieces to eat with the meat. Serve with salad, French bread and a rosé or red wine

French fried potatoes

Whether cut finely (*alumettes*), slightly thicker (*mignonettes*) or in thick fingers (*pont-neuf*), French fries (*pommes frites*) are delicious

To preserve as much goodness as possible, use a potato peeler to remove skin with very little flesh attached. Wash well

The size and shape of fries can be what you like — either thick chunky fingers, or very finely cut matchstick lengths

Deep-fat fryer should only be one-third full of oil and basket a quarter full, or oil will lose heat and fries will be soggy

The first frying blanches the fries, the second one crisps and colors them. Tip on to paper towels to drain, then serve

VEGETABLE   Serves 4

Overall timing 1 hour

Equipment Bowl, deep-fat fryer

Freezing Prepare to end of Step 2 and cool. Freeze without wrapping, then pack into freezer bags, seal and label. Freezer life: 6 months. To use: deep fry from frozen at 360°

Above: French fries — make them thick and succulent, or thin and very crispy

INGREDIENTS

1½lb	Waxy potatoes
	Oil for deep frying
	Salt

METHOD

1 Peel the potatoes and cut into ½ inch thick slices, then into sticks ½ inch wide. Alternatively, cut slices ⅛ inch thick, then cut into thin matchsticks. Put into a bowl of cold water and leave to soak for 30 minutes.
2 Heat the oil in a deep-fat fryer to 350°. Drain the potatoes and dry thoroughly. Quarter-fill the fryer basket and fry for 4–5 minutes till tender but not brown. Remove and drain on paper towels. Repeat till all the fries are blanched.
3 Make sure oil is at right temperature. Quarter-fill the fryer basket with blanched fries and fry till crisp and golden. Drain on paper towels and keep hot, uncovered, while the remainder are cooked.
4 Arrange on a warmed serving dish and sprinkle with salt. Serve immediately.

OVEN FRENCH FRIES

These are a good idea for those who don't like deep frying, but are economic on fuel only if you're using the oven to cook something else. Peel and wash 4 medium-size waxy potatoes, then cut into sticks ½ inch thick. Place in a pan, cover with cold salted water and bring to a boil. Boil for 2 minutes, then drain and pat dry on paper towels. Preheat the oven to 450°. Spread cold potatoes in a single layer on a baking sheet. Pour over 2 tablespoons melted butter mixed with 1 tablespoon oil; turn fries till coated.* Bake for 25–30 minutes, turning fries several times, till golden and tender. Drain on paper towels.

*Freeze at this stage if liked, in shallow foil containers which can go straight in the oven for cooking.

potato nests

Scrape 1½lb waxy potatoes, wash and dry. Shred coarsely using fluted blade of mandoline. Dry, divide into 4. Use one portion to line bottom part of a potato nest mold. Secure top part in place. Lower into oil heated to 360°. Fry for 4–5 minutes till crisp, then unmold. Repeat with rest.

Above: Kidneys in white wine – a simple Danish dish appreciated by everyone

Kidneys in white wine

Deliciously tender lamb kidneys only need simple treatment and, in this recipe from Denmark, they are quickly cooked and then wine, lemon juice and mustard are added to the cooking juices for a super sauce

MAIN DISH   Serves 4

Overall timing 20 minutes

Equipment Skillet

Freezing Not recommended

INGREDIENTS

1lb	Lamb kidneys
	Salt
	Freshly-ground black pepper
6 tablespoons	Butter
$\frac{3}{4}$ cup	Dry white wine
2 tablespoons	Lemon juice
2 teaspoons	Prepared Dijon-style mustard

METHOD

1 Prepare kidneys and halve. Season well with salt and pepper.
2 Melt $\frac{1}{4}$ cup of the butter in a skillet, add kidney halves and cook for 5 minutes on each side until crisped and golden. Remove from pan, arrange on warmed serving plate and keep hot.
3 Add wine to pan and cook for 2–3 minutes. Blend lemon juice and mustard and stir into pan with remaining butter and seasoning. Heat through, stirring, but do not boil.

TO SERVE

Pour sauce over kidneys and serve immediately with boiled cauliflower and buttered green beans.

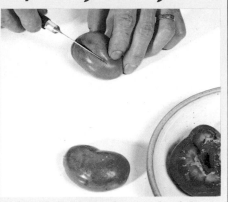

Make a deep cut on the outside of the lamb kidney without cutting it in half

Using your fingers, pull off the thin membrane that surrounds the kidney

Open the kidney and carefully snip off core in center with knife or scissors

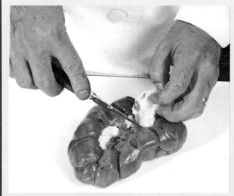

When preparing beef and veal kidney, remove the gristly core with sharp knife

Both orange rind and juice play important roles in savory dishes. While their flavor is not as astringent as lemons, the sweet/sharpness of oranges makes them a popular accompaniment for fatty meats like duck and pork, whether served in a sauce or gravy, as a garnish or in an accompanying salad. Make a deliciously sticky glaze for brushing over pork chops while broiling by mixing the juice of 1 orange with 2 tablespoons each of honey and catsup, and $\frac{1}{2}$ teaspoon powdered mustard. In salad dressings, use equal quantities of orange juice and oil with dairy salt and pepper, both freshly ground. Use with green salads and sliced tomatoes. If you're on a salt-free diet, grated rind beaten into softened unsalted butter makes a flavorful dressing for hot beans, Brussels sprouts, carrots, broiled fish — good cover for the lack of salt.

Crêpes Suzette

When Henri Charpentier created this dish at the age of 14 for his patron, Prince Albert, disaster struck when the sauce caught fire. So he added the crêpes to the sauce, added more liqueur and set it alight again!

DESSERT   Serves 6

Overall timing 50 minutes

Equipment 8 inch crêpe pan or non-stick skillet, bowl, large skillet or chafing dish

Freezing Not recommended

INGREDIENTS

2	Oranges
$1\frac{1}{4}$ cups	Flour
$\frac{1}{4}$ teaspoon	Salt
2	Eggs
$1\frac{1}{4}$ cups	Milk or water
2 tablespoons	Butter (optional)
6 tablespoons	Granulated sugar
6 tablespoons	Orange liqueur
	Oil or butter for frying
$\frac{1}{4}$ cup	Unsalted butter
$\frac{1}{4}$ cup	Confectioners sugar
3 tablespoons	Cognac

METHOD
1 Wash the oranges, finely grate the rind

Above: Crêpes Suzette — filled crêpes in a sweetened orange sauce, flamed before serving

and reserve. Squeeze out the juice and reserve. Make the batter: mix together the flour, salt, eggs, milk or water, and melted butter if wished. Stir in 1 tablespoon each granulated sugar and orange liqueur, and half the grated orange rind.

2 Cook 12 thin crêpes and reserve.* Beat the softened butter and the confectioners sugar in a bowl with the remaining grated rind and 1 tablespoon each of orange juice and liqueur.

3 Spread butter mixture over cold crêpes and roll up. Melt remaining sugar in large skillet or chafing dish over burner, stirring. Cook without stirring till pale golden. Remove from heat, carefully add rest of juice. Return to heat and stir till caramel dissolves.

4 Add the crêpes and warm through gently, spooning the caramel over them. Sprinkle the orange liqueur and Cognac over, ignite and serve immediately.

*This is best done well ahead of time as the crêpes will hold the filling better if they are cold. Cook, then cool before stacking.

The natural sweetness of oranges can be used to advantage in desserts. Instead of making sugar syrup for fresh fruit salad, use fresh, frozen or canned orange juice, toss the fruit in it, then macerate in the refrigerator to develop flavors. Fruit juice can be used to make an orange glacé icing, and it can also be added to cakes instead of milk to give an orange flavor. It especially complements chocolate. To make a quick glaze for a tart made with canned fruit, shred two strips of orange rind, add to can syrup and boil till reduced by half. Thicken with cornstarch; add yellow food coloring. Pour over tart. Orange-flavored sugar is useful for custards and other desserts which have sugar toppings browned under the broiler (*brûlé*). Shred rind finely, stir 2 tablespoons into 1 cup granulated or brown sugar, seal tightly and store in cool place.

Banana beignets

A French dish for adults who have a child-like love of fritters. For children who don't like the taste of rum, flavor the batter with lemon or apple juice instead

DESSERT   Serves 8

Overall timing 40 minutes

Equipment Measuring cup, 2 bowls, dish, deep-fat fryer

Freezing Not recommended

INGREDIENTS

2 tablespoons	Oil or water
	Milk
¾ cup + 2 tablespoons	Flour
1	Egg
¼ teaspoon	Salt
8	Large bananas
3 tablespoons	Granulated sugar
3 tablespoons	Rum
	Oil for deep frying
¼ teaspoon	Ground cinnamon
1 tablespoon	Confectioners sugar

METHOD

1 Put the oil or water into a measuring cup. Add enough milk to make ¾ cup. In a bowl, beat together the flour, egg and salt. Gradually add the mixed liquids and mix well. Cover and chill for about 30 minutes.
2 Meanwhile, peel and thickly slice the bananas. Put into a bowl and cover with 2 tablespoons of the granulated sugar, and the rum. Leave for 20 minutes.
3 Heat the oil in a deep-fat fryer to 360° — hot enough to brown, but not to burn, a cube of day-old bread in about a minute.
4 Dip banana slices in the batter and then add a few at a time to the pan. Cook until crisp and golden, then turn them over and cook on the other side. Drain on paper towels. Keep them warm while you fry the rest.

TO SERVE

Sprinkle with a mixture of cinnamon, confectioners sugar and the remaining granulated sugar. Serve immediately — they look attractive piled on a plate covered with a doily, which also helps absorb any surplus fat.

Use star tube to pipe choux paste in rings on greased squares of paper

Heat oil to fritter temperature, then carefully ease rings off the paper

Cook till rings puff up and turn golden — they should not be overbrowned

Deep-fried fancy pastries

DESSERT   Makes 16–18

Overall timing 45 minutes

Equipment Saucepan, pastry bag and star tube, waxed paper or foil, deep-fat fryer, slotted spoon, bowl

Freezing Flash freeze till firm, then pack in freezer bags or rigid container, cover, label and freeze. Freezer life: unbaked — 3 months, baked — 6 months

INGREDIENTS

1 cup	Flour
1 cup	Water
6 tablespoons	Unsalted butter
¼ teaspoon	Salt
3	Eggs
	Oil for frying
1¼ cups	Confectioners sugar
3 tablespoons	Rum
1 tablespoon	Hot water

METHOD

1 Put water and butter in a pan and heat gently until butter melts. Bring rapidly to a boil, then remove from heat. Add the flour all at once and beat vigorously. Return the pan to the heat and continue beating until the paste leaves the sides of the pan. Cool, then beat in eggs, one at a time. Heat oil in deep-fat fryer to 375°. Cut waxed paper or foil into about eighteen 4-inch squares.
2 Spoon paste into pastry bags and pipe 3 inch diameter rings onto the greased squares of paper or foil.
3 Invert squares of paper or foil, one at a time, over deep-fat fryer. Carefully ease paste off and into the hot oil, frying about 4 rings at a time. Cook for 5–6 minutes until golden, turning once. Lift out and drain on paper towels.
4 Arrange rings on serving dish. In a bowl mix together the confectioners sugar, rum and hot water and pour over rings.

Lift out rings with slotted spoon and place on paper towels to drain. When all are cooked, place on serving dish and pour over rum frosting

Roasting

Ever since the domestic oven superseded the spit, over-roasting has been one of the most popular and familiar ways of cooking cuts of meat, game birds and younger poultry. This apparently straightforward method needs care and understanding, however, if good results are to be achieved.

Lean meat is made up of muscle fibers. Each of these fibers consists of cells containing the protein myosin and a watery solution of minerals, vitamins and the "extractives" that give the meat its characteristic flavor. Fat cells, found throughout the connective tissue, are known as marbling or "invisible fat" (so called to distinguish it from the "visible fat" layers around the internal organs and under the skin). The presence of this fat certainly has an effect on the meat's flavor and juiciness, and its tenderness after cooking.

General digestibility depends not only on the amount of fat and connective tissue but on the length of the muscle fibers—the younger and less-exercised the animal, the shorter the fibers and the more tender the meat. In beef, the most suitable cuts for roasting are those from near the backbone — the sirloin, ribs and top of the round — the parts with the least movement. For lamb and pork, choose loin, leg and shoulder cuts. Lean meats such as veal or venison often need larding or barding with fat (see pages 112 and 114), whereas poultry containing a great deal of stored fat needs to have the skin pricked all over so the juices run out during cooking.

As dry heat is applied, the protein in the muscle starts to coagulate and the fat to melt. Heat gradually penetrates to the center by conduction (quicker if the meat is on the bone as bone acts like a skewer, conducting the heat through), driving the juices to the surface where they evaporate, leaving their flavors behind. The use of a rack in the bottom of the roasting pan keeps the base of the meat from frying or even stewing in the fat deposits, or from hardening, sticking and burning – though the oven heat may be moderate, the base of the pan will be much hotter. Fatty birds such as goose and duck give out a lot of fat during roasting and they need to be kept above it on a rack.

Cooking times depend on the size, type and weight of the roast, its age, density and whether it is on or off the bone. A flat piece of meat with a large surface area will cook quicker than a thicker cut of equivalent weight. Well-aged meat loses color quickly and often appears more "done" than it proves to be when tested with a skewer or thermometer. A boned, rolled, stuffed roast takes longest of all and should be turned at least once to ensure even cooking. Stuffings soak up meat juices and must reach an internal temperature of 165° so that any bacteria are destroyed. Frozen meat takes much longer to cook if unthawed and its flavor will be better if it is allowed to come to room temperature first.

There are two ways of oven-roasting. In the first, the oven is preheated to a high degree, 425–450°, and remains at this for the first 15 minutes. The oven is then turned down to a more congenial 350–375° to finish the cooking. (Continued high heat would have all the undesirable effect of overcooking – tough, dry, shrunken meat with indigestible "denatured" fat and the vitamins destroyed.) The second method uses a more moderate heat, 350°, throughout the cooking time. The lower the temperature, the slower the cooking, the less the shrinkage (meat contains 60–70% water) and greater retention of the vitamins – particularly those of the B group.

As salt draws juices to the surface, and these delay browning, it's better to add it later, or at the end of the cooking. Pepper, mustard or other spices and herbs can be added at the start. Meat starts to cook at an internal temperature of 140° – at its rarest. The protein starts to coagulate over the next 10 degrees or so – from 165–175°. The lower end of this scale indicates medium-done meat. For well-done, the thermometer placed in the coolest part of the thickest muscle, touching neither stuffing nor bone, should read at least 180°.

Carry-over cooking should always be allowed for when roasting, as the meat is still full of heat when taken from the oven. It must be left to stand for 10–20 minutes so that the fibers can relax and set and the juices redistribute themselves. This makes the meat moister and much easier to carve.

The roast is placed in a roasting pan or on a rack with a drip pan beneath so that as much of the meat as possible is exposed to the dry oven heat. The meat should be in the center of the oven so heat can circulate all around. It can be given 15 minutes at a high heat to seal in the juices and crisp the surface, and the roasting can be done at a more moderate heat; or the whole cooking can be done at moderate – the slower the roasting the less shrinkage there will be of the meat

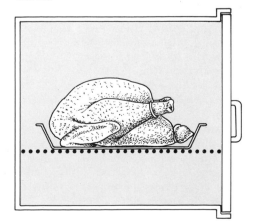

Roasting techniques

barding

Placing a layer of fat over lean meat, poultry or game before roasting to prevent the flesh from drying out during cooking; also flavors the meat and, in some cases, it is eaten with it. Use fatback for pork, bacon for poultry. Remove the barding towards end of cooking to crisp surface.

Cut fine sheets from pork fatback

Drape fat over top of roast

Secure fat in place with string

basting

Meats roasted in an oven need basting to keep them moist and to lessen shrinkage. Fat and juices which collect in the pan during cooking are scooped up at least twice during cooking time and spread over the meat. No need to baste turkeys described as self basting (they have specially added fat). With duck or goose, prick the skin before cooking; the thick layer of subcutaneous fat melts and bastes the surface without your help.

boning

Boning meat and poultry (with or without stuffing) gives it a neat shape, convenient for carving. As stuffed roasts are denser than meat on the bone (which also acts as a heat conductor) roasting time is increased by about 5 minutes per lb.

browning

Meat subjected to roasting heat will brown, but it is often suggested that leaner cuts such as beef and veal be fried in hot fat before roasting both to brown it and seal in the juices. Some cooks prefer a higher oven heat for the first 15 minutes to give the same result; this is especially good for crisping pork. Juices and sediment in the roasting pan give gravy its color so remember to scrape down sediment clinging to sides.

carving

Cut most meats across, not with the grain to get shorter fibers which are easier to digest. Lamb carves either way as there's plenty of fat between fibers to keep it tender. The closer the meat texture, the thinner it is possible to cut slices.

continued cooking

When meat leaves the oven, a meat thermometer will show the temperature at the center of a roast is still rising (by up to 60–75°) as the heat from the outside penetrates to the center and juices distribute themselves through the meat. It continues for 10–20 minutes after which the meat fibers are "set", ready for carving. Carry-over cooking is probably the reason behind instructions to cook for so many minutes per lb, plus so many minutes extra, and the food in fact could be removed from the heat for the suggested extra time – cover it lightly so heat is not lost.

defrosting

It is difficult when roasting frozen meat to achieve the state of doneness you require, and, as meats can harbor salmonellae which are not killed by freezing and the coldness of the meat will slow down the oven heat needed to kill this parasite, it is ideal to bring meats to room temperature before cooking. This is especially important with poultry and pork – thaw in the refrigerator for about 5 hours per lb. Some ovens have a special defrost setting to hurry the process, and microwaves can be used for this purpose.

doneness

The degree to which meat is cooked. It can be well done (cooked right through), medium (still pink in the center), or rare (brown outside, pink and juicy throughout). To test doneness accurately – a must with frozen meat – you need a meat thermometer. Put it in the thickest part of the muscle, away from bone or stuffing, before cooking. Poultry is ready when a skewer in the thigh flesh releases clear juices without a trace of pink. Professionals test by pressing meat surface with two fingers: spongy flesh which plumps up quickly should be rare to medium, if firm it is well done.

drawing

Technique of removing innards of feathered game and poultry after plucking. The gizzard (stomach), heart and liver are used with the neck for stock, the greenish-looking and bitter gall bladder is discarded. Some birds like snipe and woodcock are not drawn, their entrails (known as "the trail") being regarded as a delicacy.

Below: meat thermometer will give most accurate reading in thickest part of flesh

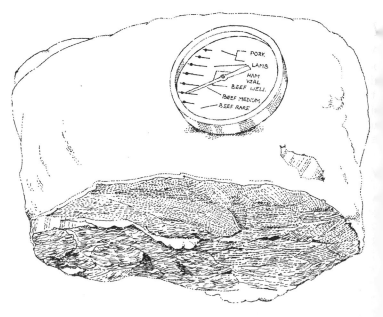

drippings

During the roasting process the fat on meat is rendered down and falls to the bottom of the pan. When, after roasting, the fat is poured off and strained into a storage jar, it will set and beneath the fat will be a layer of jellied meat juices known as drippings. Use to flavor stocks, gravies, or just spread on bread. Pommes parisienne are small potato balls cooked in melted meat jelly. Drippings from each type of meat have a specific flavor, and separate jars should be used for storage – and ideally each dripping reserved for the same type of meat it came from.

en croûte

French term meaning "in a crust". Meat is roasted to brown and seal in juices, cooled, wrapped in uncooked puff or pie pastry, chilled, then baked again.

eviscerating

Term for removing the entrails of furred game, usually rabbit and hare. After hanging head down for 1 week–10 days, the animal is skinned and slit along the abdomen to remove entrails – kidneys are left in, as is the liver but gall bladder must be cut from it. When cleaning hare, blood is saved to use as thickener for the gravy.

French roasting

A method of roasting poultry on a rack in a pan with about 1½ cups of wine or stock. For added flavor, the bird is stuffed with butter and herbs, a whole onion or lemon half.

frothing

A way of giving feathered game an appetizing crusty look: 15 minutes before the end of cooking time, baste bird, then dredge with salted flour and return to the oven. The starch grains bursting in the hot fat cause a "froth".

glazing

To baste roasting meat frequently with a sweetened mixture during the last 15–30 minutes of cooking time, giving it a glistening appearance which also adds flavor. Try maple syrup with ham; red currant jelly on lamb. For duck, mix three parts honey with one part soy sauce.

gravy

Made with the juices and sediment in the pan in which meat has been roasting. To make, pour off most of the fat, place pan over heat and when fat is hot, add flour to make a roux. Cook for 3 minutes, then gradually stir in liquid, and stir until the mixture boils, scraping down the sides of pan to draw in baked-on sediment. Cook for a few minutes till thickened and stir so all the gravy heats. Liquid can be the cooking water from vegetables (so valuable nutrients aren't wasted), stock or wine. If more color or flavor are required, add a beef bouillon cube, or a few drops of a tasty sauce such as Worcestershire.

To make gravy, first strain off most of the roasting fat. Add flour and fry for 3 minutes in same way as making a brown roux

Gradually add liquid (vegetable cooking liquid, wine, stock) and stir to remove lumps. Stir well as the gravy thickens

Frothing the surface of feathered game, or indeed any roast without a rind, gives the skin an appetizing and crusty finish

larding

Adding fat to lean meat by inserting thinnish strips along the grain of the meat, using a special larding needle. When fat is merely tucked into the skin with ends sticking out, this is called *piquage* and is done to flavor as well as moisten.

marinating

Steeping dry meat such as venison in flavored liquid before roasting to tenderize and moisten it. The added moisture causes the flesh to steam roast (see below).

plucking

Skill learned only by practice. Feathers on game and poultry are removed by hand and the ultimate object is not to break the skin (though birds that have been shot will have torn skin). Chill after hanging to make job easier – pull out body feathers first (they are easiest) against the lie of the feathers. Remove pinion feathers and others on wings with the lie, using thumb and forefinger to remove them one by one.

pricking

Do this before roasting a goose or duck (see basting).

rack roasting

Raising a roast off the bottom of a roasting pan prevents it from frying in the accumulating fat. Rack roasting is essential with fatty meats such as duck or goose.

searing

Placing roast in a very hot oven for the first 15–20 minutes to seal in juices and improve appearance before lowering the oven heat to a more congenial temperature for roasting.

seasoning

Salt draws out juices, so always add it to meat after browning or just before

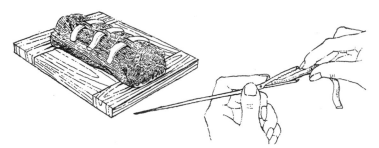

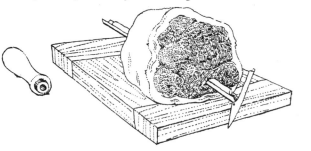

To lard meat, you'll need sheets of pork fatback (see barding, page 112) cut into strips 2 inches longer than the cut of meat. Fit strip into split end of the larding needle

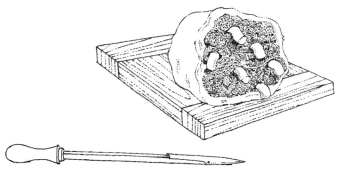

Push needle (this one is heavy-gauge variety) through meat following the grain. Undo clip to release fat, remove needle

When all the fat strips are in the meat at regular intervals the fat can be seen at both ends. It will shrink in roasting

resting

Another name for carry-over cooking or setting time after roasts come out of the oven and before they are carved.

scoring

Cutting partway through fat or meat to keep fat from shrinking and pulling meat out of shape during cooking, as with a ham. Scoring is also done to keep edges of meat from curling, and to tenderize.

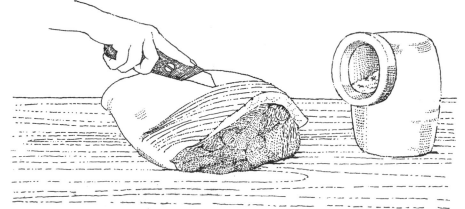

serving, or your meat will dry out. Pepper can be added at the start of cooking. Seasoned salts should be added as ordinary salt; however, other seasonings such as powdered mustard may be added at any time.

shrinkage

The longer meat roasts, the more it shrinks as moisture evaporates and fat melts. A well done roast will shrink more than one which is rare, and steam roasting will lessen shrinkage because it keeps moisture in.

skinning

To remove skin from furred game after hanging, cut off feet at first joint; cut skin down the inside of both back legs towards tail, cut off the tail, cut skin on inside of front legs. Cut skin along abdomen and remove entrails (see eviscerating). Peel off skin towards head, cut off head, then peel away the membrane covering the body. The skin is also removed from the fleshy flap on breast of lamb or veal by pulling it away in one swift movement.

spit roasting

To cook food on a revolving metal rod over a fire or hot coals. The spit may be turned by hand, but is more usually electrically operated. Ovens fitted with a rotisserie may also be used for spit roasting. To keep spit-roasted foods moist, they are basted with fat or a sauce.

Left: a very sharp knife is the best way to get even and deep cuts in the fat of a ham

steam roasting

Method of keeping moisture in meats. The roasting pan can be covered with foil or a lid, or meat can be placed in a roasting bag. Chicken can be completely encased in coarse salt – probably a link with the past when meats were cooked in clay or leaves.

studding

To add flavor, slivers of garlic or sprigs of herbs are pushed into slits made in surface of meat before roasting. Anchovies should be pushed right inside, as should oysters; strips of gherkin or carrot can be threaded in meat following the grain so that when the meat is carved it has a patterned look. For a more subtle flavor, insert a peeled clove of garlic next to the bone: the heat conducted via the bone will carry the flavor through the meat; the garlic can be removed during carving.

stuffing or dressing

Moist mixtures placed inside meat or poultry before roasting to improve flavor and prevent drying. Stuffings are usually starch based (rice, breadcrumbs) and bound with egg. Sausagemeat makes the food go further, herbs and spices add taste, dried fruit counteracts fattiness.

timing

Varies according to what is being roasted (see charts pages 122 and 124), at what stage you like to eat it (see doneness), and whether it is stuffed or not.

trussing

Boned meat and poultry is tied in a compact shape before roasting to give a neat appearance, keep stuffing in place, and encourage even heat distribution. Remove ties only after meat has set – after it has cooked and been left to stand before carving.

turning

You never turn meat which has a fat layer on top for as this melts it bastes the flesh. Lean cuts may be turned once during roasting, using tongs or a pair of spoons so as not to pierce the meat and let the juices escape. Large birds like turkeys should be started on their backs, given 15–20 minutes on each side, then turned breast side up to finish cooking.

vegetables

Raw or parboiled root vegetables (like parsnips) and tubers (such as potatoes and jerusalem artichokes) are called roasted when cooked with roasted meats, but are in fact baked as roasting is a term reserved only for meats. The fat needs to be very hot, and the vegetables well dried or they will be soggy.

weighing

If you have kitchen scales, you can weigh a boned, stuffed and rolled roast to calculate the cooking time. This is often given in roasting charts as so many minutes per pound plus a little extra. To work out how many the meat will serve, allow 6–8oz of meat per person, or 8–12oz if the meat is on the bone.

wiping

"Wash your lettuces, but leave your meat alone" . . . good advice from a French chef: meat should only be wiped before cooking because excess moisture hinders browning, and the oven heat will take longer to get through the cold layer that surface moisture creates and juices will not be sealed in.

Roasting around the world

agneau boulangère From France, lamb roasted in butter and rosemary, with onions and potatoes.

agneshka churba Bulgarian Easter dish of roasted whole lamb stuffed with rice, raisins and variety meat.

arista fiorentina From Florence, fresh pork covered in garlic, and rosemary, slowly roasted and served cold.

baron d'agneau French roast of the whole lamb minus the shoulders and head.

boeuf à la bordelaise From France, roasted sirloin of beef served with poached beef marrow in a creamy wine sauce.

caneton à l'orange Classic French dish of roast duckling with orange.

carré d'agneau persillade From France, roast rack of lamb coated with breadcrumbs, parsley and garlic.

dyrestek From Norway, venison or reindeer roasted in butter and served with a sauce of red currant jelly, sour cream and goat cheese.

dzikie gesi pieczone Wild duck or goose from Poland, rubbed with marjoram, stuffed with apples and onions and roasted in butter. Served with hawthorn berry jelly.

filet de porc en sanglier French dish of marinated, roasted pork tenderloin said to taste like wild boar.

gebraden ossenhaas Dutch fillet of beef roasted in fat with bay leaves for flavor.

gigot en braillouse From Brittany, leg of lamb covered in garlic and butter and roasted over a dish of thyme-flavored, sliced potatoes which cook in juices from the meat.

hammelkeule als wildbret From Germany, mutton roasted in sour cream to taste like venison.

kalbsbraten mit bier German method of roasting veal in beer with root vegetables.

lechazo asado From Castile, whole baby lamb roasted in fat and wine with bay leaves and served with wine, garlic and parsley sauce.

lechon From the Philippines, whole pig stuffed with tamarind leaves and spit roasted,

manzo ripieno arrosto Italian roast beef, stuffed with chicken livers, ham, tongue and cheese.

New Zealand roast lamb Fresh rosemary is inserted in the meat which is rubbed with oil and roasted slowly in a little water instead of fat.

noix de veau aux pruneaux From France, roasted rolled veal, flambéed with brandy in which prunes have soaked, and served with prune and bacon rolls.

oie rôti à la bordelaise Bordeaux roast goose, stuffed with mushrooms, goose liver, garlic and anchovy butter. A favorite dish at Christmas.

Peking duck Succulent Chinese roast duck, coated in malt, sugar and soy sauce. Bite-size pieces are eaten in crepes with plum sauce and scallions.

porcella asada Roast suckling pig from Majorca, rubbed inside and out with lemon juice and cooked in lemon juice and oil.

quaglie arrosto sul crostone From Italy, roasted quails wrapped in bacon and vine leaves, served on fried bread.

rinderfilet gartinerinart German roast of whole beef fillet wrapped in bacon, and served with sherry sauce.

roast beef and Yorkshire pudding The definitive English Sunday lunch, served with a batter pudding cooked in the hot fat from the meat. Eaten with mustard or horseradish sauce.

roast tenderloin American roast of whole fillet of beef served sliced with bordelaise sauce.

saddle of lamb with plum sauce Old Wiltshire recipe for the classic English roast of lamb. Roasted with fresh rosemary and served with red currant jelly and sauce made with plums cooked in wine vinegar and fresh mint.

Thanksgiving turkey The traditional American bird roasted for a favorite holiday, served with other harvest foods.

zharennyi porosenok Roast suckling pig cooked the Russian way with mushrooms and onions and served with buckwheat.

Carving

Carving at the table can often be an undignified grapple rather than skillful portioning of a roast so that there is little or no waste. Some people prefer to carve in the kitchen to speed up the serving and to ensure that the arrangement on the plates is attractive. A large roast, however, can make a marvelous centerpiece for a meal and the carver, with the right information and a little practice, can present the portions without problems.

You have to know your meat, for it is the position in which the bones lie that governs the carving. Before the meat is roasted feel out the size and length of the bones and decide whether they should be loosened or removed. Boning and rolling meat (see page 118, and 121 for poultry) is one way to simplify carving, although this sort of preparation does take time and raw meat is more difficult to remove from bones than cooked. But the removal of just one bone can speed up the presentation – the blade in a shoulder of lamb, for example, or the bone in the thick end of a leg of pork or lamb which get in the way of the knife. Rib roasts need to be chined as the backbone is impossible to cut through with a carving knife. These simple procedures can make roasted meat and poultry as easy to carve as a loaf of bread.

Cuts of meat and whole birds should be compact and neat in shape, for firmness makes for easier carving. More firming occurs too after cooking when the meat is left to rest before carving.

Most meat is carved against the grain for the shorter fibers are more tender and easier to chew. Carving is usually done at right angles to the bone, either vertically with large cuts, or horizontally with smaller one. Generally beef is carved into thin slices, pork, lamb and poultry into thicker slices. Large birds like goose and turkey are carved in much the same way as chicken; remove the legs and carve the thick thigh meat into slices. The irritating shape of the duck carcass makes traditional carving a problem, so poultry shears give better results. Small game birds are also best cut into serving portions with shears.

Major contributors to the success or failure of carving are the tools. A sharp carving knife which slices easily through the meat is less of a danger than a blunt one which requires force behind it in order to cut. Carving forks should have a safety guard to protect the hand if the knife should slip. Sometimes it is easier to carve a roast by not using a fork but rather by grasping a handy bone – but do remember to carve away from your hand, not towards it. A carving board with metal spikes will hold a roast steady and firmly for carving.

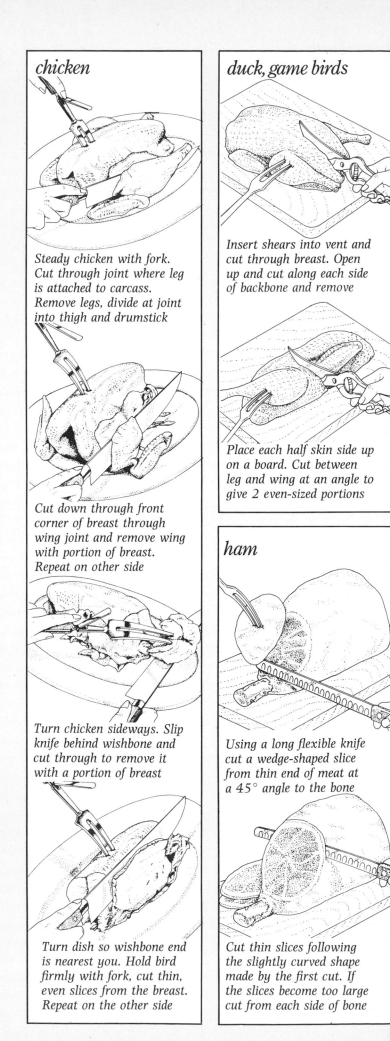

chicken

Steady chicken with fork. Cut through joint where leg is attached to carcass. Remove legs, divide at joint into thigh and drumstick

Cut down through front corner of breast through wing joint and remove wing with portion of breast. Repeat on other side

Turn chicken sideways. Slip knife behind wishbone and cut through to remove it with a portion of breast

Turn dish so wishbone end is nearest you. Hold bird firmly with fork, cut thin, even slices from the breast. Repeat on the other side

duck, game birds

Insert shears into vent and cut through breast. Open up and cut along each side of backbone and remove

Place each half skin side up on a board. Cut between leg and wing at an angle to give 2 even-sized portions

ham

Using a long flexible knife cut a wedge-shaped slice from thin end of meat at a 45° angle to the bone

Cut thin slices following the slightly curved shape made by the first cut. If the slices become too large cut from each side of bone

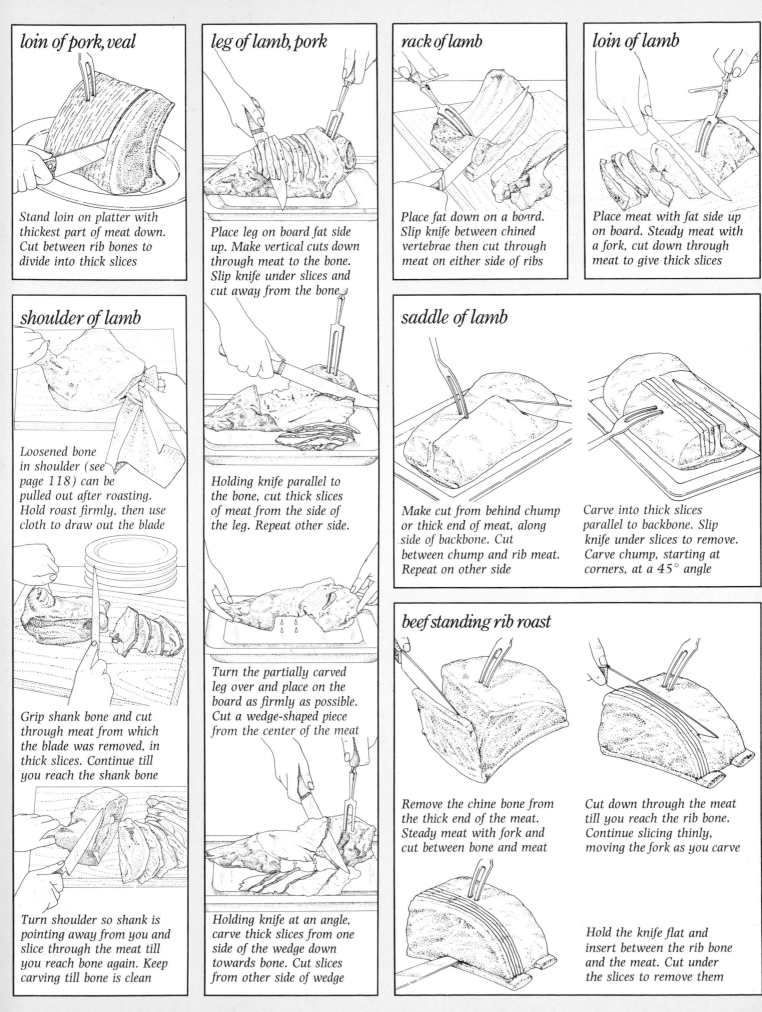

loin of pork, veal

Stand loin on platter with thickest part of meat down. Cut between rib bones to divide into thick slices

leg of lamb, pork

Place leg on board fat side up. Make vertical cuts down through meat to the bone. Slip knife under slices and cut away from the bone

Holding knife parallel to the bone, cut thick slices of meat from the side of the leg. Repeat other side.

Turn the partially carved leg over and place on the board as firmly as possible. Cut a wedge-shaped piece from the center of the meat

Holding knife at an angle, carve thick slices from one side of the wedge down towards bone. Cut slices from other side of wedge

rack of lamb

Place fat down on a board. Slip knife between chined vertebrae then cut through meat on either side of ribs

loin of lamb

Place meat with fat side up on board. Steady meat with a fork, cut down through meat to give thick slices

shoulder of lamb

Loosened bone in shoulder (see page 118) can be pulled out after roasting. Hold roast firmly, then use cloth to draw out the blade

Grip shank bone and cut through meat from which the blade was removed, in thick slices. Continue till you reach the shank bone

Turn shoulder so shank is pointing away from you and slice through the meat till you reach bone again. Keep carving till bone is clean

saddle of lamb

Make cut from behind chump or thick end of meat, along side of backbone. Cut between chump and rib meat. Repeat on other side

Carve into thick slices parallel to backbone. Slip knife under slices to remove. Carve chump, starting at corners, at a 45° angle

beef standing rib roast

Remove the chine bone from the thick end of the meat. Steady meat with fork and cut between bone and meat

Cut down through the meat till you reach the rib bone. Continue slicing thinly, moving the fork as you carve

Hold the knife flat and insert between the rib bone and the meat. Cut under the slices to remove them

117

Boning meat

There are two main reasons for removing bones from inside meat – to make room for a stuffing which extends the flavor and serving capacity of the meat, and to make carving and serving easier. Stuffing, if placed in the cavity of a shoulder of lamb after only the blade bone has been removed, plumps up the flesh and gives a more substantial roast, easily carved into slices. Meats to be rolled around a stuffing should be large and bone free to make the most of both flesh and stuffing. Breast of lamb and veal are used this way.

Succulent loin roasts well and serves more if the rib bones are removed – if left in, carving is restricted to the width of the chops. When taken out with the backbone, the meat is supple enough to roll with or without a stuffing, and carving into slices is simple.

Sawing through rib bones where they join the backbone at right angles is called chining; this is often done by the butcher so the meat can be cut into chops between the ribs without the carver having to try to get through the backbone. Chining is done to rack of lamb, standing rib roast of beef, and pork or veal loin.

While some bones don't get in the way of carving, awkward ones should be removed before roasting for neater carving – the odd shaped bone in the end of leg of pork and lamb, if taken out, leaves a straight fleshy thigh to carve.

Whatever the meat, the boning method is always the same. Feel the bone to get an idea of its shape and size, then slip a knife between it and the meat and cut the meat away in short sharp strokes, keeping the blade against the bone so no meat is wasted. Sometimes you have to work your way right around a bone inside a roast so it can be removed; this is called tunneling.

shoulder of lamb

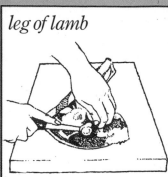

Place shoulder skin side down on board with the arm bone towards you. Slit meat along length of arm bone, cutting and scraping away the meat from both sides of the bone

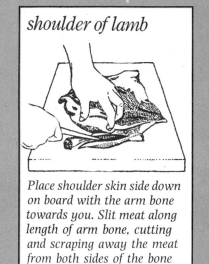

Bend bone to break it from ball and socket, remove. Using tip of knife loosen round arm bone by tunneling around it. When you can go no further turn shoulder so narrow side faces

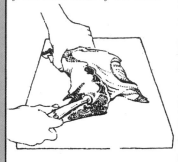

Make small feathery cuts into meat on both sides of blade bone. Cut gristle at top to remove blade bone. Now you should be able to pull out the round arm bone from other side

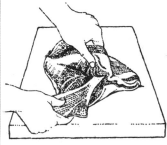

Tuck in the arm meat to make neat shape, then, using fine string and needle, stitch to close opening. Stuff other opening, sew up to close

leg of lamb

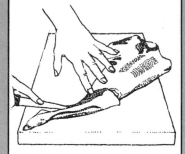

Trim away top fat, then cut on either side of hip bone with short sharp strokes so it can be pulled out. The hip bone is not included in the sirloin end of lamb, only whole leg

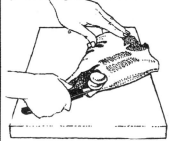

About halfway along side feel for shank joint, make cut to sever it from leg bone. Make short sharp cuts around shank bone turning meat inside out if necessary to remove it

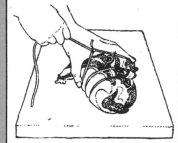

To prevent cutting skin, start at shank end and tunnel around ball joint. When halfway into meat, do same at the other end till the bone is able to be pulled out

Cut out small bone above cut made in shank. Tuck shank meat into main part, secure with skewer. Tie string at intervals, remove skewer

stuffing a half-boned shoulder

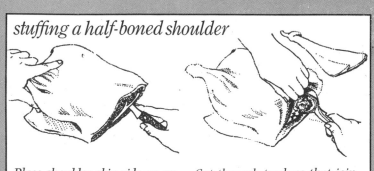

Place shoulder skin side up on board. Locate end of blade bone and insert knife. Cut the meat away from the bone above and below, right to end of roast

Cut through tendons that join blade to arm bone, then twist the bone and pull it out. Spoon in stuffing, packing firmly to plump meat. Sew up opening

crown roast and guard of honor

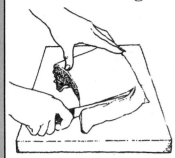

1 You will need two racks from the same lamb so they match for joining. The backbones should be chined. Place one rack skin side up on board and with a sharp knife cut a 2 inch wide strip of fat and meat covering the thin end of the bones. Do the same with the other rack so they look even and neat

2 Stand the rack upright with skin facing you. With a sharp thin bladed knife cut down between the rib tips, scraping them to remove all the meat and to leave them both clean and well separated. Do the same with the other rack — the rib tips are what give these roasts their attractive finished appearance

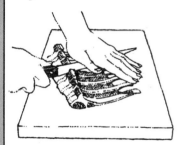

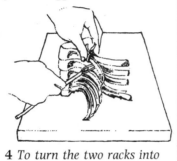

3 Place rack skin side down on board. Position the knife in a natural groove between the ribs, then thump the back of the blade or press down hard to separate the bones and cut a little way into the fleshy eye of meat below — this is necessary so that the rack can be curled into a semi-circle. Repeat till all grooves in both racks are cut through

4 To turn the two racks into a crown roast, place them on their ends back to back and with skin sides touching. Now use a trussing needle and fine string to join together the end ribs. Place in upright position and bend each rack so it forms a semi-circle and the base of the ribs with their eyes of meat separate. Sew other end

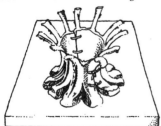

5 The cavity of the crown roast is now ready to be stuffed. Pack in stuffing of sausage-meat, mixed herbs and onions bound with egg and bread-crumbs, then smooth top. Ends of rib bones should be wrapped in foil strips to prevent burning during roasting. Before serving remove foil, decorate with chop frills

6 To make a guard of honor roast (which gets its name from the crossed swords used to form an arch on special military occasions), place racks upright with insides facing. Press one set of rib tips between the other so they intertwine. Tie racks together in several places underneath. Wrap bone tips with foil before roasting

breast of lamb, veal

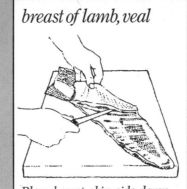

Place breast skin side down. Lift top flap of flesh (the diaphragm). With flat of blade against rib bones, use short sharp strokes to separate flap without detaching it

Use tip of the knife to locate where bones come to an end under the flap, then use feathery strokes to scrape meat from them to free end of row of bones

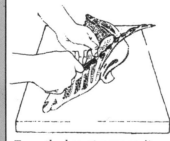

Turn the breast over so it is pointing away from you with bones to the left. Cut flesh downwards so the row of bones, joined at base, can be removed in one piece

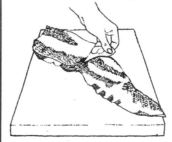

With breast skin side down and flap in original place, lift corner of thick skin covering it, tear off with one swift pull. Stuff, roll, tie

loin of pork, lamb

Place loin fat side down on board with rib tops towards you. Cut downwards on either side of the bones just far enough into meat to clear the underside of the bones

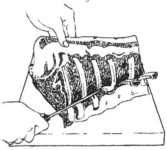

Place loin upright with thickest part down. Slip the knife between meat and bones. Scrape down backs of bones to free them, pull meat away with other hand

Continue to scrape till meat is flat on board and back-bone (chine bone) is revealed. Cut meat away with short strokes till all bones can be removed in one piece

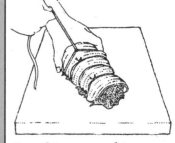

Turn loin over so fat side is out. Roll into a compact shape and tie at regular intervals with string

119

Preparing poultry and game

Roasting is the best way of cooking young poultry and game. The methods for each differ slightly but the basic preparation is similar.

Poultry is best cooked within a day or two of killing (frozen birds are merely suspended in time), but most game birds are hung for between several days and two weeks to improve the flavor and to tenderize the meat (it also makes plucking easier). Poultry is always drawn before roasting but some small game birds are cooked with their entrails and sometimes their heads intact (though the eyes and crop are removed).

Game birds suitable for roasting are lean and are barded or protected by a cover of some sort before they are roasted. In some cases the fat is removed before the end of cooking time to allow the skin to brown — frothing with flour and seasonings will hasten the browning and prevent the bird drying out while uncovered.

Light-fleshed game birds are roasted till well done but those with darker flesh are usually served rare or underdone. Poultry is generally trussed either to keep a stuffing inside or to give a good shape. When the strings are removed, the bird is easily carved. Before roasting, poultry and game birds should not be washed but wiped over with a damp cloth. Pat them dry with paper towels. Large birds can be boned and stuffed to make them more interesting to eat and to provide contrast to the flavor of the meat. Boned birds can be reshaped by careful stuffing — often only the carcass is removed leaving the leg and wing bones in so the bird can be carved into thick slices. Sometimes the boned wings and legs are pulled inside the bird and the sheet of meat can be wrapped around a stuffing and sewn into a neat shape before roasting. This method gives an attractive centerpiece as well as a roast that's simple in the extreme to carve. Boning might seem tricky, but it does reduce effort at serving time.

Stuffings for poultry and game vary enormously. Tiny game birds need but a grape or a clove-studded onion, a good pinch of fresh herbs or crushed juniper berries — all of which are used only for flavor and are discarded before serving. Larger birds with a high proportion of fat are best given flavor-making but discardable stuffings. The stuffing in large birds like turkey, capon and chicken, even goose, is part and parcel of the end result, and extra time must be allowed to ensure that the stuffing cooks right through.

plucking and drawing game

After the game bird has been hung for the time it takes to make it tender, place on newspaper-covered bowl or board. Pull out body feathers first, then rest with fingers or tweezers

Cut off head, roll back neck skin and cut off neck (keep for stock). Slit neck skin, loosen windpipe and gullet with fingers

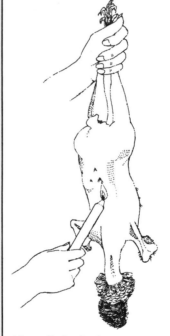

After all the feathers are out and before drawing, singe any stubborn quills using either a lighted candle, a taper or if necessary a low gas flame

Make a slit above vent to enlarge it, slide in fingers and remove innards. Don't break gall

stuffing under the skin

Only possible with fresh bird. Pinch skin all over, then lift and work it carefully away from the meat. Don't tear skin

Arrange pats of flavored butter or slices of truffles on meat, then ease skin back over the bird, smoothing as you go

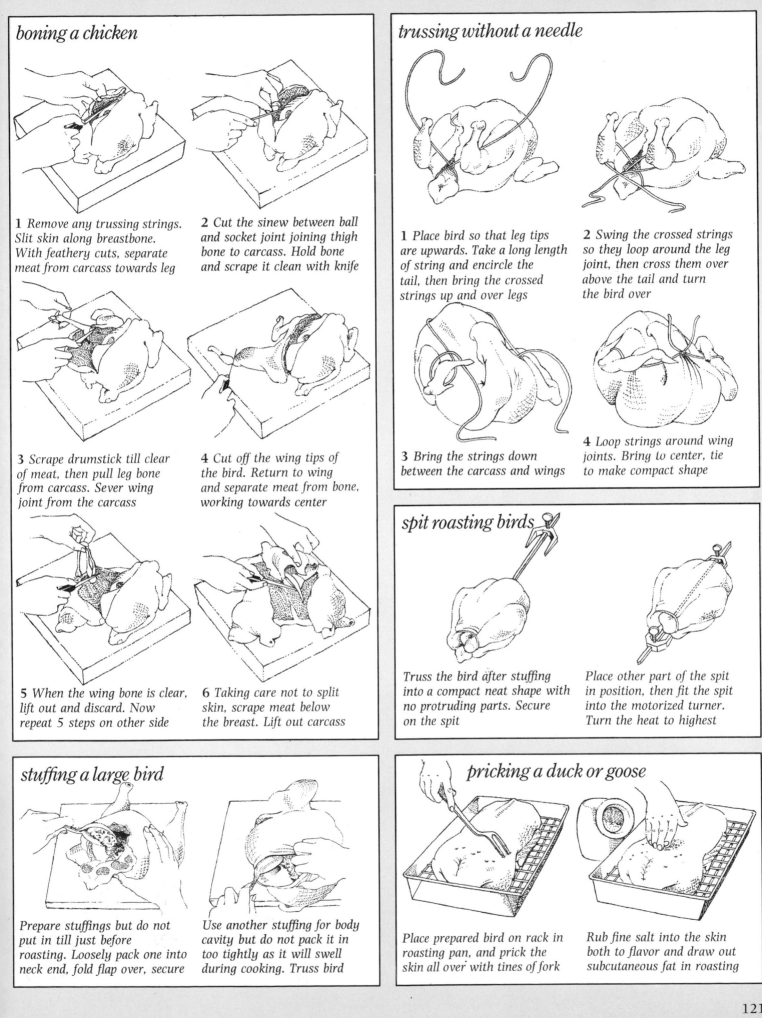

boning a chicken

1 Remove any trussing strings. Slit skin along breastbone. With feathery cuts, separate meat from carcass towards leg

2 Cut the sinew between ball and socket joint joining thigh bone to carcass. Hold bone and scrape it clean with knife

3 Scrape drumstick till clear of meat, then pull leg bone from carcass. Sever wing joint from the carcass

4 Cut off the wing tips of the bird. Return to wing and separate meat from bone, working towards center

5 When the wing bone is clear, lift out and discard. Now repeat 5 steps on other side

6 Taking care not to split skin, scrape meat below the breast. Lift out carcass

trussing without a needle

1 Place bird so that leg tips are upwards. Take a long length of string and encircle the tail, then bring the crossed strings up and over legs

2 Swing the crossed strings so they loop around the leg joint, then cross them over above the tail and turn the bird over

3 Bring the strings down between the carcass and wings

4 Loop strings around wing joints. Bring to center, tie to make compact shape

spit roasting birds

Truss the bird after stuffing into a compact neat shape with no protruding parts. Secure on the spit

Place other part of the spit in position, then fit the spit into the motorized turner. Turn the heat to highest

stuffing a large bird

Prepare stuffings but do not put in till just before roasting. Loosely pack one into neck end, fold flap over, secure

Use another stuffing for body cavity but do not pack it in too tightly as it will swell during cooking. Truss bird

pricking a duck or goose

Place prepared bird on rack in roasting pan, and prick the skin all over with tines of fork

Rub fine salt into the skin both to flavor and draw out subcutaneous fat in roasting

Roasting meat

Roasting has to be one of the easiest cooking methods — you need to do very little to a roast during the whole process and so long as the meat is prime, the end results will be thoroughly enjoyed. Meat can be studded with herbs or garlic, rubbed with a little oil if a crisp skin is wanted, or boned and stuffed to make it go further. After this it goes into the oven and cooks at a recommended temperature for a time calculated by weight — and even basting isn't always necessary as most roasts have natural fat which keeps the meat moist. Shrinkage can be a problem as a roast contains between 60 and 70% water which in the heat of the oven is driven off, drying up the fibers. Using roasting bags or foil will prevent this for they keep steam in — do remember to unwrap for the last 30 minutes of cooking time so the roast becomes nicely browned.

FOOD	SEARING TEMP	ROASTING TEMP	ROASTING TIME IN MINUTES PER LB	+ EXTRA MINS
BEEF				
chuck blade roast				
rare		350°		+25
medium				+30
well done				+35
boneless chuck eye roast	(fried off)			
rare				+30
well done				+40
tenderloin				
rare		425°		
well done				
rib roast				
rare		350°		+25
medium				+30
well done				+35
boned and rolled				
rare				+30
medium				+35
well done				+40
rump roast, boneless				
rare	425°	375°		+15
medium				+20
well done				+25
sirloin tip roast				
rare				+15
medium				+20
well done				+25
boned and rolled				
rare				+20
medium				+25
well done				+30
top round roast				
rare	(fried off)	350°		+25
medium				+30
well done				+35

The 15 minute searing time should be included in the overall roasting time; lean meats should be barded, others basted during roasting. If using a meat thermometer, the internal temperature when cooked will be: beef, rare 140°; medium 160°; well done 170°; lamb 175°; pork 180°; veal 175°

FOOD	SEARING TEMP	ROASTING TEMP	ROASTING TIME IN MINUTES PER LB					+ EXTRA MINS
			0	10	20	30	40	
LAMB								
rack (rib roast)		350°						+30
guard of honor								+30
crown roast								+30
breast, boned and rolled								+35
boned, stuffed and rolled								+40
leg, whole								+30
boned and stuffed								+40
loin roast								+35
boned and rolled								+40
boned, stuffed and rolled								+45
saddle, whole								+35
boned and rolled								+40
shoulder, square cut								+30
boned and rolled								+40
boned and stuffed								+45
PORK								
fresh pork sides, rolled	450°	375°						+40
stuffed and rolled								+45
thick end, boned and								
rolled								+40
leg (fresh ham), whole								+35
boneless								+35
loin, roast								+35
boned and rolled								+40
boned, stuffed and rolled								+45
boneless top loin								+35
blade (Boston) roast								+40
boneless blade roast								+40
tenderloin, stuffed								+25
VEAL								
rib roast	375°	350°						+25
breast, boned and stuffed								+30
leg, sirloin roast								+25
round roast								+30
loin roast								+35
boned and rolled								+40
boned, stuffed and rolled								+45
shoulder roast								+30
boned and rolled								+35
boned and stuffed								+40

cook's know-how

Roasting is usually done at two temperatures — the first sears, the second cooks the meat till tender. Another method of roasting keeps the oven heat at moderate for the whole time — and eventually the method you use all boils down to personal taste. In New Zealand, shoulder and leg of lamb roasts are roasted at 300° for 45 minutes per pound and with water in the pan instead of fat. It cuts down shrinkage, ensures tenderness.

Roasting poultry and game

Roasting is probably the best method of cooking young poultry, feathered game and some furred game. The skin of turkey, chicken, duck and goose becomes crisp and is a major feature in the look and taste of the end result. Chicken and turkey should be draped with fatty bacon or rubbed with butter and basted often. Duck and goose need to be pricked all over so their excessive fat can escape and baste at the same time. Game birds are lean, don't require a lot of cooking but do need barding (as does venison) with a thin layer of pork fat or bacon which should be tied or skewered in place and removed for the last 10 minutes so the top can brown.

FOOD	SEARING TEMP	ROASTING TEMP	ROASTING TIME IN MINUTES PER LB (except where otherwise stated)	+EXTRA MINS
black game		400°	overall timing	
capercaillie (Scottish grouse)			overall timing	
capon				+20
chicken				+20
stuffed				+20
boned and stuffed				+25
duck	400° for 20 mins	350°		+20
stuffed				+25
goose				+30
stuffed				+35
grouse		400°	overall timing	
guinea hen				+15
stuffed				+20
hare, saddle, stuffed		350°		+30
mallard duck		425°	overall timing	
partridge	450° for 10 mins	400°	overall timing	
pheasant				+15
stuffed				+20
pigeon		400°	overall timing	
prairie hen			overall timing	
ptarmigan (grouse)		425°	overall timing	
quail	450° for 5 mins	350°	overall timing	
rabbit, saddle				+10

FOOD	SEARING TEMP	ROASTING TEMP	ROASTING TIME IN MINUTES PER LB (except where otherwise stated)	+EXTRA MINS
			0　10　20　30　40	
snipe (rare*)		425°	overall timing	
squab		400°	overall timing	
teal (rare*)			overall timing	
turkey, stuffed		350°		
5—8lb				+17
8—11lb				+15
11—15lb				+14
15—20lb				+13
25—30lb				+11
venison, marinated, haunch		325°		+20
loin				+25
saddle				+30
Rock Cornish game hen		400°	overall timing	
woodcock			overall timing	

*always served underdone, never roasted right through

Below: Poultry and game birds all ready for roasting. They are from left to right, from the top: hen pheasant, plumper and with more tender flesh than the cock; guinea hen, a dry bird with a taste reminiscent of both chicken and pheasant; chicken, bigger fleshier ones are called capons; turkey, great for special occasions and for feeding a lot of people; gray-legged or common partridge, generally regarded as the best for eating; red-legged partridge, slightly larger than the gray; mallard duck, or teal, rated highly for its flavor; grouse, probably the most popular game bird; and quail, one of the smallest; pigeon, wild woodpigeons are gamier than the birds bred for the table, and young ones are called squabs; Rock Cornish game hen, for an individual serving

cook's know-how

Stuffings are used in roasts to extend serving capacity, and also to keep the meat moist or to act as an antidote to fattiness. Poultry and game should be well thawed before being stuffed and cooked. If possible, weigh roasts after stuffing and then calculate the cooking time, for it will require extra time to reach the dense center of stuffing. Duck is rarely stuffed for it gives off too much fat — a clove studded apple or a whole onion will help flavor and can be discarded on serving.

Roast chicken with spinach stuffing

Probably the favorite roast in many countries, chicken needs a moist, well-flavored stuffing to contrast with the sometimes bland meat

Make stuffing by mixing spinach, cheeses, breadcrumbs, butter, garlic, nutmeg

Spoon stuffing into chicken – don't pack tightly or oven heat won't cook it through

MAIN DISH   Serves 6

Overall timing 2¼ hours

Equipment Saucepan, bowl, string, roasting pan, skewer

Freezing Not recommended

INGREDIENTS

1½ lb	Spinach
6 tablespoons	Butter
½ cup	Ricotta or cottage cheese
½ teaspoon	Freshly-grated nutmeg
¼ cup	Grated Parmesan cheese
2 cups	Soft breadcrumbs
1	Garlic clove
1	Egg
	Salt
	Freshly-ground black pepper
3¼ lb	Roaster chicken

METHOD

1 Preheat the oven to 400°.
2 Trim and thoroughly wash the spinach. Place in a saucepan with only the water that clings to the leaves, cover and bring to a boil. Cook for 5 minutes shaking the pan occasionally. Drain thoroughly in a colander, then chop. Put into a bowl.
3 Add 2 tablespoons of the butter and the Ricotta or cottage cheese and beat together with a wooden spoon. Stir in the nutmeg, Parmesan and breadcrumbs. Peel and crush the garlic and add with the egg and plenty of seasoning. Mix well.
4 Wipe the chicken with a damp cloth, then pat dry. Spoon the stuffing inside the chicken, then truss securely.
5 Place the chicken in a roasting pan and rub skin with butter. Roast for 1¾ hours, basting twice during cooking, till the juices run clear.
6 Remove chicken from the pan and place on a warmed serving platter. Leave to rest for 10 minutes. Make gravy from the pan juices in the usual way and pour into a sauceboat. Remove the strings from the chicken before carving.

VARIATION

To roast the chicken in an electric roaster, prepare it in the same way but instead of rubbing chicken with the butter, heat butter in a skillet. Fry the chicken, turning it frequently till browned all over. Remove to the roaster and cover with the lid, leaving vent open for a crisp finish. Roast for about 1½ hours, then test for doneness in the usual way. As with conventional roasting, potatoes, parsnips or pumpkin can be "roasted" in the fat around the chicken for the last hour of cooking time; greens can be added to bake in the steam for last 20–30 minutes of cooking time.

Below: Roast chicken with spinach stuffing – to cook in the oven or an electric roaster

Surprise roast veal

A roast from Italy with a superb mixture only revealed on carving — it makes a wonderfully different dish for a very special occasion

Make the "roast" by layering pounded veal, pork, chicken breasts, ham, omelette

Form into tight roll to enclose filling, then tie at intervals with fine string

MAIN DISH   Serves 10

Overall timing $3\frac{1}{4}$ hours

Equipment Waxed paper, meat mallet, bowl, skillet, fine string, roasting pan

Freezing Not recommended

INGREDIENTS

2lb	Slice of veal rump
$1\frac{1}{2}$lb	Slice of pork leg (fresh ham)
2	Chicken breasts
2	Eggs
	Salt
	Freshly-ground black pepper
7 tablespoons	Butter
$\frac{1}{4}$lb	Prosciutto slices
$\frac{3}{4}$ cup	Sweet sherry
3 tablespoons	Flour
2 cups	Veal stock or broth

METHOD

1 Wipe and trim the veal, removing any skin. Place between 2 sheets of dampened waxed paper and pound to a rectangle about 12×9 inches.
2 Wipe pork and chicken breasts, removing bones and skin from both. Pound pork to the same size as the veal. Pound chicken breasts to $\frac{1}{4}$ inch thickness.

Below: Surprise roast veal — combination roast suitable for a celebration

3 Beat the eggs with 1 tablespoon water and seasoning. Heat 1 tablespoon butter in a skillet, add the eggs and make a thin omelette. Remove and leave to cool.
4 Preheat the oven to 375°.
5 Spread the veal on a board and season. Cover with remaining ingredients in this order — pork, half the prosciutto, omelette, chicken breasts and the remaining prosciutto, seasoning each layer.
6 Roll the veal tightly to enclose the filling and place seam down. Tie at 1 inch intervals with fine string and place in a roasting pan. Rub the remaining butter over the veal and pour the sherry around it.
7 Roast for 15 minutes. Reduce the temperature to 350° and baste the veal with the juices. Cook for a further 2 hours, basting every 30 minutes to make a glaze.
8 Lift out the veal, place on a serving platter and leave to rest for about 20 minutes before carving.
9 Pour off all but 3 tablespoons fat from the pan, retaining the juices. Heat the fat in the pan, add the flour and stir over a low heat for 1 minute. Gradually stir in the stock and bring to a boil stirring constantly. Simmer for 5 minutes, season to taste, then pour into warmed sauceboat. Remove strings from veal and carve into thick slices. Serve with the gravy, baked potatoes and green vegetables.

Roast beef and Yorkshire puddings

Britain's most famous roast — luscious, tender sirloin removed from the bone and rolled. Studding with garlic is not traditional, and is of course optional. It does, however, enhance the flavor of the meat very well. The batter puddings absorb all the beef drippings as they rise in the heat

Make deep slits at regular intervals in the rolled roast and insert fine garlic slivers

When drippings are sizzling in the muffin tins, fill each about two-thirds full with batter

MAIN DISH   Serves 9

Overall timing 2¼ hours

Equipment Small knife, roasting pan, bowls, sifter, muffin tins

Freezing Not recommended

INGREDIENTS

4lb	Boned and rolled sirloin tip roast
2	Garlic cloves
¼ cup	Beef drippings
1¼ cups	Flour
	Salt
2	Large eggs
1½ cups	Milk
¼ teaspoon	Powdered mustard
	Freshly-ground black pepper
1½ cups	Beef stock or broth

METHOD

1 Preheat the oven to 425°.
2 Wipe the beef and pat dry. Peel the garlic and cut into thin slivers. Cut deep slits at regular intervals in the fat around the meat. Insert a sliver of garlic into each slit and place the meat in a roasting pan. Add the drippings.
3 Roast for 15 minutes. Reduce the temperature to 375° and cook for 1 hour for rare beef (1 hour 25 minutes for medium, 1¾ hours for well done).
4 Meanwhile sift 1 cup of the flour with ½ teaspoon salt into a bowl and make well in the center. Add eggs and mix with a wooden spoon, gradually adding the milk. Beat to a smooth batter and chill.
5 Mix together 1 tablespoon of the remaining flour, the powdered mustard and seasoning. Froth the beef 15 minutes before the end of cooking time — baste with the hot fat and quickly sift the flour mixture over. Return to the oven to complete cooking.
6 Baste beef to complete frothing; remove to a serving platter. Cover and leave to rest in a warm place for about 30 minutes. Increase the oven temperature to 425°.
7 Spoon a little drippings from the roasting pan into each muffin tin. Put into the oven to heat for 5 minutes till smoking hot. Quickly pour batter into tins so that it sizzles, and return to oven. Bake for about 20 minutes till well-risen and brown.
8 Make the gravy with the stock while the puddings cook. Serve the beef carved in fine slices.

Left: Roast beef and Yorkshire puddings — complementary textures and tastes

Spit roast lamb with mint

The sweetness of lamb is enhanced by a piquant marinade and fresh mint

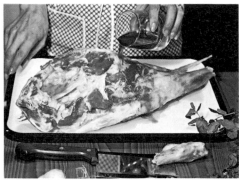

Place the prepared leg of lamb in a shallow dish and pour over the marinade

Sprinkle with finely chopped garlic and mint, then leave to absorb all flavors

After 2 hours marination, drain lamb, then secure meat on the spit forks

MAIN DISH Serves 8–10

Overall timing 3 hours plus 2 hours marination

Equipment Shallow enameled or glass dish, drippings tray

Freezing Not recommended

INGREDIENTS

5lb	French-style leg of lamb
6 tablespoons	Olive oil
6 tablespoons	Red wine vinegar
4	Garlic cloves
2	Large sprigs of fresh mint
	Freshly-ground black pepper

METHOD

1 Remove the sawn end of the leg bone from the lamb. Wipe the meat with a damp cloth. Pat dry and place in a shallow enameled or glass dish.

2 Pour the oil over and rub it into the meat. Pour the vinegar over. Peel and roughly chop the garlic cloves. Wash and chop the mint.

3 Sprinkle garlic and mint over the lamb with plenty of pepper and rub into the meat. Leave to marinate in a cool place for 2 hours turning occasionally.

4 Drain the lamb. Thread one of the spit forks onto the spit, then push the rod lengthwise through the lamb along the side of the bone till it is impaled on the fork.

5 Thread the other fork onto the spit, pushing it into the meat. Tighten the screws of the forks so the meat is held firmly in position.

6 Position the spit on the rotisserie in the oven (or on a barbecue) with a tray underneath to catch the drippings. Set to the highest temperature (or follow the manufacturer's instructions). Roast for $2\frac{1}{2}$ hours. Prick with a skewer to test for doneness.

7 Turn off the rotisserie and remove the spit. Pull the forks and spit out of the meat, and allow it to rest for about 20 minutes before carving in the usual way.

8 Serve with saffron rice and a tossed mixed salad.

Below: Spit-roast lamb with mint — a dish with a delicious summer flavor

Roast turkey with brandied stuffing

Brandy is used to effect in this dish — to flavor the stuffing and the pan juices used for basting. The result is a tender, moist meat that's as succulent cold as it is hot. To complete this festive meal serve a delicious chestnut purée with the turkey

MAIN DISH   15 servings

Overall timing 4½ hours

Equipment Mixing bowl, roasting pan with rack, small baking dish, saucepan

Freezing Not recommended. If using frozen turkey make certain that it is completely thawed

INGREDIENTS

	Stuffing
1	Onion
2	Shallots
1lb	Sausagemeat
2 tablespoons	Chopped parsley
1 cup	Chopped mixed nuts
⅓ cup	Golden raisins
2 teaspoons	Dried mixed herbs
	Salt
	Freshly-ground black pepper
2 cups	Soft brown breadcrumbs
¼ cup	Butter
¼ cup	Brandy
1	Egg
	Other ingredients
12–14lb	Turkey
2 tablespoons	Butter
	Oil
	Salt and pepper
½lb	Bacon slices
1	Bouillon cube
1¼ cups	Water
¼ cup	Brandy
	Bouquet garni
	Turkey giblets
2 tablespoons	Flour

METHOD

1 Chop onion and shallots; add to other stuffing ingredients in a mixing bowl and mix well together.
2 Use half to stuff turkey. Roll the rest into balls and place in a small baking dish. Dot with butter; leave in cool place.
3 Preheat the oven to 450°.
4 Brush turkey all over with oil. Rub salt and pepper in well.
5 Place rack in roasting pan and arrange half the bacon slices on top. Put turkey, breast down, on bacon. Arrange remaining bacon slices on top of turkey. Roast for 20 minutes.
6 Remove from oven and baste turkey well with the pan juices. Dissolve bouillon cube in the water and add to pan with brandy, 1 teaspoon salt and bouquet garni. Cover turkey legs with foil.
7 Return to oven and reduce temperature to 400°. Roast for a further hour. Baste every 15 minutes.
8 Remove turkey from the oven, and turn it breast side up. Brush with melted butter. Return to 350° oven and continue to roast slowly, basting regularly, for about 2 hours. An hour before the end of cooking time, place dish of extra stuffing in oven. At the same time cook 2lb pork link sausages – put in roasting pan below turkey.
9 To test for "doneness", insert a skewer into the thick part of the leg

Right: Roast turkey with brandied stuffing — a great dish for a time of celebration

and if the juices are clear, not red, the turkey will be ready. If not, return to oven for 15 minutes.

10 Put turkey onto a serving platter and leave in a warm place for 20 minutes, to allow meat to rest and to make carving easier. Bring turkey giblets to a boil in 2½ cups water. Simmer for 15 minutes.

11 Pour off all but 2 tablespoons of the fat in the roasting pan. Remove bouquet garni. Over heat, stir flour into fat in roasting pan, then cook for 1 minute. Remove from heat and stir in strained giblet stock. Return to heat and bring to a boil, stirring. Adjust seasoning. Strain gravy into a warm gravy boat.

Roast potatoes

Crisp and savory roast potatoes are traditionally cooked and served with roast meats in Britain

VEGETABLE	Serves 4

Equipment Saucepan (optional), roasting pan

Freezing Not recommended

INGREDIENTS

2lb	Waxy potatoes
	Salt
½ cup	Lard or drippings

METHOD 1
Peel potatoes, cut into even-size pieces and wash. Place in pan, cover with cold salted water, bring to a boil and cook for 5 minutes. Drain in colander and cool slightly. Turn in hot fat in roasting pan till coated. "Roast" in 400° oven for about 1 hour, turning once, till crisp and golden. Or arrange in fat around roasting meat 1–1¼ hours before end of cooking time. This method is not recommended for floury potatoes.

METHOD 2
Peel potatoes; cut into even-size pieces. Wash and dry thoroughly. Leave as is, or scratch the surface with a fork, or toss in a bag containing a little seasoned flour and shake off excess. Turn prepared potatoes in hot fat in roasting pan (or arrange around roast) and bake for 1¼–1½ hours, turning once, till crisp and golden.

CHESTNUT STUFFING

With a sharp knife, slit 1lb chestnuts from base to point, then cook in boiling water for 5 minutes. Leave to cool a little, then peel and skin. Place chestnuts in a pan, cover with 2 cups milk, add ¼ teaspoon salt and cook for 30 minutes. Lift out chestnuts and chop finely. Place in bowl with ½lb sausagemeat, 1 chopped onion, 1 chopped stalk of celery, ½ cup finely chopped bacon, grated rind of 1 lemon, 1 tablespoon sherry, 1 tablespoon chopped parsley, 3 tablespoons golden raisins and 1 cup soft white breadcrumbs. Add lots of salt and freshly-ground black pepper, then combine with a beaten egg. Use to stuff turkey.

Chestnut purée

Whole chestnuts are a traditional accompaniment to the Christmas turkey. For a change, try this savory purée — it goes well with any poultry, in fact

SAUCE	Serves 6–8

Overall timing 1¾ hours

Equipment 2 large saucepans

Freezing Freeze without wrapping, then pack in rigid container. Freezer life: 6 months. To use: thaw in refrigerator for 12 hours, then place in greased dish, cover with greased foil and reheat in 350° oven for 40 minutes

INGREDIENTS

1lb	Chestnuts
½ teaspoon	Salt
½	Small onion
2	Stalks of celery
2½ cups	Milk
¼ cup	Butter

METHOD
1 Bring 1 quart of water to a boil in a large pan. With a sharp pointed knife score each chestnut right around, from the base to the pointed end. Place chestnuts in the boiling water and cook for 5 minutes.

2 Remove from heat and leave to cool a little, then peel the chestnuts and place them in another suacepan with the salt and chopped onion and celery. Pour over half the milk.

3 Half cover and simmer gently for 45 minutes, adding more milk during cooking, if necessary, so that the chestnuts don't dry out.

4 Drain the chestnuts and reserve any cooking liquid. Place the chestnuts in a blender or food processor with the butter and 3 tablespoons of the cooking liquid. Process until soft and smooth.

5 Put the purée into a warm serving dish and shape into a mound. Mark with a fork. Spoon over a little of the cooking juices from roast meat and serve as an accompaniment to roast turkey, pork or chicken.

VARIATION
While the purée is still warm, beat in ¾ cup heavy cream, and season with salt and freshly-ground black pepper. Serve immediately with boiled poultry.

Grilling

Broiling is a good cooking method for foods of high quality which have enough moisture content to prevent them drying out during cooking. The heat is capable of reaching very high temperatures which reach the surface of the food by means of "heat waves". Radiated heat from any source is very efficient and care must be taken not to overcook the food. Continued high heat — as in any other form of cooking — toughens muscle fibers and destroys vitamins so food for broiling must be tender to begin with, of even thickness, and need only relatively brief cooking to keep evaporation to a minimum.

Dryer and leaner cuts of meat, poultry and thick-fleshed fish benefit in both succulence and flavor if they are tenderized beforehand in an acid/oil marinade which softens the fibers of the meat.

The conventional broiler should always be preheated for 5–10 minutes to achieve the high heat required to sear and seal the food. The broiler rack is *not* preheated (remember to remove it) and should be lightly greased before food is placed on it to prevent sticking.

It is better to regulate the intensity of heat by lowering the broiler pan rather than turning down the heat. At the start of cooking, the rack should be about 3 inches below the heat source for most foods, though the thinner they are the nearer the heat they should be. In gas flame broilers, which get hotter than electric ones, the rack should be 4–5 inches below the heat source.

Broiling is a technique often used in combination with other methods. Foods are often almost completely cooked in an oven, then transferred to a hot broiler for a few seconds or 1–2 minutes to give the dish an appetizing brown finish. Savory sauce-coated dishes — especially fish — are completed in this way so they bubble and crisp, and *gratin* dishes with their thick layer of crumbs are treated similarly. Desserts topped with a layer of sugar are "flashed" under the broiler to caramelize before serving. Almonds are toasted to give them extra flavor in baked foods, and hazelnuts must be toasted to remove their skins. Breadcrumbs are browned for use in various ways; and bread is broiled with a savory topping for a quick snack.

Pan broiling is not unlike dry frying or griddling. A thick-based, flat pan with characteristic ridges across it, is placed over heat and when hot, chops or steaks are placed on it and pressed against the metal so the surface is seared. Any fat that runs out is poured away (the pan usually has a channel into which it runs) and the food is turned to cook on the other side.

Infra-red broilers are designed to cook food very fast — the original "minute" steak for example. Infra-red rays are high energy heat waves shorter than microwaves, but longer than those that make up visible light beyond the red end of the spectrum (hence the name). In infra-red broilers, the rays are direct and pass through any vapor formed to penetrate the food; the closer the food is to the heat source the quicker it will cook. This has mostly been exploited by snack bars where fast food is the order of the day, but now contact broilers have entered the home from providing extremely speedy cooking facilities. Electrically operated, the broilers have two, usually ridged, plates which close over the food and cook it in 20 to 30 seconds.

hot

A distance of about 5 inches from the heat is recommended for cheese (too high a temperature makes it stringy), and for steaks that have been seared on both sides and are lowered to finish cooking

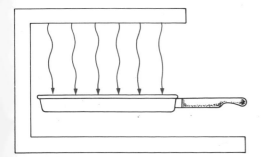

hotter

The middle position (about 4 inches from the heat) is best for meats which are over an inch thick or do not have a flat surface. The pan can be lowered to hot after food is seared

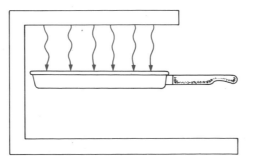

hottest

The top and fiercest position (2 inches from the heat) is used for thin and very tender foods. Always regulate the heat's intensity by lowering the pan, rather than reducing heat at source

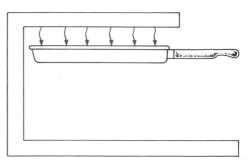

Broiling techniques

accompaniments

Foods which are broiled or barbecued have their flavors and juices sealed in but need accompaniments which will add extra moisture, basically to make the eating easier. **Savory butters** are the classic accompaniment to broiled meat and fish. Butter, unsalted or lightly salted, is left to soften, then is mixed with flavorings such as fresh herbs with or without lemon juice, pounded anchovy fillet, shrimp or other shellfish, garlic, paprika, orange, mustard or a strong blue cheese like Roquefort. The butter is shaped into rolls about $1\frac{1}{2}$ inches in diameter, wrapped in foil and chilled. To serve, cut into $\frac{1}{4}$ inch pats and place on hot food. **Sauces** provide good contrast to meats cooked over charcoal or broiled. Spiciness and piquancy are prized in barbecue sauces – the marinade is often used as the sauce base with added ingredients such as chopped green ginger root, chutney, chili peppers and garlic.

barbecue

To grill food correctly the heat must be just right. If using charcoal or shaped briquets, the fire must be lit about 1 hour before so the temperature is right for cooking. Place the palm of your hand 1 inch above the grill rack and if you can hold it there and count to three or even five the temperature's not high enough. Charcoal is ready to cook on when it is covered with a whitish ash. Before placing the food on the rack, sprinkle the fire with fennel twigs, sprigs of thyme, marjoram or rosemary – the herby flavor will reach the food via the charcoal's heat. A foil lining (shiny side down) in the fire bowl helps in the cooking and makes the cooled charcoal easy to remove.

basting

This is done to give the food good gloss and taste. Cover a broiler rack with foil, turning it up at the edges so the cooking juices don't fall into the pan where they can't be reached. Create boat shapes with foil for corn on the cob and place up to 2 tablespoons butter in each. As it melts and the corn is occasionally turned in it, the butter moistens the kernels. White fish fillets can be dotted with butter or sprinkled with lemon juice, or both. Lean meats like kidneys, liver and veal should be wrapped in or covered by bacon slices, the fat from which will baste the meats. A bulb baster or $\frac{1}{2}$ inch bristle brush is good for brushing over melted butter or marinade. Too much fat on barbecued food will cause a lot of flare; too much marinade will douse the fire. When cooking a mixed grill, baste after the food has been turned, and don't lower the heat but widen the distance between the pan and the heat so any fat on the broiler pan won't be in danger of catching alight. Generally speaking, basting should be done in moderation when broiling or barbecuing – foods chosen for this method of cooking are inherently tender and moist and their fat content should prevent them from drying out during the quick cooking.

blanching

Onions and peppers, which don't cook as quickly as meats, are best blanched for 2–3 minutes in boiling water before being threaded onto skewers for kabobs. Sausages which have a high fat content benefit from blanching which prevents any spitting when they're broiled or barbecued. Place in saucepan, cover with cold water and bring just to a boil. Quickly pour away water and leave to cool. Chicken portions need up to 30 minutes cooking so that juices run clear when pierced with a skewer. This can be a long time in barbecuing, so blanch as sausages but simmer for 10 minutes. Dry, cool and chill if necessary, but bring to room temperature before cooking.

blistering

Method of removing plastic-like outer skin from peppers. Place under hot broiler till skin blisters and burns. Leave to cool under damp cloth, then peel away charred parts.

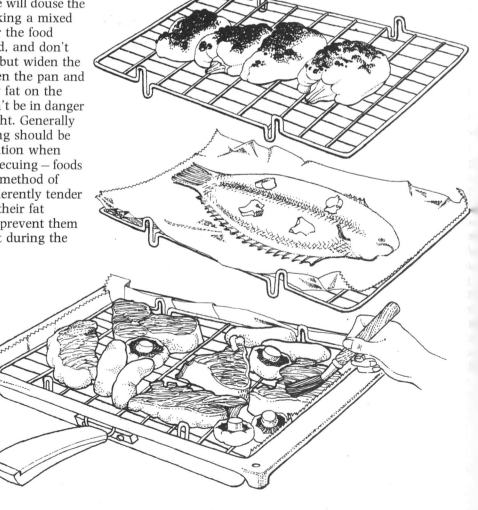

branding

This is done to foods so they look as though they have been grilled over bars. Heat four or five metal skewers under the broiler, then press on top of fish or sweet omelette to create a brown "lattice" effect.

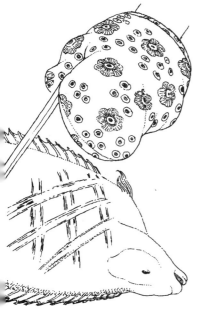

caramel topping

This is the method used to give a quick sweet topping to well chilled desserts, usually to provide a crisp contrast to a soft texture. The dessert in a heatproof dish is covered with ¼ inch layer of white or brown sugar and placed about 4 inches below a preheated broiler. The sugar melts and caramelizes, forming a thin, hard sheet of brittle toffee — keep your eyes on it or it will burn. The sugary crust which is called *brûlée* in France can be made ahead, then wrapped in wax paper and stored, or frozen, to be added to desserts as needed just before serving. Cut rounds the same size as dish or ramekins out of foil and grease well with butter. Press on ¼ inch thickness of brown sugar and place rounds on baking sheet. Put under preheated broiler (don't take your eyes off them) until caramelized. Invert rounds onto wire rack and leave to cool slightly, then peel caramel off the foil. Cool before wrapping.

continued cooking

Broiled foods continue to cook in residual heat even though they have been removed from the heat source. This is particularly true of foods cooked on metal skewers — they'll carry on cooking until the skewers are taken out.

doneness

Almost ungrammatical term for the stages at which foods are ready to be eaten. How long a food cooks depends on its thickness, the temperature of the broiler or barbecue, and the personal preference of the eater.

Chicken is done when the thickest part is pierced with a fine skewer and the juices run clear.

Steak uses the rule of the finger: very rare (*bleu*) is cooked just long enough to seal both surfaces and when pressed with a forefinger will feel very spongy because it is almost raw; rare (*saignant*) is turned as soon as drops of blood appear on top side and will feel spongy because it is underdone and mostly pink inside; medium (*à point*) has both surfaces well sealed and feels firm as the heat has almost penetrated to the center which will be rose pink; well done (*bien cuit*) has brown surfaces, is very firm to the touch and juices are clear because there isn't a trace of pink inside. For very thick steaks to be well done they need to be baked.

Fish fillets cook quickly skin side down — there's no need to turn them and they are cooked when easily pierced with tip of knife.

Fish steaks need turning; they should be tender when pierced with knife tip and there's no sign of reddish juices.

Whole fish should be tender when pierced right through to the bone and there's no sign of reddish juices.

Potatoes can either be "baked" in charcoal or on spikes which will help heat penetrate to the center. They are cooked when tip of knife pierces them easily.

frozen foods

Most foods should be thawed before they are broiled. It is especially important with chicken and turkey, and with thick steaks which will not cook evenly unless brought to room temperature. Very thin slices of steak, however, sometimes benefit from not being thawed — if using an infra-red broiler, for example, which has heat enough to penetrate quickly. Some commercially frozen foods (such as fish sticks) are in fact better cooked from frozen — always check directions on the package though.

gratin

The French name given to dishes on which a thin, golden brown crust is formed under a high heat from a broiler or in an oven. Foods cooked this way are usually coated with a sauce, then topped with cheese or breadcrumbs, or both, which sizzle and brown and create the appetizing finish. The topping also protects the food underneath.

greasing

Greasing or oiling the rack or metal skewers will prevent food from sticking. The rack is not usually preheated but can be if you wish food to be branded. Heated or not, it should be lightly greased before food is placed on it.

pan juices

These are used for basting or can be poured over before serving. Or they can be used as the basis for a sauce to serve with the broiled food. Fat from chops can be strained and used for frying or roasting.

preheating

Infra-red and conventional broilers need to be heated for 5–10 or even, in some cases, 20 minutes before cooking begins or the surface of the food will not be seared and the texture will be dry, hard.

salamander

It sounds like a fish but is in fact a flat round or oval metal "plate" with a long handle which is heated and placed on top of dishes to brown them before serving. The name is also used to describe the large broiler used in restaurant kitchens for the purpose.

searing

This is the reason why the broiler heat must be initially high — to sear and seal the surface of the food, keeping in as many as possible of the juices which contain the goodness and flavor. This is also called "seizing" as the heat sets the surface.

seasoning

Always a bit of a problem when foods are cooked quickly, and while there are several schools of thought on the matter, it usually all boils down to personal preference. If added in advance of cooking, salt draws juices to the surface of the food and these juices will form a steam layer which causes the food to stew rather than broil while the inside is dry rather than moist. If the outside is well seared before the salt is added it will flavor without being absorbed. If you add salt just before the food goes under the heat it also won't have time to do any drawing out. Pepper, paprika, mustard and other dry seasonings don't have the same effect as salt and can be used as a flavorful coating. Remember that if you leave food sprinkled with salt to stand, the moisture will end up on the plate, not in the food.

skewers

These are the lengths of metal used for broiling or barbecuing. Longer and thicker versions of the tiny skewers used for securing rolled meats for roasting, they are also known as *brochettes* (French) and kabobs (Turkish). Long sword-like ones often have decorative end pieces which are metal as well and should be turned with a gloved hand. Some have wooden handles which should be a good idea as wood doesn't conduct heat, but it does burn, and care must be taken if using them on barbecues. Fine lengths of bamboo are used as skewers for Southeast Asian *satays*. Inexpensive, they have sharply pointed ends so the meat goes on easily, and are usually used once only. Meats for kabobs and satays are cut into small pieces and are nearly always marinated. They are quickly cooked and rarely need basting. If broiling instead of barbecuing, foil boat shapes can be made to hold the kabobs and some marinade so that as the kabobs are turned (several

times over a fairly short period) the marinade will baste the food. This isn't possible on a barbecue as the foil would prevent the heat reaching the skewered foods. Foods are arranged on the skewers so that dry is next to fat and colors look appetizing. Bacon, pork fat, tomatoes, pineapple cubes have good moisture; onions, peppers, mushrooms provide color and texture contrast. Seafoods like scallops, prawns, shrimp and clams can be skewered. Dried fruits such as apricots and prunes should be soaked before skewering. They make an unusual dessert or can be combined with savory foods. You can only eat hot food from bamboo skewers; slide food from metal skewers with the back of a fork onto plate or into buns or pitta bread.

slashing

A technique used when broiling whole round fish. Several diagonal cuts are made at intervals in the sides of the fish so that the heat can penetrate faster. Once the bone is hot it distributes heat as well. Butter can be rubbed onto the skin so that it crisps during cooking. Whole fish should be placed about 3 inches from the heat source, and after turning, the pan can be lowered to slow down the cooking — the temperature of the broiler itself should not be reduced.

spatchcock

Comes from old English meaning "dispatch cock", a method of killing and cooking in a hurry. It has now come to mean flattening small chickens or game birds so they can be cooked evenly. With poultry shears cut along both sides of backbone, snip backbone out. Turn bird breast side up and open out, then with heel of the hand or rolling pin press down on ribs to break them and flatten bird. Make into a neat compact shape by tucking in the legs and wings, then thread onto skewers which aid in the turning (see page 140).

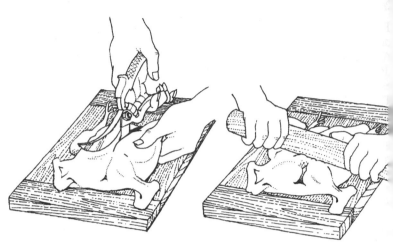

tenderizing

Broiling is not the method of cooking suited to meat or poultry that has tough connective tissue for the heat is too fierce and too fast. Prime quality foods that it does suit are tender in the first place, but sometimes certain things are done to ensure their tenderness.

Pounding will benefit thin steaks for the fibers will soften and the steak will cook quickly.

Commercial tenderizing powder may be sprinkled over. Though most types contain monosodium glutamate, this should not be used by itself as a tenderizer for it will draw juices out of the meat.

Fresh fruit such as papaya or pineapple tenderize as well as flavor — arrange on steak and refrigerate for 2–3 hours. Bring to room temperature before cooking.

Marination adds moisture and flavor to foods to be broiled. Marinades usually contain oil, an acid such as wine, wine vinegar or lemon juice and seasonings (garlic, peppercorns, paprika, onions, herbs). During broiling they are used for basting or can be the base for the accompanying sauce. Plain yogurt is also a good tenderizer — after marination it is not used for basting, but can be used in a sauce.

All foods should be surface dried after marination or they will cook in steam rather than being sealed by the broiler's heat. Broiling can cause cheese to become stringy and rubbery so to ensure tenderness it is best to shred it.

toasting

Toasting is near to broiling in that it uses high heat, but it is only used to seal a surface and not to cook the center of a food. Yeasted foods (breads, rolls, muffins) are toasted to give them a brown finish, and to warm them through. Breadcrumbs are toasted to dry them out, hazelnuts so that the skins can be rubbed off, and almonds to release their flavor. Melba toast is made by toasting slices of bread on both sides, splitting them, then toasting the uncooked sides. The fine slices crisp and dry in the process.

trimming

Fat on chops and steaks shouldn't be trimmed off before broiling as it adds flavor and moistness to the meat. Fatty bacon or ham steaks will curl up at the edges and the fat should be snipped at intervals to prevent this happening.

turning

Turning is done with tongs or a spatula when broiling. A fork or knife pierces the flesh and allows juices to escape.

Thin fish fillets should be placed on the greased rack skin side down. Cooking is quick and no turning is necessary.

Whole fish should be slashed and turned once.

Steak needs to be seared for 1 minute, turned and cooked according to preference, then turned back to first side to finish cooking.

Chops are done in the same way as steak. The first side cooked is the best side for serving.

Kabobs need to be turned several times to ensure even cooking of all surfaces.

Vegetables, unlike meats, are broiled, bottom side first, turned, basted and finished on the serving side. Special racks to hold corn on the cob and potatoes are available for barbecues.

Sausages should be turned several times. Prick or blanch before broiling to release fat.

Rotisseries are used with broilers or barbecues to turn the food automatically. They are either battery or electrically operated.

waffles

These are thought to have developed from the unleavened bread wafers used in church services. They are round or heart shaped and are made in "irons" which have indentations to create a holey design in the cooked waffle. The batter is more buttery and thicker than that used for pancakes, and the irons shouldn't need greasing.

Broiling around the world

andruty Polish wafer made on waffle irons. **Andruty migdalowe** has grated almonds added.

angels on horseback English savory of oysters wrapped in bacon, skewered, broiled and served on toast or fried bread. **Devils on horseback** are prunes stuffed with chutney.

Arbroath smokies Scottish smoked haddock sold in pairs and often called "tied tailies".

arni souvlakia Chunks of lamb skewered, broiled and often served with vegetables. Also known in its native Greece as kabob.

asticciole alla calabrese Italian dish of beef rolls stuffed with Mozzarella cheese and sliced pork sausages, skewered with bread and bay leaves and broiled.

au vert pré French accompaniment for broiled meats comprising *allumette* potatoes, watercress and maître d'hôtel butter.

beurre à la broche Chilled pats of breadcrumb-coated herby butter broiled and served with poached fish in France.

blawn fish Broiled dish from the Orkney Islands, to the north of Scotland, of air dried (wind "blawn") white fish.

broccoli med frankfurterkorv Swedish specialty of broccoli, frankfurters and cheese, broiled.

brochettes de veau French skewered dish of veal with bacon and mushrooms. **Rognons à la brochette** are kidney kabobs.

cargolade Provençal mixed grill with snails, meat and sausages.

ciğer kabob Turkish specialty — skewered liver is wrapped in caul (thin membrane from pig's stomach), broiled and served with a garlic and vinegar sauce.

coquilles St Jacques en brochettes Breton specialty of scallops and bacon broiled on skewers.

côtes de porc à l'ardennaise French broiled pork chops with crushed juniper berries.

côtes de porc Vallée d'Auge French pork chops broiled, and served with shallots and a cider and Calvados sauce.

crème brûlée Old English chilled sweet egg custard; topped with sugar and broiled.

elgbiff stekt på grill Norwegian broiled elk steak.

esterházy rostélyos Hungarian way of lightly broiling steaks, then frying with vegetables and adding sour cream and paprika.

funghi alla graticola Italian large mushrooms broiled with garlic, olive oil and marjoram.

gaufres Crispy Belgian and French vanilla waffles eaten with syrup, honey or cream.

graddyafflor Swedish sour cream waffles.

gratin French dishes with a rough crust made with butter, breadcrumbs and/or cheese.

homard flambé French whole broiled lobster flambéed in brandy or whisky. Called **Dublin lawyer** in Eire. **Lobster Thermidor** is the classic broiled lobster dish, named after the French revolutionaries' word for November.

huîtres comme à Bordeaux Splendid mix of tiny broiled sausages eaten with ice-cold oysters, bread and chilled wine.

kebapcheta Bulgarian kabobs of tiny garlic-flavored meatballs.

la micishja Corsican way of broiling skewered strips of goat, often over a wood fire. The drippings fall into a pan of garlic-rubbed bread, eaten with the meat.

langostinas a la plancha Large Spanish deep-sea prawns with red shells and black spots which are broiled and eaten hot.

London broil American dish of broiled flank steak, thinly sliced across the grain to serve.

melba toast Thin slices of toasted bread, named after famous Australian singer Dame Nellie Melba.

poor man of mutton Scottish dish of blade-bone cut of mutton, either broiled or spit roasted.

psari tis skaras Greek for broiled fish. **Psari me rigani** or **psari riganato** is white fish or sardines sprinkled with olive oil, lemon juice and oregano before broiling.

queue de porc grillée French dish of boned pig's tail stuffed with forcemeat, pressed, then brushed with melted butter, rolled in breadcrumbs and broiled.

raznjići Yugoslav version of kabobs usually made with pork, veal or lamb and served with rice and chopped raw onion.

rostélyos roston koritessel Hungarian broiled steak with mushrooms and other vegetables.

sate (Indonesian)/**satay** (Malaysian) Southeast Asian marinated meat on bamboo skewers, broiled and served with a spicy peanut sauce. **Sate ajam** is chicken, **sate kambing** is lamb, **sate babi** is pork.

scrowled pilchards Specialty of Cornwall, England — the fish are salted overnight, then grilled ("scrowled") over a fire.

shashlyk Russian kabobs with marinated lamb or mutton, onion and bay leaves.

shish kebab Originally a Turkish dish but well known all over the Balkans (the Yugoslavs call them **šiš ćevap**). Cubes of meat are skewered and broiled, often over charcoal. Other ingredients such as bay leaves, onion, mushrooms, and tomato can be added. The word kabob is widely used to cover any skewered food, but in Turkish means lamb or mutton.

sole à la niçoise Broiled sole Mediterranean style with tomatoes, garlic, lemon wedges, ripe olives and anchovies.

uskumru kebabi Turkish mackerel kabobs — the fish is marinated in salt, pepper, parsley and fennel and skewered with bay leaves. **uskumru kulbastisi** is marinated mackerel broiled and served with chopped parsley, raw onion and lemon juice.

ventresca Sardinian specialty of thin slices of stomach of tuna fish, brushed with oil and broiled.

voltaire French way of serving *oeufs en cocotte*. Eggs are baked with chicken purée, covered with white sauce and Parmesan and browned under the broiler.

Welsh rabbit or rarebit Popular British dish of cheese on toast. Though there's no rabbit involved the theme continues with **buck rarebit** which has poached eggs on top of the cheese!

Broiling

Whether you are broiling in the kitchen or barbecuing out of doors, food should always be at room temperature before you begin — the dampness of frozen foods prevents the necessary searing and sealing. Foods cooked by broiling should be of the best quality, for the whole point of using this method is to cook quickly — and tough fibered meats will become tougher and tasteless. The overall cooking times are based on one turning, and have been worked out on different distances from the heat source. These will, of course, depend on your broiler. If you wish to cook a food more slowly, don't turn down the heat, but lower the pan from it — if the outsides have been sealed at the hottest position the juices won't be drawn out. Remember to preheat the broiler, and to place the food on a greased or oiled rack.

FOOD	PAN POSITION			TIME IN MINUTES				
	HHH	HH	H	0	5	10	20	30
almonds, sliced, to toast								
anchovies								
bacon, slices								
bananas								
bass, whole								
bread, to toast								
cheese, as topping								
chicken, quarters								
legs								
kabobs								
Cornish game hens, flattened								
halves								
crumpets/muffins, to toast								
flounder, small whole								
grapefruit								
guinea fowl, flattened								
ham, steaks								
hamburgers								
hazelnuts, to toast								
herring, whole								
kidneys, halved								
kippers								
lamb, sirloin chops								
rib chops								
loin chops								
kabobs								
lobster, halves								
mackerel, whole								
mullet, whole								
mushrooms								

Abbreviations for position of broiler pan: HHH close as possible to heat source; HH midway from heat source; H furthest from heat source (see explanation with drawings page 133)

FOOD	PAN POSITION			TIME IN MINUTES				
	HHH	HH	H	0	5	10	20	30
mussels, skewered								
partridge, flattened								
peppers, to skin								
perch, small whole								
pigeon, flattened								
pineapple, rings								
porgy, whole								
pork, rib chops								
loin chops								
sardines/sprats, whole								
sausages, large								
links								
skinless								
scallops, skewered								
sole, small whole								
steak, ½ inch rare								
medium								
well done								
1 inch rare								
medium								
well done								
Chateaubriand, medium								
T-bone								
kabobs								
tomatoes, halves								
trout, whole								
turkey, wings								
veal, sirloin chops								
rib chops								
loin chops								

Broiled game hens with bacon pilaf

Small game hens are flattened then skewered to keep their shape and to aid turning during cooking

MAIN DISH Serves 4

Overall timing 1¼ hours

Equipment Poultry shears, rolling pin, 8 long skewers, foil, brush, large saucepan with lid

Freezing Not recommended

Using sharp poultry shears cut on both sides of backbones, remove. Press birds to flatten

Make birds compact, then push skewers in so they pass through wings, breasts and legs

Brush birds with marinade 15 minutes before cooking. Brush again after turning

Right: Broiled game hens with bacon pilaf — simple-to-prepare meal with Oriental touch

INGREDIENTS

4 × ¾lb	Cornish game hens
¼ cup	Course-grain mustard
	Cayenne
2 teaspoons	Worcestershire sauce
1 teaspoon	Vinegar
6 tablespoons	Oil
	Salt
	Freshly-ground black pepper
	Pilaf
1	Large onion
¼lb	Bacon slices
1	Green pepper
¼ cup	Butter
1 cup	Long grain rice
2 cups	Chicken stock or broth
	Salt and pepper
1	Bunch of watercress

METHOD

1 Wipe the Cornish game hens. Place one breast down on a board. Using poultry shears, cut along one side of the backbone, then along the other side to remove it cleanly from the body.

2 Turn the hen breast side up and open out. Using a rolling pin or the heel of the hand, press down on the breast to break the ribs and flatten the bird. Flatten the remaining game hens in the same way.

3 Tuck the wing tips under the bird. Fold the legs so they lie as flat as possible. Push a skewer through the wing, then the breast and the other wing. Skewer the legs in the same way so the birds are kept flat.

4 Line the broiler rack with foil and arrange the hens on it skin side down. Mix the mustard, pinch of cayenne, Worcestershire sauce, vinegar, oil and seasoning together. Brush half over the birds and leave to marinate for 15 minutes.

5 Meanwhile, to make the pilaf, peel and chop the onion. Dice the bacon. Wash, deseed and chop the pepper. Heat the butter in a large pan and fry the onion with the bacon till golden.

6 Preheat the broiler. Stir the rice into the bacon and fry for 1 minute till transparent. Add the stock and seasoning and bring to a boil, stirring. Cover and simmer for 10 minutes.

7 Broil the game hens for 10 minutes, 3 inches below the heat. Stir the chopped pepper into the rice, cover and cook for a further 5–8 minutes till the liquid is absorbed and the rice is tender.

8 Turn the hens carefully with skewers, brush with remaining marinade. Broil for a further 8–10 minutes till tender.

9 Arrange the rice on a large warmed serving dish and fluff with a fork. Place the hens on top, pull out the skewers and serve immediately, garnished with watercress.

Brochettes d'agneau

LUNCH OR SUPPER   Serves 4

Overall timing 20 minutes

Equipment Saucepan, 4 skewers

Freezing Not recommended

INGREDIENTS

6oz	Fresh pork sides
2	Onions
2lb	Boned shoulder of lamb
2 tablespoons	Oil
2 tablespoons	Tomato paste
	Salt
	Freshly-ground black pepper

METHOD

1 Put the pork in a saucepan, cover with water and bring to a boil. Drain pork well and cut into strips. Heat the broiler and line broiler pan with foil.

2 Peel and quarter the onions. Cut lamb into bite-size pieces. Thread lamb, pork and onion alternately onto skewers.

3 Mix oil, tomato paste, salt and pepper together.

4 Brush brochettes well with oil mixture. Cook for 10 minutes under broiler, turning frequently. Serve hot.

Kabobs à l'orientale

LUNCH OR SUPPER   Serves 6

Overall timing 1 hour

Equipment Bowl, 6 skewers

Freezing Not recommended

INGREDIENTS

1½lb	Boned shoulder of lamb
1lb	Lean veal
½ cup	Oil
¼ cup	Lemon juice
1	Large garlic clove
	Cayenne
	Salt
	Freshly-ground black pepper
12	Pearl onions
4	Tomatoes
1	Eggplant
12	Cubes of bread
6	Small bay leaves
6	Mushrooms

METHOD

1 Cut lamb and veal into bite-size pieces.

2 In a bowl, mix together the oil, lemon juice, crushed garlic, a pinch of cayenne, and salt and pepper. Add the meat and leave to marinate for 30 minutes, stirring frequently.

3 Peel onions. Quarter tomatoes and cut eggplant into pieces. Heat the broiler and line broiler pan with foil.

4 Drain meat and thread onto skewers with bread, onions, bay leaves, tomatoes, eggplant and mushrooms (flute them if liked, see page 240).

5 Cook kabobs under broiler for 15 minutes, turning and basting with marinade frequently. Serve hot.

Below: Kabobs à l'orientale — spectacular looking and superb tasting blend of marinated meats, herbs and vegetables, all basted and cooked under the broiler

Barbecued chops

Leaving meat to soak in marinade breaks down any tough fibers and the flavors also permeate the meat. They are then sealed in by the instant searing of direct heat from a barbecue

MAIN DISH   Serves 4

Overall timing 20 minutes plus marination time

Equipment Bowl, pitcher

Freezing Not recommended

INGREDIENTS

4		Pork chops
		Marinade
1		Large onion
2	tablespoons	Lemon juice or vinegar
2	tablespoons	Oil
½	teaspoon	Powdered mustard
2	teaspoons	Worcestershire sauce
½	teaspoon	Salt
½	teaspoon	Freshly-ground black pepper
1	teaspoon	Sugar
½	teaspoon	Paprika

METHOD

1 Place pork chops in bowl. Peel and grate the onion and place in pitcher. Add rest of marinade ingredients, mix well, then pour over chops. Leave to marinate for 1 hour in a cool place, turning chops at least twice.

2 Cook chops on barbecue (or under hot broiler), occasionally brushing chops with marinade. Serve with mixed salad, dressed with vinaigrette flavored with fresh dill or other herb of choice.

Below: Barbecued chops – marinated to give a delicious, slightly sweet and sour taste

Above: Cheeseburger — a hamburger dressed up with slices of cheese and tomato and broiled

Cheeseburgers

Becoming the top family favorite around the world, hamburgers taste even better with melted cheese

LIGHT LUNCH OR SUPPER　　　　Serves 4

Overall timing 30 minutes

Equipment Large bowl

Freezing Not recommended

INGREDIENTS

1	Large onion
1 lb	Ground beef
3 tablespoons	Soft breadcrumbs
⅓ cup	Milk
	Salt
	Paprika
1 teaspoon	Powdered mustard
	Oil
4	Small tomatoes
4	Slices of Cheddar cheese
4	Hamburger buns

METHOD

1 Heat the broiler. Peel and finely chop onion. In a large bowl, mix together the onion, ground beef, breadcrumbs and milk. Season with salt, a pinch of paprika and mustard. Leave for 10 minutes.
2 Make 4 hamburgers from the mixture. Brush with oil. Cook for 5 minutes on each side under the broiler.
3 Remove from heat. Top with slices of tomato and strips of cheese. Put hamburgers back under the broiler till the cheese melts. Serve in warm buns.

Ham steaks with pineapple

Glazing with a mixture of sugar, pineapple juice and mustard gives ham steaks a deliciously sweet flavor with a hint of piquancy

MAIN DISH　　　　Serves 4

Overall timing 30 minutes

Equipment Kitchen scissors, saucepan

Freezing Not recommended

INGREDIENTS

4	¼ inch thick ham steaks
2 tablespoons	Butter
16oz	Can of pineapple rings
2 tablespoons	Soft brown sugar
½ teaspoon	Powdered mustard
	Watercress

METHOD

1 Preheat the broiler and line the broiler pan with foil. Snip through the fat on the edges of the ham steaks at 1 inch intervals.
2 Place on the broiler pan. Melt the butter in a saucepan and brush a little over each steak. Broil the ham for a minute on each side, then move further away from heat and cook for 4 minutes.
3 Meanwhile, drain the pineapple rings, adding the syrup to the saucepan. Add the sugar and stir over a gentle heat till it dissolves.
4 Bring to a boil and boil rapidly till reduced by two-thirds. Add the mustard.
5 Turn the ham over and brush liberally with the glaze. Broil for a further 4 minutes.
6 Arrange 2 pineapple rings on each ham steak and brush with the glaze. Broil for a further 3 minutes till golden.
7 Arrange on a warmed serving platter, garnish with watercress and serve immediately with sauté potatoes and peas or a green salad.

Slit trout along the backbone from just behind head to just in front of tail. Cut flesh from bones, snip out backbone

Broiled trout with cucumber

A dish to delight fish fanciers. Because the bone is removed, the trout is easy to eat — and there's more space for the delicate stuffing

MAIN DISH   Serves 2

Overall timing 45 minutes

Equipment Kitchen scissors, saucepan, brush

Freezing Not recommended

Place pocket side down on rack, brush with melted butter, then cook for 2–3 minutes about 2 inches from heat

Turn trout over, brush with pan juices, arrange stuffing in pockets and broil for 4–5 minutes till crisp, golden

INGREDIENTS

2 × ¾lb	Whole rainbow trout
6	Scallions
2	Stalks of celery
8 inch	Piece of cucumber
½lb	Drawn butter
2 teaspoons	Chopped fresh dill weed
¼ cup	Soft white breadcrumbs
	Salt
	Freshly-ground black pepper
	Lemon wedges

METHOD

1 Wash the trout and dry on paper towels. Insert a sharp knife on one side of the fin on the trout's backbone. Slit the fish open along the backbone from the tail.

2 Using short knife strokes, cut the flesh away from the bones. Make another slit along the length of the fish on the other side of the fin and scrape the flesh away from the bone. Snip the bone at both ends and remove.

3 Cut a little further into the flesh till the entrails are visible. Remove carefully and discard. Pull the head sharply to one side to open one gill, then snip it out with kitchen scissors. Repeat on the other side.

4 Prepare the second trout in the same way so each has a large pocket to hold the stuffing. Remove broiler rack and brush with oil. Preheat the broiler.

5 Wash and trim the scallions and cut into ½ inch lengths. Wash, trim and thinly slice the celery. Peel the cucumber, cut in half lengthwise and scrape out the seeds with a teaspoon. Cut into ¼ inch thick slices.

6 Melt the butter in a saucepan. Place the trout with the skin side up on the boiler rack so the pocket is held open underneath. Brush a little butter over and broil about 2 inches away from the heat for 2–3 minutes.

7 Meanwhile add the scallions and celery to the remaining butter and fry, stirring, over a high heat for 2–3 minutes till golden. Remove from the heat and stir in the cucumber, chopped dill, breadcrumbs and plenty of seasoning.

8 Turn trout over carefully and brush with juices from the pan. Arrange the stuffing in the pockets of the fish and cook for a further 4–5 minutes till the trout is tender and the breadcrumbs are crisp and golden.

Broiled trout with cucumber — serve garnished with lemon wedges and dill

Line tart pan, prick base, then bake "blind" for 10 minutes on a heated cookie sheet

Peeled and cored apple halves are sliced but keep their shape. Arrange in pastry shell

After baking and chilling, sprinkle top with sugar, brown under hot broiler

Apple brûlée tart

Lusciously rich dessert combining rich pastry, halved apples and a cream and egg custard. The crisp topping is created under the broiler

DESSERT   Serves 6–8

Overall timing 1¼ hours plus chilling

Equipment 2 bowls, foil, cookie sheet, 9 inch ceramic tart pan

Freezing Not recommended

INGREDIENTS

	Pastry
1¾ cups	Flour
½ cup	Butter
2 tablespoons	Sugar
	Grated rind of 1 lemon
1	Egg
	Water to mix
	Filling
4	Large apples
4	Egg yolks
½ teaspoon	Vanilla extract
1¼ cups	Heavy cream
	Topping
6 tablespoons	Sugar

METHOD

1 Sift the flour into a bowl and cut in the butter till the mixture resembles fine breadcrumbs. Stir in the sugar and the lemon rind and make well in center.

2 Add the egg and mix with a palette knife, adding a little cold water if necessary to bind to a soft but not sticky dough. Knead lightly till smooth and shape into a ball. Foil-wrap and chill for 30 minutes.

3 Preheat the oven to 375°. Put a cookie sheet in to heat up. Roll out the dough on a lightly floured surface and use to line the tart pan. Crimp the edges to emphasize the flutes, and prick the base several times with a fork. Bake "blind" on the cookie sheet for 10 minutes.

4 Meanwhile, peel the apples, cut in half vertically and remove the cores. Place apple halves flat side down and cut into ¼ inch thick slices, keeping them together in their halves.

5 Remove the tart shell from the oven and reduce the temperature to 325°. Arrange the apple halves flat side down in the tart shell, with one in the center, fanning out the slices so they lie fairly flat.

6 Put the egg yolks and vanilla in a bowl and gradually beat in the cream. Pour carefully over and around the apples. Press apples down.

7 Bake for about 30 minutes till custard is set.

8 Remove tart from the oven and leave to cool. Chill for several hours.

9 Preheat the broiler. Sprinkle the remaining sugar over the tart in an even layer to cover the surface completely. Broil about 1 inch from heat for 3–4 minutes, turning dish as necessary so sugar browns evenly. Serve.

Apple brûlée tart – hot, crunchy top contrasts well with the cold flan

Braising and casseroling

Braising comes from the French *brasier*, which the dictionary defines as "to stew in a closed vessel" – but this isn't completely true. A tightly closed and heat-retaining pot is used (earthenware or cast iron being perhaps the favorites) but the food inside doesn't stew. The process could be better described as steam baking for the nutrients and flavors are kept inside the food during the cooking and are not drawn out into the liquid as in stewing. In braising the liquid is kept to a minimum – between 1–2½ inches up the side of the food. Braising is kind to poultry past its prime, older game birds, rabbit and hare, it flatters the uncertain (stringy vegetables like celery and swiss chard, bulbous fennel and roots of uncertain age). The completely tough, such as very old poultry and medium grade meats require long slow cooking in lots of liquid and are not suitable for braising. But it makes a wonderful difference to meats which are low in natural fat (venison, for example) so that you end up with meat that resembles a roast and, because the meat is so moist, it is as good cold as it is hot.

There are several stages of the process of braising. Meat or poultry can be marinated first; this helps to break down some of the tougher connective tissue between the muscle fibers. If the marination time is to be long (3–5 days), the marinade is brought to a boil to discourage bacteria and to stop fermentation that would otherwise occur in that time. The boiling also draws out the fullest possible flavor from the vegetables, herbs and spices into the liquid.

The marinade is often strained to form part of the cooking liquid. Any remaining marinade can also be used at the end to extend the gravy – if there's too much it can be reduced to concentrate it, or it can be thickened. The next important part of braising

is the mirepoix. Butter, bacon fat, or a combination of butter and oil is used to brown the meat on all sides, then the diced vegetables and other flavorings are "sweated" until soft in the same fat. The meat is placed on the vegetables, the pot is covered tightly and braising begins. To keep the steam in, the lid should fit well. If it doesn't, cover the pot with a double thickness of foil and place the lid on top.

If the pot is being cooked on top of the stove, the heat must be kept low, or the liquid will bubble and become a stew which is not the purpose of the exercise. A diffuser helps spread the heat, and the mirepoix protects the bottom of the meat. Generally speaking, it is better to braise in the oven (this is probably how the term pot roasting began), at low to moderate temperature – 325–350°. The all-round heat ensures evenness of cooking and, though the temperature is less than that used for roasting, heat penetration is greater because of the steam generated inside the closed pot. Also the steam condenses on the lid and sides of the pot and falls back onto the food to baste it.

In some braised dishes, there is often no browning at the start because the end result is required to be white – these are called white braised dishes and usually contain veal, fish or lamb. Vegetables aren't browned either and are braised in butter with only the smallest amount of liquid added (this is called *à l'étouffée* in France).

Meats with little natural fat should be larded before cooking as fat is needed to keep the flesh moist during cooking. It is very difficult to obtain rare beef by braising, and it is certainly only possible with the near-to-prime cuts like top round. By this method, meats are cooked right through so they are both tender and moist at the end. When braising red cabbage added acid is needed (apples or vinegar) to

preserve the color otherwise it will turn blue/purple.

Braising is an ideal cooking method for large cuts of meat and whole birds. Casseroling, on the other hand, is better for pieces of poultry and meat cup up into bite-sized pieces. Like braising, cheaper cut of meat can be used because the long, slow cooking tenderizes them and adds flavor.

For most casseroles the meat and vegetables are first browned in butter, bacon fat, or a combination of butter and oil. The hot stock or cooking liquid is then added. Whereas a braise cooks in the steam generated from a small amount of water, a casserole actually cooks in the liquid so it should come at least two-thirds of the way up the side of the food in the casserole dish.

The casserole is then brought to simmering point, covered with a tightly-fitting lid and transferred to the oven (it can also be cooked on top of the stove). The meat and vegetables cook gently in the liquid. The flavors in a casserole always intensify during cooking so season lightly to begin with.

The cooking liquid is thickened with either a beurre manié or a flour/cornstarch/arrowroot paste when the casserole is done, or the meat is tossed in seasoned flour before it is browned.

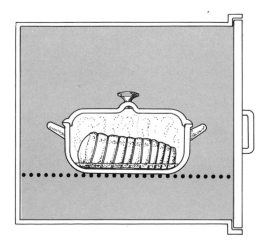

Braising and casseroling techniques

acidulation

An acid such as vinegar, wine or lemon juice is used when braising or casseroling meats with touch muscle fiber as it helps soften it.

basting

Necessary during marination and toward the end of braising when the liquid may have reduced to very little. In marination, the meat is turned several times over a set period so that all sides of the meat are given the benefit of the soaking liquid.

braise

A dish of meat, game, poultry, or vegetables produced by braising. If it is described in a recipe title as: *blanc*, the foods are not browned first; *blond*, the foods are lightly browned; or *brun*, the foods are well browned first.

braising

A method of cooking which uses both dry and moist heat. It is sometimes called frying/steaming, pot roasting or steam baking. Steam plays a major part in the cooking and keeps the food moist. The foods for braising should be largish, and cooking can be done on top of the stove, or slowly (3–4 hours) in the oven at 300°. At 350° you halve the time. Large cuts of meat can be cooked on top of stove or in the oven at 325°. Braised fish needs a short cooking time.

browning

This is the first stage of braising in which foods are fried to brown them. While large cuts of meat or whole birds need only just to fit the pot in which they'll be braised, they need more space when being browned as they have to be turned. The more unwieldy the shape, the more awkward this is to do – a fork can be slipped under the string of a rolled roast but shouldn't otherwise be used as the prongs will pierce the skin and release juices. Large wooden spoons which can be firmly grasped are best to use.

casseroling

Method of cooking cut-up pieces of tough but cheaper meat, poultry or vegetables in more liquid than used for braising. Cooking is done slowly on top of the stove, or in the oven at 300–325°. The food is not always browned first. Thickening is done either when the casserole is cooked or when meat is browned. In braising overcooking gives dry, stringy results; in casseroles too much liquid is created.

covering

Tight-lidded pots are essential to braising and casseroling, as the steam and its condensation on the lid is important in keeping the food moist. A pot-size round of foil with a $\frac{1}{4}$ inch hole cut in the center can be placed on top of food when braising to prevent the pieces above the liquid from drying out. To stop steam escaping, cover pot with foil, then the lid; or use luting paste.

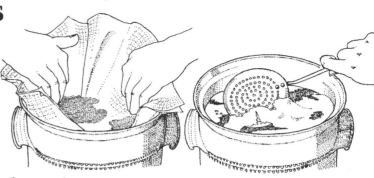

degreasing

As cheaper cuts of meat contain quite a bit of fat, it melts during braising and casseroling and needs to be removed before gravy is made or liquid is thickened. If cooking is done in advance the fat will set and can be lifted off. To draw off liquid fat, place pieces of paper towel on top, changing them as fat is absorbed. Or use a skimmer which is brushed across the liquid. Always pour away excess fat after foods have been fried at the start.

cutting up

Poultry and game are braised whole and cut up before serving. In casseroling, they are cut up to lessen cooking time.

drying

Any meat for braising or casseroling should be dried well before frying, or it will start to stew in the liquid instead of browning quickly.

flavorings

A bed of sweated diced vegetables is the most usual flavoring method. A bouquet garni (fresh or dried) can also be added, or a fine paring of orange or lemon peel. Ground spices should be fried with the meat to release their flavors – but be sparing with them.

jugging

Old English method of braising hare so named because it was originally done in a large earthenware jug.

larding

Method of ensuring succulence in lean cuts of meat. Thin strips of fat (lardons) are inserted into meat parallel with grain with a larding needle (*lardoire*) and should protrude about $\frac{1}{2}$ inch at each end of meat to allow for shrinkage during braising. With venison, small strips of fat are threaded over the outside so it looks like a hedgehog.

liquid

For best results in flavor terms, the liquid in braises and casseroles is usually wine, stock, cider, beer or strained marinade, though water can be used with a mirepoix. When braising, heat liquid to simmering point before adding, so its heat can be held by the lid. The liquid should only cover a third of the food. In a casserole, the liquid should come two-thirds up the side of the food.

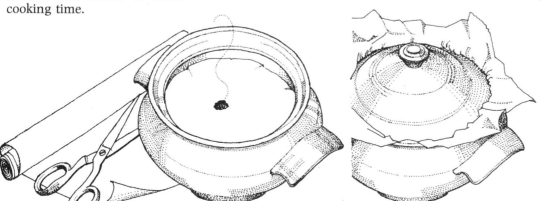

luting paste

A flour and water dough which is used to make an airtight seal between the lid and rim of a casserole to trap steam inside when cooking in the oven. Mix 1 cup flour with 4–5 tablespoons of cold water to make stiff paste. Roll into sausage shape, place around rim and press lid on top. After cooking, scrape off the paste, clean off the rim before serving.

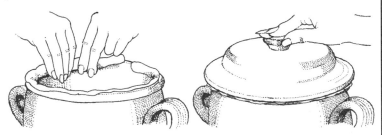

marinade

Flavored liquids in which flesh foods are steeped before braising. The marinade should be cooked if meat is left to stand for 2 or more days. Long marination, for example with venison, requires the marinade to be reboiled and cooled every 2 days.

Food in a marinade must be kept in a cool place, in the refrigerator if necessary. Use a deep non-metal bowl so as much of the meat as possible is covered. Cover bowl during marination and turn food at least twice a day so steeping is even. Strain marinade if using in the braising — marinades for strong-tasting meats are rarely used in the cooking because of the exchange of flavors.

mirepoix

Diced vegetables such as carrots, onions, celery, sweated in butter (mirepoix au maigre) or bacon fat (mirepoix au gras) on which meat or whole vegetables are braised.

pressing

During braising, collagen (connective tissue) breaks down and makes the meat tender, and because there's so little liquid the collagen will cause it to jell when cool. Meat chilled under a heavy weight will be encased in jellied gravy and will be easier to slice.

pot roasting

Another way of describing braising of roasts of meat.

reheating

The exchange of flavors as braises and casseroles cool and rest makes food cooked this way taste better 1 or 2 days after making. Store in refrigerator, and reheat by bringing to a boil. Stir occasionally to ensure mixture is heating right through, and to prevent sticking on the bottom.

seasoning

Sometimes salt and pepper are added in the form of seasoned flour at the frying stage, as are spices, but generally you should taste and adjust seasoning before serving as flavors intensify as liquid reduces.

sweating

Term used when diced vegetables are cooked in fat. The pan is covered and the vegetables aren't usually browned. To brown meat, remove vegetables and return later with the liquid, then braise.

thickening

Can either be done via seasoned flour used to coat the meat for frying and which breaks down in the liquid during cooking; or flour/cornstarch/arrowroot can be blended with water and stirred into liquid at end of cooking. A grated floury potato can be added 20 minutes before end of cooking to thicken liquid; a cooked potato can be riced and added 5–10 minutes before. Rice or pasta can be cooked in the liquid to absorb some of it, but allow longer than usual cooking time.

Braising around the world

aillade de porc Pork and garlic casserole from Southern France.

arni me spanaki avgolémono Lamb casserole from Greece with spinach and lemon sauce.

bayrisch kraut Bavarian dish of cabbage braised in white wine and vinegar, with caraway seeds and bacon.

beckenoffe Alsatian braise of pork, lamb and vegetables.

beef olives English dish of thin slices of beef, stuffed and rolled, then braised.

bigos From Poland, a casserole of meats, sausages, apples, sauerkraut and wine.

boeuf chasseur French braise of beef, wine, mushrooms.

boeuf bourguignon Classic casserole from France of beef cooked in Burgundy's red wine.

boeuf en daube Classic French braise of marinated beef with wine.

carbonades flamandes From Belgium, beef braised in beer, vinegar and brown sugar.

cassoulet Classic dish found in most parts of Southern France. Navy beans, goose, pork, mutton, duck and vegetables are layered in a large pot (usually earthenware), covered and cooked in the oven.

coq au vin Classic French casserole of chicken and wine.

csirke paprikás Hungarian casserole of chicken with paprika, stock, sour cream.

dolmathes Greek specialty of braised stuffed vine leaves.

estouffade de boeuf A Provençale casserole of beef, with wine, tomatoes, garlic and olives. **Estouffat** comes from the Languedoc and is made with dried beans and pork.

faisan à la Périgueux From Périgord, pot roasted pheasant with truffles and wine.

fischeintopf German "one-pot" dish of cod with olives, capers.

fricandeau à l'oseille French pot roast of veal with sorrel and stock.

gulyàs Hungarian national dish better known as goulash. Beef is casseroled with paprika, caraway seeds, vegetables and herbs.

guvetch Romanian national dish of braised mixed vegetables.

hochepot gantoise From Belgium, brisket of beef cooked in stock with variety meats and sausages.

Irish stew In fact a casserole of lamb chops and potatoes.

karjalan paisti Finnish casserole of pork, lamb and beef with gherkins.

Lancashire hot-pot From England, middle neck of lamb casseroled with kidneys and onions, and sliced potatoes.

manzo stufato Italian braise of beef and red wine.

marinebraten From Austria, beef braised on a bed of sliced vegetables with wine.

maiale ubriaco Literally intoxicated chops! Pork chops are browned, covered with wine, then braised till most of the wine has been absorbed. A specialty of Tuscany.

milchbraten German pot roast of beef cooked with milk.

mou de porc à la ménagère French casserole of pork lights (lungs) cooked "housewife style" with vegetables and stock.

navarin printanier From France, lamb casserole with spring vegetables.

ossu bucco Classic Italian braise of thick slices of shank of veal (with central core of marrow).

ragoût à l'anglaise French method of braising meat, fish or poultry with onion, potatoes.

ratatouille Mixed vegetable casserole from South of France.

sauerbraten German and Austrian dish of beef marinated in vinegar and wine, then pot roasted with raisins and red currant jelly.

stiphado Greek beef and onion casserole similar to France's **estouffade** and **daube**. Vinegar is used both as a tenderizer and flavoring agent during cooking, or stirred in at end.

Braising and casseroling

Braising and casseroling will produce tender moist foods, ready to be served straight from the pot. Be careful when calculating the liquid — you need very little for braising and enough to come two-thirds up the side of the food in casseroles. The cooking times recommended on the chart can only be approximate as the end result will depend on how big or small the cubes of meat are, how tightly rolled and compact a roast is, whether it is being cooked in the oven or on top of the stove. Even the length of the frying time can make a difference to the overall cooking time, for if the pan is not hot enough, juices will be drawn out and the food will take longer to brown. There are a lot of ifs and buts in this type of cooking and the best results do come from carrying out each stage well — see the Cook's know-how, right. At the end of braising, the rich liquid should be used as gravy — either mash the mirepoix in to thicken, or strain and thicken liquid (see page 152). Serve with sliced meat.

FOOD	Type	TIME IN MINUTES / TIME IN HOURS
beef, top round/flank		
up to 3lb	B	per lb+30 mins
3½lb and over	B	per lb+25 mins
bottom round, cubed	C	
rump, 6oz steaks	B	
cubed	C	
fresh brisket		
up to 3lb	B	per lb+45 mins
3½lb and over	B	per lb+40 mins
6oz tip steaks	B	
short ribs, up to 3lb	B	per lb+40 mins
3½lb and over	B	per lb+35 mins
chuck, up to 3lb	B	per lb+45 mins
6oz steaks	B	
cubed	C	
boneless shoulder		
up to 3lb	B	per lb+40 mins
3½lb and over	B	per lb+35 mins
6oz blade steaks	B	
celery, hearts	B	
chicken, whole	B	per lb+30 mins
quarters	C	
fish, whole	B	per lb+20 mins
fillets	C	
ham (cured pork)		
smoked shoulder, up to 3lb	B	per lb+25 mins
3½lb and over	B	per lb+20 mins
smoked hock, 2lb	B	
smoked arm picnic		
up to 3lb	B	per lb+25 mins
3½lb and over	B	per lb+20 mins
smoked loin, 1½lb	B	
hare, portions	C	
hearts, beef, sliced	C	
veal, whole	B	
sliced	C	

TIME IN MINUTES: 0 5 10 20 30 40 50   TIME IN HOURS: 1 2 3

B braised; C casseroled

Calculate braising and casserole cooking times after frying. Cooking can be done in the oven at 325°, or casseroles can be cooked over low heat on top of the stove

FOOD		TIME IN MINUTES							TIME IN HOURS		
		0	5	10	20	30	40	50	1	2	3
hearts, continued											
lamb, whole	B										
sliced	C										
pork, whole	B										
sliced	C										
kidneys, beef, sliced	C										
lamb, shoulder/leg, cubed	C										
stuffed shoulder	B					per lb + 25 mins					
neck slices	C										
stuffed rolled breast	B					per lb + 30 mins					
leeks, small whole	B										
liver, beef, sliced	C										
lamb, sliced	C										
pork, sliced	C										
onions, medium whole	B										
pearl	B										
oxtail, pieces	B										
pheasant, whole	B										
quarters	C										
pigeon	C										
pork, fresh sides,											
sliced	C										
cubed	C										
fresh feet	C										
rabbit, portions	C										
root vegetables, whole	B										
sliced	C										
snipe/woodcock	B										
tongue, veal, whole	B										
lamb, whole	C										
beef, whole	B				per lb + 20 mins						
turkey, up to 10lb	B										
portions	C				per lb + 45 mins						
veal, stuffed rolled breast	B										
riblets	C										
venison, cubed	C										

cook's know-how

During relatively long braising or casseroling, flavors can intensify so you should be sparing at the start with seasonings and taste and adjust before thickening. Flavoring by way of a mirepoix is best of all — dice a variety of vegetables and sweat them in butter or bacon fat. Remove to brown the meat. Keep the lid tightly on the pot throughout the cooking so as not to disturb the steam.

Mirepoix au maigre

Use this mirepoix or *brunoise* for braising vegetables, shown below, or use it to bring out the flavor of large cuts of meat

Overall timing 20 minutes

Equipment Saucepan

Freezing Not recommended

INGREDIENTS

$\frac{1}{4}$ lb	Carrots
1	Onion
1	Stalk of celery
$\frac{1}{4}$ cup	Butter
$\frac{1}{4}$ teaspoon	Dried thyme
1	Bay leaf
	Salt
	Freshly-ground black pepper

METHOD

1 Scrape and wash the carrots; peel the onions; trim and wash the celery. Pat dry with paper towels and cut vegetables into small cubes.
2 Melt the butter in a saucepan and add the vegetables. Cover and fry gently for 10 minutes without browning.
3 Add the dried thyme, bay leaf and salt and pepper. Mix well, cover and simmer for a further 5 minutes.

Halve celery hearts lengthwise, place on mirepoix and add $\frac{1}{2}$ inch stock

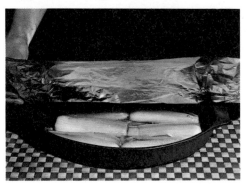

Cover and bake at 350° for 1$\frac{1}{4}$ hours till tender when pierced with the tip of a knife

Braised beef with mirepoix

This uses a double quantity of mirepoix au maigre. Prepare the vegetables, and set aside. The butter for the mirepoix is first used to seal the meat

Above: Braised beef with mirepoix — meat made tender and juicy by long, slow braising

MAIN DISH   Serves 6–8

Overall timing 2$\frac{3}{4}$ hours

Equipment Fine string, flameproof casserole, strainer, 2 saucepans, blender (optional)

Freezing Not recommended

INGREDIENTS

2$\frac{1}{2}$ lb	Boneless beef chuck eye roast
	Salt
	Freshly-ground black pepper
3 tablespoons	Flour
1 tablespoon	Tomato paste
$\frac{2}{3}$ cup	Red wine
$\frac{2}{3}$ cup	Beef stock or broth
1$\frac{1}{2}$ lb	Potatoes

METHOD

1 Preheat the oven to 325°. Wipe and trim the meat and tie into a neat shape with fine string – or ask the butcher to do this for you.
2 Season the flour and turn the meat in it till lightly coated. Shake off any excess. Heat $\frac{1}{2}$ cup butter in the casserole and fry the meat quickly till browned on all sides. Remove from the pan and reserve.
3 Add the prepared vegetables to the pan and stir till coated with the butter. Cover and sweat the vegetables for 5 minutes, shaking the pan frequently to prevent sticking.
4 Stir in the tomato paste, red wine and stock or broth. Return the meat to the pan. Season, cover and cook in the oven for 2 hours till the meat is tender.
5 Meanwhile, peel and wash the potatoes and cut into chunks. Cook in a saucepan of boiling salted water till tender. Drain the potatoes and keep hot.
6 Remove the meat from the pan and keep hot. Pour the cooking liquid through a strainer into a saucepan. Reserve half the vegetables. Rub the remaining vegetables through the strainer into the liquid, or purée in a blender till smooth.
7 Remove the string from the meat. Cut meat into thick slices and arrange on a warmed serving platter with the potatoes. Reheat the sauce, taste and adjust the seasoning. Spoon a little over the meat slices.
8 Stir the reserved vegetables into the sauce, heat through and spoon over the potatoes. Serve immediately with spinach or broccoli spears.

Above: Braised pork chops—succulent this way

Braised pork chops

Apples add extra interest to this mid-week dish. Buy the chops as a roast or separately

MAIN DISH   Serves 4

Overall timing 55 minutes

Equipment Heavy-based pan or flameproof casserole with lid

Freezing Not recommended

INGREDIENTS

4	Pork chops
	Salt
	Freshly-ground black pepper
2	Tart apples
2	Onions
2 tablespoons	Butter
$\frac{1}{3}$ cup	Water
2 teaspoons	Worcestershire sauce
	Fresh parsley

METHOD

1 Dry meat and season with salt and pepper. Peel and core apples. Cut into eighths. Peel onions and cut into rings.
2 Melt butter in pan and brown the meat on all sides. Add water and sauce, cover and cook for 10 minutes. Turn chops over. Add apples and onions. Reduce heat, cover and cook for a further 30 minutes.
3 Garnish with parsley and serve with creamed potatoes in a separate dish.

Braised oxtail

A hearty and nourishing meal. Cook the oxtail the day before, then skim to remove grease before the vegetables are added and the braising process completed

MAIN DISH   Serves 4

Overall timing $4\frac{1}{4}$ hours

Equipment Flameproof casserole, skillet

Freezing Not recommended

INGREDIENTS

2lb	Chopped oxtail
2 tablespoons	Oil
$\frac{2}{3}$ cup	Dry white wine
3 tablespoons	Brandy
	Salt
	Freshly-ground black pepper
$\frac{1}{4}$ lb	Bacon
$\frac{1}{4}$ lb	Pearl onions
3	Carrots
2	Small turnips
1	Garlic clove
	Celery leaves

METHOD

1 Preheat the oven to 300°.
2 Wash and dry the oxtail. Heat the oil in the casserole and fry the oxtail for 10 minutes, turning the pieces frequently till well browned. Pour the fat into a skillet.
3 Add the wine and brandy to the oxtail, season, cover, and cook in the oven for $2\frac{1}{2}$ hours.
4 Meanwhile, dice the bacon. Peel the onions. Scrape and slice the carrots. Peel and slice the turnips.
5 Heat the fat in the skillet and fry the bacon and vegetables, stirring. Peel and crush the garlic and add to the oxtail with the bacon and vegetable mixture, salt, pepper and a handful of celery leaves. Mix well, cover and cook for a further hour till the meat is tender.
6 Taste and adjust the seasoning. Serve immediately with creamed potatoes.

VARIATION

Use a full-bodied red rather than a white wine and add 2 tablespoons tomato paste before braising oxtail.

Below: Braised oxtail – flavored with white wine and brandy. The spirit can be set alight after adding if you like as this will help remove excess fattiness

West Indian carbonade

Where a boned weight is given in a recipe, this means the amount of meat required after the bone's removed. For this sweet-sour dish that serves 6 to 8, you'll probably need meat from 2 shoulders of lamb

MAIN DISH Serves 6–8

Overall timing 2 hours

Equipment Flameproof casserole

Freezing Not recommended

INGREDIENTS

3	Large onions
2 tablespoons	Oil
¼ cup	Butter
3lb	Boned shoulder of lamb
⅓ cup	Dry white wine
3 tablespoons	Tomato paste
	Bouquet garni
⅔ cup	Stock or broth
	Salt and pepper
	Potatoes
	Sweet potatoes
	Stalk of celery
	Zucchini
	Apples
	Pears

METHOD

1 Peel and slice onions. Heat oil and butter in flameproof casserole, add onions and cook until transparent.
2 Trim meat and cut into chunks, add to the onions and cook over high heat till browned on all sides. Add the wine, tomato paste, bouquet garni, stock or broth, salt and pepper. Stir well, cover and cook over low heat for about 50 minutes.
3 Peel potatoes and sweet potatoes and cut into chunks. Wash and chop celery and zucchini. Add to casserole, cover and continue cooking for 30 minutes.
4 Peel and core apples and pears and cut into small pieces. Add to casserole and cook for another 10 minutes. Remove bouquet garni.

TO SERVE

Take the carbonade to the table in its cooking pot or pour into a warm tureen. Serve it hot with crusty bread, or, to make it go further, serve it with rice.

Garlic chicken

A true dish of the Mediterranean – it uses a whole bulb of garlic! If your predilection for garlic is less, reduce the amount, keeping in mind that the garlic taste is important

MAIN DISH Serves 4

Overall timing 1¾ hours

Equipment Flameproof casserole with lid, small bowl

Freezing Not recommended

INGREDIENTS

8	Chicken legs and wings
¼ cup	Butter
1 tablespoon	Oil
	Salt and pepper
1	Whole garlic bulb
⅔ cup	Dry white wine
2 cups	Hot milk
1 teaspoon	Cornstarch
2 tablespoons	Light cream
¼ teaspoon	Cayenne

METHOD

1 Wash chicken pieces and dry well on paper towels.
2 Heat half the butter and the oil in a casserole. Add the chicken and brown on all sides. Season with salt and pepper and cook for 10–15 minutes over a low heat. Remove chicken from pan and keep warm.
3 Peel and crush all the garlic cloves. Add remaining butter to casserole and cook garlic over a low heat, stirring with a wooden spoon till soft.
4 Add the wine, bring to a boil and cook for 3 minutes. Replace chicken in casserole and pour in hot milk. Cover and simmer for 20–30 minutes.
5 Blend the cornstarch and cream in a bowl. Stir in tablespoons of cooking liquid from casserole and add cayenne. Stir cream mixture into casserole and simmer for 2–3 minutes.

TO SERVE

Put chicken pieces into a warmed serving dish and spoon sauce over. Serve with green beans and mashed potatoes.

West Indian carbonade – a taste of the Caribbean made with lamb, apples, pears, zucchini and sweet potatoes

Russian rib chop casserole

Pork rib or loin chops may be used in this casserole. Sour cream adds piquancy

MAIN DISH   Serves 4

Overall timing 30 minutes

Equipment Flameproof casserole

Freezing Not recommended

INGREDIENTS

1lb	Potatoes
2 tablespoons	Oil
4	Pork rib chops
	Salt and pepper
3 tablespoons	Water
¼ lb	Button mushrooms
1 teaspoon	Garlic salt
⅔ cup	Sour cream
2 tablespoons	Chopped parsley

METHOD

1 Peel potatoes and cut them into very small, thin pieces. Melt the oil in the casserole and fry the potatoes for 5 minutes. Remove from pan.
2 Season chops with salt and pepper, add to casserole and cook for 1 minute on each side. Drain excess fat. Add water, cover and cook for 10 minutes.
3 Wipe and slice mushrooms. Add to casserole with fried potatoes and garlic salt and cook for a further 10 minutes.
4 Stir in sour cream and 1 tablespoon of the chopped parsley. Heat through. Sprinkle with remaining parsley just before serving.

Chicken chasseur

Tarragon, a herb well suited to chicken, is a good complement to a chasseur sauce: double the quantity if using fresh instead of dried herbs

MAIN DISH   Serves 4

Overall timing 1½ hours

Equipment Flameproof casserole

Freezing Make as Steps 1–3. Cool, pack into rigid container, cover, label and freeze. Freezer life: 4 months. To use: thaw for 3 hours then heat slowly but thoroughly

Above: Russian pork chop casserole — pork chops, potatoes, mushrooms and sour cream

INGREDIENTS

½lb	Mushrooms
4	Shallots
2 tablespoons	Butter
1 tablespoon	Oil
2½lb	Chicken portions
2 tablespoons	Flour
1 cup	Dry white wine
⅔ cup	Chicken stock or broth
1 tablespoon	Dried tarragon
1 tablespoon	Tomato paste
	Bouquet garni
	Salt and pepper

METHOD

1 Wipe and slice mushrooms. Peel and slice the shallots.
2 Heat the butter and oil in the casserole and cook mushrooms and shallots over a high heat. Add the chicken portions and brown on all sides. Sprinkle with flour. Cook for 1–2 minutes, stirring all the time, till flour colors.
3 Add the wine and the stock or broth, half the tarragon, the tomato paste, bouquet garni, salt and pepper. Bring to a boil, stirring. Cover and simmer slowly for about 1 hour.
4 Place on a hot serving dish and sprinkle with remaining tarragon. Serve with boiled or sauté potatoes.

German-style braised partridges

Young partridges are usually roasted, but older birds should be braised or casseroled to make the flesh tender and draw out all the flavor

MAIN DISH   Serves 6

Overall timing 1 hour

Equipment Wooden toothpicks, flameproof casserole, metal ladle, saucepan

Freezing Not recommended

INGREDIENTS

6	Dressed partridges
	Salt
	Freshly-ground black pepper
6	Bacon slices
$\frac{3}{4}$lb	Carrots
2	Onions
6 tablespoons	Butter
1 tablespoon	Chopped parsley
1 teaspoon	Chopped basil
1 teaspoon	Chopped sage
1	Bay leaf
$1\frac{1}{4}$ cups	Light stock or broth
$\frac{1}{4}$ cup	Brandy
2 teaspoons	Cornstarch
$\frac{2}{3}$ cup	Sour cream

Below: German-style braised partridges — gently cooked in a herby sauce, flamed with brandy and enriched with sour cream

METHOD

1 Wipe the partridges and season inside and out. Wrap a bacon slice around each and secure with a toothpick.
2 Scrape and wash the carrots and cut into matchstick lengths. Peel and chop the onions. Heat the butter in the casserole and fry the partridges quickly till browned on all sides Remove from the pan and reserve.
3 Add the carrots and onions to the pan and fry for 3 minutes. Return the partridges to the pan, add the herbs, stock or broth and season to taste. Cover and simmer for 30 minutes till the partridges are tender. Remove pan from heat. Warm brandy in ladle, ignite and pour over partridges.
4 When flames have died down, strain the cooking liquid into a saucepan. Blend the cornstarch with 2 tablespoons cold water and stir into the saucepan. Bring to a boil, stirring constantly. Add the sour cream and heat through gently without boiling. Taste and adjust the seasoning.
5 Arrange the partridges on a warmed serving dish, discarding the bay leaf. Arrange the carrots and onions around the partridges. Pour the sauce into a warmed sauce boat and serve immediately with sauté potatoes.

Casseroled grouse

This is a good dish to serve at a small dinner party as the preparation is done well in advance and the grouse is then left to cook gently. It's good, too, because served in this fashion you need only two grouse for four servings — an advantage with such an expensive bird

MAIN DISH   Serves 4

Overall timing $2\frac{1}{2}$ hours

Equipment Large flameproof casserole with tight-fitting lid

Freezing Not recommended

INGREDIENTS

$\frac{1}{4}$lb	Piece of slab bacon
2	Carrots
2	Stalks of celery
2	Shallots
2	Dressed grouse
1	Garlic clove
$1\frac{1}{4}$ cups	Chicken stock or broth
$\frac{2}{3}$ cup	Red wine
1	Bouquet garni
	Salt and pepper

METHOD

1 Preheat oven to 325°.
2 Cut bacon into cubes and cook over moderate heat in casserole for 10 minutes until fat has melted. Meanwhile, wash, scrape and slice the carrots and celery and peel and slice the shallots.
3 Add grouse to bacon fat and brown on all sides, then remove from casserole. Peel and crush garlic and add to casserole with vegetables. Reduce heat and sauté gently for 10 minutes. Add stock or broth, wine, bouquet garni, salt and pepper. Stir well.
4 Place grouse in casserole, cover and cook in oven for $1\frac{1}{2}$ hours. Remove lid, increase heat to 350° and cook for a further 30 minutes.
5 Remove birds and keep warm. Strain cooking liquid and reduce over high heat until thickened. Pour into gravy boat. Place grouse on warmed serving dish, garnish with halved broiled tomatoes and serve with rice or mashed potatoes. Accompany by an orange salad with small bunches of watercress tossed in orange juice and a little oil

Boeuf à la mode

This is a classic French, full of flavor, dish. It can be made well ahead of time as it reheats extremely well. The sauce can be made two ways — but if you intend freezing it, it's best not to add the cream and brandy

MAIN DISH　　　　　　Serves 8–10

Overall timing　3 hours plus marination

Equipment　Large bowl, large heavy-based flameproof casserole

Freezing　Cool meat, wrap well. Put sauce in rigid container and cover. Freezer life: 2 months. To use: thaw for 24 hours in refrigerator, place meat and sauce in casserole. Cook for 1 hour, in 400° oven

Above: Boeuf à la mode — tender, tasty meat served with pearl onions and sliced carrots

INGREDIENTS

4lb	Beef pot roast
	Freshly-ground white pepper
	Salt
6oz	Pork fat with skin
1	Large onion
3	Stalks of celery
3	Carrots
1	Garlic clove
	Fresh parsley
2	Bay leaves
	Fresh thyme
1½ cups	Red or white wine
2 tablespoons	Butter
2 tablespoons	Oil
1	Pig's foot
½ cup	Water
1 tablespoon	Tomato paste
2 tablespoons	Cream (optional)
1 tablespoon	Brandy (optional)
¾lb	Pearl onions
1lb	Carrots

Assemble all ingredients. A bouquet garni can be used instead of the fresh herbs

Rub beef with pepper and salt. Slice pork fat, secure around beef with string

Cover beef with chopped onion, celery, 3 carrots, crushed garlic, herbs, wine

After overnight marination, dry meat. Brown in casserole in hot butter/oil mixture

Add marinade, halved pig's foot, water, paste. Cover and cook gently for 2½ hours

Remove beef from casserole. Discard foot. Strain cooking juices, cool and skim

To thicken, either reduce juices, or whisk in beurre manié over gentle heat

Cream, brandy can be added to sauce with already-cooked onions and carrots (optional)

157

Braised carrots with cream

VEGETABLE Serves 4

Overall timing 1¼ hours

Equipment Flameproof casserole with tight-fitting lid

Freezing Do not add cream. Place in rigid container, cover, label and freeze. Freezer life: 3 months. To use: thaw, then heat in covered pan. Stir in cream and cook uncovered for 2–3 minutes

INGREDIENTS

2lb	Carrots
4	Small onions
1	Clove
1	Garlic clove
¼ cup	Butter
1	Bouquet garni
	Salt and pepper
2 tablespoons	Light cream

METHOD
1 Scrape, wash and thinly slice the carrots. Peel and quarter the onions. Stick a clove in one of the quarters. Peel and crush the garlic.
2 Melt butter in flameproof casserole over low heat and add carrots, onions, garlic, bouquet garni, salt and pepper. Cover and cook for 1 hour over low heat. Remove clove and bouquet garni.
3 Stir in cream, bring to a boil and simmer, uncovered, for 2–3 minutes. Serve.

Braised pearl onions

VEGETABLE Serves 4

Overall timing 45 minutes

Equipment Bowl, flameproof casserole

Freezing Not recommended

INGREDIENTS

1lb	Pearl onions
½ cup	Butter
1	Bay leaf
1 teaspoon	Sugar
1 teaspoon	Tomato paste
¼ cup	Light stock or broth or white wine
	Salt
	Freshly-ground black pepper

Braised Jerusalem artichokes are cooked in lemon-flavored broth

METHOD
1 Soak the onions in boiling water for 5 minutes to loosen the skins. Peel and dry. Heat the butter in the flameproof casserole and fry the onions over a low heat with the bay leaf for about 10 minutes, stirring till transparent.
2 Sprinkle in the sugar and fry gently for a further 5 minutes. Add the tomato paste and stock or wine and simmer for 5 minutes till just tender.
3 Discard the bay leaf and season to taste. Serve immediately with the cooking juices spooned over.

Braised artichokes

Jerusalem artichokes cooked gently in a stock made piquant with lemon juice

VEGETABLE Serves 4–6

Overall timing 50 minutes

Equipment Saucepan or flameproof casserole

Freezing Prepare to the end of Step 3. Cool, pack in foil container, cover, label and freeze. Freezer life: 3 months. To use: reheat slowly from frozen

INGREDIENTS

1	Large onion
2lb	Jerusalem artichokes
¼ cup	Unsalted butter
1 tablespoon	Oil
1¼ cups	Chicken stock or broth
1 tablespoon	Lemon juice
	Salt
	Freshly-ground black pepper
2 tablespoons	Chopped parsley

METHOD
1 Peel and finely chop the onion. Prepare artichokes but leave whole.
2 Heat the butter and oil in a saucepan or casserole and fry the onion until transparent. Add the artichokes and cook gently, stirring, for 5 minutes.
3 Add the chicken stock or broth, lemon juice and seasoning. Cover and cook for about 30 minutes until tender.
4 Lift artichokes out of liquid, place in a warm serving dish and keep hot. Boil the cooking liquid till reduced by half. Taste and adjust seasoning. Stir in parsley, pour over artichokes and serve.

Casseroled rabbit

Rabbit pieces, marinated, cooked in wine and served with peppery sauce.

MAIN DISH   Serves 8

Overall timing 2 hours plus 12 hours marination

Equipment Bowl, flameproof casserole

Freezing Make as Steps 1–5, reducing cooking time to 1 hour 10 minutes. Cover, label and freeze. Freezer life: 4 months. To use: reheat slowly from frozen and proceed as Steps 6–7

INGREDIENTS

	Marinade
2	Onions
2	Carrots
3	Garlic cloves
1	Bouquet garni
1 tablespoon	Coarse salt
10	Peppercorns
10	Juniper berries
2 cups	Red wine
	Other ingredients
4lb	Prepared rabbit pieces
¼ cup	Butter
2 tablespoons	Oil
	Salt and pepper
¼ cup	Flour
2 cups	Chicken stock or broth
3 tablespoons	Gin
6	Juniper berries

METHOD

1 To make the marinade, peel and cut onions into wedges; scrape and cut carrots into large pieces; peel and bruise garlic and place in bowl with remaining ingredients. Add rabbit, cover and leave to marinate for 12 hours, turning meat occasionally.

2 Remove rabbit from marinade and drain. Strain marinade and reserve.

3 Preheat the oven to 375°.

4 Heat butter and oil in large casserole, add rabbit and fry over high heat until brown on all sides. Season.

5 Sprinkle flour over mixture in casserole, stirring. Gradually add stock and reserved marinade. Bring to a boil, stirring. Cover and cook in the oven for 1½ hours or until tender.

6 Lift rabbit pieces out of the sauce and arrange on warmed serving dish.

7 Warm gin in a ladle and set alight. Pour into casserole. Lightly crush juniper berries and add to sauce. Bring to a boil, stirring. Adjust seasoning and pour the sauce over rabbit.

Navarin

One of the classic French stews, Navarin was a good, solid casserole to make at the end of winter with less than tender lamb and the last of the root vegetables. This version, however, is superb for summer with lamb and fresh vegetables providing succulence and flavor. Though the completed dish is not recommended for freezing, you can freeze at the end of Step 3 and add the vegetables when reheating

MAIN DISH   Serves 6

Overall timing 1¾ hours

Equipment Flameproof casserole

Freezing Not recommended

Navarin of lamb – a delicious stew that uses inexpensive blade or arm chops with onions, carrots, turnips and peas to make a tasty and nourishing family meal

INGREDIENTS

2½lb	Lamb blade or arm chops
¼ cup	Butter
4	Small onions
1 tablespoon	Flour
2 cups	Stock or broth
3 tablespoons	Tomato paste
1	Bouquet garni
	Salt and pepper
1lb	Carrots
1lb	Turnips
1lb	Potatoes
1½lb	Fresh peas
1 tablespoon	Chopped parsley

METHOD

1 Trim meat. Heat butter in casserole, add lamb and brown on all sides.

2 Peel and quarter the onions. Add to casserole and fry gently for 5 minutes. Sprinkle flour over and cook, stirring, for 2 minutes.

3 Gradually stir in the stock or broth. Add tomato paste, bouquet garni, salt and pepper and bring to a boil. Cover and simmer gently for 45 minutes.

4 Scrape and chop carrots. Peel turnips and cut into cubes. Add to casserole and cook for 15 minutes.

5 Meanwhile, peel potatoes and cut into chunks. Shell peas. Add potatoes to casserole and cook, covered, for 10 minutes, then add peas and cook for a further 20 minutes. Remove bouquet garni and adjust seasoning. Garnish with parsley and serve hot.

Baking

Baking takes place in an oven of any size, and food is cooked by dry heat, modified by the presence of water in the foods being cooked which converts to steam.

The hot air, less dense than cold, rises and as it comes in contact with the cooler oven walls and food it cools slightly, starts to fall, meets the heat and rises again. As the oven is an enclosed box the air gets hotter and the rise and fall creates convection currents.

Changes in food occur at specific temperatures and baking times are determined by the amount of moisture in, and the density of, the food. To ensure the correct air temperature is maintained, a thermostat or sensing device is fixed into the oven, and this works in conjunction with the temperature selector on the control panel outside the oven. Some ovens have exposed burners or open elements which give a high radiant effect. But as all ovens are made of metal the walls get hot and give off a certain amount of radiant heat which contributes to the browning and crisping of the food surface. At the same time, the shelves, baking sheets and dishes absorb heat and this helps cook the food by conduction.

All ovens have to have a venting system for, if they were totally sealed, the steam wouldn't escape and in the humid atmosphere the food would not crisp. The position of vents in an oven differs according to the model and even the fuel used, but they are arranged so as not to lose more heat than is necessary. In gas ovens, vents are also needed to remove the waste of combustion.

Forced air ovens differ from the conventional in that they have a motor-driven fan which increases the movement of the hot air and enables food to cook more quickly. This circulation also gives the same temperature throughout the oven and food cooks at a guaranteed temperature regardless of shelf position. In conventional ovens, heat zones are created — the selected temperature is thermostatically controlled in the center (which is why recipes suggest that dishes should be cooked in this position), and it will be hotter above and cooler below (by how much depends on the oven), but it enables foods to be cooked at the same time at different speeds. Forced air ovens are useful when baking cakes or pastries where temperature is crucial; for other baking, zones have advantages.

Ovens today are very well insulated which means they can be placed alongside a refrigerator if necessary when space is at a premium, and also that the walls heat up more quickly and maintain the heat. A major selling point of many ovens is that they need little or no preheating, an obvious boon in both time and fuel-saving terms. Automatic systems, which allow foods to be baked or roasted hours after you've prepared them and when you are in an entirely different place, have become almost standard. In cooking in an oven there are two basic temperatures: that of the oven and the food. (Temperature of the food would only be that of the oven if all moisture had evaporated — and the food was ruined.) Conventional ovens have a temperature range from 150° (used for drying herbs, fruit and vegetables) to 550° (rarely used except for flash baking (baked Alaska, some pizzas).

Forced air ovens have varying scales. They may give a range from 100–380° — which, say the manufacturers, is the approximate equivalent of the maximum temperature in a conventional oven thus giving the same results but at lower temperatures — or between 150° and 540°. Some gas fan ovens indicate temperature by numbers or words, and the temperatures will not always have a clear-cut equivalent in Celsius or Fahrenheit. With all ovens it is important to be guided by the manufacturer's instructions.

Conventional

As the air in the oven is heated, it rises, then cools when it comes in contact with oven walls, falls and rises again. The selected temperature is accurate in center of oven; is higher above, cooler below

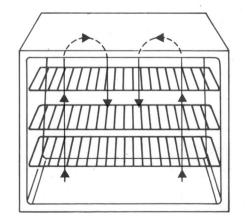

Forced air

A motorized fan at the back of the oven keeps hot air moving around, ensuring a uniform heat throughout and eliminating zones. The fan makes heating instant so little or no preheating is necessary. These ovens are called fan or fan assisted

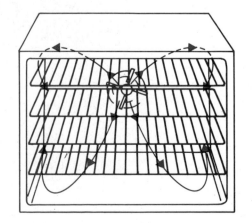

Bread baking techniques

Baking your own bread and rolls gives you greater control over the nutritional content, and opportunity to find the tastes and textures you like. Wholewheat and wheatmeal flours add flavor, color and texture as well as providing essential roughage, but as they have less gluten their leavening qualities are more limited than strong white flours. A mixture of the two is often more suitable, and a little fat will give a better crumb. In terms of temperature, bread making is exactly opposite to pastry making — warmth and moisture are essential to activate yeast, which is then able to work on flour creating the carbon dioxide which makes dough expand in the oven's heat. When the temperature of the dough reaches 130°, the yeast cells die, but have worked the leavening magic. Yeast's potential is restrained by freezing (it can be stored for 1 year), and the dried version has a shelf life of six months. Handy formulas to remember are:

   1 package active dry yeast=0.6oz cake compressed yeast. This will raise:
   2 cups flour for enriched doughs (fruit, eggs and extra sugar slow down yeast);
   3 cups wholewheat flour; or
   6 cups strong bread flour.

Breads are cooked in a hot oven in temperatures ranging between 400° and 450°. Enriched doughs are cooked at the lower end, plain white doughs at the upper.

Don't store bread in anything airtight — mold will develop if moisture can't escape.

crustiness

Brush bread with salty water during baking; or put pan of hot water in bottom of oven for two-thirds of baking time, then remove.

doneness

Turn loaves out of pans and tap underside with knuckles. If loaf sounds hollow, it's cooked. If it doesn't, return to pan and cook longer.

enriched doughs

Made by incorporating flour with yeast in a batter, then eggs, sugar, fruit are added for rolls and cakes.

flours

White or wholewheat flours high in gluten (they are described as strong) are used in bread making as it stretches when gas produced by yeast expands in the oven heat.

glazing

Beaten egg yolk gives crusty finish, holds toppings in place. Sweetened milk is brushed on freshly-cooked, still hot rolls to give a shiny, sticky surface.

hand hot

Describes temperature of milk or water used in bread making — if you can put your whole hand in, the yeast won't die.

kneading

Dough must be pushed and pulled to develop gluten. Place on lightly floured surface and stretch dough — use heel of one hand to push away, knuckles of the other to pull toward you. Fold, give dough a quarter turn, repeat — by hand it takes up to 10 minutes for dough to

become smooth and elastic, much less using an electric mixer with dough hook.

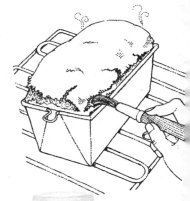

oven spring

This occurs as dough expands in oven heat before yeast is killed off and gives loaves a "torn" look above top of pan. After 20 minutes when loaf has set in shape you can glaze this part with egg yolk, then leave loaf to cook.

proving yeast

Dried yeast is sprinkled on to hand hot water or milk in which a little sugar has been stirred till dissolved and left until frothy. Fresh yeast is crumbled in, stirred and when dissolved is ready to use.

punching down

During first rising, dough expands unevenly and gas needs to be punched out so dough returns to original size.

second rising

After the first rising, the dough is punched down and shaped. It is placed in or on greased pans and covered completely with oiled plastic wrap or a damp dish towel and left till doubled in size — either in a warm place (not too hot or yeast will be killed) or overnight in refrigerator. Some say the more slowly the dough rises, the more even bread's texture after baking.

shaping

Loaves can be made pan shaped, braided or cottage shaped (press wooden spoon handle through to work surface so top won't fall off). To make rolls, knead dough pieces. To shape, cup hand over dough and rotate it anticlockwise, gradually

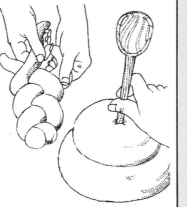

straightening fingers till ball is smooth. Let rise in/on greased pans, then glaze.

unleavened breads

Breads made without any leavening agent (chapatis). Flat bread like pitta and naans are leavened.

Breads around the world

baguette Traditional French loaf. Literally a rod or wand, this describes its shape. The thinner version is called **ficelle** (string).

Boston bread American cake-like bread flavored and colored by molasses and served with Boston baked beans.

challah World-famous Jewish braided loaf glazed with egg and topped with poppy seeds.

chapati Indian unleavened bread eaten with curry.

cornbread Popular bread of both the US and the Balkans. **Spoonbread** is special cornbread traditionally eaten at Thanksgiving.

ensaimada Light, fluffy Mallorquin breakfast bun.

grissini Italian crunchy bread sticks.

kümmelbrot Rich German bread with caraway seeds. The dough also contains a high proportion of fat and eggs.

makowiec Polish fruit and nut loaf topped with poppy seeds.

matzos Jewish unleavened bread, a part of the ritual Passover service, which look rather like plain crackers.

naan Flat Pakistani leavened bread baked pressed on the sides of beehive-shaped tandoor oven.

pannetone Italian bread/cake rich with fruit and eaten on festive occasions.

pitta Oval-shaped Middle Eastern flatbread which when slit on one side makes a pocket shape. **Pide** is Turkish soft, white and round flatbread.

pumpernickel Heavy and moist German black rye loaf eaten finely sliced.

semit Egyptian bread rings covered in sesame seeds.

tsoureki Greek enriched snail-shaped Easter loaf which has a dyed hard-cooked egg in the center.

Sweet and savory baking techniques

Protein foods and cereals react particularly well to the different heats that can be maintained in the oven. Starchy foods such as rice, cereals and beans cook very successfully in the controlled heat by the absorption method — their starch grains rupture and they can absorb cooking liquid without any risk of burning. Lean foods like fish and veal can be wrapped and the all-round heat ensures tenderness while full flavor is retained. Hams respond well to steam baking and can be topped with a glistening, appetizing glaze.

The heat has to be right for foods such as eggs in sweet and savory dishes, for over-cooking will spoil the end result — the tiny streams of air bubbles that appear in custards are an indication that the oven was too hot, or the mold in which they were baked heated too quickly. Water baths slow down the cooking of delicate foods and lessen the effect of the heat. Baking is kind, too, to meats that are ground to break down their connective tissue, for this reduces the cooking time and keeps them succulent. Foods with a sauce or topping of breadcrumbs to protect them can be cooked quickly at a high temperature, with just the right amount of browning occurring.

baking in a brick

When baking fish or chicken in a terracotta brick, soak top and bottom of the brick in cold water for 30 minutes before cooking, then drain and dry. No other liquid is needed as moisture will turn to steam in baking. Place brick in cold oven (never preheated) set to temperature.

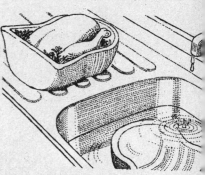

coagulation

The name given to the "setting" of eggs during cooking. The white sets at about 140°, the yolk about 149°. Egg custards and beaten egg toppings must set undisturbed by movement.

covering

Many baked foods (except those that need browning or crisping) are covered to make them tender. Edible coverings are: sauces which add flavor and color as well as keeping the food moist; mashed potatoes; breadcrumbs moistened with butter or cheese; and uncooked tomatoes which release their juices and baste the food — most of these are cooked in shallow dishes. When using foil to cover food, use it shiny side inside or it will reflect heat away.

glazing

Brushing a glaze over baked meats such as ham or chops adds flavor and improves appearance. It should be done toward the end of cooking as most glazes are sugary and will burn if cooked too long.

molding

Although many baked dishes are cooked in and served from the same dish, some are baked in molds and are unmolded when hot, or after chilling, to look decorative. Eggs are molded by breaking them into "nests" made by hollowing out vegetable purées (mashed potatoes, spinach) or meat mixtures, and are baked till set.

package baking

Excellent method for individual servings of foods like veal cutlets and fish which are low in fat and need to be protected from the heat. Paper wrappers are easily made by cutting a large heart shape out of parchment. Place the food on one half, add herbs and other flavorings, then dot with butter. Bring other side over and roll edges together to seal. The packages should be baked on a wire rack so heat can circulate all around.

Vine, spinach and lettuce leaves make very good edible wrappings for foods needing protection during baking. Blanch leaves to soften.

planking

Baking meat on a wooden board which scorches slightly in the oven's heat giving the meat a smoky flavor. Generally thought to be an American innovation, but meat was planked in Britain long before the Pilgrim Fathers set sail. Planks, made of kiln-dried oak, are oiled and made very hot before meat is placed on. Popular method for thick steaks such as Chateaubriand which are seared under the broiler first, and cooking is completed in a very hot oven. Mashed potatoes piped around prevent the plank burning.

reheating

The oven's even heat is an efficient method of reheating but food will dry out unless extra liquid is added, or the food covered and cooked in a water bath to create a steamy atmosphere.

steam baking

All baked foods cook in their own steam, but when extra liquid is poured around a bird or large fish and the container is covered, the food cooks by steam baking.

temperature

The correct temperature is a crucial factor when baking some foods. Eggs can curdle or set rock hard; fish and meats will dry out and fall to pieces if heat's not right.

water baths

Used with egg custards, to create a steamy, moist atmosphere in the oven and to prevent the temperature of the food rising above boiling point.

Sweet and savory bakes around the world

aardappel purée met ham en uien Dutch dish of chopped ham layered with mashed potato and onions.

äggkrans From Sweden, baked egg custard rings with meat fillings.

baked mackerel with rhubarb Specialty of the west of England, fish are baked with herbs and cider, served with a rhubarb and cider sauce. **Maquereaux en papillotes** is Belgian baked mackerel with fines herbes in paper.

barbounia sto harti From Greece, red mullet baked *en papillote* with olives, lemon and marjoram.

bitki po russki Russian dish of meatballs baked with a border of sliced cooked potatoes, with sour cream sauce and cheese.

Boston baked beans Famous American dish of white beans baked with pork and molasses.

cockelty pie From Ireland, cockles with vegetables in pastry.

crap umplut Romanian dish of whole carp baked with garlic, herbs and root vegetables.

crème caramel Classic custard from France baked in a mold in a bain-marie (water bath).

dolma kroum Algerian stuffed cabbage leaves baked with chickpeas and rice.

Exeter pudding Old English dessert made with eggs, rum, butter and breadcrumbs poured over fruity sponge and blackcurrant jam.

faggots Traditions dish from the north of England made of pig's lights, liver, breadcrumbs, onions and herbs baked in pig's caul.

falscher hase Means "false hare" in German, it is made with chopped meat, eggs, onions and capers, rolled in breadcrumbs, baked.

fidget pie From the Welsh borders, potatoes, onions, apples and diced bacon under pie pastry.

filetti di tacchino in pasta sfoglia From Italy, turkey breasts baked in pastry with ham, mushrooms.

gnocchi al forno Italian bake of semolina rounds covered with egg yolks and milk, then cheese.

keshy yena coe cabaron From Curaçao in the Dutch West Indies, hollowed out Edam cheese stuffed with onions, tomatoes, breadcrumbs, raisins, olives and shrimp and baked till cheese is soft.

moussaka Best known of the Balkan dishes – ground lamb, eggplant and onions baked with a rich cheese sauce.

pepes ikan Indonesian dish of whole fish baked with garlic, chili powder, shallots, coconut.

Fruit and vegetable baking techniques

Baking is one of the best ways of cooking fruit and vegetables so their characteristics change in a desirable way. Whole vegetables baked in their skins retain their flavor and nutritive value as they cook in their own steam and the dry oven heat makes the skins crisp, golden and delicious to eat. Moisture needs to be added to vegetables and fruit if peeled and sliced as they have no method of retaining their own.

Many fruits are used as eatable containers for a wide variety of stuffings. Some fruits need additional sweetness, often supplied by the stuffing, together with a contrasting texture such as cereals or nuts. Many vegetables, too, can be stuffed, once central seeds are removed, to improve both texture and flavor.

Because many vegetables are similar to fruit in texture, even though they differ in taste, they both can be treated the same way in baking. The Belgians have their sweet leek flan (*flamiche*), we Americans our sweet pumpkin pie, and in Provence Christmas Eve would not be complete without *tarte sucrée aux épinards*, a combination of spinach, crème pâtissière and mixed glacé fruits. In France, whole baked apples are just as popular as turnips with roast duck, and baked pears are traditionally served with roast reindeer in Norway.

basting

The low fat content of fruit and vegetables can cause them to dry out in baking. If cut up with or without skin and placed around a roast, they need to be basted once or twice during cooking with the pan juices. Baked fruit needs basting with syrup, or with the pan juices if being served as a savory.

blanching

Many vegetables are blanched before baking to reduce the cooking time, or to make them easier to prepare for stuffing. Vegetables such as peppers and soft-shelled squash like zucchini are quickly blanched in boiling water. Tomatoes are blanched to remove skins before being sliced and baked.

coating

Done to tender foods like fruit to prevent collapse during baking. Pastry makes a protective covering for whole apples or pears, as does meringue. In pies with pastry above and below, fruit doesn't need to be cooked first for even though the temperature is high, it is protected. Bread-crumb and sugar toppings known as *streusel* also protect fruits baked in tarts.
Skins of vegetables are the

best protection – rub washed and dried potatoes with a butter wrapper to make them crisp and prevent wrinkles.

coring

The innermost parts of fruit and vegetables are not always edible, and are frequently removed to make space for a stuffing. Cooked stuffings are generally used so the cored fruit or vegetable will bake more quickly. The core of Belgian endive which can be bitter is sometimes removed before the *chicons* are wrapped in ham, covered with sauce and baked. Not-so-prime root vegetables (eg, parsnips and carrots) often have a coarse, woody core which can be removed with an apple corer before baking.

deseeding

Part of the coring technique as the seeds are attached to the fibrous inner parts. When preparing tomatoes for stuffing and baking, scoop out the seeds with a teaspoon, taking care not to break the flesh.

parboiling

Vegetables which require longer cooking time to make them tender are often parboiled to give them a head start in baking. Halved or quartered potatoes, turnips and parsnips are parboiled for just a few minutes – if the precooking time is too long the moisture content will be driven out of the vegetables and they will absorb too much fat in baking. Some vegetables are parboiled when they are to be baked in a sauce because the sauce would spoil in the long cooking needed to tenderize the vegetables.

peeling

Peels are often essential to the end result when fruit and vegetables are baked – stuffed tomatoes, for example, would give up in the heat if the skins were removed. Chunks or wedges of pumpkin are best baked in their skins.

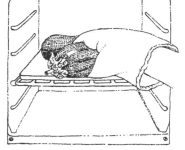

pricking

Done to fruit and vegetables either to prevent skins bursting, or to help heat penetrate quicker. Whole apples are scored around their circumference so that as they expand and become foamy, the skin can lift slightly. Hard vegetables are pricked with a skewer or fork.

purée

Fruit and vegetables can be baked in their skins so that the inside will become dry and fluffy and easy to purée. Eggplants are baked whole till wrinkled and tender, then the skin can either be peeled away and the flesh chopped, mashed or puréed for use in soups or dips (one dish cooked in this way is known as *caviar d'aubergines*). Score the skins but do not core whole apples when baking to make a dry purée. The flesh can be sieved to remove seeds and "maiden's fingernails" (the tough bits of the core). Apples puréed in this manner have excellent flavor.

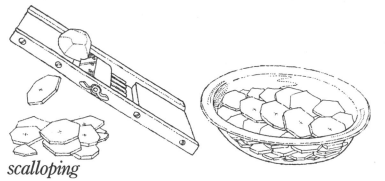

scalloping

Not cooking on scallop shells, but a term for sliced, layered vegetables baked in milk or cream. The vegetables have to be thinly sliced (to cook through) and layered in a shallow dish. Most of the liquid is absorbed as the vegetables cook.

skewering

As most foods are poor conductors of heat, metal skewers are pushed through them so that as the metal heats, the oven's heat will get right into the middle, reducing the cooking time by almost one-third.

steam baking

All fruit and vegetables contain a high proportion of water which is converted to steam and is forced through the cells making them tender. In steam baking extra liquid is added and the dish is covered during baking. Fruit and vegetable mixtures lightened with whisked egg whites (soufflés) or set with egg (molded custards) are placed in a water bath to slow down the cooking.

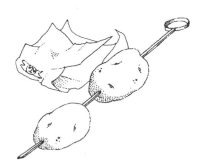

stuffings

These have several important functions when baking fruit and vegetables – they bulk them out, make them even more moist, and provide contrasting texture and flavor. With vegetables that have been blanched, a cooked stuffing is usually used so the baking time is lessened. Stuffings make vegetables much more substantial and with added protein can become a whole meal.

Fruit and vegetable bakes around the world

alivenci Traditional Romanian dish of baked cabbage leaves, layered with corn and buttermilk and served hot with sour cream sauce.

Anglesey eggs Welsh dish of baked leeks, potatoes and cheese.

bruciate briache An Italian dessert of baked, peeled chestnuts, sugared, soaked in rum and set alight. The name means "burning drunkards"!

couronne du Barry Cauliflower, Béchamel and Gruyère cheese baked in a ring mold.

Molmeh sib Persian first course or side dish of baked apples with meat and split pea stuffing.

fasoeil al fùrn Italian version of baked beans. They are cooked overnight with pork rinds, garlic, parsley and spices.

flamiche (or **flamique**) Flemish flan with leek and cream filling.

gratin dauphinois A French dish of sliced potatoes baked in eggs, milk and Gruyère cheese.

imam bayildi Turkish dish of halved stuffed eggplants, baked, then left to cool to room temperature before eating.

Jansson's frestelse Literally Jansson's temptation, a luscious Swedish dish of potatoes, onions and anchovies baked in thick cream and eaten as an appetizer.

minestra di lattughe Italian baked dish of lettuces stuffed with veal, sweetbreads and brains.

parmigiana di zucchini Italian zucchini dish with Mozzarella and Parmesan, and basil-flavored tomato sauce. Any baked dish containing a good helping of cheese is called Parmigiana.

pastinake-pudding A German parsnip pudding made by baking mashed parsnips with breadcrumbs, eggs, butter, sugar, rum.

pisang goreng An Indonesian side dish of savory baked bananas.

pommes cendrillon French baked potatoes (the name means Cinderella's potatoes) with cheese.

sarma Serbian cabbage rolls stuffed with meat and rice, baked with stock or tomato paste. In Israel they're called **holishkes.**

sheikh el mahshi betingan Arab baked eggplants with a meat and pine nut stuffing.

stoemp Flemish baked dish of potatoes, leeks and eggs.

sweet potato pone An American dish from the South, eaten with ham. Sliced sweet potatoes are baked with butter, sugar, raisins.

tarten riwbob A traditional Welsh rhubarb pie.

timbalo di rigatoni Sicilian baked pasta with eggplants.

Pastry baking techniques

All pastries are mixtures of flour, fat and water and the different types are produced by altering the proportions of each ingredient, the method of making and the cooking temperature. The handling of the ingredients and the mixed dough is very important — lightness of touch, speed of work and the coolest of conditions are essential for successful pastry making.

It is the protein in the flour — the gluten — and how it is treated that determines whether pastry will be short and crumbly, or flaky. In short pastries the fat surrounds the gluten so that it doesn't set in long strands when it comes in contact with the water used to bind the dough. (Because it literally shortens the strings, fat for pastry is often called shortening.) The light kneading that follows makes the dough smooth enough to roll, and the pastry crisp and brittle. Over-handled pastry will be tough, as will pastry with too much water and too little fat. Eggs improve color and flavor of pastry and because they are emulsifiers also make the dough easier to work. Sugar adds sweetness and gives pastry extra shortness.

With flaky pastries the development of the gluten strands is needed to make the layers. Water in the dough is converted to steam in the oven heat, pushing up the layers, and the starch grains burst and absorb the fat before the pastry sets in layers. Careless rolling and shaping, stretching or over-handling will make the pastry shrink and it won't rise to five times its thickness when baked.

Hot water pastries like choux and hot water crust are different in that partial cooking takes place before they go into the oven. The water makes the choux puff up, and makes hot water crust malleable.

aerating

This is done by manual or chemical means to introduce air and lightness to puffed and suet pastries. The sifting of flour, and lifting fat and flour together when rubbing in, adds air as does rolling and folding dough with butter. Air is introduced to suet crust chemically by a mixture of one part of baking soda and two parts of cream of tartar (known as baking powder) which form carbon dioxide gas which raises the mixture.

baking blind

Method used for baking a pie crust before filling, to stop the base from rising. After lining and shaping, prick the base with a fork to release air trapped underneath. Press foil or parchment paper into shape of case and cover with rice or dried beans. Partially baked crusts are used when a liquidy filling is cooked in them (eg, stewed fruit) and fully baked crusts are needed when a precooked filling only requires reheating (eg, vol-au-vent) or for tarts eaten cold. Partially baked crusts go into the oven for 10 minutes to "set", then the lining and beans are removed and the empty crust returned to the oven for 5 minutes to dry and color base. It can then be filled and immediately returned to the oven.

chilling

This is necessary to firm the fat content of dough making it easy to roll. Cover or wrap to prevent a skin forming and place in the refrigerator for 30 minutes. This is especially important for puffed pastries as the successful rising of the flaky layers depends on the even distribution of firm cold fat between layers of dough. In the oven's heat the fat melts and the cold air trapped between the layers expands, forcing the pastry to rise.

crimping

Means of giving a decorative shell-like edge to a tart or pie which also seals the dough to the container or lid to the pastry base. Press thumb into dough, make dent alongside with back of knife. Repeat around edge. Used for all kinds of pastry, and is especially effective with puff pastry in conjunction with fluting.

fat

This determines the flavor of pastry and the method of incorporating it gives characteristic textures.

flours

All-purpose flour is used for all pastries except for suet crust, which needs self-rising in order to make a more doughy pastry.

Strong bread flour is better for puffed pastries as it contains more gluten and stretches well.

Wholewheat flour can be used to make pie pastry, but as it contains bran which laps up water, it can be heavy and tough. Lighter results are obtained by using self-rising whole-wheat flour, or half white self-rising flour and half wholewheat.

fluting

This is done to establish layers in puffed pastry before baking to help in the rising. Place a finger flat on top of dough and using a sharp knife make light horizontal cuts in the side of the dough. Move finger along and repeat till all the edge is cut.

folding

This is done to the dough of puffed pastries to incorporate fat and air by repeatedly rolling and folding to create layers of pastry which will rise in thin light flakes when baked. Chilling in between rolling and folding is essential so fat doesn't melt into the layers.

glazing

This is done before baking to give a sheen and color to pastry. If pastry edges have been fluted, don't brush these with glaze as it will prevent the layers separating. Egg yolks mixed with salt give a golden color to savory pies and hot water crusts. Lightly forked egg whites can be brushed onto sweet pies and tarts and sprinkled with sugar. Puff pastry looks splendid when glazed with beaten yolk or the whole egg. Heated and sieved apricot jam is sometimes used on tarts and on base of pastry to prevent filling soaking in (lightly forked egg white can be used in the same way). When decorating pastry, dip the pieces into beaten egg to glaze and give stickability.

incorporating fat

Rubbing in is the method used for pie pastry. Fat should be firm but not hard and cut into small pieces or coarsely grated if straight from the refrigerator. Lift mixture with fingertips only above bowl or cold work surface, rubbing lightly between thumbs and fingertips, then letting it fall back into the bowl. This is done until the mixture looks like fine bread-crumbs — shake bowl occasionally so large pieces of fat come to the surface. Dough should be handled as little and as lightly as possible as over-rubbing makes large oily crumbs and tough pastry.

Cutting in is like rubbing in but uses a pastry blender or two knives to incorporate fat. The advantage of this method is that the dough stays cool and the pastry will be light.

Rolling and folding is the method used with puffed pastries. When making puff, half the butter is rubbed in, and the remainder is kept as a block, placed on the rolled dough and by folding and rolling and chilling five times altogether is slowly incorporated to create layers of dough and fat.

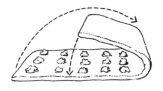

For flaky pastry, a quarter of fat is rubbed in to make a dough, and the rest is added a third at a time, dotted over two-thirds of the rolled-out dough. The dough is folded, sealed, rolled and chilled in sequence to create the layers of dough and fat.

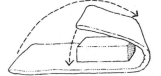

Stirring is method used with grated or shredded suet — it's added to flour and mixed in with a palette knife. When making pastry with corn oil the oil and water are stirred together before flour is added.

Melting method is required for hot water crust and choux. Hot water crust is made by melting lard in water and pouring it into flour to give a malleable dough for shaping (keep it warm while using it). In choux the flour is added to the melted butter and water, then stirred over heat to partially cook it.

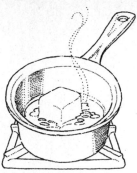

One-stage pastry. The quickest and easiest way to make pie pastry. The fat, flour and water are mixed together with a fork. More water is used than in conventional pie pastry, which helps the mixture combine more easily.

kneading

Unlike bread making which requires much pummeling to stretch the dough, in pastry making kneading is done to smooth. The touch should be light — bring outside edge into center, rotating dough anticlockwise until bottom and sides are smooth. Turn over and roll up or wrap and chill.

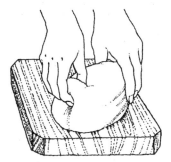

leavening agents

Air, steam and carbon dioxide gas expand in the oven's heat and, as cold air expands more dramatically than hot air, pastry needs to be cold when it goes into the oven. Suet pastry has baking powder in the flour to help it rise.

lining a flan ring

A flan ring is a circle without a base which is placed on top of a greased upturned cookie sheet, Roll the dough to a size big enough to cover base and sides of ring. Roll dough around rolling pin, lift it over the ring and unroll. Ease the dough into base and up sides, then roll the pin over the top to cut off excess. Fill to cook or bake blind. The pastry will have shrunk when cooked so that the ring can be lifted up and off. The crust can then be moved off the cookie sheet with two spatulas and placed on a plate ready for serving.

proportions

In most pie pastry, the proportions are half fat to flour. In sweet pie dough, sugar is added and the amount of butter is increased to just over half. Puff pastry has equal quantities of fat and flour. Flaky and rough puff pastry uses three-quarters fat to flour. Hot water crust uses a third fat to flour. Suet crust uses half suet to flour. Do not over-flour the work surface as this will alter the ingredient proportions.

relaxing

This means letting the dough "rest" before rolling to allow the gluten in the flour to contract, making pastry less likely to shrink. A pastry-lined ring or pan can be relaxed in the refrigerator for 30 minutes before baking.

removing a flan ring

After the tart has cooked, the pastry will have shrunk in a little. Grasp the ring firmly on either side, shake to loosen, then lift straight up, being careful that the bottom of the ring doesn't knock the top edge of the pastry. Use two broad spatulas to lift the tart onto a serving plate.

rolling

The way pastry is rolled is important. It's only turned over once — after kneading. Always roll in short sharp strokes in one direction only — away from you — but not to the edge, as this will make it thinner than the rest. Rotate dough one half turn to the left after each short rolling, so gluten is evenly stretched. If dough is over-stretched in any direction, it will cause the pastry to shrink when baked.

sealing

This is done to secure pastry to a container, a lid to a base or when enclosing a filling inside dough. Brush container rims or pastry edges with water or beaten egg, then press together. Crimping also helps to seal edges. The term is also used when edges of folded puffed doughs are dented with the rolling pin to seal in fat during rolling and folding processes. To do this, use the end of the pin to make light indentations.

temperature

All pastry needs to be cooked in a fairly hot oven. Pastry cooked in too low a heat will be tough and heavy. If too hot, the outside will brown while the inside stays soggy. A hot oven, usually about 425°, is essential for puffed pastries.

trimming

When trimming pastry for a tart or pie, use a sharp knife to cut away the surplus, cutting away from you and turning the dish slowly. Puffed pastries should be trimmed with a very sharp knife to restore the layers which may have been flattened during rolling.

trimmings

Decorative shapes can be cut out of the surplus dough, dipped in beaten egg and arranged on the pastry. When making decorations from puff pastry, cut the strips so that the layers all go in one direction. The shapes can be cut with a knife or fluted cutter. Flute them all around so that the layers can rise as evenly as the pastry.

Pastries around the world

Aberdeen butteries From Scotland, a cross between Danish pastries and croissants.

bakewell tart From England, crust filled with jam and almonds.

baklava From Greece and Middle East, sweet, nut-filled phyllo pastry, soaked in syrup.

Banbury cakes From Oxfordshire, England, puff pastry filled with spices, currants and candied peel.

bànitsa Savory Bulgarian tart made with phyllo pastry.

börek Tiny Middle Eastern pastries made in variety of shapes with savory or sweet fillings.

boeuf en croûte French dish of beef tenderloin wrapped in puff pastry and baked. **Beef Wellington** is the English version. Liver pâté is often spread on the beef.

courting cake Large jam tart from Yorkshire, England.

croissant French crescent-shaped crisp and flaky rolls made with yeast dough rolled out like flaky pastry.

Eccles cakes Small pastry cakes from England, similar to Banbury but without the candied peel.

éclair From France, choux pastry filled with crème pâtissière.

empanadas From Spain and South America, turnovers filled with meat, fish or vegetables.

gantois Belgian, spicy iced pastries, layered and covered with greengage, then apricot jam.

gâteau St Honoré A Parisian specialty, the base is made of pâte brisée, sides of choux balls, and filling is crème pâtissière.

hamantaschen Three-cornered Jewish pastry filled with poppy seeds, nuts, raisins and honey.

kadaif Arab in origin, cream or nut-filled pastry soaked in syrup.

kadin göbeği Means "ladies navels" in Turkish, they are cup-shaped pastries with custard filling.

likky pie Pie of leeks, bacon, cream and eggs covered with suet crust, from Cornwall, England.

linzertorte From Austria, raspberry jam in cinnamon flavored pastry with a lattice topping.

ma'amoul Moroccan pastries stuffed with dates.

mille-feuilles French layered puff pastries with crème pâtissière and jam filling. **Napoleon slices** have glacé icing on top, are filled with whipped cream, jam.

Oldbury tarts English small hot water crust tarts filled with gooseberries and brown sugar.

palmiers French crisp, sweet cookies made from puff pastry.

pasticcio di tortellini all'emiliana Meat and stuffed pasta in a layered pie from Bologna, Italy.

pirozski Small Russian turnovers filled with savory stuffings.

Pithiviers French puff pastry cake with creamy almond filling.

profiteroles From France, choux paste balls filled with cream and served with chocolate sauce.

tiddy oggy Another name for Cornish pasty, filled with meat and diced potatoes, carrots, onions.

Wienerbrød Danish puff pastries with different fillings/toppings.

Cookie baking techniques

Cookies, apart from a few exceptions, are cooked quickly and become crisp after they are taken out of the oven and are placed on a wire rack to cool. Like cakes they are a combination of fat, flour, sugar and eggs and can be of various textures. Macaroons, for example, are made with whisked egg whites, sugar and ground almonds and are more like meringues. Cookies made by creaming butter and sugar have a good crumb and are designed to melt in the mouth — these are the ones that are often joined together with a filling and are called kisses, or *braisers* in France. The Germans have made a specialty of cookie making, and Christmas Eve would not be complete without a selection of *springerle*, delightfully decorated spicy shapes. In Scotland the large decorated rounds (which are broken into wedges) or fingers of shortbread are traditional Christmas fare.

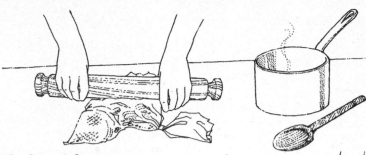

baked crumb crust

Making a crust of cookies is an excellent alternative to pastry. Usually graham crackers are used, but any will do — including the bits at the bottom of the cookie jar. If they have gone soft, dry them out at 350° for 15 minutes, or toast them under the broiler. They need to be crushed evenly and finely — put them in a plastic bag, close it and then bash it with a rolling pin. Butter is melted till frothy (as in enriched dough, just over half of butter to the amount of cookies) and then the two are mixed together in a bowl. The hot, moist crumbs are pressed into a greased springform pan to cover the bottom and sides. Roll a jar against the edges to make them smooth, thcn chill for 20–30 minutes. Bake with or without filling at 350° for 20 minutes. To fill with a cold filling, let crust cool, add filling and chill to set before removing from pan.

Run knife around edge of cake, place on jar and release clip to drop ring. Use spatula to separate cake from pan base

chilling

Cookies which are handled a lot are like pastries in that they should be cold when they go into the oven — the colder the air trapped in the dough, the more the cookies will expand in the heat, giving a lighter texture. After rolling out and cutting cookies, place on greased sheet and chill for 20–30 minutes.

cooling

Cookies are cooked quickly and often appear slack and soft after they come out of the oven — and this is as it should be! Let them cool or rather "set" for about 30 seconds, then use a spatula to lift them onto wire racks where air can circulate all around and crisp the cookies. Exceptions to this rule are cookies that need to be shaped while hot, eg, brandy snaps, tuiles.

creaming

Method used in cookie making where there is high proportion of fat; when it is creamed with the sugar it helps to dissolve it.

glazing

Crackers are brushed lightly with forked egg white or milk before baking. Cookies can be glazed after baking, while still hot, with thin water frostings.

icebox cookies

This cookie dough is rolled into a log shape and kept in the refrigerator for 12–24 hours before being thinly sliced for baking. They could be called convenience cookies, for the wrapped roll can be stored in the refrigerator for 10 days to 2 weeks and you can cut off $\frac{1}{8}$ inch slices and bake them when you want at 400° on a greased cookie sheet for about 10 minutes. Made with more than $\frac{1}{2}$ cup of fat to 4 cups flour, they are short and delicate cookies which crisp when cooling on a rack. The roll (make it about 2 inches in diameter) can be made up of two differently colored doughs, rolled out, placed on top of each other and rolled up — when cut they make pin-wheels. Or the roll can be coated with crushed cereals or finely chopped nuts. The rolls also freeze well but should be thawed in the refrigerator to soften to a stage where they can be cut into thin slices.

melting

Used for cookies which contain molasses, corn syrup or honey, this method gives a chewy texture. The fat and syrup are heated, then cooled before being stirred into the dry ingredients.

molding

Decorative molds are used to give a pattern to cookies — Scottish thistle on shortbread, people shapes on the German *springerle* (both are Christmas specialties). Cookies can also be hand molded into shapes like knots, twists.

piped cookies

Soft creamed mixtures can be piped into shapes (see shaping). To freeze, pipe onto cookie sheet, freeze uncovered, then lift off sheet and pack in freezer bags. Bake from frozen on greased cookie sheet.

rolling out

Method used for flat cookies which are pricked with a fork before baking to prevent them rising. Dough should be rolled to a uniform thickness ($\frac{1}{4}$–$\frac{1}{2}$ inch). Roll dough away from you using short, sharp movements. Never turn dough over, and bake rolled side up.

sandwiching

Method of joining two like cookies together with cream, jam or frosting. Often known as kisses or *braisers*.

shaping

Cookies can be shaped by piping with a large tube (Viennese fingers, *petits sablés*), or with a cookie press — a metal syringe with interchangeable disks for creating stars and other shapes. Cookies can be stamped out with cutters; firm doughs can be pressed into bowl of deep spoon, then shapes turned onto greased cookie sheet for baking. Dough can be made into a long even sausage, chilled, then sliced with a sharp knife to make rounds for baking. Creamed mixtures can be placed in rocky piles.

spreading space

Soft doughs with a high fat content will spread more than those that have been rolled and cut. Cookies made by the melting method spread most, some getting a lacy texture this way. Leave 1–2 inches all around shapes on cookie sheets.

storage

Always store cookies on their own in a jar made airtight if necessary with plastic wrap under the lid. A sugar cube stored in the container will absorb any moisture – for it is moisture that makes cookies lose their crispness. Cookies with a high egg white content (eg, macaroons) don't store well.

temperature

Apart from shortbread which is dried out in a coolish oven so it doesn't color, cookies are usually baked for a short time in a moderate to hot oven – 350–400°.

texture

Generally speaking cookies are crisp and have a crumbly or chewy texture. Fruit, nuts, oats, syrup all affect texture.

unbaked cookies

Often made with whole or crushed breakfast cereals formed into rocky shapes with melted shortening, syrup or chocolate. They're put in the refrigerator to set.

Cookies around the world

abernethy cookie Named after its Scots creator, chief surgeon at Bart's Hospital, London, in the 19th century, it has caraway seeds as major flavoring.

American toll house cookies Everybody's favorite – rich, buttery cookies full of chocolate chips and chopped walnuts.

baisers Literally "kisses", cookies joined together with frosting.

baseler leckerli Swiss fruit and honey cookies.

Bath olivers Thin English crackers for cheese.

brandy snaps Originally Flemish, they are very thin, crisp curls shaped after cooking.

buñuelos Mexican deep-fried honey cookies.

Cornish fairings From south west England, cookies made with ginger, spices and syrup.

crumiri Arc-shaped cornmeal cookies from Piedmont, Italy.

darazsfeszek Litterally "wasps nests" in Hungarian, they are yeast cookies enriched with butter, almonds and raisins.

Easter biscuits Spicy English cookies with currants.

flapjacks Scottish and English bar cookies made of oats, brown sugar, butter and golden syrup.

galettes bretonnes Buttery cookies from Brittany.

garibaldis From England but of Italian origin, thinnish spicy cookies with currants.

gingerbread men Ginger cookies shaped like men, originally from Lancashire, England. Gingerbread women are also made today (equal opportunities in baking!).

Grasmere gingerbread Ginger finger cookies from the English Lake District.

kaerlighedskranser From Denmark, rich buttery cookie rings.

karvekjeks From Norway, a rich caraway cookie made with brandy and dredged with sugar.

kipfeln Austrian crescent-shaped almond cookies for coffee time.

kniplingskrager Danish "lace" cookies made with oats.

kurabiye A Turkish cookie of yogurt, cornmeal, egg, sugar.

langue de chat Crisp cookies from France shaped like cats' tongues.

lebkuchen-herzen Heart-shaped German cookies flavored with ginger, topped with chocolate frosting and preserved ginger.

macaroon Imported from Italy to France in the 16th century, light cookie made of ground almonds, egg whites and sugar.

makagigi Polish almond and honey cookies.

mantecados Spanish cookie flavored with rum or wine.

melogarida Thin Greek cookies made with honey and walnuts.

melting moments Australian shortbread-type "kisses" which are joined with jam or fruity flavored frosting.

papparkakor Swedish ginger cookies flavored with molasses and cinnamon.

pastas de almendras mallorauinas Almond cookies from Majorca.

pogacsa Hungarian cookie garnished with salted almonds.

pryaniki Traditional Russian cookies shaped like animals.

sablé Rich French cookies made with equal amounts of sugar and butter, several egg yolks, flour.

shortbread Buttery and short Scottish cookie popular at Christmas. The dough is pressed into a round mold to give it a decorative imprint, then is turned out and baked. Shortbread fingers are pricked on top.

springerle German festive cookies flavored with spices or lemon.

tuiles Fine French cookies like brandy snaps but shaped on rolling pin.

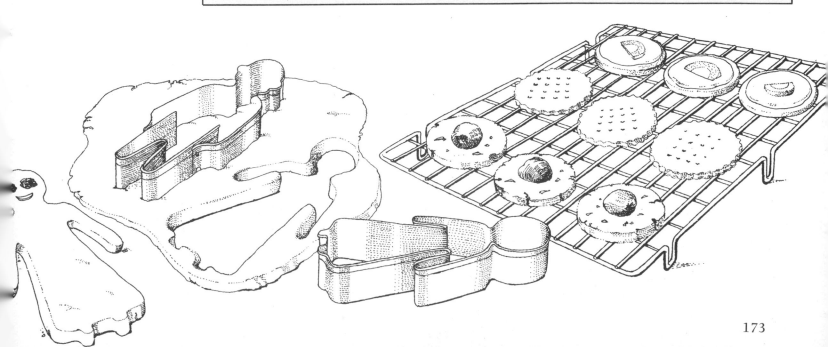

Cake baking techniques

The word cake comes from Arabic and has been adopted in many countries to describe baked combinations of fat, flour, sugar and eggs (though some are made without fat or egg). The texture of the finished cake depends on the proportions of the ingredients and the method of combining them. In order to be light to eat, most cakes are required to rise so air must be incorporated during mixing by sifting, creaming or beating, or by adding baking powder. Those heavy with fruit are the exception and the space they occupy in the pans before they go into the oven will be similar to what comes out after baking. Before starting a cake making session, gather together all the utensils and ingredients — bring eggs and butter to room temperature, sift dry ingredients, prepare any dried fruits and grease and line pans so that the cake can be put into a moderate to hot oven as soon as possible after mixing. Cake mixtures will lose added air if left to stand.

aerating

Increasing the volume of a cake's ingredients by incorporating air — manually by beating or sifting, chemically by a leavening agent such as baking powder. The air expands in the oven's heat and stretches the protein in eggs and flour.

beating

A method of beating egg, or an egg-based mixture with a hand, rotary or electric beater to incorporate air (increasing volume) and, if necessary, blend the different ingredients. Egg whites to be folded in should be stiff and glossy.

chiffon cakes

Also called feather, these are light, sponge-like cakes made with vegetable oil, baking powder and beaten egg white.

consistency

The degree of density of an uncooked cake mixture. For a sponge, the eggs and sugar are beaten together until thick and the beater, when lifted, leaves a trail that lasts up to 20 seconds. Mixtures made by melting method have the consistency of thick batter. Creamed mixtures have two consistencies: light and fluffy like thick cream when fat and sugar are beaten, soft dropping (it will flick easily from a spoon) when all ingredients are combined. Rubbed-in mixtures won't drop unless flicked from the spoon.

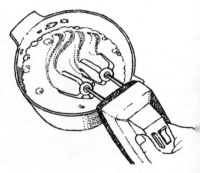

The beater trail on sponge mixes should last 20 seconds

cracking

The surface of a moist cake splits if there is too little liquid in the mixture. If a cake peaks in the center, the mixture in contact with the sides of the pan cooked before steam and hot air helped it to rise.

creaming

Beating solid fats, like butter or block margarine in a bowl with a wooden spoon, electric mixer or food processor to incorporate air and increase volume, gradually adding sugar to get a fluffy mixture. Beaten eggs are then added gradually (if curdling occurs stir in a little sifted flour as well), followed by sifted dry ingredients.

doneness

The point at which a cake is ready to be removed from the oven. Sponges are cooked when they shrink away slightly from the side of the pan, and the center springs back if pressed lightly with a fingertip. A fine skewer inserted into the center of creamed or fruit cakes will have nothing clinging if the cakes are cooked.

cooling

Ideally, a freshly-baked cake should stay in its pan until it has cooled to 140° as it breaks if handled warm. Allow a minimum of 10–15 minutes cooling time, then turn out onto a wire rack. The exception is a jelly roll which cools rapidly because of its shallowness, and will only roll well when warm. To turn sponges out so tops aren't marked, cover rack with waxed paper. Invert cake onto it, place another rack on top, then quickly flip them so cake base is on rack.

flours

Soft wheat (low protein) flour much refined, is used for most cakes to give a soft, tender crumb. Self-rising, white or brown, contains a standard quantity of baking powder; all-purpose flour can be used without baking powder (when beaten egg whites are leavening agent), or it can be added. Wholewheat can be combined with half self-rising flour, or baking powder can be added.

folding-in

Blending two ingredients, one of which is beaten eggs, with a gentle folding motion so that air doesn't escape from the eggs (the lighter is added to the heavier). Gently rotate bowl clockwise as you move a large metal spoon down contour of the bowl, under mixture, up the other side and then over the top (so spoon is hollow-side down). Continue till evenly mixed (don't forget the mixture stuck to the spoon!).

greasing and flouring

Most pans, especially ring molds which are difficult to line, should be brushed with melted fat or oil (or rubbed with a butter paper), lightly sprinkled with flour, and then the excess flour shaken out to prevent sticking.

melting

A cake making method in which fat and liquid ingredients (often corn syrup or molasses), are melted together in a saucepan, cooled, then poured onto dry ingredients, before adding eggs. The final mixture has a batter-like consistency and the cooked cakes are moist and sticky.

one-stage

An easy method for making all cakes (except fatless sponges) brought about by the invention of soft margarine. All the ingredients are beaten together and extra baking powder aids rising.

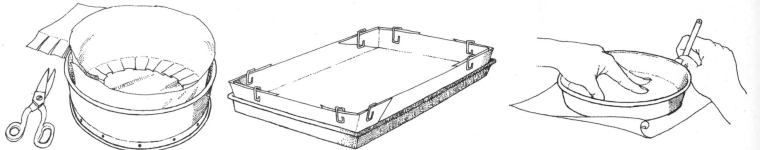

preparing pans

For many cakes, after greasing the bottom is lined with parchment paper – use the pan as a guide when cutting. Deeper pans used for cakes with long cooking times require a parchment lining for the sides: cut long strip 2 inches higher than the depth, fold one long edge in 1 inch then make cuts at intervals. Place cut edge down in greased pan, then grease paper. To protect rich fruit cakes from drying out, tie strips of brown paper around outside of pan and stand pan on a newspaper covered cookie sheet. Line greased jelly roll pans with a parchment case made with one sheet of paper; make 45° angle slits into corners, fold edges in 1 inch, then raise to make a 90° angle at corners. Secure with paper clips.

rubbing in

Technique of mixing fat into flour, working lightly with the fingertips, to achieve a breadcrumb-like texture, as in pastry.

sinking

Sometimes a cake sinks in the middle as it cools and the texture becomes dense, with a sunken appearance and heavy consistency. This can be because of an excess of liquid or leavening agents, or because the oven was too cool. Turning the cake upside down and coating the underside will disguise its appearance. Alternatively, fill the hollow in the top with fruit or cream. Cakes rise in the center (peak) if the oven's too hot.

sticking

Until a cake has cooked right through, the mixture sticks to the sides of the pan (see doneness). Those most likely to stick have a high proportion of sugar and egg whites.

storage

Only fruit cakes improve with age, but most will stay fresh if stored with care. Fatless sponges, though, should be eaten the day they are made, or frozen. Plain cakes should be placed in an airtight container to prevent drying out. Cream-filled cakes should be stored in the refrigerator. Wrap rich fruit cakes in foil immediately after cooling and leave up to six weeks to mature; if spirits are added, storage life is longer.

texture

The "feel" and appearance of a cake, which varies according to air, moisture and fat content: sponge-type cakes are light, and fluffy, those with molasses moist and sticky. If a melted cake is close textured, the mixture was beaten for too long; if dry, it's short of liquid or cooked in too hot an oven. A cookie texture in a sponge was caused by too little beating of eggs, not folding the flour in lightly enough, or the oven was too hot. A heavy-textured creamed cake was possibly caused by insufficient creaming of fat and sugar. A well-baked creamed cake should have a "tender crumb" – it should cut cleanly and leave only a few crumbs on the plate.

unmolding

Still-warm cakes are brittle so need careful handling (see cooling). Moist, high-fat ones should generally be left to cool in their pans. Sponges are unmolded immediately. Peel off lining from all cakes by tearing it down the middle to avoid catching the cake's edges. Where the sides of a pan are unlined, run a palette knife around the edges of the cake before unmolding.

Cakes around the world

American bread torte Crumbly buttery cake made with toasted breadcrumbs, pecans.

baked Alaska American dessert of cake and ice cream surrounded by egg whites baked till meringue browns but ice cream doesn't melt.

bara brith Spicy speckled tea bread from Wales, raised with yeast or buttermilk.

barm brack Traditional Irish fruity cake made with tea.

biscuit de Savoie In fact a plain, fatless whisked sponge from France.

brownies Moist American chocolate cakes with walnuts.

cikolatali pasta Rich Turkish chocolate cake with creamy filling.

devil's food Rich chocolate cake from U.S. **Angel food cake** is white.

diostekercs Hungarian yeast cake eaten at Easter.

dobos torta Rich, caramel topped layered cake from Hungary.

far breton Prune and batter cake from Brittany. Eaten warm.

fat rascals Spicy teacakes from Yorkshire eaten with butter.

génoise Egg-rich but basic sponge cake from France used for many gâteaux. **Petits génoises aux noisettes** are hazelnut flavored.

gugelhupf or **kugelhopf** Austrian yeast cake baked in a fluted tin.

lamingtons Australian specialty – chocolate frosted sponge oblongs covered in coconut.

lardy cake Old English spice cake made with lard, raisins.

Madeira English cake made to be eaten with Madeira wine.

Madeleines Classic small French shell-shaped cakes.

parkin Oatmeal and ginger cake from the north of England.

Sachertorte Famous Austrian gâteau of chocolate sponge lightened with beaten egg whites.

savarin Ring shaped yeast cake from France soaked in syrup.

Schwarzwalder Kirschtorte Germany's famous Black Forest gâteau made with cookies, chocolate sponge, cherries and cream.

simnel cake Rich English fruit cake with almond paste middle.

Stollen Rich, fruity, festive yeast cake from Germany.

Streusel cake Popular European cake topped with buttery crumbs.

ugat dvash Spicy honey cake from Israel.

yogurt tatlisi Turkish yogurt cake soaked in syrup and served warm.

Baking with microwaves

In time and energy saving terms, microwaves have become top kitchen aids, but to use them requires a rethink about how food must look in order to excite the digestive juices. Practice and a spirit of adventure should produce excellent results. Microwave cook books are readily available but with a little experimentation you should be able to adapt your favorite recipes.

The more sophisticated microwave ovens include devices which will brown foods, but less expensive standard models give an end result that looks different from that which we've come to accept via conventional ovens.

Microwaves are not conventional (though they can be combined with the conventional — for the best of both worlds) and they offer extraordinary opportunities for cooking discoveries. First of all, they shouldn't really be called ovens for although they look similar, and indeed cannot begin working till the door is tightly closed, they can boil, bake, steam, stew, roast and broil.

Microwave ovens have different wattages (500, 600 and 700) — the lower the wattage, the longer the cooking time. They can be free-standing (for use on a counter top) or built in (in which case space for ventilation has to be allowed for). Ovens differ from each other in their controls and versatility, and much is dependent on what is called the energy pattern — the way the waves bounce off the metal walls. The more even the pattern of the bounce, the less you have to stir or turn the food during cooking.

The invisible waves ignore everything that isn't metal and concentrate on the moisture, fat and sugar in the food, causing the molecules to move back and forth at more than 2,000 million times a second. It is this which generates heat and cooks the food without the oven itself getting hot.

The waves penetrate the food to a depth of about 2 inches and with dense foods, such as a roast of meat, the heat created in the outer part is conducted to the center. Dishes holding the food get hot and this also helps the cooking. Dishes used in a microwave can be made of anything except metal (including a metal trim) for microwaves cannot pass through and will bounce off. Porous earthenware can be used but as it tends to have a high moisture content, the waves will concentrate on heating that up and fewer will get to the food.

Apart from these two materials though, anything goes in, and the containers can go from oven to the table saving dish washing (scrambled eggs can be cooked in the serving dish). Microwave ovenware is widely available, and improvization is easy for all sorts of shapes and sizes of containers are useful. Teacups, for example, can be used for poaching eggs or to hold cup cakes cooked in paper cases which will need support. And instead of cases you could use unwaxed cardboard drinking cups with the bases cut off. Cardboard (without any wax coating) is great microwave stuff — a Battenburg cake, for example, which conventionally has to be made in separate pans, can be made in one cardboard shape divided down the middle, then the colors cut and arranged in the checkerboard pattern. Paper, too, can be put to good use especially with warming or reheating.

Plastic works well in microwave ovens but choose the thermoplastic for the longer cooking operations (not everything takes only minutes to cook) in which high temperatures will be achieved. Plastic wrap and boil-in bags can be used but they should be punctured so steam can escape — don't use plastic storage bags for the heat of the food will shrivel them. And don't seal up parcels with metal ties, or use metal skewers to truss poultry.

Glass (not crystal containing lead — that's metal in another form) should only be used with quick cooking, and never with anything with a high fat or sugar content for the food's high temperature will crack the glass.

Wood can take short bursts in the oven but in long cooking will lose natural oils and could split or warp.

Aluminum foil is metal and cannot be used to cover or wrap. It can, however, be used to mask poultry wingtips or other thin parts which might overcook. It should not touch the oven interior for it will cause arcing — flashes of blue light reminiscent of *Star Wars*.

Natural fibers, such as cotton (never man-made synthetic ones) make a good wrapping for food being warmed (a very quick process).

If you use conventional methods to brown food which has been cooked by microwaves, the containers should not be ones that will catch fire, crack or melt under a broiler or in a hot oven.

Because microwaves make an excellent ally of a freezer, containers that will go from one to the other and then to the table make a lot of sense.

If ever in doubt about a container, try this test: place 1 cup of water in the oven in the "test" container. Microwave on full power for 15 seconds for plastic, $1\frac{1}{4}$ minutes for non-plastics. If the water in the cup is warm but the test container cool it is suitable. If the water is cold and the test container hot, then it is absorbing the microwave energy and is not suitable.

A cup of coffee or hot chocolate can be put into the oven and is warmed and ready to drink in merely seconds!

Right: a microwave oven to place on counter top and thaw food in only minutes

White bread

Use this recipe to make bread to any shape (braids, loaves, rounds). You can also add $\frac{1}{4}$ cup of wheatgerm to the mixture with the flour or brush top with salted water and sprinkle it on before baking

BREAD   Makes 2 small loaves

Overall timing 3 hours minimum

Equipment 2 bowls, plastic bags, loaf pans

INGREDIENTS

5 cups	Strong bread flour
2 teaspoons	Salt
1 tablespoon	Lard
0.6oz	Compressed yeast *or*
1 pkg	Active dry yeast *and*
1 teaspoon	Sugar
2$\frac{1}{4}$ cups	Warm water

METHOD

1 In a bowl, mix the flour and salt then rub in the lard.

2 In another bowl, blend the compressed yeast with the warm water. If using dry yeast, dissolve the sugar in the warm water and sprinkle the yeast on top. Leave till frothy, about 10 minutes.

3 Add the yeast liquid to the dry mixture and work to a firm dough that leaves the bowl clean, adding a little extra flour if needed.

4 Place the dough on a lightly floured surface and knead by folding the dough towards you, then pushing down and away from you with the palm of your hand. Give the dough a quarter turn and repeat the kneading process. The dough should be kneaded till it feels firm and elastic, not sticky. It will take about 10 minutes.

5 Make dough into a ball and place in a lightly oiled plastic bag.

6 Leave the dough to rise till it doubles in size and springs back when lightly pressed with a floured finger.

7 Place the dough on a lightly floured board, divide into two, then flatten each piece firmly with the knuckles to knock out the bubbles. Knead to make a firm dough.

8 Shape the loaves then place each in a greased 5 × 3 × 2 inch loaf pan. Place inside a lightly oiled plastic bag and put aside till the dough rises just above the tops of the pans — 1–1$\frac{1}{2}$ hours at room temperature. Preheat the oven during this time to 450°.

9 Bake the loaves for 30–40 minutes or until the loaves shrink slightly from the sides of the pans and the crust is deep golden brown. For a crustier loaf, unmold the loaves onto a cookie sheet and bake for a further 5–10 minutes.

Quick cottage loaf

Adding 25mg of vitamin C (ascorbic acid) to the yeast makes it work faster and cuts down the making time. The tablets can be bought at drug and health food stores

BREAD   Makes 1 loaf

Overall timing 1$\frac{1}{2}$ hours

Equipment Bowl, mixing bowl, baking sheet or loaf pan

INGREDIENTS

1.2oz	Compressed yeast
1 cup	Warm water
25mg	Vitamin C
1 tablespoon	Lard
5 cups	Strong bread flour
2 teaspoons	Salt
1 teaspoon	Sugar

METHOD

1 Blend the yeast with the warm water. Crush vitamin tablet and add to the yeast liquid.
2 Rub the lard into the flour, salt and sugar. Add the yeast liquid and mix to a dough that leaves the bowl clean.
3 Place the dough on a lightly floured board or work surface and knead till smooth and elastic.
4 To shape dough into a cottage loaf, divide it into two pieces with one about a third bigger than the other. Shape both into rounds, place smaller one on top. Press handle of wooden spoon through center of both pieces. If preferred, shape dough into rolls.
5 Place on baking sheet and cover with oiled plastic wrap. Leave loaves 40–50 minutes, rolls 25–30 minutes.
6 Brush top with beaten egg or dust with flour. Bake in a preheated 450° oven. Loaves bake for 30–35 minutes, rolls for 15–20 minutes.

Soda bread

Quick to make as no rising time is needed. Use either strong bread flour or half strong white and half wholewheat. If you use buttermilk, reduce the cream of tartar by half

BREAD   Makes 1 loaf

Overall timing 1 hour

Equipment Bowl, baking sheet

INGREDIENTS

4 cups	Strong bread or white and wholewheat flour
1 teaspoon	Salt
2 teaspoons	Baking soda
4 teaspoons	Cream of tartar
2 tablespoons	Fat
1¼ cups	Milk or buttermilk

METHOD

1 Sift the flour, salt, soda and cream of tartar into a bowl.
2 Rub in the fat and add enough milk to make a soft dough. Place the mixture on a floured board or work surface and knead lightly for a minute.
3 Shape into a ball and place on a greased baking sheet. Mark with a cross, cutting almost to the base of the dough.
4 Bake in a preheated 425° oven for 40–50 minutes till well risen, lightly browned and firm underneath.

Below: **1** *Wholewheat loaves, round, rolls and flower pot* **2** *White braid with poppy seeds, small loaf* **3** *Black round* **4** *Soda round* **5** *Rolls with cumin* **6** *Quick cottage loaf* **7** *Milk rolls and shapes*

Curry cookies

INGREDIENTS   Makes 20

1 cup	Flour
½ teaspoon	Baking powder
1 teaspoon	Curry powder
¼ cup	Butter
¼ cup	Grated Parmesan cheese
1	Egg yolk
¼ cup	Milk
¼ teaspoon	Salt
	Cayenne
½ teaspoon	Hot mustard

METHOD
1 Preheat the oven to 425°. Grease cookie sheet. Sift flour, baking powder and curry into bowl. Rub in butter and Parmesan.
2 Beat together egg yolk, milk, salt, a pinch of cayenne and mustard, then stir into flour mixture, with a knife. Knead to smooth dough, then roll out to ¼ inch thickness. Cut rounds with fluted cutter, place on sheet, glaze with beaten egg white. Bake for 10 minutes. Cool on wire rack.

An array of cookies to make: 1 Coconut surprises 2 Curry cookies 3 No-cook acorns 4 Lemon crisps 5 Galettes bretonnes 6 Peanut crunchies 7 Piped and unpiped petits sablés 8 Fruit and nutties

Coconut surprises

INGREDIENTS   Makes 35

4	Egg whites
¾ cup	Sugar
2 cups	Shredded coconut
¼ cup	Self-rising flour

METHOD
1 Preheat the oven to 375°. Grease cookie sheets. Beat egg whites till very stiff. Gradually add sugar, then very carefully, using a figure of eight cutting and folding motion, fold in coconut and flour.
2 Place small spoonfuls of mixture on sheets. Leave at least 1–2 inches space all around each cookie so they can expand without merging and sticking together. Bake for 15–20 minutes. Lift off sheets and cool on wire rack.

Lemon crisps

INGREDIENTS   Makes 50

¾ cup	Softened butter
1 cup	Confectioners sugar
1 teaspoon	Salt
2 teaspoons	Grated lemon rind
3½ cups	Flour

METHOD
1 Grease cookie sheets. Cream butter, sugar, salt and lemon rind in a bowl. Mix in three-quarters of the flour, then place mixture on board and work in rest of flour to make a smooth dough.
2 Shape into roll about 10 inches long and 2 inches in diameter. Wrap in foil and chill for 2 hours.
3 Preheat the oven to 400°. Cut dough into 50 slices. Place on sheets and bake for 10 minutes. Cool on wire rack, then decorate with lemon frosting and sugared lemon slices.

No-cook acorns

INGREDIENTS   Makes 24

1	Egg
1 cup	Ground almonds
½ cup	Confectioners sugar
½ cup	Granulated sugar
¼ cup	Ground rice
1 teaspoon	Lemon juice
	Almond extract
	Green food coloring
¼ cup	Chopped walnuts
	Candied angelica

METHOD
1 Separate egg. Mix almonds, both sugars and ground rice to a firm paste with yolk. Add lemon juice, a few drops of

almond extract and food coloring. Work mixture till evenly colored.

2 Divide mixture into small balls then roll into acorn shapes, forming ridge with spoon handle near blunt end. Lightly beat egg white and dip in acorns up to ridge. Roll firmly in chopped nuts. Add angelica stalks. Chill for 30 minutes.

Galettes bretonnes

INGREDIENTS   Makes 25

1¼ cups	Flour
	Pinch of salt
½ cup	Confectioners sugar
6 tablespoons	Melted butter
1	Egg
1 teaspoon	Vanilla extract

METHOD

1 Preheat the oven to 400°. Grease cookie sheets. Sift flour, salt and sugar into a bowl. Make well in center and pour in butter. Separate egg. Add yolk and vanilla to bowl and quickly mix to dough. Knead into a ball, wrap and chill for 10 minutes.

2 Roll out dough to ¼ inch thickness. Cut into 2 inch rounds and place on sheets. Ridge tops with fork, brush with beaten egg white (not necessary if frosting). Bake for 10 minutes, cool on sheets. Frost and decorate.

Peanut crunchies

INGREDIENTS   Makes 30

6 tablespoons	Margarine
¾ cup	Sugar
1	Egg
1½ cups	Raw peanuts
1 cup	Shredded coconut
1½ cups	Self-rising flour
1 tablespoon	Cocoa

METHOD

1 Preheat the oven to 375°. Grease cookie sheets. Cream margarine and sugar till light and fluffy, add egg and beat. Stir in peanuts, coconut, flour and cocoa to stiff mixture.

2 Roll into 30 balls and place on cookie sheets. Leave spreading space. Bake for 15 minutes. Cool on wire rack.

Fruit and nutties

INGREDIENTS   Makes 36

½ cup	Margarine
1 cup	Brown sugar
1	Egg
1½ cups	Self-rising flour
½ teaspoon	Vanilla extract
¾ cup	Chopped nuts
1 cup	Glacé cherries

METHOD

Preheat the oven to 375°. Grease cookie sheets. Combine ingredients as Peanut Crunchies, saving half the cherries for decoration. Form mixture into 2 rolls 6 inches long. Cut each into 18 slices, bake for 15 minutes.

Petits sablés

INGREDIENTS   Makes 25

1¼ cups	Flour
¼ teaspoon	Salt
¾ cup	Confectioners sugar
6 tablespoons	Softened butter
2–3	Egg yolks

METHOD

1 Preheat the oven to 375°. Grease cookie sheets. Sift flour, salt and sugar into a bowl. Work in butter with a fork to breadcrumb-like texture.

2 If not piping mixture, mix in 2 egg yolks, then form dough into a ball. Wrap and chill for 1 hour (freeze at this stage, if liked). Roll out dough to ¼ inch thickness. Cut out rounds, prick tops, place on cookie sheets.

3 If piping mixture, mix in 3 yolks. Place mixture in pastry bag with large tube and form high rosettes on sheets (flash freeze now, if liked). Bake both cookies for 10–12 minutes (more if frozen). Cool on cookie sheets.

Walnut and orange cake

This is made by the creaming method (all in one cakes are an extension of this). The texture is fine and close — the method is also used to make pound cakes, cup cakes and victoria layer cakes

DESSERT

Overall timing 1 hour 50 minutes

Equipment 7 inch round deep cake pan, mixing bowl

Freezing When cold, wrap, label and freeze without frosting in a rigid container. Freezer life: 6 months.
To use: thaw in wrapping for 3 hours

Below: Walnut and orange cake — pound-type cake with fruit and nut flavorings

INGREDIENTS

$\frac{3}{4}$ cup	Margarine
$\frac{3}{4}$ cup	Sugar
3	Eggs
	Grated rind of $\frac{1}{2}$ orange
$\frac{1}{2}$ cup	Chopped walnuts
2 cups	Flour
$1\frac{1}{2}$ teaspoons	Baking powder
	Pinch of salt
$\frac{1}{4}$ cup	Orange juice

METHOD

1 Preheat the oven to 325°. Grease the pan well. Line the bottom with parchment paper and grease again.
2 Beat the margarine in a bowl till light. Gradually add the sugar and continue beating till pale and fluffy.
3 Add the beaten egg, a little at a time, beating well after each addition. Add walnuts and grated orange rind. Sift and fold in the flour, baking powder and salt, alternating with the orange juice. When the mixture is smooth and will flick easily from a spoon put into the pan and smooth top with a spatula. Bake for $1\frac{1}{4}$–$1\frac{1}{2}$ hours, or until a skewer inserted in the cake comes out clean.

Margarine and sugar are beaten till pale and fluffy, then beaten eggs are added

Sifted flour, orange juice and walnuts are folded in carefully with a metal spoon

Spoon the creamy mixture into a deep pan that's been well greased and bottom-lined

Smooth the top with a spatula before baking so the cake will cook evenly on top

Dobos cake

A Hungarian confection which combines soft golden sponges with chocolate butter cream and a thin topping of caramel. The caramel is spread on and left to set so that it provides a crunchy contrast — mark it into portions while soft to make the cutting and serving easier

DESSERT   Serves 8

Overall timing 1¼ hours

Equipment 2 bowls, 4 8-inch layer cake pans (or use 2 twice), double boiler, small saucepan

Freezing Prepare the cake to the end of Step 7. Pack in rigid container, cover, label and freeze. Freezer life: 2–3 months. To use: thaw at room temperature, then complete Step 8

INGREDIENTS

4	Eggs
½ cup	Sugar
1 cup	Flour
1	Sachet of vanilla sugar
¼ cup	Lemon juice
½ teaspoon	Grated lemon rind
2 teaspoons	Water
2 tablespoons	Melted butter
	Chocolate cream
⅔ cup	Softened butter
1¼ cups	Confectioners sugar
3	Egg yolks
4 squares	Semisweet chocolate
¼ cup	Water
	Caramel
⅓ cup	Sugar
3 tablespoons	Water

METHOD

1 Preheat the oven to 375°. Grease the cake pans.
2 Separate eggs. Put the whites in a large bowl and beat till mixture forms soft peaks that turn downwards. Add the egg yolks and beat in. Add the sugar to the egg mixture and continue to beat until the mixture is thick and creamy.
3 Sift the flour and vanilla sugar over the beaten mixture and fold in gently until thoroughly mixed. Add half the lemon juice, the lemon rind, water and butter and fold in.
4 Pour a quarter of the mixture into each of the cake pans. Gently spread out to the edges.
5 Bake for 7–10 minutes, until the cakes are pale golden but still soft. Gently lift them on to a wire rack or a wooden board to keep them flat and cool.
6 To make the chocolate cream, beat together the butter, sugar and egg yolks. In a double boiler or a bowl over a pan of water, melt the chocolate with the water, then beat into the butter cream.
7 Reserve the piece of cake with the best surface for the top. Spread chocolate cream evenly on the remaining 3 cakes, then stack them on top of each other. Place reserved cake on top.
8 To make the caramel, stir the sugar and water in a small saucepan until sugar melts. Heat until it turns golden. Stir in the remaining lemon juice and remove from heat. Pour it over the cake, spreading it evenly with a knife brushed with oil. Mark caramel topping into 8 portions to make cutting easier when set, then leave for 30 minutes before cutting and serving.

Below: Gingerbread — moist and rich cake

Gingerbread

The melting method used here gives the classic moist gingerbread texture

ANYTIME   Cuts into 9 squares

Overall timing 1¼ hours

Equipment Bowl, saucepan, 7 inch square pan *or* 8 inch round pan

Freezing When cold, wrap, label and freeze. Freezer life: 6 months. To use: thaw in wrapping for about 2 hours

INGREDIENTS

2 cups	Flour
1 teaspoon	Baking soda
1½ teaspoons	Ground ginger
3 tablespoons	Molasses
⅓ cup	Corn syrup
6 tablespoons	Margarine
⅓ cup	Brown sugar
2	Eggs
2 tablespoons	Milk

METHOD

1 Preheat the oven to 325°. Sift flour, soda and ginger into bowl.
2 Place molasses and corn syrup in saucepan with margarine and brown sugar. Heat till melted.
3 Beat eggs and milk. Pour melted ingredients, then beaten eggs into dry ingredients. Mix to thick batter, pour into greased pan bottom-lined with parchment. Bake for 1 hour.

Chicken with grapes in pastry

Chicken is boned to provide a meaty casing for the bacon, veal and pork sausagemeat filling made extra moist with seedless purple grapes. After it is sewn up, the chicken is wrapped in thinly rolled pastry and baked

MAIN DISH Serves 6

Overall timing 2 hours plus boning

Equipment 3 bowls, trussing needle, fine string, baking sheet

Freezing Not recommended

INGREDIENTS

	Pastry
4 cups	Flour
	Salt
½ cup	Butter
½ cup	Lard
	Other ingredients
1 cup	Soft breadcrumbs
6 tablespoons	Milk
¼ lb	Bacon
½ lb	Ground veal
¼ lb	Pork sausagemeat
	Salt
	Freshly-ground black pepper
½ lb	Seedless purple grapes
3½ lb	Roaster chicken
2	Eggs

METHOD

1 To make pastry, sift flour and salt into a bowl; rub in fats till mixture resembles fine breadcrumbs. Stir in enough cold water to make a soft but not sticky dough. Knead lightly till smooth; foil-wrap and chill for 30 minutes.

2 Meanwhile, soak breadcrumbs in milk for 10 minutes. Finely chop the bacon and put into a bowl with the ground veal and sausagemeat. Add plenty of seasoning and mix well. Wash and dry the grapes. Remove any trussing strings from the chicken.

3 Bone the chicken (see page 121, or ask the butcher to do this for you). Spread boned chicken out on a board with skin side down. Pull leg and wing flesh through to the inside, remove any sinews.

4 Squeeze breadcrumbs and mix into the meats with one of the eggs. Stir in the grapes. Spread stuffing along center of chicken and fold chicken around it to make a neat, compact shape entirely enclosed by the skin.

5 Using a trussing needle and fine string, sew up the chicken. Preheat the oven to 400°. Beat remaining egg lightly in a bowl.

6 Roll out dough to rectangle large enough to enclose chicken. Place chicken, sewn side up, on dough and fold ends in and sides over. Brush edges with beaten egg and press to seal. Turn chicken over and place seam down on a greased baking sheet. Brush beaten egg all over.

7 Bake for 1¼ hours, covering lightly with foil once the pastry has browned. Push a thin skewer into the center of the chicken to check that juices run clear. If they don't, cook for further 15 minutes.

8 Transfer carefully to a serving dish. Serve hot or cold, cut into thick slices, accompanied by mixed vegetables or a selection of salads.

VARIATION

Plump 1½ cups large golden raisins in white wine, then drain and use in filling instead of grapes. Add ½ cup finely chopped pine nuts as well.

After boning the chicken, pull leg and wing flesh through to inside and trim away any sinews. Spread stuffing along the center

Fold chicken around stuffing to make neat, compact shape. Wrap in pastry and use beaten egg to seal joins and to glaze

Below: Chicken with grapes in pastry. Tender meat, succulent filling and a crisp coat add up to a splendidly different meal

Puff pastry

Butter is the vital ingredient for the light layers of crispness used to hold sweet and savory fillings

PASTRY

Overall timing 3¾ hours including chilling time

Equipment Waxed paper, rolling pin

Freezing Wrap in freezer wrap or foil, label and freeze. Freezer life: 3 months. To use: thaw for about 8 hours in refrigerator

INGREDIENTS

2¼ cups	Flour
	Salt
½ cup	Softened butter
¾ cup	Chilled water
½ cup	Hard butter

METHOD

1 Place flour, salt and half the softened butter, cut into pieces, on clean work surface. Work the ingredients with your fingers till mixture is like crumbs.
2 Make a well in center of crumbs and add rest of softened butter. Pour in water and mix quickly to a dough. Cover and chill for 1 hour.
3 At the end of this period, place hard butter between 2 sheets of waxed paper. Roll out to a rectangle about 5 × 3 inches.
4 On a lightly floured surface, roll out dough to a rectangular shape about 10 × 8 inches. Remove waxed paper and place butter in the middle of the dough. Fold in the top and bottom thirds of the dough to enclose butter in a parcel.
5 Give the dough a half turn so that side seam is on your left. Roll out to a rectangle about 5 × 14 inches. Fold in top and bottom thirds of dough as before. Wrap and chill for 15 minutes.
6 Repeat rolling, turning and folding 4 more times, chilling between rolling.
7 Roll out dough to rectangle for a last time. Bring the 2 small sides to the center, then fold in half like a book. Cover and chill for 1 hour.

TO USE

After final chilling, roll out dough to ¼ inch thickness then cut out as required. Glaze with beaten egg or milk for savory dishes. Puff pastry should be cooked in a preheated 450° oven for about 15 minutes.

Filet de boeuf en croûte

A splendid dish which uses the best of ingredients — tender melt-in-the-mouth beef and pastry. Follow each step scrupulously for perfect results

MAIN DISH   Serves 6

Overall timing 1½ hours plus cooling and chilling

Equipment Fine string, roasting pan, baking sheet, bowl

Freezing Not recommended

INGREDIENTS

2¼ cups	Home-made puff pastry or
1lb	Package frozen puff pastry
3lb	Beef tenderloin
1	Garlic clove
2 tablespoons	Softened butter
	Salt
	Freshly-ground black pepper
1 tablespoon	Chopped fresh thyme or
1 teaspoon	Dried thyme
½ cup	Smooth liver pâté
1	Egg

METHOD

1 Preheat the oven to 425°. Thaw pastry dough if not using home-made.
2 Trim the meat of all fat and then tie into a neat shape with fine string. Make tiny slits in the beef with the tip of a sharp knife and insert slivers of peeled garlic. Spread the butter over the beef, season and sprinkle with half the thyme. Place in roasting pan and roast for 10 minutes.
3 Take the meat out of the pan, place on a wire rack and leave to cool completely. Remove the string from the meat. Roll out the dough to a large rectangle just over twice the size of the meat.
4 Place the meat on one half of the dough and brush the dough edges with water. Spread the pâté over the top of the beef, and sprinkle with remaining thyme. Fold dough over to enclose beef, and seal edges. Trim around 3 sides of dough and, if liked, make a hole in the top. Place on dampened baking sheet.
5 Cut decorative shapes out of the dough trimmings, dip them into the beaten egg and arrange on the dough. Glaze all over with the egg and chill for 1 hour. Make a funnel from foil and place in top of parcel if liked.
6 Preheat the oven to 425°.
7 Bake pastry-covered meat for 35 minutes till well risen and golden. Place on a warmed serving dish, garnish with watercress and serve, cut into thick slices.

Pâté de campagne

A rich, glazed country pâté — pork, bacon and chicken are flavored with brandy, allspice, nuts and truffle

APPETIZER OR LUNCH   Serves 8–10

Overall timing 3½ hours plus marination and overnight chilling

Equipment Grinder or food processor, bowls, terrine with lid, roasting pan, saucepan, foil

Freezing Make to end of Step 7, remove from terrine and discard fat. Wrap in double thickness of foil, label and freeze. Freezer life: 1 month. To use: remove wrappings, replace pâté in terrine and thaw overnight in refrigerator. Glaze with gelatin mixture and leave to set before serving

INGREDIENTS

1 lb	Fresh pork sides
1 lb	Lean pork
¼ lb	Bacon slices
2 tablespoons	Brandy
	Salt
	Freshly-ground black pepper
¼ teaspoon	Ground allspice
1 lb	Chicken breasts
1	Boneless pork chop
	Thin slices of fresh pork fat
2	Eggs
2	Slices of black truffle (optional)
2 tablespoons	Chopped pistachios (optional)
1	Bay leaf
	Luting paste (see page 149)
1 teaspoon	Unflavored gelatin
⅔ cup	Light stock or broth

METHOD

1 Wipe and trim pork sides, removing any bones. Cut into small pieces. Cut 4 thick strips from the lean pork and reserve. Cut the rest into small pieces. Dice the bacon.
2 Grind the pork and bacon pieces into a large bowl. Add the brandy, salt, pepper and allspice. Mix well and leave to marinate for 2 hours, stirring occasionally.
3 Meanwhile, wipe and bone the chicken breasts, discarding the skin, and cut into thick strips. Wipe the pork chop and cut into strips. Cut a little of the pork fat into strips and reserve. Use the rest to line the terrine, leaving enough overhanging to cover the pâté.
4 Preheat the oven to 375°. Add the eggs to the ground meat and mix well. Spread half the mixture in the terrine, pressing it down well. Arrange the strips of pork, chicken and fat on top and sprinkle with the sliced truffle and pistachios, if using.
5 Spread the remaining ground meat over, smooth the top and place the bay leaf in the center. Fold the overhanging fat over the top to enclose the meat.
6 Cover with the lid, sealing it with luting paste according to the instructions on page 149. Stand the terrine in a roasting pan containing 1 inch hot water and bake for 2 hours.
7 Remove luting paste. Pour the liquid from the terrine into a bowl and reserve. Leave the pâté to cool.
8 Lift the pâté out of the terrine. Remove and discard the fat. Wash the terrine and replace the pâté. Dissolve the gelatin in the stock, then stir in the liquid from the terrine.

Below: Pâté de campagne — tasty pâté that takes time to make but is well worth it. Serve with crusty bread and gherkins

9 Pour over the pâté, cover with foil and place weights on top. Chill overnight. Serve, cut into slices, from the terrine with crusty bread and gherkins or sliced dill pickles.

Grind pork and bacon pieces, then marinate in brandy, salt, pepper and allspice for 2 hours. Add eggs and mix well

Line terrine with pork fat and spread half the ground mixture in. Press down well. Arrange the pork and chicken strips on top

Sprinkle chicken and pork strips with sliced truffle and pistachios (if used). Spread the remaining ground meat over and add bay leaf

Fold overhanging fat to enclose meat. Cover, seal and bake for 2 hours. Pour out liquid, cool pâté and discard fat. Glaze with stock and gelatin, cover, add weights and chill

Olive and caper pizza

In this Italian pizza, the light crisp texture of the potato-based dough contrasts well with the piquant topping of olives, tomatoes and capers

LUNCH OR SUPPER   Serves 4

Overall timing 1 hour 40 minutes

Equipment Saucepan, bowl, 9 inch pizza pan

Freezing Not recommended

INGREDIENTS

2	Potatoes
	Salt
2 cups	Self-rising flour
¼ cup	Butter
¾ cup	Tomatoes
4	Anchovy fillets
1 tablespoon	Capers
¼–½ cup	Ripe olives
¼ cup	Milk
	Freshly-ground black pepper
2 teaspoons	Dried oregano
1 tablespoon	Olive oil

METHOD

1 Peel potatoes and cut into small chunks. Cook in salted water till tender.
2 Meanwhile, put the flour into a bowl and rub in the butter till the mixture resembles fine breadcrumbs. Blanch, peel and chop tomatoes. Desalt and chop anchovy fillets. Drain capers. Pit olives.
3 Preheat the oven to 425°. Grease pizza pan.
4 Drain potatoes and mash well. Stir into rubbed-in mixture. Add milk and mix to form a soft dough. Knead lightly till smooth.
5 Roll out dough and use to line pan. Arrange tomatoes, anchovies, capers and olives on top. Sprinkle with salt, pepper and oregano.
6 Sprinkle olive oil over and bake for about 55 minutes till well risen and golden. Cut into wedges to serve.

Pizza succulenta

From Italy, a pizza using the favorite soft cheese Mozzarella which melts without flowing

LUNCH OR SUPPER   Serves 6

Overall timing 1 hour 10 minutes

Equipment 2 bowls, saucepan, 11 inch pizza pan

Freezing Cool pizza and flash freeze, then wrap in foil, seal and label. Freezer life: 3 months. To use: unwrap, brush with oil and reheat in 400° oven for 30–40 minutes

INGREDIENTS

1¼ cups	Strong bread flour
½ teaspoon	Salt
1½ teaspoons	Active dry yeast
½ teaspoon	Sugar
½ cup	Warm water
1 tablespoon	Brandy
3 tablespoons	Oil
¼ lb	Mushrooms
1	Garlic clove
16oz	Can of tomatoes
1 teaspoon	Dried oregano
	Salt
	Black pepper
¼ lb	Cooked ham
6oz	Mozzarella cheese
	Small can of anchovy fillets

METHOD

1 To make the base, put the flour and salt into a large bowl and leave in a warm place. Place yeast in a small bowl and add the sugar and warm water. Cover and leave in a warm place for about 10 minutes or until frothy.
2 Make a well in the flour, add the yeast mixture and brandy and mix to a soft dough. Cover with a damp cloth and leave in warm place for 30 minutes.
3 To make topping, heat 2 tablespoons of the oil in a saucepan. Wipe and slice mushrooms and fry gently for 3 minutes. Add peeled and crushed garlic, drained tomatoes and oregano and season well. Preheat the oven to 475°.
4 Knead the dough gently on a floured surface, roll out and line greased pizza pan. Cover with tomato mixture.
5 Finely chop the ham and scatter over. Arrange sliced cheese, then drained anchovies on top. Sprinkle with remaining oil and bake for 30 minutes. Serve immediately with a green salad in a lemony vinaigrette dressing.

Cheese soufflé

The attractive garnish is achieved with cheeses – Gruyère or processed – which hold their shape because they are very slow to melt in heat

LIGHT LUNCH OR SUPPER   Serves 4

Overall timing 45 minutes

Equipment Saucepan, 1½ quart soufflé dish

Freezing Not recommended

INGREDIENTS

	Sauce
2 tablespoons	Butter
¼ cup	Flour
1½ cups	Milk
	Salt and pepper
	Grated nutmeg
	Other ingredients
4	Eggs
	Salt
	Squeeze of lemon juice
¼ lb	Gruyère cheese

METHOD

1 To make the sauce, gently melt butter in a pan. Remove from heat, stir in flour, then gradually blend in the milk. Return to heat and bring to a boil, stirring continuously. Season with salt, pepper and a pinch of nutmeg and cook for 2–3 minutes until thick and smooth, stirring all the time. Remove from heat.
2 Preheat the oven to 400°. Grease the soufflé dish.
3 Separate eggs. Beat whites with a pinch of salt and lemon juice to a very stiff, meringue-like texture.
4 Slice a little of the cheese, cut out 7 diamond shapes for the garnish and set aside. Shred remaining cheese, stir into sauce with egg yolks, then carefully fold in a little of the beaten whites to lighten. Fold remaining whites carefully into yolk mixture.
5 Pour mixture into soufflé dish. Run a knife blade around the sides of the dish and arrange cheese shapes on top like the petals of a flower. Bake for 20–25 minutes. Serve immediately.

VARIATION

You can use Cheddar cheese instead of Gruyère in this recipe, but you will also need 2 slices of processed cheese to make the diamond shapes for garnish – a garnish made from Cheddar would sink into the soufflé as it cooked.

Above: Cheese soufflé – a choice of cheeses to make the petal-shaped topping

Beat together egg whites, lemon juice

Combine sauce, egg yolks, shredded cheese

Lighten yolk mixture with beaten whites

Fill soufflé dish with combined mixture

cook's know-how

Processed cheese is produced by melting, pasteurizing, flavoring and repacking ripe and unripe Cheddar-type cheese. It is particularly good for cooking as the fat does not readily melt away on heating and there's less chance of overcooking it.

Run knife around edge of dish, then garnish

Cheesey baked potatoes

These potatoes retain two different textures — the flesh left in them stays firm, the scooped-out centers beaten with cheese, butter and milk and then replaced, become smooth and savory as the cheese melts, contrasting well with the texture of the skin. Ground paprika adds a final splash of color

VEGETABLE   Serves 6

Overall timing   2 hours

Equipment   6 metal skewers, baking sheet, 2 bowls

Freezing   Not recommended

INGREDIENTS

6 × ½lb	Potatoes
6 tablespoons	Melted butter
	Salt
	Freshly-ground black pepper
⅓ cup	Cottage or cream cheese
5 tablespoons	Milk
2 teaspoons	Paprika

Below: Cheesey baked potatoes — with a fluffy cheese filling cooked till golden

Cut cross in baked potatoes, fold skin back carefully, scoop out flesh into bowl

Spoon butter, cheese and milk mixture into shells, top with mashed potato mixture

Sprinkle liberally with paprika, return to baking sheet. Bake for further 15 minutes

METHOD

1 Preheat the oven to 400°.
2 Scrub and dry the potatoes and push a metal skewer lengthwise through each one. Brush potatoes with a little melted butter and place on a baking sheet. Bake for 1–1¼ hours till tender.
3 Take the potatoes out of the oven, remove skewers and cut a cross in the top of each. Lift the center of each cross and scoop out some of the flesh. Put the flesh into a bowl and mash with a fork. Add half the remaining melted butter and mix thoroughly. Season well.
4 Mix the cheese, milk and rest of the butter in a bowl and beat till creamy. Spoon into the potatoes and cover with the mashed potato mixture. Sprinkle with paprika and salt.
5 Replace the potatoes on the baking sheet and bake for about 15 minutes till the topping is golden. Arrange on a serving dish and serve immediately.

freezing know-how

Leftover plain baked potatoes can be frozen, although with the reheating time it is not worth baking them specially for freezing. Cut the potatoes in half lengthwise and scoop out the flesh. Mash it with a little butter and seasoning (finely-grated cheese can be added if liked) and pile it back into the shells, packing it in firmly. Wrap closely in foil, seal, label and freeze for up to 3 months. Place the foil-wrapped potatoes in half lengthwise and potatoes on a baking sheet and reheat in a preheated 400° oven for about 30 minutes (or while another dish is cooking). Unwrap the potatoes, place on the sheet and bake for a further 10–15 minutes till browned.

Choose 12 large apricots, wash and dry them and carefully remove the pits

Chop almonds, macaroons and candied peel, mix into custard and add cinnamon

After apricots have cooked for 30 minutes, spoon red currant syrup over them.

Baked apricots

A simple but delicious way of serving apricots when they are in season. As they freeze well, you can store them away for a mid-winter treat. You'll get an equally appetizing result if you use peaches, pears or nectarines instead of the apricots

DESSERT   Serves 6–8

Overall timing 1 hour

Equipment 2 small saucepans, baking sheet or shallow baking dish

Freezing Prepare to end of Method, Step 5. Cool, flash freeze, then pack in a rigid container, seal and label. Freezer life: 3 months. To use: remove from container and place on baking sheet. Heat in 400° oven for 15 minutes, then carry out Step 6

Above: Baked apricots – a creamy, nutty filling and a red currant and Kirsch sauce

INGREDIENTS

12	Large apricots
1¼ cups	Milk
2 tablespoons	Imported Bird's English dessert mix
1 tablespoon	Sugar
1 cup	Blanched almonds
5oz	Macaroons
¼ cup	Candied orange peel
	Pinch of ground cinnamon
6 tablespoons	Red currant jelly
¼ cup	Kirsch (optional)
¼ cup	Water

METHOD

1 Preheat the oven to 400°. Wash, dry and halve apricots. Remove the pits.
2 Prepare the custard according to package instructions, using the milk, dessert mix powder and sugar. Cool quickly by standing the pan in cold water. Stir the custard frequently.
3 Chop almonds, macaroons and candied peel finely, mix into the custard and add cinnamon.
4 Grease a baking sheet or shallow baking dish. Arrange the prepared apricot halves on it.

5 Fill apricot halves with custard mixture. Bake for 30 minutes.
6 Meanwhile, mix together the red currant jelly, Kirsch, if you are using it, and water in a small pan over a low heat. Spoon syrup carefully over the apricots and return to oven for a further 10 minutes.

TO SERVE

Serve hot with whipped cream, or leave to cool, then chill and serve with ice cream or with a bowl of whipped cream.

Baked coffee caramel ring

A variation on the theme of the much appreciated crème caramel. The added coffee and liqueur or brandy gives the custard a slightly darker color and delicious flavor. The custard is baked in a bain-marie to slow down the cooking and prevent bubbles forming in the mixture

The milk is heated till almost boiling, then the black coffee is stirred in well

The milk/coffee is beaten into egg/sugar mixture; placed in caramel-lined mold

After baking and overnight chilling, the set custard and runny caramel is unmolded

DESSERT   Serves 6

Overall timing 2 hours plus cooling and overnight chilling

Equipment 2 saucepans, pastry brush, 1½ quart mold with funnel, bowl

Freezing Not recommended

INGREDIENTS

1 cup	Sugar
⅔ cup	Water
8	Eggs
4 cups	Milk
⅔ cup	Strong black coffee
3 tablespoons	Kahlua or brandy

METHOD

1 Put all but 4 tablespoons of the sugar into a saucepan with the water and stir over a low heat till the sugar dissolves. Wash any sugar crystals on the sides of the pan into the syrup with a pastry brush dipped in cold water.

2 Stop stirring and bring to a boil. Boil steadily till a deep golden brown. Pour into the mold, turning it so the bottom and sides are coated with caramel.

3 Preheat the oven to 325°. Put the eggs and remaining sugar into a large bowl and beat together lightly. Put the milk into a pan and heat till almost boiling, then pour in the coffee and stir well.

4 Pour onto the eggs in a thin stream, beating constantly. Add the Kahlua or brandy, then strain the custard into the caramel-lined mold.

5 Stand the mold in a roasting pan containing 1½ inches hot water. Cover the mold with foil and bake in the oven for about 1¼ hours till custard is set.

6 Remove from the oven and leave to cool completely. Chill overnight.

7 To unmold custard, place mold on the table and put a deepish serving dish over it. Hold the dish and mold together and turn them over. Put the dish on the table and lift off the mold carefully. Serve immediately with whipped cream.

VARIATION

To make individual custards, line each mold with caramel, then divide custard between them. Cover each mold with foil and place in roasting pan with ½ inch hot water. Bake at 350° for 45 minutes till custards are set. Chill overnight, and unmold to serve.

Left: Baked coffee caramel ring — superb tasting dessert to serve with cream

Preserving

There are many advantages to preserving your own food at home: economy, quality, variety and satisfaction, to name but a few. Home preserves are usually cheaper than manufactured varieties and definitely superior in quality. With many people growing their own produce, local markets and the advent of "pick-your-own" farms, it is possible to obtain cheap foods when they are plentiful to make economical preserves for the kitchen cupboard as well as delightful presents. Making your own preserves is also very rewarding and fun for all the family — from gathering the foods, through the preparation and craft of the old cooking skills which produce delectable smells that waft through the house, to the end product of neatly labeled and stacked produce on the shelves.

Months later, when the preserve is finally opened, the delicious aroma, color, texture and flavor bring back all the pride and pleasure of the making.

However, preserved foods will not keep forever. Properly preserved and stored, they will be safe to eat for several years, but gradually the quality of flavor, color and texture deteriorates. For best results use the preserves within a year and then there will be room to store the next season's produce.

Foods deteriorate and decay because of the "breaking down" activity of chemical substances called enzymes naturally present in the foods, and the growth of micro-organisms (yeasts, molds and bacteria) which attack the tissues.

The organisms causing decay need food, warmth and moisture in order to multiply and so the principles of preserving are based on depriving them of these essentials. Heat will destroy the organisms, while cold, dehydration and chemical action will inactivate them. Either one or a combination of these methods is used to preserve foods. Once the organisms have been destroyed, the food must be sealed and stored to prevent further organisms reaching it.

There are many ways of preserving foods: dry storage is a temporary method, which is only suitable for foods that keep well — apples and pears (wrapped individually in newspaper), root vegetables (layered in light sand in a box), onions, shallots and garlic (hung up), nuts (packed in a ventilated container). All should be stored in cool, airy places.

Drying is one of the oldest, simplest and most effective methods of preserving food. All the moisture is removed from the food so that micro-organisms and enzymes cannot live. In hot, dry climates, foods are still dried naturally by the sun and wind, but modern techniques use artificial heat and ventilation. Dried food quickly deteriorates if allowed to become moist again so it must be stored carefully.

All sorts of food can be dried — meat, fish, fruit, vegetables, eggs, milk. However, for home drying the most practical foods to use are fruits, vegetables and herbs. The drying process is also used for some smoked foods and with glacé fruits.

Canning needs sufficient heat to destroy micro-organisms and enzymes. Careful control of the temperature and processing time is essential and containers which completely exclude air are necessary to prevent recontamination after processing.

Refrigeration provides sufficiently low temperatures to preserve food by temporarily retarding the growth of micro-organisms, but it does not inactivate them.

Freezers have a basic temperature of 0° which prevents micro-organisms and enzymes activating; and during storage the temperature must be kept below this.

Edible chemicals in the form of sugar, salt, vinegar and alcohol make foods uninhabitable for micro-organisms if added in sufficient concentrations. Sugar concentrations of 40–50% will prevent growth of bacteria, but 65% is necessary for jams to prevent some years and molds growing during storage.

Salt is used in sufficient quantities to remove moisture from the food by attraction. It may be used dry or in solution as a brine and it is often used as a preliminary stage to pickling vegetables in vinegar, or for foods before smoking.

Vinegar's high acid content acts as a preservative for pickles and chutneys, and also contributes to their flavor.

Alcohol in the form of spirits — being a concentration of sugar — can be used to preserve fruits, and for making liqueurs.

Sulfuring is a cold method of preserving, useful when there are gluts of fruit and time's too short for heat processing. There are two methods of sulfuring. The simplest is to soak cut fruits in a sulfite solution; with this method the fruit may become waterlogged and lose some water-soluble nutrients. The second method dries fruit in a box using the fumes from burning dry sulfur. The burning sulfur produces sulfur dioxide that penetrates the fruit evenly.

Sulfuring preserves the color of drying fruits whose flesh would normally darken when exposed to air (apples, peaches, pears, etc.) and prevents mold in storage.

Once the science of preserving is understood, making delicious preserves is easy and rewarding. Throughout the year, there is always some food that can be usefully and interestingly preserved for eating another day.

Pickling techniques

Although pickles, relishes and chutneys are now traditional preserves in many countries their origin is ancient. Pickling was known in Greek and Roman times and chutneys were developed in India. Pickles and chutneys are great fun to make and not difficult, so it is an ideal starting point for those who have never tried preserving before. All sorts of fruits and vegetables, spices and flavorings can be included to make a wide variety of preserves. They make delicious accompaniments to cold cuts, bread and cheese and can be used to make interesting salads and hors d'oeuvre.

No special equipment is needed except canning jars and a boiling-water-bath canner. Pans made of brass, copper or iron should not be used, as vinegar corrodes these metals. An enameled kettle is the only suitable pan for pickles and relishes. **Pickles** are made from raw or lightly cooked fruit and vegetables preserved in vinegar and salt, sugar and spices. Relishes are a close cousin, the difference being that for pickles the vegetables and/or fruits are left whole or cut to a specified size and for relishes they are chopped.

Vegetables for pickling are first brined (layered with salt or steeped in a salt and water solution) for at least 24 hours. The salt extracts the water from the vegetables, which would otherwise dilute the vinegar and therefore reduce its preservative quality, and it also makes the vegetables crisp.

Fruits are not brined as their acid content is needed for preservation, but are usually lightly cooked before being preserved in sweetened vinegar.

Brining — vegetables must be prepared by being washed, peeled, trimmed and then chopped or sliced as necessary. Pickling, dairy or kosher salt should be used as refined table salt may cloud the pickle.

Wet brining — place the whole or cut up vegetables in a large bowl and pour over a brine solution. Float a plate on top so that the vegetables are completely immersed in the solution. A solution of $\frac{3}{4}$ cup of pickling salt dissolved in 2 cups boiling water and then strained is sufficient to brine 1 pound of vegetables. Skim the scum from the brine every day.

Dry brining is used for vegetables with a high water content such as squash and

Dry brining is done by layering prepared vegetables with salt in a large stone crock

cucumber. Layer the vegetables with salt in a large stone crock and cover. Allow $\frac{1}{2}-\frac{3}{4}$ cup of salt for every pound of vegetables. Brine vegetables for 24 hours, then drain off the salt water, rinse and drain the vegetables well.

Vinegar can be any type: malt, distilled, wine or cider, as long as it has an acetic acid content (the sour element in vinegar) of at least 5%. You can buy special pickling vinegar which has an 8% content. For the best pickles the vinegar should be flavored with spices or herbs — whole spices and whole fresh herbs are recommended as they keep the vinegar clear. Vinegar may be bought already spiced or with herbs, but you can get a better flavor if you make your own (and save yourself money!). Combine 1 cinnamon stick and a bay leaf with 1 tablespoon of each of the following: cloves, mace blades, allspice berries and peppercorns. For the best flavor, place the spices and 1 quart vinegar in a bottle, seal well and leave to steep for 1–2 months, shaking occasionally. Alternatively, place the spices and vinegar in a saucepan, cover and bring to a boil. Remove from heat and leave to steep for 2–3 hours, then strain. For a hot spiced vinegar, add 1 tablespoon hot red pepper flakes and mustard seed. Never use ground spices for these cloud the pickle. To make herb vinegar, half fill a bottle with sprigs of fresh herbs (parsley, thyme, sage, tarragon, rosemary, mint). Fill up the bottle with either white wine vinegar or distilled malt vinegar. Seal and leave to steep in a warm place for at least 2 weeks. Strain before using.

Filling the jars should be done by tightly packing the brined or cooked fruit or vegetables into clean canning jars without squashing or bruising. Drain off any excess water from the bottom of the jar. Pour flavored vinegar over the vegetables or fruit to cover completely. Food that is packed raw into jars will give a crisper pickle as the fruit and vegetables hold their shape better. Food that is partially or fully precooked produces a softer pickle, which can be packed in the jar more closely. Space, called headroom, must be left between the top of the liquid and the lid to allow for expansion or for the liquid bubbling up during processing in the boiling-water-bath. The usual headroom is $\frac{1}{2}$ inch for pickles.

After adding the flavored vinegar, run the blade of a knife down between the food and the side of the jar at several places. This will release any air bubbles that might have been trapped. There is more likelihood of air bubbles if the food has not been cooked, but be sure to check both types of packs – raw and cooked.

With a scalded clean cloth, wipe off all vinegar and food from the rim of the jar –

this could prevent a perfect seal. Place the wet rubber ring in position, then add the metal or glass lid (unless using self-sealing 2-piece screwband metal closures which don't have rubber rings). Old-style mason jars and jars with 3-piece glass closures should have their bands or caps counter turned slightly to allow the jar to vent during processing.

Process in a boiling-water-bath (page 199) to ensure sterilization and a good seal. Raw pack food should start processing in hot but not boiling water to be sure the jars don't crack. Pint jars are usually processed for 10 minutes.

Chutney is a sweet and sour condiment made from a mixture of fruit and/or vegetables, which are cooked to a pulp and preserved with vinegar and sugar with the addition of salt and spices. Many different ingredients can be included to give a wide variety of flavors, from sweet to sour, from hot to mild. Ground or whole spices may be used, although whole spices are usually removed before canning, except for seeds such as mustard. Slightly over-ripe or blemished fruits and vegetables may be used as long as the damaged parts are discarded during preparation.

To make chutney the fruit and vegetables should be washed and peeled or skinned if necessary. Cut into small pieces and place in a large enameled kettle. Add the vinegar, sugar and spices and cook slowly, stirring until the liquid evaporates and the chutney is reduced to a pulp. It should be the consistency of jam, with no

free liquid on the top, and will thicken slightly on cooling. It does not, however, jell like a jam. Long, slow cooking is important to break down the fibers of the vegetables and fruit and to bring out the flavor. It can take from 1–4 hours, although 2 is more usual – it all depends on the size of the kettle and the type of fruits or vegetables used.

Different types of vinegar or sugar give different flavors and colors. Even white sugar will give a darkish colored chutney when cooked for a long time, so if a pale chutney is desired, add the sugar near the end of cooking with some of the vinegar. (This method can also be used for fruit and vegetables with tough skins as the sugar has a hardening effect.)

Pour the hot chutney into sterilized canning jars using a wide-mouth funnel and cover at once while still hot with sterilized 2-piece screwband lids. Turn each jar over for a few moments after it has been capped, then turn upright again. Clean the outside of the jars, label and store in a cool, dry, dark place.

Some mild chutneys may be eaten immediately, but most chutneys improve on maturing for a few months and should keep well if stored properly.

Sauces and catsups are made from the same ingredients as chutneys, but are sieved or processed in a food mill to give a smooth, thinner consistency. Sauces and catsups, unlike chutneys, should be processed in a boiling-water-bath as for pickles and relishes.

Jam-making techniques

Home-made jams, jellies and marmalades are probably the most popular way of preserving fruits. All are preserves of cooked fruit boiled with sugar till they set, but different methods are used to produce a variety of flavors, textures and colors. All require pectin and acid (and in an ideal world, where fruits contained equal amounts of both, there would be no failures) plus the right quantity of sugar.

Pectin is a natural gum-like substance present in varying proportions in the cells of fruit and is drawn out by acid to form a jell when boiled with sugar.

High pectin fruits are: baking apples, gooseberries, citrus fruits, black and red currants, damsons and other firm plums, quinces and cranberries. Pectin stock which can be used to pep up fruit lacking in this essential is made from gooseberries or crab apples.

Medium pectin fruits are: raspberries, loganberries, blackberries, soft plums and apricots.

Low pectin fruits are: strawberries, rhubarb, cherries, pears, peaches, pineapple, melon and grapes.

All fruits contain the sort of pectin needed for jam making when they are underripe. Low pectin fruits can either be combined with others which have a larger amount, or 1 tablespoon lemon juice per pound of fruit can be added.

If doubtful about a fruit's setting quality, test before adding the sugar. Place 1 teaspoon of the boiled juice in a cup, cool, then add 1 tablespoon rubbing alcohol. Swill gently to combine. A jelly-like clot will form if there's plenty of pectin; two or three lumps will mean moderate pectin and lots of little pieces will indicate low pectin. If the content is moderate or low, continue to simmer to concentrate the pectin by evaporation but add 2 tablespoons lemon juice or $\frac{2}{3}$ cup of commercial liquid pectin to 4 pounds of fruit.

Acid, either present in the fruit or added to it, extracts the pectin from the cells and improves flavor and clarity of the jam. It also helps to prevent crystallization of the sugar by breaking it down quickly.

Sugar is vital to the keeping qualities of jams, jellies and marmalades and it should make up 60% of the finished weight. Too much will cause crystallization, too little will give a poor set (and can cause mold to form).

Because of the high acid content in high pectin fruits, extra sugar may be needed to sweeten, but generally 2 cups is added for each pound of fruit. Any kind of sugar may be used, but unless otherwise specified, this should be assumed to be refined white cane or beet sugar. Any froth should be skimmed off with a slotted spoon once or twice during the rolling boil (see also page 48). And before any sugar is added check that fruit skins have completely softened or the sugar will toughen them.

Jell point is the point at which jam will set to the spreading consistency expected and the kettle should be removed from the heat while the tests are made. The *saucer test* is used for jam: put a dollop on a cold saucer and leave to cool slightly. In 3–5 minutes a skin should form which will wrinkle when pressed with a finger (see also page 49). The *sheet test* is best for jellies which reach setting point more quickly: remove a little from the kettle with cold metal spoon. Allow to cool a little, then tilt spoon so that most of the mixture falls back into the kettle: the rest should thicken on the spoon and run together to form a sheet.

Temperature of jelly when done is 8° above boiling point, and jam 9° above (usually 220 or 221°). But the boiling point of water (212° at sea level) may vary with a change in altitude or barometric pressure, so test the boiling point in your kitchen first. If using a thermometer dip it into hot water before putting it into the boiling fruit and don't let it touch the bottom of the pan or you'll get a false reading. After jell point has been reached, leave jam to stand for 5 minutes so the fruit distributes itself evenly. These tests are not necessary when commercial pectin is used. Just follow the package instructions.

Jam Choose your fruits and prepare them. Some can be left whole; pitted fruit can be halved and the pits skimmed off during boiling. Place fruit in kettle and cook gently, stirring occasionally, till soft and pulpy. Soft, juicy fruits need no extra water, whereas harder fruits need added water and a longer cooking time. Add extra acid and pectin at this stage if necessary, then the measured amount of sugar. Stir over a medium heat till sugar is dissolved, then bring to a boil. Increase heat and boil rapidly, taking care not to let it boil over, for 10–15 minutes. Remove pan from heat and begin to test for jell point (unless using commercial pectin). When it has been reached, skim, then ladle into jars.

The jars should be hot and sterilized. Ladle or pour the hot jam into them, leaving $\frac{1}{2}$ inch of headroom. Wipe the rims with a scalded, clean cloth, then cap. Process in a boiling-water-bath (page 199), then complete the seals if necessary. Label and store in a cool, dark, airy place.

Jelly is made in a similar way to jam but the cooked fruit is strained before boiling with the sugar to give a sparkling clear preserve. It takes longer to make than jam and yields fewer jars. Wash the fruit and remove any damaged parts. Leave on stalks, cores, peel, etc. as these will be strained off later and will add to the flavor. Large fruits should be cut into chunks. Cook with water (depending on type of fruit, see jam) till mushy. Scald jelly bag and suspend over bowl. Pour pulp into the bag and leave it to drip through – preferably overnight. Do not squeeze the bag at all for this will cloud the jelly.

Measure the juice, place in kettle and bring to a boil. For every $2\frac{1}{2}$ cups of juice add 2 cups of sugar (or $1\frac{3}{4}$ cups for low pectin fruits). Stir until dissolved, then boil rapidly till jell point is reached. Start testing after 3 minutes if the fruit is a high pectin one. Skim – last traces may be removed with paper towels if necessary or by pouring through damp cheesecloth, but work quickly as the jelly will begin to set. Pour into hot jars, then seal with the lid or melted paraffin wax.

Marmalade is a jam of citrus fruits, made in much the same way as jam, except that the peel is included and as citrus peel takes longer to cook and soften, more water is required. It can vary from a thick, chunky consistency to a clear jelly with or without shreds of peel.

Bitter Seville oranges are the most traditional for marmalade (sweet orange skin gives a cloudy appearance and the pith does not turn as translucent as that of the bitter oranges). Unfortunately, Seville oranges are a winter fruit, but may be frozen or canned for use later in the year. Other citrus fruits may be used – lemons, tangerines, grapefruit, limes – to give a wide variety of interesting marmalades which can be made any time through the year. All citrus fruits are high in pectin and acid. Even the seeds are used, tied in a cheesecloth bag and cooked with the fruit. They are removed before adding the sugar.

There are several different ways of preparing and softening the fruit and each way gives a different consistency and appearance. Choose whichever method is most convenient to you and which type of marmalade you prefer. In general, for 3 pounds fruit, add $3\frac{1}{2}$ quarts of water and 6 pounds (12 cups) sugar to make about 10 pounds of marmalade.

Method 1 gives a thick, chunky marmalade and is the easiest. Wash the fruit, cut in half and squeeze out the juice into a large kettle, reserving the seeds. Slice the peel, without removing the pith, into either thick or thin shreds depending on the type of marmalade desired, then add to the fruit juice along with the seeds tied in a cheesecloth bag. Pour over the measured quantity of water and bring to a boil. Reduce the heat and simmer for 1–2 hours until the peel is very soft and disintegrates when pressed between two spoons. Remove the cheesecloth bag, pressing the juice back into the pan. Add the sugar and proceed as for jam.

Method 2 gives a similar consistency to the previous method, but the fruit is cooked whole, then cut up before adding the sugar (it is a rather messy operation). Wash the fruit, prick all over and place whole in a large kettle. Cover with the water and bring to a boil. Reduce the heat and simmer for $1\frac{1}{2}$–2 hours until the peel is very soft (or cook in a casserole in a coolish oven for 4–5 hours). Remove fruit with a slotted spoon and cut up with a knife and fork, thinly or thickly as desired. Tie the seeds in cheesecloth, return to the liquid and boil for 5 minutes to extract the remaining pectin before removing. Add the sliced fruit with any juice to the boiling liquid, then add the sugar and continue as for jams.

Method 3 is mostly used for the thick-skinned fruits, such as grapefruit, and the pith is removed before canning. Wash the fruit and thinly pare off the colored part with a potato peeler so that the pith is left on the fruit. Cut the peeled rind into shreds. Either cut the fruit in half and squeeze out the juice or cut off the pith and slice or coarsely chop the flesh. Place the shredded rind in a large kettle with the fruit juice or chopped flesh. Tie the seeds and pith in a cheesecloth bag and add to the kettle. Pour in the measured water and bring to a boil. Reduce the heat and simmer for 1–$1\frac{1}{4}$ hours until the rind is very soft. Remove the cheesecloth bag, pressing the juice back into the kettle. Add the sugar and continue as for jams.

Pressure cooking is ideal for saving time and fuel in the usually long process of softening fruit for marmalades. Prepare fruit by any of the methods given and place in the pressure cooker without the trivet and with only half the amount of water stated in the recipe. Bring to High (15lb) pressure and cook for 10–20 minutes depending on the type and preparation of the fruit. Reduce pressure slowly, then remove the lid. Add the sugar and continue as for jams, using the open cooker as a kettle. Many pressure cookers will only make 5 pounds marmalade at once so do check the manufacturer's instructions.

Freezers can be used to store fruit for marmalade so you can make it out of season – prepare it by any of the methods and pack into freezer bags. It can go straight into the kettle from frozen, but as the pectin quality can be reduced in freezing, combine the frozen with up to one-third of fresh fruit (lemons or grapefruit which are available all year round). Freezer life of marmalade fruit is 1 year, but the longer it is frozen the more the pectin quality is reduced.

No-sugar jams, jellies and marmalades can be made for diabetics if a sugar substitute is used. Many are available and all vary in their sweetening power (experiment is the only guide). Add it after the fruit has been softened with or without water (as jam making) plus 1 tablespoon of lemon juice for every pound of fruit. Leave till just warm, measure amount, then stir in 4 teaspoons dissolved unflavored gelatin for each $2\frac{1}{2}$ cups. Bring gently to boiling point, then pour into warmed sterilized jars, cover and seal. The storage life of this type of jam is only 2 months and, once opened, it should be stored in the refrigerator.

Canning techniques

Canning is a traditional way of preserving fruits by heat treatment. Unless you have a pressure canner, home canning of vegetables, meat and fish is not recommended as they do not contain sufficient acid to prevent the growth of bacteria which causes botulism — they require a much higher temperature than is achieved with a boiling-water-bath processing to guarantee sterilization. Fruits, including most tomatoes, however, contain sufficient acid to be safely canned at home. The fruit is heated in canning jars in order to kill all spoilage micro-organisms and enzymes present in it, so that it is sterilized. An airtight seal is made during the processing to prevent further micro-organisms from entering and contaminating the fruit. It is very important to process the jars accurately to preserve the fruit. It may appear complicated at first, but once the rules have been mastered, it is a very simple and rewarding process.

There are several different types of bottles used. Wide-neck canning jars have metal or glass lids separated from the jars by a rubber ring. Bailed jars are secured by a metal spring clip which allows air and steam to escape during processing and keeps the lid in position during cooking to form a vacuum. Others are secured by a metal or plastic screw-band which is screwed on lightly during processing and tightened during cooling to form a vacuum. All jars and lids must be clean with no chips or cracks, while metal lids and rubber rings must only be used once to ensure a perfect seal.

Only best quality fruit should be canned. Wash and prepare fruit according to type and preference, eg, hull soft fruits, trim gooseberries and currants, remove pith and peel from citrus fruits and cut into segments or slices; apples and pears should be peeled, cored and cut into halves, quarters or slices and immersed in acidulated water to prevent browning; pitted fruit can be bottled whole, or halved and pitted. Fruit may also be blanched or soaked in syrup or even stewed or puréed before being packed tightly into jars.

Sterilize the jars, then pack the fruit lightly into them, pressing down gently with a wooden spoon handle, being careful not to bruise the flesh. Water or syrup may be used to fill up the jars, or brine (well salted water) for tomatoes, or soft fruit can be dry-packed with sugar. Syrup produces a better color and flavor but causes the fruit to rise in the bottles. Use 1 cup of sugar to $2\frac{1}{2}$ cups of water, stir gently over low heat until sugar is dissolved, add any flavoring such as orange or lemon, liqueurs, spices, and boil for 1 minute. Pour the liquid over the fruit in the jars, tilting to exclude any air bubbles. Fill the jars one at a time, setting the jar on a tray or newspaper to catch the drips and overflows. Space, called headroom, must be left between the top of the food and/or liquid and the lid to allow for expansion or for the liquid bubbling up during processing.

Run the blade of a knife down between the food and the side of the jar at several places. This will release any air bubbles that might have been trapped. There is more likelihood of air bubbles if the food has not been cooked (raw pack), but be sure to check both raw and hot packs. With a scalded clean cloth, wipe the sealing rim of the jars. Sterilize rubber rings in boiling water before fitting onto the jars, then cover with lids and clips or screwbands (these should be loosened a quarter turn to prevent bursting during processing).

After the jars have been processed, you may have to complete the seals on some types. The modern mason jar with its 2-piece screwband metal closure will seal itself as it cools, and the screwband should never be tightened after processing. (These closures are also called dome, snap, and self-sealing.) However, jars with one-piece zinc caps or 3-piece screwband caps with separate rubber rings have to be screwed till tight after processing. Bailed jars have their seals completed by snapping down the lower bail on the shoulder of the jar after processing.

Let the jars cool overnight, then check the seals to ensure that a vacuum has formed. On modern mason jars, the metal lids of the 2-piece screwband closure will have snapped down, pulled in by the vacuum. Any lids that are not pulled in, but that stay down when pressed, should be given a tougher test. Remove the screwband and carefully lift the jar by its lid (do this over a towel in case the jar drops and breaks or spills its contents). If the lid remains attached, a vacuum has formed. If the lid comes away from the jar, the food must be reprocessed or eaten up as soon as possible. Bailed jars and old-style masons with zinc caps can be tested by tilting them so that the food presses against the closure: if bubbles form and rise through the food, or moisture appears at the sealing point, the seal is not good. Test flat glass lids by gently removing the screwbands and tilting the jar to check for bubbles or moisture seepage. As above, any jars

whose seal is in question should be given the tough test of lifting the jar by the lid. Wash and dry bails and screwbands if they have been removed. Do not replace them because doing so could twist the lid just enough to break the seal. Wipe down the outside of the jars and label clearly. Store in a cool, dry, dark place. To open the jars, remove screwbands, insert a knife between the rubber seal and the jar and prise off the lid — a stream of air bubbles will enter when the seal is broken. If difficult to open, stand jars in hot water for a few minutes.

If you see signs of any of the following before the jar is opened, it is unfit (or even dangerous) to eat: seepage around the seal, mold around the seal or in the contents of the jar, small bubbles in the contents, cloudy liquid, shriveled or spongy-looking food, food very dark or an unnatural color. If when the jar is opened, there is fermentation, mold, a musty or disagreeable smell, or shiny food, the contents is not safe to eat. It must be destroyed so that it cannot be eaten by people or animals. Burn it, if possible. Otherwise, put the food, jar and closures in an enameled kettle, cover with water and add $\frac{1}{4}$ cup strong detergent and a household disinfectant. Bring to a boil and boil for 20 minutes. Remove the jars and closures, then flush everything else down the toilet. Undamaged glass lids and jars may be used again if they are sterilized. Strong-acid foods such as fruit, including most tomato products, and vinegared things such as pickles, can be safely processed in a boiling-water-bath. The canner for this is a large, round, deep kettle made of heavy enameled ware or stainless steel. It has a rack in the bottom on which the jars are placed (this keeps the jars from coming into direct contact with the heat of the kettle as well as allowing the boiling water to circulate during processing).

To prepare the boiling-water-bath, half fill the canner with water, put the rack in place and put over heat on the stove. Also heat a large teakettle of water. While the water is heating, prepare the food for canning. Pack it into sterilized jars and cap the jars. If using a raw pack where the food is cold, the jars must not be placed in boiling water as they could crack, so add cold water to the canner if necessary. Hot pack jars can safely go into boiling water. Arrange the jars in the canner so they do not touch the sides and are about 1 inch apart. Pour enough extra hot water into the canner to bring the level to 2 inches above the tops of the jars. Cover and bring the water to a full rolling boil, then process for the required time (see chart on next page). The water must boil fiercely for the entire processing time, and constantly cover the top of the jars.

The steam-pressure method of processing is done in generally the same way as the boiling-water-bath, except that the processing is done in a pressure canner. Low-acid foods such as vegetables, meat, poultry and fish can be canned at home only by using a pressure canner.

A pressure canner is like a pressure cooker, only larger. It is usually made of cast aluminum, and has a tight-fitting lid that is fastened down with clamps or a twist-groove system. It is fitted with a pressure gauge, open vent and safety valve, and it has a rack in the bottom on which the jars are placed.

The manufacturer's instructions should be followed carefully when using a pressure canner, but in general, here is the procedure to follow: put about $1\frac{1}{2}$ inches warm water in the canner and heat, uncovered. Meanwhile, prepare the food for canning, pack it into sterilized jars and cap. Place the jars in the canner on the rack, not touching, and cover tightly. Continue heating, leaving the vent open to allow all air trapped inside the canner to escape. When the steam has been issuing from the vent for 7–10 minutes, close the vent and bring the pressure up to 10 pounds. As soon as this pressure has been reached, begin timing the processing (see chart on the next page). Do not allow the pressure to fall below the required level; if it does, bring it up to 10 pounds again and start the timing from scratch (the food will not be harmed). At the end of the processing time, remove the canner from the heat and let cool until the pressure drops to zero. Open the vent slowly, then when all steam has stopped coming from the vent, remove the lid. Lift out the jars and complete the seals if necessary. Don't worry if the contents of the jars is still bubbling. An important point to remember about steam-pressure canning is not to leave the canner unattended during processing.

Cover the fruits with boiling liquid, up to the required level — the recipe will specify the headroom to be left

After processing, let cool overnight, then test seal. For really tough test, remove screwband or bail and lift by lid

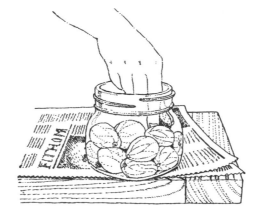

Pack the prepared fruit into the jars so that most of the space is filled but without pressing so hard that fruit bruises

With bailed canning jars, rubber ring is pressed on, lid secured with clamps

Canning times

PROCESSING IN A BOILING-WATER-BATH

FOOD	PREPARATION	PACK	HEADROOM	PROCESSING TIME IN MINUTES Pint jars	Quart jars
apples	peel, core and slice; treat with anti-discoloration solution	hot	$\frac{1}{2}$ inch	15	20
applesauce	chunky or smooth; pack very hot	hot	$\frac{1}{2}$ inch	10	10
apricots	halve and pit; slice if liked	hot	$\frac{1}{2}$ inch	20	25
berries, soft*	clean and hull if necessary	raw	$\frac{1}{2}$ inch	15	20
berries, firm**	bring to boil with $\frac{1}{2}$ cup sugar to each quart of fruit, then remove from heat and let stand 2–4 hours; reheat slowly before packing	hot	$\frac{1}{2}$ inch	15	20
cherries, sweet	pit if liked; prick to prevent bursting; for hot pack, cook with sugar ($\frac{3}{4}$ cup to each quart of fruit)	raw or	$\frac{1}{2}$ inch	20	25
		hot	$\frac{1}{2}$ inch	20	25
figs	cover with boiling water and simmer 5 minutes	hot	$\frac{1}{2}$ inch	85	90
grapes	remove from stems; for hot pack, bring to boil in sugar syrup	raw or	$\frac{1}{2}$ inch	15	20
		hot	$\frac{1}{2}$ inch	15	20
citrus fruit	peel, removing all white pith, then segment	raw	$\frac{1}{2}$ inch	10	10
nuts***	bake in 275° oven until dry but not brown	hot	$\frac{1}{2}$ inch	20	20
peaches	skin, halve and pit; slice if liked	raw or	$\frac{1}{2}$ inch	25	30
		hot	$\frac{1}{2}$ inch	20	25
pears	peel, halve or quarter and core; simmer in sugar syrup for 2 minutes	hot	$\frac{1}{2}$ inch	20	25
pineapple	peel and core; slice, cut into wedges or chop	hot	$\frac{1}{2}$ inch	15	20
plums	prick if canned whole, otherwise halve and pit	raw or	$\frac{1}{2}$ inch	20	25
		hot	$\frac{1}{2}$ inch	20	25
rhubarb	trim and cut into $\frac{1}{2}$ inch pieces; mix with $\frac{1}{2}$ cup sugar to each quart of fruit and let stand 4 hours, then bring to a boil	hot	$\frac{1}{2}$ inch	10	10
strawberries	layer with sugar ($\frac{1}{2}$ cup to each quart of fruit) and let stand 2–4 hours, then simmer 5 minutes	hot	$\frac{1}{2}$ inch	10	15
tomatoes****	peel and leave whole	raw	$\frac{1}{2}$ inch	40	50
	peel and cut up; simmer in own juice for 5 minutes	hot	$\frac{1}{2}$ inch	15	20

*Blackberries, blueberries, boysenberries, gooseberries, loganberries, raspberries.   **Currants.   ***Keep water level in canner well below tops of jars during processing.   ****Add $\frac{1}{4}$ teaspoon fine crystalline citric acid or 1 tablespoon white vinegar to pint jars, and $\frac{1}{2}$ teaspoon citric acid or 2 tablespoons white vinegar to quart jars, before capping and sealing. Cut up tomatoes may be processed in a pressure canner, without added acid. See chart below.

PROCESSING VEGETABLES IN A PRESSURE CANNER

VEGETABLE	PREPARATION	PACK	HEADROOM	PROCESSING TIME IN MINUTES Pint jars	Quart jars
asparagus	remove scales and tough ends; leave whole or cut into 1 inch pieces; for hot pack, blanch for 3 minutes	raw or	$\frac{1}{2}$ inch	25	30
		hot	$\frac{1}{2}$ inch	25	30
beans, green	trim and leave whole or cut up; for hot pack blanch 5 minutes	raw or	$\frac{1}{2}$ inch	20	25
		hot	$\frac{1}{2}$ inch	20	25
beans, lima	shell; for hot pack blanch 1 minute	raw or	$\frac{3}{4}$–1 inch for pints; $1\frac{1}{4}$–$1\frac{1}{2}$ inches for quarts (depending on size of beans)*	40	50
		hot	1 inch	40	50
beets	boil 15–25 minutes till skins slip off; slice or dice	hot	$\frac{1}{2}$ inch	30	35
broccoli	trim and cut into 2 inch pieces; blanch 3 minutes	hot	1 inch	30	35
carrots	peel, then slice, dice, etc.; for hot pack, blanch 10 seconds	raw or	1 inch*	25	30
		hot	$\frac{1}{2}$ inch	25	30
celery	trim and cut into 1 inch pieces; blanch 3 minutes	hot	1 inch	30	35
corn, whole kernel	husk ears and cut off kernels; for hot pack blanch 10 seconds	raw or	1 inch*	55	85
		hot	1 inch*	55	85
greens	wash, tie in cheesecloth and steam 10 minutes till wilted	hot	$\frac{1}{2}$ inch	70	90
onions, white	choose uniform size (1 inch diameter); peel and blanch 5 minutes	hot	$\frac{1}{2}$ inch	25	30
peas, green	shell; for hot pack blanch 10 seconds	raw or	1 inch**	40	40
		hot	1 inch**	40	40
peppers, sweet	core, seed and leave whole or cut up; blanch 3 minutes	hot	1 inch*	35	45
squash, summer	trim and slice; for hot pack blanch 10 seconds	raw or	1 inch*	25	30
		hot	$\frac{1}{2}$ inch	30	40
squash, winter	peel, seed and cut into 1 inch pieces; blanch 10 seconds	hot	$\frac{1}{2}$ inch	55	90
tomatoes	peel and cut up; simmer in own juices 5 minutes	hot	$\frac{1}{2}$ inch	15	20

*Add enough boiling liquid to the jars to come well over the top of the vegetables — usually to $\frac{1}{2}$ inch headroom.
**Add boiling liquid to the jars to come well below the level of the vegetables — to $1\frac{1}{2}$ inches headroom.

NOTE: To blanch, cover the vegetable with boiling water and bring the water back to a boil. Start the timing for blanching when the water reaches boiling point again.

Curing and drying techniques

Curing and drying are both very ancient methods of preserving food by natural elements of sun, wind and smoke. Modern techniques are more sophisticated and salting is sometimes carried out in conjunction with smoking.

Drying is a process by which all the moisture from the food is removed, usually by heat so that micro-organisms cannot grow and enzymes (chemical substances which bring about the deterioration of food) are inactivated. Many types of foods can be dried, but for home drying it is really only practical to dry fruits, vegetables and herbs.

No special equipment is necessary: any warm, well-ventilated place can be used such as a cool oven. Or go outdoors and use the drying power of the sun. Foods need to be in a single layer and have free circulation of air around them – a temperature of 120–150° is ideal.

Fruit should be fresh, ripe and undamaged. Prepare it according to type: peel, core, pit; cut into halves, quarters, rings or slices as desired. Apples and pears and other fruits that brown should be immediately immersed in anti-discoloration solution. Dissolve pure crystalline ascorbic acid in cold water, coat each piece of fruit as it is prepared, then pat dry before drying. Place the prepared fruit in single layers on slatted wooden trays or wire racks lined with cheesecloth and leave in a warm place to dry. The fruit should be warmed to the right temperature slowly to prevent the skin from hardening and drying time will depend on the temperature and type and size of fruit – it could take from a few hours to several days. If using an oven, leave the door ajar for circulation of air and do not allow the temperature to exceed 150°.

When the fruit is completely dry (when pressed between fingers, no moisture will come out), allow to cool before packing into boxes lined with waxed paper. Store in a very dry, cool place.

To reconstitute dried fruit, soak in a bowl of water overnight, then simmer till tender.

Vegetables – the simplest vegetables to dry are legumes, beans, mushrooms, onions and garlic. All are dried by similar methods to fruits, but green vegetables are first blanched to preserve their color. Onions and garlic are braided into strings and hung up to dry. Mushrooms may be sliced or threaded whole on strings or sticks and covered with a cheesecloth sleeve.

Herbs – for the best flavor, pick the herbs just before they reach flowering stage on a warm dry day. Tie them in bundles and hang them upside down in a warm airy place. The sprigs can also be dried in a cool oven.

Smoking was originally used as a means of preservation in conjunction with salting and drying, but is now used more as a way of flavoring food rather than for extending its keeping time. Home smoking is done in a bought or home-made smoke box. There are two basic methods of smoking and with both food may be salted and/or dried before smoking to preserve it longer.

Hot smoking is a method of cooking and flavoring food such as fish, bacon, sausages, hamburgers, steaks etc, and is done in a small smoke box. When put over the heat, smoke builds up inside the box and cooks the food. Most foods take about 20–30 minutes to cook and may be eaten hot or cold. Hot smoked food does not keep any longer than other cooked foods unless it is pre-salted.

Cold smoking is a viable form of preservation as the food is dried and salted before being smoked. Larger equipment is necessary so that large pieces of meat and fish can be hung over the smoke in an enclosed area, allowing smoke to circulate freely around the food without cooking it. The temperature should be 70–90° and the process may take 24 hours.

Freezer techniques

Freezing in the first part of this century was altogether different from today – frozen foods were often transformed out of all recognition by the slow methods used. In the 1920s, the American scientist, Clarence Birdseye, discovered that food needed to be frozen fast to retain its original texture, and invented a way of doing this. Since then, freezing has become the most popular method of food preservation and salting, pickling and canning, which change the flavor, texture and appearance of the food, have taken second place

If food is placed in a freezer in prime condition, frozen, stored and thawed correctly, it should come out in the same condition as it went in, retaining all its original qualities and nutrients. With very few exceptions, this can be said of all foods – and no other method of preservation can claim to have such perfect results.

As a means of preserving food, freezing is nothing new – prehistoric man froze surplus meat by packing it in ice and snow, a primitive but effective method using natural elements. By the middle ages things had become a little more sophisticated. Food was stored underground in ice houses – very deep holes which were insulated and packed with ice. These were reached from nearby dwellings by underground tunnels, and packed with fresh ice every winter so that food could be preserved for the following summer. The system worked well if the summer wasn't too hot! With the industrial revolution in the late 19th century came many new developments in food preservation, canning being the most important. At the same time, the arrival by ship of the first frozen lamb from South America (1878), Australia (1880) and New Zealand (1882) caused quite a stir. From then on, mechanical freezing came to stay: manufacturers rushed to make the latest designs of refrigerators, ice safes and freezing machines, and cook books began to praise such appliances in the late 1890s.

Until the late 1960s freezer-owning families were few and far between: exceptionally large families, or those who produced food for a living, might possibly have owned one but the rest of us managed without. But as domestic freezers became cheaper to buy and were designed to fit into the average home, their advantages became quickly apparent.

For the working wife, being able to buy in quantity once every few months and prepare meals in advance, a freezer means greater freedom for leisure activities. Another advantage of quantity buying, of course, is that with careful planning it is quite possible to save a considerable amount on the family budget. You can take advantage of cheap offers and seasonal gluts to stock your freezer. For instance, buying a wholesale side of beef cuts the cost of the more expensive cuts considerably.

Owning a freezer for most of us is rather like owning a car – it's only when it breaks down that you wish you knew more about the workings. In fact, the running of a freezer is a little less complicated than a car, because correctly installed freezers from reputable manufacturers rarely go wrong.

To freeze food is to change it from being either liquid or pliable to solid, and by so doing to arrest (though not completely stop) the organic processes that would normally cause it to age, deteriorate and eventually rot. To do this, a freezer must have three basic components: an evaporator, compressor and condensor. These are connected by tubing, through which a refrigerant mixture circulates. It is this system of motor units and tubing which transfers the heat from the food inside the cabinet to the outside. The refrigerant passes first through the evaporator, where it is converted into a gas, then it goes into the compressor, at the same time drawing off heat from the food. The compressor forces the gas into the condensor, which in turn converts the gas back into a liquid and the cycle starts all over again. The condensor is the part that actually transfers the heat from the inside of the cabinet to the outside, and there are three different types. The most common is the skin-type condensor, which is between the inner and outer linings of the freezer and transfers the heat through the walls. The other less common types are fan assisted and static plate condensors.

During the freezing process the water

small ice crystals

When freezing is fast, small ice crystals form in an even pattern between the tissues of food so they remain intact

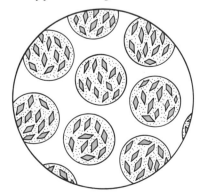

large ice crystals

If the temperature is not low enough and freezing is slow, large uneven crystals break up tissues and damage the food

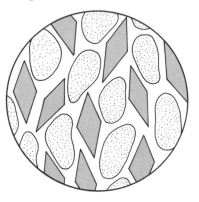

between the tissues in food turns to ice crystals which occupy more space than water and, if too large, will damage the tissues, having an adverse effect on the texture of food when thawed. To keep the ice crystals as small as possible, the freezing process must be as quick as possible, which means the temperature must be lower than the normal 0° required for keeping frozen foods frozen. This temperature, achieved by means of the sharp freeze switch, or quick-freeze shelf, depends on the overall loading capacity of the freezer and the amount of food to be frozen (see fast freezing page 201). It is this ability to freeze fresh food at lower than 0° that distinguishes a freezer from a conservator. A conservator looks almost identical to a freezer, but it must never be confused with it, as it can only store food and can't freeze it.

Ice boxes or freezer sections in refrigerators are like conservators and can store ready-frozen foods for limited periods – these are calculated by frozen food dealers who err on the safe side, so food stored for longer will not be harmful but may have lost color, flavor or texture, or have dried out. Frozen food dealers have quick turnovers and strict rotation of stock, and their freezing and storing conditions are ideal compared with freezing at home.

You and your freezer

To make your freezer work for you, you have to be sure of the role it will play in your life. Freezers work at their best when filled to capacity, and you waste money if you haven't time to keep it full

In the 1960s, all home freezers were the basic box or chest type, modeled on the large cabinets and conservators used by caterers (the "deep freeze" as they were known and are still called by some today). With increase in interest in freezing, demands arose for smaller, compact units that could fit into the average size town house (as opposed to the large farm-houses where freezers were popular) and would blend happily with other kitchen furniture. This resulted in the upright freezer, designed to look like a refrigerator and take up about the same amount of space.

Chest and upright freezers work on exactly the same principle. In economical terms, chest freezers are cheaper than uprights. They are less expensive to buy and give more storage space; they also use less electricity and are therefore cheaper to run (cold air is heavier than warm, so very little cold air is lost when the lid is opened). With an upright freezer, every time you open the door, the cold air literally falls out and warm air from the room enters to replace it, causing a bigger build-up of frost than in a chest freezer. This also activates the motor more frequently and makes it costlier to run. At least in an upright the food is more visible and less time is needed to locate what you're looking for. Equally important in choosing a freezer is its capacity – it is essential to establish

before you buy whether the freezer will store enough for your requirements and thus justify its existence in your home. Conversely, do remember that it is pointless buying too large a freezer and running it half full; this increases the running costs.

As a rough guide, each cubic foot will hold about 20 pounds of food, and 6 cubic feet should be allowed for each member of the family. This is a conservative estimate, however, and more space should be allowed if you grow and freeze your own produce, intend to invest in quantity buys, or entertain frequently on a large scale. Always remember, a freezer should work for you, not the other way around. When choosing a site for your freezer, the surface must be level and strong enough to take the weight of the unit fully loaded. Any damp will not only cause the cabinet to rust but will attack the unseen metal parts underneath. The whole area must be cool and well ventilated or the running of the motor will be affected.

Precautions should include blocking off the freezer plug so it cannot be accidentally disconnected, and investing in a freezer insurance policy to protect contents as well as the unit. Keep the telephone number of the repairman in an easily accessible place – on the freezer door is best – so you can call immediately in an emergency.

chest freezer

When you lift the lid of a freezer filled to capacity, warm air bounces off the cold, still and dense air in the unit. If the storage level is lower, warm air will enter and will activate the motor

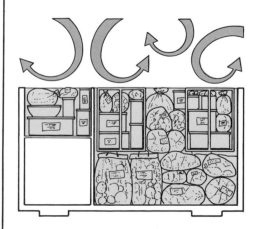

upright freezer

When door is opened, cold air falls out (literally at your feet), warm air rushes in, so close door as quickly as possible. Shelves should be protected by shields

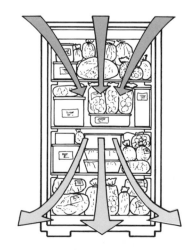

Freezing techniques

air

The exclusion of air from packages is essential before sealing to prevent dehydration, discoloration and freezer burn. Air trapped inside packs containing animal fats causes rancidity; with vegetable fats it causes oxidation. Air also circulates in freezers that aren't packed to capacity and the motor has to work over-time to cool it. Keep the freezer as full as possible to minimize running costs.

batch cooking

To cook a large quantity or "batch" of the same food especially for the freezer, then divide and pack into portions to freeze for future use. There are two ways to batch cook: either cook extra portions when preparing a meal and freeze the surplus, or have special sessions to "feed" the freezer. Ideal foods for batch cooking are cakes, pastry-based dishes, soups, stews.

blanching

The scalding process by which enzyme action is halted in vegetables and some fruits. Enzymes are a natural protein present in food and, unless inactivated by the extreme heat of blanching, will continue to work during freezing and eventually cause loss of ascorbic acid (vitamin C), flavor, color and texture. The initial blanching causes vegetables to lose a small amount of ascorbic acid, but this is counteracted during storage: if blanching was omitted, the loss would eventually be greater – and the longer the storage, the greater the loss. Blanching before freezing simply holds enzymes in a state of suspended animation; once thawing commences, the enzymes spring back to life. All thawed food must there-fore be treated as fresh.

To blanch vegetables: place about $\frac{1}{2}$ pound vegetables in a blanching basket and immerse completely in about 4 quarts of boiling salted/acidulated water. Return to a boil quickly, then calculate blanching time from the moment the water reboils. Plunge basket and vegetables immediately into ice-cold water for the same length of time as boiling to prevent further cooking, then drain thoroughly before packing. The same blanching water can be re-used 6 or 7 times, as this improves vitamin C retention. Some vegetables can be blanched over steam, but this takes longer and is not recommended for leafy green vegetables. Blanching times are on page 210/11.

blast freezing

The very fastest method of freezing and only effectively done by commercial freezers. Butchers will blast freeze fresh meat for you, usually if you buy a whole carcass and it is cut into manageable pieces for cooking.

brick freezing

Not to be confused with pre-forming where shapes are created by freezing, this method saves space and containers because a large amount (of say a stew) can be frozen, then turned out and cut into meal-size blocks with a freezer knife and wrapped in foil for storage. Do the same with bulk buys of frozen food.

bulk buying

To buy large quantities of food for the freezer at reduced prices for bulk. Most common "bulk buys" are fruit and vegetables from farms and markets, animal carcasses from butchers, and special bulk or catering packs from freezer centers and large supermarkets.

chain cooking

Similar to batch cooking in that several dishes are prepared for the freezer at the same time, With chain cooking, the same basic ingredients are used to start the "chain", then divided up and made into a selection of dishes by adding different ingredients to each part.

cooling

Before packaging for the freezer, food must be as cool as possible or moisture in the form of steam will be retained. This, and the warmth of the food, causes large ice crystals to form between the tissues of the food which will damage them. "To cool quickly" means to remove heat from food as fast as possible. The most efficient method is to stand pans and dishes of food in bowls of ice cubes or ice-cold water.

covering

All food must be covered before freezing to protect it from freezer burn and prevent it from drying out. All containers should therefore have sealable lids or covers to prevent moisture escaping and air entering.

dating

Before placing food in the freezer, it should be marked with the date of freezing and, more importantly, the date by which it should be eaten. These dates should then be recorded with the details of the food in a freezer logbook.

Line bottom of freezer with newspaper, put in bowl of hot water, then close door/lid

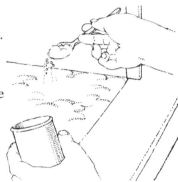

To defrost quickly, sprinkle baking soda over ice

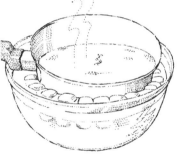

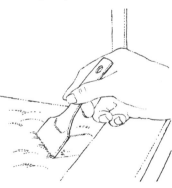

When ice is loose, scrape it off with a plastic spatula

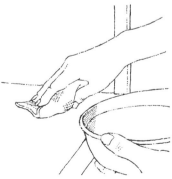

After removing ice and water, clean inside of freezer with mild solution of baking soda and water. Wipe dry

defrosting

This is the removal of frost from the inside of the freezer cabinet. If the frost is allowed to build up indefinitely, the freezer's motor will have to work overtime in order to regulate the temperature. Some freezers have an automatic defrosting device, but most have to be defrosted manually, about once or twice a year if a chest freezer, three or four times if an upright or combination refrigerator/freezer with two doors. Check the build-up of frost from time to time; if more than $\frac{1}{4}$ inch thick, it is time to scrape it off (see distilled water) or to defrost the cabinet. Most freezer owners defrost when stocks are low, and also take the opportunity of cleaning the inside of the cabinet at the same time.

To defrost and clean a freezer:

1 Choose a cold day if possible (evening in warm weather).

2 Unplug the freezer, if instructed to do so.

3 Remove food and baskets/shelves from cabinet, then pack food quickly in insulated bags or wrap in newspapers, blankets or rugs. Keep in a cool place (outside in winter). If convenient, some food can go in the refrigerator or its freezer.

4 Line the bottom of freezer with thick newspapers, then place a bowl of hot water inside the freezer and close the lid or door. Wait until the ice begins to loosen, then scrape off gently with a plastic (not metal) spatula. Remove the ice from the paper as you work. Once all the ice is removed, wash the inside of the freezer with a solution of 2 teaspoons baking soda to $2\frac{1}{2}$ cups of water. Wipe dry. Close lid or door, plug in again and sharp freeze for 30 minutes before replacing food. Keep on sharp freeze for 4–6 hours or until temperature registers 0°.

5 An alternative and quicker method is simply to sprinkle neat baking soda on the ice inside the cabinet. This breaks down the ice; and makes bowls of hot water unnecessary.

discoloration

Discoloration most frequently occurs with fruit, although some vegetables and the flesh of fish also discolor in the freezer. Salt or acid added to blanching water helps prevent vegetable discoloration. Lemon juice keeps the flesh of fish white. Fruits with a low vitamin C content change color and darken more quickly than others; this can be counter-acted by the addition of antioxidants. For syrup packs, add the juice of 1 lemon to 3 cups of water, or $\frac{1}{4}$ teaspoon of crystalline ascorbic acid dissolved in $2\frac{1}{2}$ cups of water. For dry sugar packs, use 1 teaspoon of ascorbic acid to 2 cups of sugar. Exposure to air is the prime cause of discoloration; therefore, fruit should be prepared for freezing as quickly as possible.

distilled water

Keeping the frost down in a freezer gives you this handy by-product which can be used in a steam iron for it has no minerals to dry out as scale. Frost is formed when moisture in the air trapped inside the freezer condenses on the walls (removing it several times a year keeps defrosting down to an annual event). Scrape it off with a plastic spatula into a bowl and leave to melt. Strain before storing.

freezer burn

Spoilage occurs when food is exposed to air in the freezer due to inadequate wrapping or packaging. Freezer burn is a form of dehydration, or the loss of moisture and juices from food; it appears as grayish-white or brown patches on the food surface. Irregularly-shaped parts of meat and poultry are particularly susceptible to freezer burn. Although unsightly, it is not harmful and bad patches can be cut off after thawing if necessary.

headroom

Refers to the space between the surface of food and the lid of a rigid container. It is essential to leave headroom with all liquids, as these expand during freezing and will force off the container lid if packed to the brim. Food then becomes exposed to air and will spoil. Headroom varies according to size and shape of container, but is usually $\frac{3}{4}$–1 inch. Leave more headroom in narrow containers. When freezing stews and casseroles in which chunks of meat and vegetables are likely to float to the surface and suffer freezer burn, roll or crumple waxed paper into small balls, then place on surface of food – this will keep all solids below the surface of the liquid.

ice glazing

An unusual method of freezing whole raw fish and bottles of spirits (usually vodka and schnapps which are tradition-ally served ice cold in tiny glasses). Fish is ice glazed to protect the skin and to prevent air getting to the flesh. Freeze without wrapping until solid, then dip quickly in cold water and refreeze. Repeat this process again

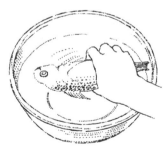

To ice glaze whole fish, freeze, dip in water, refreeze

Repeat dipping and freezing till well glazed, then overwrap

and again until the ice is about $\frac{1}{4}$ inch thick, then overwrap for storing.

To ice glaze spirits, stand bottle upright in a suitably-sized metal container, then fill with water up to the shoulder. Rose petals and leaves can be "set" in the ice to give a decorative look to the finished glaze. Freeze until solid – but do not leave in the freezer for more than 24 hours. Though the freezing temperature of alcohol is lower than that of water, if left for any longer it will start to freeze, will expand and the bottle will shatter. To remove bottle from glazing pan, place it under hot water till you are able to pull the bottle free. The hot water can be used to create attractive channels in the ice. Wrap base in a napkin to serve. This method is not suitable for any other liquids.

Place chosen spirit (vodka or schnapps) in large can and fill with water to shoulder of bottle

Freeze – but not for more than 24 hours. Place under running hot water to remove the can

interleaving

A method of separating pieces, portions and slices of food so that they freeze individually. Place double sheets of freezer wrap between each chop, steak or hamburger, etc, then freeze together in one container or package. When frozen in this way, individual portions can be taken out and the package resealed and stored again.

Stack hamburgers, interleaving each one for easy removal

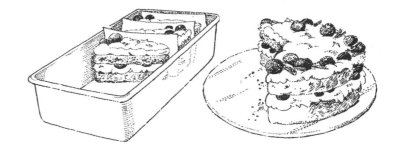

Portions of a large cake can be taken out and eaten as needed if interleaved in a rigid container. Cover, label, freeze

open freezing

Also known as flash freezing. A method of freezing food uncovered on trays to (1) keep individual pieces separate so they do not freeze in a solid mass and (2) keep delicate, decorative and soft-textured foods intact. Line trays/baking sheets with foil or parchment, then spread food (fruit, vegetables, rosettes of whipped cream, etc) on top so they aren't touching. Freeze until solid, then remove from tray and pack in bags. Vegetables and fruits can be open frozen at home to produce "free-flow" packs as sold commercially. Simply shake out the exact amount required. Cakes with decorations of cream or frosting are best packed in a rigid container after open freezing. Always remove them from the container before thawing or the elaborate design could be spoiled.

overwrapping

All foods must be wrapped before storing in the freezer, to prevent air entering and moisture escaping. Certain foods benefit from over-wrapping, ie, wrapping in a double thickness of foil or, in the case of rigid containers, double wrapping and sealing in a freezer bag. Over-wrapping in this way is used to prevent cross-transference of flavors and odors from one food to another, or to give added protection to protruding bones on poultry and meat, etc. Overwrapping also protects against possible puncturing and heavy handling during a search for a lost food.

oxidation

Connected with rancidity in fatty foods. If food is not correctly wrapped for freezing, oxygen from the air passes into the fat cells of food during storage in the freezer, causing it to develop a spoiled taste and smell. Any vitamin A present in the food will also be destroyed.

preforming

A way of packaging food for the freezer into usable quantities and/or uniform shapes and sizes. A preformer is any kind of rigid container that is lined with a freezer bag (or boil-in-bag). Fill bag with food, freeze until solid, then remove bag from preformer, seal and return to freezer. Preformers can thus be used indefinitely. The shape of the preformer determines the shape of the freezer package, so choose ones with straight sides. Casseroles are ideal for preforming. Use the casserole dish as a preformer by lining it with foil, leaving a large overhang all around for later sealing. Open freeze, then remove from dish, seal and overwrap. When required, unwrap, remove the block and replace in same dish for reheating.

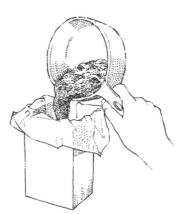

refreezing

As a general rule, once food has thawed it should not be refrozen. Raw meat, poultry, fish, fruit and vegetables can only be refrozen if they are cooked first before returning to the freezer. Thawed food should be cooked as quickly as possible, and not kept for longer than one would normally expect to keep any fresh food before eating/cooking. Cooked dishes that have thawed should be reheated and cooled before refreezing. Dairy products, and foods containing them (eg, pastries and cakes filled with cream), should not be refrozen.

refreshing

A term used with breads, pastries and cookies which, after thawing, need to be put into a preheated 400° oven for a few minutes to crisp them whether they are to be served hot or cold.

rotating stock

Home freezer owners should rotate stock constantly, to enjoy frozen food at its best and within its recommended storage period. Use a logbook to record dates by which food should be eaten.

sealing

To make packages airtight and prevent oxidation (see opposite), correct sealing is essential before freezing. Rigid containers with suction lids present no problem, nor do snap-on and screwband lids. Foil that is molded around solid food needs no further sealing. Food in freezer bags must have air excluded before sealing, and this can be done in several ways: suck out air with a clean drinking straw, use a special mechanical freezer pump or alternatively squeeze out air with the hands, working from bottom to top. Once air is excluded from bag, seal with wire closures or ties, freezer tape, heat sealing unit or iron. The exception to the exclusive air rule is uncooked bread dough. It should be placed in an oiled bag which will allow the dough to rise a little when it goes into the freezer, and to rise further after it comes out and has thawed. Allow plenty of time for this as the yeast cells need time to awaken. Remove ties to expand bag, close again.

To remove air, use a straw to suck it out before tying bag

special freezer pump can be used to draw out all the air

sharp freezing

The lowering of the temperature inside the freezer in order to freeze fresh or cooked foods as quickly as possible. Sharp freezing is essential if ice crystals between tissues of food are to be kept small and to suspend enzyme action quickly, so that food will not deteriorate. Switching to "sharp freeze" (also sometimes called super, automatic or extra cold) overrides the thermostat, causing the motor to run continuously and lower the temperature inside the cabinet. All freezers are capable of freezing at least 10% of their loading capacity in 24 hours, some can freeze more. Also consult manufacturer's handbook for length of time to use the sharp freeze switch when freezing food (this can vary between 2 and 24 hours depending on type and quantity of food). This is important to ensure that frozen food already in the cabinet does not partially thaw when unfrozen food is placed next to it.

vacuum packs

Only applicable to commercial packaging, usually of pork products. Vacuum packing excludes air, giving food a longer storage life than usual freezer wrappings. Without vacuum packing, storage life of bacon is much shorter than other meats, due to its high fat and salt content (salt accelerates rancidity in animal fat).

wet sugar pack

A method of packing soft juicy fruits to draw out oxygen from the cells. Whole, sliced and crushed fruit can be packed in this way, the most common method for freezing berries. Mix fruit and sugar gently together until sugar has dissolved, then pack in a rigid container, or pack fruit and sugar in equal layers directly into container. Quantity of sugar varies according to tartness of fruit, but usually $\frac{1}{2}$—$\frac{3}{4}$ cup of sugar is sufficient for every pound fruit. Leave $\frac{3}{4}$ inch headroom before sealing the box.

wrapping

Can be done in a variety of ways depending on the food's shape and whether or not it is fragile. Smallish fruits and vegetables are best in freezer bags, while large foods which might be knocked, crushed or broken by careless handling or storage need the protection of rigid containers. Sheet wrapping can be used for more regularly-shaped and sturdy foods which have nothing protruding, and the two techniques used for making sure all air is excluded and all surface covered are called the butcher wrap and drugstore fold.

drugstore fold

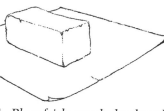

1 *Place fairly regularly-shaped food on a large foil rectangle*

2 *Lift up the two long sides, bring to the top. With edges meeting, make one sharp fold*

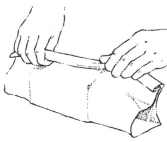

3 *Continue to fold the foil till it reaches the food — this presses out the air*

4 *Fold in foil at both sides, seal on top with freezer tape*

butcher wrap

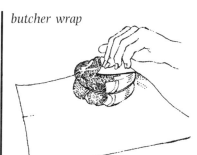

1 *Place awkwardly-shaped food on a large square of foil*

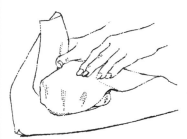

2 *Slide one corner of foil so it covers the food*

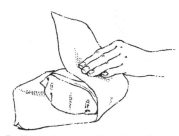

3 *Turn in one side, then the other so food is nearly hidden. Fold foil back on itself neatly*

4 *Bring fourth corner to top, press to exclude air, then seal*

Freezing fresh meat, fish and poultry

Major protein foods such as meat, fish and poultry have a definite place in a freezer, especially when bought in bulk to provide a reliable food source for several weeks. (In the process you save money and also reduce the time spent shopping.) Before buying in bulk, you must know how much fresh food your freezer can freeze at a time (usually 10% of the total capacity in 24 hours). If the amount you want is too great, or your freezer can't reach the state of coldness necessary, it is best to buy from a butcher or farmer who will blast freeze it for you after it's been divided, wrapped and labeled.

FOOD	PREPARATION
BEEF roasts	Remove surplus fat. If possible, saw off protruding bone ends or bone whole roasts to economize on space. Roll and tie boned roasts, but do not stuff
steaks	Remove surplus fat. Cut no more than 1 inch thick, cut into serving pieces
boneless meat for stewing	Remove surplus fat, sinews and gristle. Slice or cut into 1 inch cubes
ground beef	Only freeze lean ground beef. Leave loose, or shape into burgers or meatballs with onion, herbs, spices, etc
LAMB roasts	Remove surplus fat. If possible, saw off protruding bone ends or bone whole roasts to economize on space. Roll and tie boned roasts, but do not stuff
chops	Trim bone ends. Remove skin and surplus fat
meat for stew and boneless leg	If stew meat has bones, chop into serving pieces, including bones. Cut leg into slices or 1 inch cubes. Remove surplus fat, skin and gristle
PORK roasts	Remove surplus fat. If possible, saw off protruding bone ends or bone whole roasts to economize on space. Roll and tie boned roasts, but do not stuff before freezing
chops, spareribs	Remove surplus fat
boneless tenderloin	Remove surplus fat, sinews and gristle. Leave whole or cut into 1 inch cubes
ground pork	Only freeze very lean pork. Leave loose, or shape into burgers or meatballs with onion, herbs, spices, etc

PACKAGING	STORAGE TIME	TO USE
Wrap individual roasts in sheet wrapping. Pad protruding bones and use drugstore fold or butcher wrap. Seal, label and freeze	12 months	Thaw in wrappings in refrigerator for 8–10 hours per pound, or at room temp for 3–4 hours. Or cook from frozen for approx twice normal time until 165° on meat thermometer at center of roast
Wrap individually or interleave with doubled freezer wrap. Pack together in freezer bags. Seal, label and freeze	12 months	Thaw in wrappings in refrigerator overnight, or at room temp for 2–3 hours. Or broil or fry thin steaks from frozen for approx twice normal time
Pack in usable quantities in freezer bags. Seal, label and freeze	8 months	Thaw in wrappings in refrigerator overnight. Use thawed juices with liquid in recipe. Or stew when partially thawed for slightly longer than normal time
Pack loose ground beef in usable quantities in freezer bags. Wrap burgers individually or interleave with doubled freezer wrap. Pack together in freezer bags. Open freeze meatballs, then pack together in freezer bags. Seal, label and freeze	3 months	Thaw loose ground beef in wrappings in refrigerator overnight, or cook when partially thawed for slightly longer than normal time. Cook burgers, etc from frozen
Wrap individual roasts in sheet wrapping. Pad protruding bones and use drugstore fold or butcher wrap. Seal, label and freeze	12 months	Thaw in wrappings in refrigerator for 8–10 hours per pound, or at room temp for 3–4 hours. Or cook from frozen for approx twice normal time until 185° on meat thermometer at center of roast
Wrap individually or interleave with doubled freezer wrap. Pack together in freezer bags. Seal, label and freeze	12 months	Thaw in wrappings in refrigerator overnight, or at room temp for 2–3 hours. Or broil or fry from frozen for approx twice normal time
Pack in usable quantities in freezer bags. If meat has many bones, pack in rigid containers. Seal, label and freeze	8 months	Thaw in wrappings in refrigerator overnight. Use thawed juices with liquid in recipe. Or cook when partially thawed for slightly longer than normal time
Wrap individual roasts in sheet wrapping. Pad protruding bones and use drugstore fold or butcher wrap. Seal, label and freeze	9 months	Thaw in wrappings in refrigerator for 8–10 hours per pound, or at room temp for 3–4 hours
Wrap individually or interleave with doubled freezer wrap. Pack together in freezer bags. Seal, label and freeze	9 months (spareribs 6 months)	Thaw in wrappings in refrigerator overnight, or at room temp for 2–3 hours. Or broil or fry from frozen for approx twice normal time
Wrap whole individually in foil, then overwrap in freezer bags. Pack cubes and slices in usable quantities in freezer bags. Seal, label and freeze	9 months	Thaw in wrappings in refrigerator overnight. Use thawed juices in liquid in recipe. Or cook when partially thawed for slightly longer than normal time
Pack loose ground pork in usable quantities in freezer bags. Wrap patties individually or interleave with doubled freezer wrap. Pack together in freezer bags. Open freeze meatballs, then pack together in freezer bags. Seal, label and freeze	3 months	Thaw loose ground pork in wrappings in refrigerator overnight, or cook when partially thawed for slightly longer than normal time. Cook patties, etc from frozen

(continued)

Meat Whole carcasses can mean an expensive capital outlay so you want to be sure you're buying the best quality, as well as the sort of meat you like to eat. The butcher or farmer will divide it as you want, but with a pig you get a head (not something everyone appreciates), and with beef a lot of huge bones and fat which can be used for stock or rendered down for drippings (both activities requiring time which not every freezer owner has to spare).

The whole carcass works out less costly because prime and poorer grades of meat are included, and the price will probably be an average of both. Package deals can sometimes be arranged on just steaks, or chops, or roasts — shop around to find the options. When freezing fresh meats in bulk, check the manufacturer's instructions about when the sharp freeze button should be switched on. As to amount, allow 2 cubic feet of space for every 20 pounds boneless meat; twice the space for meat on the bone. Freezer centers and some supermarkets specialize in blast-frozen bulk packs which might not give the origin of the fresh product, but will have been frozen and stored by the best methods.

Poultry and game Unless you live in the country or have a source of supply which provides you with fresh birds, most poultry and game is bought already frozen. Before freezing, it is hung (if necessary), dressed, plucked or skinned, trussed, or divided into pieces. Never stuff poultry or game before freezing — because of its bulk it might not thaw sufficiently to allow heat penetration during cooking and any micro-organisms in the birds or stuffing will not be destroyed. Once poultry and game have thawed, cook immediately; never refreeze uncooked.

Fish These are among the most highly perishable of foods and must be frozen within 12 hours of being caught (or 24 at the very most if they have been stored on ice). Fish bought from a fish market should not be frozen as it may have been frozen and thawed once already. Scale, clean, wash and dry whole fish; ice glaze to preserve skin. Wash and dry fillets before freezing. Overwrap fish well to prevent cross-flavoring.

FOOD	PREPARATION
VEAL roasts	Remove any surplus fat. If possible, saw off protruding bones or bone whole roasts to economize on space. Roll and tie boned roasts, but do not stuff
chops, cutlets	Trim bones and any surplus fat. Pound cutlets
ground veal	Leave loose, or shape into patties or meatballs
VARIETY MEAT	Clean and remove fat/suet, sinews, skin, gristle, etc. Wipe dry. Leave whole or slice/chop/cube according to type and possible future use
SAUSAGES/ SAUSAGEMEAT	Only freeze when very fresh. Avoid highly seasoned or spicy products
BACON, HAM ham roasts	Only freeze when very fresh, lean and mild-cured. Remove surplus fat if possible. Saw off any protruding bone ends or bone whole roasts to economize on space. Roll and tie boned roasts
bacon slices	Only freeze when very fresh, lean and mild-cured. Remove surplus fat if possible. Commercial vacuum packs are best for freezing
POULTRY AND GAME whole birds	Wash inside and out, then dry thoroughly
giblets	Remove from bird. Discard sac from gizzard. Separate liver. Wash and dry thoroughly
cut up birds	Separate whole birds into halves, quarters, drumsticks, breasts, etc. Wash and dry thoroughly
game animals	Remove entrails as soon as possible. Hang, skin, draw and dress as required. Leave whole or cut up
FISH white fish	Only freeze very fresh fish, 12–24 hours after catching. Clean, remove scales and fins. Cut off heads, tails and remove skin if wished. Wash and dry thoroughly. Leave small fish whole, cut large fish into steaks or divide into fillets
oily fish	Only freeze very fresh fish, 12–24 hours after catching (mackerel within 12 hours). Clean, remove scales and fins. Leave whole, or cut off heads and tails, split open and bone. Wash and dry thoroughly. Large fish can be cut into steaks
smoked and cured fish	Only freeze freshly-smoked fish that has not been previously frozen and thawed. Leave whole or separate into fillets, removing all visible bones. Skin if wished
SHELLFISH oysters, scallops	Freeze as soon as possible after removal from sea. Wash shells, open and remove meat. Discard inedible parts. Retain liquid. Wash edible meat quickly in lightly salted water
prawns, shrimp	Freeze as soon as possible after removal from sea. Cook in boiling salted water for 2–6 mins, shell and devein. Wash claws and tails of large shellfish in salted water, dry thoroughly, but do not cook
crabs, lobsters	Freeze as soon as possible from live state. Prepare and cook before freezing as for serving fresh

PACKAGING	STORAGE TIME	TO USE
Wrap individual roasts in sheet wrapping. Pad protruding bones and use drugstore fold or butcher wrap, seal, label and freeze	12 months	Thaw in wrappings in refrigerator for 8–10 hours per pound, or at room temp for 3–4 hours. Or cook from frozen for approx twice normal time until 165° on meat thermometer at center of roast
Wrap individually or interleave with doubled freezer wrap. Pack together in freezer bags. Seal, label and freeze	12 months	Thaw in wrappings in refrigerator overnight, or at room temp for 2–3 hours. Or broil or fry chops from frozen for approx twice normal time. Thin cutlets hardly need thawing: cook from frozen for a few minutes longer than usual
Pack loose ground veal in usable quantities in freezer bags. Open freeze/interleave patties, etc, pack in freezer bags	3 months	Thaw loose ground veal in wrappings in refrigerator overnight, or cook when partially thawed for slightly longer than normal time. Cook patties, etc from frozen
Wrap individually or interleave whole items, pieces or slices with freezer wrap. Pack together in freezer bags. Pack chopped or cubes in usable quantities in freezer bags. Seal, label and freeze	3 months	Thaw in wrappings in refrigerator overnight, or at room temp for 2–3 hours. Or cook from frozen, taking care not to overcook
Open freeze sausages, then pack together in freezer bags. Pack sausagemeat in usable quantities in freezer bags. Seal, label and freeze	2–3 months	Cook sausages from frozen or thaw in refrigerator overnight, whichever is most convenient. Thaw sausagemeat in wrappings in refrigerator overnight
Wrap individual roasts in sheet wrapping. Pad protruding bones and use drugstore fold or butcher wrap. Seal, label and freeze	2 months	Thaw in refrigerator for 24 hours or at room temp overnight. Or cook from frozen for approx twice normal time until 170° on meat thermometer at center of roast
Wrap in usable quantities in freezer wrap. Seal, label and freeze. Place vacuum packs straight in freezer	2 months (smoked); 2–3 weeks (unsmoked); 2½ months (vacuum packs)	Thaw in wrappings in refrigerator overnight, or 2–3 hours at room temp
Pad protruding bones. Pack whole birds in freezer bags	9 months (turkey and chicken) 4–6 months (duck and goose) 6 months (game birds)	*All birds must be thawed before cooking.* Thaw in wrappings in refrigerator, allowing approx 5–6 hours per pound
Pack in freezer bags, keeping liver separate. Seal, label and freeze	2–3 months	Thaw in wrappings in refrigerator overnight. Or use from frozen to make stocks, gravies, etc
Wrap in individual pieces in freezer wraps, then pack together in freezer bags. Seal, label and freeze	As for whole birds (above)	Thaw in wrappings in refrigerator for 12–15 hours. Or cook from frozen or partially thawed, allowing up to twice usual cooking time
Wrap whole small animals in sheet wrapping or freezer bags, padding any protruding bones. Wrap individual pieces in freezer wrap, then pack together in freezer bags	8 months	Thaw in wrappings in refrigerator, allowing approx 5–6 hours per pound for whole birds, 12–15 hours total thawing time for pieces
Wrap whole fish individually in freezer wrap, then pack several together in freezer bags. Wrap steaks and fillets individually or interleave with doubled freezer wrap and pack in freezer bags. Seal, label and freeze	3–4 months	Thaw whole fish in wrappings in refrigerator overnight. Cook steaks and fillets from frozen, allowing extra cooking time
Wrap large whole fish, boned fish and steaks individually or interleave with freezer wrap, then pack together in freezer bags. Pack small whole fish in usable quantities in freezer bags	2 months	Thaw whole fish in wrappings in refrigerator overnight. Cook boned fish and steaks from frozen, allowing extra cooking time. Thaw small whole fish in refrigerator for 1 hour until separate
Wrap whole fish and fillets individually or interleave with doubled freezer wrap. Pack together in freezer bags. Seal, label and freeze	3 months	Thaw in wrappings in refrigerator overnight
Pack meat and liquid together in usable quantities in rigid containers. Place crumpled waxed paper between surface of liquid and lid of container to keep fish submerged. Seal, label and freeze	3 months	Cook from frozen, taking care not to overcook. To serve oysters raw, thaw in refrigerator for 6 hours. Eat as soon as possible after thawing
Pack in usable quantities in freezer bags. Seal, label and freeze	2 months	Cook from frozen, taking care not to overcook. To serve cold, thaw in wrappings in refrigerator for 2–3 hours. Uncooked claws and tails can be cooked from frozen, then shelled
Pack lobsters and dressed crabs in shells. Cover with freezer wrap, then overwrap in freezer bags. Or remove meat from shells and pack in rigid containers (pack white and brown crab meat separately). Seal, label and freeze	2 months	Cook from frozen, taking care not to overcook. To serve cold, thaw in wrappings in refrigerator for 2–3 hours for crab, 6 hours for lobster

Freezing vegetables

Nearly all vegetables will freeze successfully. It is vitally important to freeze them at their freshest — after harvesting is ideal, or within a few hours at the most. Most vegetables should be blanched first to stop the enzymes from reacting in the freezer resulting in loss of flavor and color. Difficult vegetables are those with a high water content or a soft, delicate texture.

Avocados should be frozen as pulp mixed with lemon juice or cream cheese, or as a soup.

Jerusalem artichokes should be boiled, then made into a purée.

Mushrooms can be frozen whole but keep longer if sliced and sautéed in butter, or made into duxelles.

Potatoes should be cut into French fries and part cooked before freezing, or mashed and formed into croquettes or piped into duchess shapes. New potatoes should be parboiled.

Sweet potatoes and **pumpkin** should be baked, boiled or puréed for freezing.

VEGETABLE	BLANCHING TIME IN MINS	PACKAGING	STORAGE TIME IN MONTHS	TO USE
artichokes, globe, whole	5–7	RC/FB	6	thaw RT (4 hrs) use as fresh
hearts	2–5	RC/FB	6	thaw RT (4 hrs) use as fresh
asparagus, bundles	2–4	RC	9	thaw RT steam 2–4 mins
beans, lima, shelled	2–3	FB	12	boil from frozen 3–5 mins
green, Italian, whole	1–2	FB	12	boil from frozen 5–7 mins
green, sliced	1–2	FB	12	boil from frozen 5–7 mins
broccoli, spears	2–4	OF/FB	12	boil from frozen 3–7 mins
brussels sprouts, whole	2–4	OF/FB	12	boil from frozen 4–8 mins
cabbage, green/white, shredded	1	FB	6	boil from frozen 5–8 mins
red, shredded	1	FB	12	thaw RT use as fresh
carrots, baby new, whole	3	RC/FB	12	boil from frozen 4 mins
old, sliced	2	RC/FB	12	thaw RT add to casseroles
cauliflower, florets	3	OF/FB	6	boil from frozen 4 mins
celeriac, diced/sliced	1	FB	6	thaw RT/cook from frozen
grated	2	FB	6	add frozen to casseroles
celery, chunks	3	FB	6	add frozen to casseroles
chili peppers, seeded	1	FB	6	thaw RT/use frozen in casseroles
corn, husked ears	2–8	OF/FB	12	thaw RT (5–6 hrs)/R overnight use as fresh
kernels	—	FB	12	cook from frozen
eggplant, sliced	4	RC/IL	12	thaw RT/R use as fresh
fennel bulb, quartered	3–5	FB	6	boil from frozen
horseradish, grated	—	RC	6	thaw RT/R use as fresh
kale (curly), leaves	1	FB	12	boil from frozen 4–6 mins
kohlrabi, large sliced/diced	2	FB	12	thaw RT use as fresh
small whole	3	FB	12	thaw RT use as fresh
leeks, large sliced	3	FB	6	use frozen in casseroles
small whole	4	FB	6	boil from frozen 6–8 mins
mushrooms, whole	—	OF/RC	1	cook from frozen
okra, small whole	3	FB	12	cook from frozen/boil 6–8 mins
onions, chopped	1	FB/OW	3	add frozen to casseroles
small pearl	2	OF/FB/OW	3	add frozen to casseroles

VEGETABLE	BLANCH-ING TIME IN MINS	PACKAGING	STORAGE TIME IN MONTHS	TO USE
parsnips, sliced	2	FB	6	boil from frozen/thaw RT add to casseroles
peas, podded	1	OF/FB	12	boil from frozen 4 mins
pepper, chopped/sliced	2	OF/FB	6	thaw RT (1–2 hrs)/use frozen in casseroles, salads
whole (seeded)	3–4	OF/FB	6	thaw RT (1–2 hrs) use for stuffing/baking
rutabaga, diced	2	FB	12	boil from frozen/thaw RT add to casseroles
salsify (scorzonera), cut into short lengths after blanching	2	FB	12	thaw RT (2 hrs) cook from frozen
shallots, whole	2	OF/FB/OW	3	thaw RT use as fresh
snow peas, whole	½–1	FB	6	boil from frozen 3–4 mins
spinach, leaves	2	FB	12	cook from frozen
purée	–	FB	12	cook from frozen
squash, large summer, chunks	2	RC	6	steam from frozen 1–2 mins
swiss chard, leaves	2	FB	12	boil from frozen 7 mins
ribs (stalks)	3	FB	12	boil from frozen 7 mins
white turnips, large sliced	2	FB	12	boil from frozen/thaw RT add to casseroles
small whole	4	FB	12	boil from frozen 5–10 mins
zucchini, large sliced	1	OF/FB	12	thaw RT (2 hrs) use as fresh
small whole	1	OF/FB	12	boil from frozen 4 mins

NB: blanching and boiling times vary according to size of vegetable

Abbreviations: RC rigid container; FB freezer bag; IL interleave; OF open freeze; OW overwrap; RT room temperature; R refrigerator

cook's know-how

Salad vegetables have a high water content and go limp in a freezer. But if there is a glut you can freeze them to use other than raw.

Beets should be boiled and skinned and can be left whole, sliced or diced to be used later as a hot vegetable with a white sauce or spicy dressing.

Cucumber can be frozen as a soup or as a purée for sauces, dips.

Endive should be blanched for 5 minutes, and left whole or sliced. It can be served hot, with sauce, or braised with other vegetables.

Lettuce hearts can be frozen to use later in soups.

Winter radishes are like turnips and should be diced and blanched for 2 minutes. Use as a hot vegetable with sauce.

Scallions should be frozen whole and chopped for use in stir-fried dishes.

Tomatoes should be made into juice, purée or sauce for freezing.

Freezing fruit

Preserving fruit by freezing takes less time and effort than canning. Their high water content causes a structure change but this can be used to advantage — soft fruits in a sugar pack, for example, produce juice during thawing and the mix can be folded into whipped cream to make a mousse, or poured over ice cream. Ripe, unblemished stone fruits can be halved or sliced straight into a cold sugar syrup (see cook's know-how right) and the flesh, though softened, retains enough texture to rival commercially canned fruit. Fruit must be of the best quality for sugar or syrup packs; squashy or overripe ones should be puréed. Speed in preparation is especially important with fruits that have a pale-colored flesh likely to brown when cut. Keep lemon juice handy to sprinkle over if necessary. Pears and guavas are so prone to discoloration that they are best cooked before freezing. Bananas can only be frozen if combined with other ingredients (eg, in ice cream, or cheesecake). Thaw fruit in its unopened pack and use when still slightly frozen.

FRUIT	METHOD OF FREEZING	PACK-AGING	STORAGE TIME IN MTHS	TO USE
apples, tart, pulp/purée		FB/RC	8	use from frozen/thaw RT (1 hr) reheat/use in cooked dishes
slices/rings	OF/MS	FB/RC	12	use from frozen/thaw RT (1 hr) use as fresh
apricots, peeled, halves	MS	RC	12	thaw R (3 hrs) use in fruit salads, etc
blackberries, whole	OF/PD/M–HS	FB/RC	12	use from frozen/thaw RT (2 hrs) use as fresh
blueberries, whole	OF/PD/M–HS	FB/RC	12	use from frozen/thaw RT (2 hrs) use as fresh
cherries, black/red, pitted	M–HS	RC	12	thaw RT (3 hrs) use as fresh
citrus fruits, whole	PD	FB	12	thaw RT (1–2 hrs) use as fresh
segments/slices	OF/PD/L–MS	RC	12	thaw RT (2 hrs) use as fresh
cranberries, whole	OF/PD/M–HS	FB/RC	12	use from frozen/thaw RT (2 hrs) use as fresh
currants, black/red/white, whole	OF/PD	FB/RC	12	use from frozen/thaw RT (2 hrs) use as fresh
crushed/purée		FB/RC	12	thaw RT (1 hr) reheat/use in cooked dishes
dates, fresh, pitted	OF/PD/LS	FB/RC	12	thaw RT (1 hr) use as fresh
elderberries, whole blanched (30 secs)	OF/PD	FB/RC	12	thaw RT (2 hrs) use as fresh
figs, fresh, whole unpeeled	OF/PD	FB/RC	12	thaw RT (1–2 hrs) use as fresh
whole peeled/sliced	L–MS	RC	12	thaw RT (1–2 hrs) use as fresh
gooseberries, whole	OF/PD	FB/RC	12	use from frozen/thaw RT (2 hrs) use as fresh
purée (cooked)		FB/RC	12	thaw RT (1 hr) reheat/use in cooked dishes
grapes, seedless, whole and in bunches	OF/PD	FB/RC	12	thaw RT (2 hrs) use as fresh / thaw RT (2 hrs) use in fruit salads, etc
large, halved and seeded	LS	RC	12	
huckleberries, whole	OF/PD/HS	FB/RC	12	thaw RT use as fresh
kiwifruit, skinned and sliced	PD	RC	6	use partially frozen in fruit salads, etc
loganberries, whole	OF/PD/MS	FB/RC	12	use from frozen/thaw RT (2 hrs) use as fresh
crushed/purée		FB/RC	12	thaw RT (1 hr) reheat/use in cooked dishes

Abbreviations: OF open freeze; LS light syrup; MS medium syrup; HS heavy syrup; PD pack dry, with or without syrup according to taste and future use; FB freezer bag; RC rigid container; FW freezer wrap; RT room temperature; R refrigerator

FRUIT	METHOD OF FREEZING	PACK-AGING	STOR-AGE TIME IN MTHS	TO USE
lychees, shelled and seeded	HS	RC	12	use partially frozen in fruit salads, etc
mangoes, peeled and sliced	MS	RC	12	thaw R (1–2 hrs) use partially frozen in fruit salads, etc
melon, balls/cubes	HS	RC	12	thaw R (3 hrs) use partially frozen in fruit salads, etc
nectarines, peeled and pitted, halves/slices	HS	RC	12	thaw R (3 hrs) use partially frozen in fruit salads, etc
peaches, peeled and pitted, halves/slices	HS	RC	12	thaw R (3 hrs) use partially frozen in fruit salads, etc
pears (firm eating)/cooking peeled, halved, cored, quarters/slices	HS	RC	12	thaw RT (3 hrs) use in fruit salads, etc
persimmons, chunks/slices	HS	RC	12	thaw R use partially frozen
purée (cooked)		FB/RC	12	thaw RT reheat/use in cooked dishes.
pineapples, peeled, slices/ cubes/wedges	PD/LS	RC	12	thaw RT (3 hrs) use as fresh
crushed with sugar		RC	12	thaw RT (3 hrs) use as fresh
plums, whole	OF/PD	FB/RC	6	thaw RT (2–3 hrs) use as fresh
halved and pitted	PD/MS	RC	12	thaw RT (2 hrs) use as fresh
purée (cooked)		FB/RC	12	thaw RT (1 hr) reheat/use in cooked dishes
quinces, peeled, cored, sliced and poached		RC	12	thaw RT use partially frozen
raspberries, whole	OF/PD	FB/RC	12	use from frozen/thaw RT (3 hrs) use as fresh
purée (uncooked)		FB/RC	12	thaw RT (3 hrs) use as fresh
rhubarb, chunks blanched (1 min)	PD	FB/RC	12	use from frozen/thaw RT (3 hrs) use as fresh
strawberries, small whole	OF	FB/RC	12	use partially frozen
large sliced	PD	RC	12	thaw RT (1–2 hrs) use as fresh
purée (uncooked)		RC	12	thaw RT (1–2 hrs) use as fresh

cook's know-how

When making a sugar pack, layer the fruit in a rigid container with sugar — $\frac{1}{2}$–$\frac{3}{4}$ cup to each pound of fruit. Soft fruit, berries and fresh currants can be open frozen without sugar and put into freezer bags to make free-flow packs. Purées can either be cooked or uncooked, with or without sugar. Syrup packs can be light, medium or heavy. Light is made with $\frac{1}{2}$–$\frac{3}{4}$ cup of sugar to $2\frac{1}{2}$ cups of water; medium, 1–$1\frac{1}{2}$ cups sugar; heavy, 2–$2\frac{1}{2}$ cups sugar. Heat sugar and water, stirring till dissolved, then boil for 2 minutes. Leave to cool before using. You need to make up quite a lot, well in advance, as the fruit must be completely covered in the rigid containers (leave $\frac{3}{4}$ inch headroom). Balls of crumpled waxed paper can be placed on top of syrup to prevent fruit rising.

Freezing problem food

Some foods need to be dealt with in a special way so they freeze well. **Eggs, hard-cooked** (whole, chopped or sieved) go tough and rubbery in a freezer. **Fresh eggs** can't be frozen in their shells (they crack), but can be lightly mixed with a fork with salt or sugar – remember to note which on the label to prevent wrong use later. Mix egg yolks the same way; whites need no addition.
Cream, milk and yogurt should not be used to thicken soups or stews to be frozen – when boiled after thawing unsightly curdling will occur. All, however, can be frozen as part of a cooked or uncooked filling (quiche,

cheesecake). Heavy cream (with a butter fat content of not less than 40%) can be lightly whipped with sugar to store, or piped into rosettes. Whipped cream can be used to coat a cake – but only for short term freezing or it will be tacky.
Butter cream (made with butter and confectioners sugar) freezes well and is best for filling and decorating. Cakes filled with jam will go soggy in the freezer.
Cold soufflés and mousses made with cream and egg whites and set with gelatin freeze well, as gelatin stops large ice crystals forming.
Pastry, if it is to be served hot after freezing, has to be refreshed in the oven which can result in over-cooked pastry and filling. Uncooked pie shells glazed with egg white (to prevent sogginess) are a good standby

for filling when needed with a sweet or savory mix. Storage times of pastry dishes vary. With pastry it is the same as the fat content; if filled, the filling governs the time. Bacon or smoked fish, for example, are high in salt (this causes rancidity) and storage time is less than a filling made with eggs and vegetables. Most cooked **bread** stores splendidly (crusty loaves will lose their crust after 1 week). Doughs, however, need care. Yeast should be doubled for some of the cells will be killed before the dough freezes and extra ensures raising after the dough thaws. Dough allowed to rise before freezing is often not as successful as dough packed and frozen soon after making.
Casseroles, stews and soups are best without too much seasoning,

FOOD	PREPARATION	PACKAGING	STORAGE TIME	TO USE
bread loaves, unrisen dough	increase yeast by 50%, knead lightly, package immediately	FB (large greased)	1 month (white/brown) 1½ (enriched)	reseal bag to allow room for rising at RT (6 hrs), punch down, rise again, bake
risen dough	increase yeast by 50% when making. After first rising, punch down, place in greased baking pan or foil	FB (large greased)	1 month	thaw RT, rise before baking
partially baked, homemade commercial	cool leave in original wrappings	FB/F OW/FB	4 months 2 months	bake from frozen, allowing extra time bake from frozen to manufacturer's instructions
baked, homemade commercial (not crusty)	cool freeze as fresh as possible	FB/F FB/F	6 months (white/brown) 4 (enriched)	thaw RT (3 hrs)/refresh from frozen in F in hot oven for 45 mins
sliced	leave in original wrappings	OW/FB	6 months	thaw RT (3 hrs)/toast slices from frozen
rolls, etc	cool/freeze as fresh as possible	IL/RC	1 month (white/brown) 1½ (enriched)	thaw RT (1 hr)/refresh from frozen in F in hot oven for 15 mins
butter	keep in original wrapping	OW/FB	3 months (salted) 6 (unsalted)	thaw R (overnight)
cakes, plain and fruity, large and small	make in usual way, cool	FB/IL slices	4–6 months 10 (fat free)	thaw RT (1–4 hrs)
fancy, with butter cream or cream	avoid synthetic flavorings, don't decorate with nuts, fruit	OF/RC/IL slices	3 months 2 (cream)	thaw RT (1–4 hrs)
casseroles/stews, cooked	do not thicken, cool quickly	RC/FB/PF/F	1–3 months	reheat from frozen/thaw R (overnight), then reheat
cheese, hard	divide into usable quantities	FW/OW/FB	3–4 months	thaw RT (overnight)
soft	divide into usable quantities	FW/OW/FB	6 months	thaw R (overnight), then RT
cottage	keep in cartons	OW/FB	4–6 months	thaw R (overnight), stir before use
cookies, unbaked dough	pipe/shape on trays form into long rolls	OF/RC F	6 months 6 months	bake from frozen thaw R (1–2 hours), slice, bake
baked	cool	IL/RC	6 months	thaw RT refresh in hot oven if necessary
cream, heavy or whipping (at least 40% fat content)	chill and whip lightly with 2 teaspoons sugar per 1½ cups	RC	6 months	thaw R stir/whip before use
rosettes	whip with sugar, pipe onto trays	OF/RC	3 months	thaw RT (30 mins)

or strong-flavored root vegetables and aren't thickened (this should be done when reheating).
Unfreezables include: unstabilized yogurt, buttermilk, cream with less than 40% butter fat, milk that isn't homogenized, clear fruit gelatins (they go cloudy), custards (they separate), mayonnaise (it curdles), aspic toppings (they become murky).

Right: a lage chest freezer which filled to capacity can take 350 pounds of food, and can freeze 71 pounds fresh food in 24 hours.

FOOD	PREPARATION	PACKAGING	STORAGE TIME	TO USE
eggs, whole/yolks	mix with salt/sugar according to future use ($\frac{1}{2}$ teaspoon to 6 eggs)	RC	6 months	thaw RT
whites	no beating, no additions	RC	6 months	thaw RT
ice cream	divide into usable quantities	RC	3 months	do not allow to thaw, "soften" home-made ice creams, sorbets in main body of refrigerator before serving
margarine, hard and soft	keep in original wrapping	OW/FB	12 months	thaw R (overnight)
milk, homogenized	do not freeze in bottles	RC	1 month	thaw R (overnight)
pastry, uncooked dough	divide into usable quantities/blocks	FB	3–6 months	thaw R (overnight)/RT (2–3 hrs) use as fresh
uncooked pies, tarts, quiches, etc	prepare in foil dishes, brush pastry with egg white before filling	OF/FB/F	1–3 months (according to filling)	cook from frozen in foil containers, allowing extra time
uncooked lids/shells, etc	make to fit pie pans	OF/IL/FB	3–6 months	cook from frozen/thaw RT, use as fresh
cooked pies, tarts, quiches, etc	make in foil containers, cool	FB/F	1–6 months (according to filling)	thaw RT (3 hrs) refresh to serve hot, taking care not to overcook
puddings, baked (sponges, charlottes, betties, etc)	make in foil containers	FB/F	3 months	reheat from frozen, allowing extra time
steamed (sponge and suet crust)	make in foil containers	FB/F	3 months	reheat from frozen, allowing extra time
sauces, apple, sweet (fruit, chocolate), tomato, espagnole, white (béchamel, mornay, soubise), bread, meat	make in bulk/divide into usable quantities/keep seasoning and thickening to minimum	RC	12 months (sweet/fruit/tomato) 6 (espagnole/white) 3 (bread/meat)	thaw RT then reheat if necessary/reheat from frozen, beat vigorously during reheating before serving
shortening	divide into usable quantities	OW/FB	6 months	thaw R (overnight)
soups	do not thicken/do not add eggs, cream, yogurt or milk/skim off all fat/keep seasoning to minimum	PF/RC	3 months	reheat from frozen/thaw RT/thicken or add cream or milk on reheating/adjust seasoning
stocks	make in usual way, skim off all fat, boil till reduced to one-third	RC/ICT	3 months	reheat from frozen/thaw RT/add cubes to casseroles, stews

Abbreviations: OF open freeze; RC rigid container; OW overwrap; FB freezer bag; FW freezer wrap; F foil;
IL interleave; PF preform; ICT ice cube trays; R refrigerator; RT room temperature

Tutti-frutti conserve

Seven different fruits cooked in white wine are used to make this luscious jam. For best results, it's advisable to use a candy thermometer to test accurately for setting point

PRESERVE   Makes about 8lb

Overall timing 45 minutes

Equipment Large kettle, sterilized canning jars and lids, ladle

Freezing Not recommended

Storage Cool, dark place

INGREDIENTS

½lb	Strawberries
½lb	Cherries
½lb	Raspberries
½lb	Blueberries
1lb	Fresh pineapple
½lb	Pears
½lb	Plums
1¼ cups	White wine
6 cups	Sugar
¼ cup	Brandy

METHOD

1 Prepare and chop fruit, discarding the pits. Put chopped fruit into kettle with the wine and cook gently until soft, stirring frequently. Skim off any remaining pits that rise to the surface.
2 Add sugar to the kettle and stir till it dissolves, then boil rapidly for about 10 minutes. Test for jell point. Stir in brandy.
3 Ladle jam into sterilized jars. Cover, leaving ½ inch headroom, and process for 10 minutes in a boiling-water-bath.

Four fruit jam

When soft fruits are in season, this is a good jam to try. The currants will need stringing — to do this, hold the branch in one hand and pull the currant-bearing stalks through the prongs of a fork

PRESERVE   Makes about 6 jars

Overall timing 1 hour

Equipment Large kettle, sterilized canning jars and lids, ladle

Freezing Not recommended

Storage Cool, dark place

Above: Tutti-frutti conserve — a colorful, rich and fruity jam

INGREDIENTS

1lb	Cherries
1lb	Red currants
1lb	Strawberries
1lb	Raspberries
2½ cups	Water
8 cups	Sugar
2	Lemons

METHOD

1 Wash fruit. Pit cherries; string currants and pick them over; hull strawberries and raspberries.
2 Put the water in a large kettle, add the sugar and heat gently, without stirring, until sugar dissolves.
3 Increase heat. When syrup begins to bubble, add the cherries. Bring back to a boil, then reduce heat and boil (but not vigorously) for 20 minutes.
4 Add the strawberries, boil for 10 minutes, then add red currants. After 5 minutes, add the raspberries and juice from lemons. Boil for a further 10–15 minutes.
5 Skim surface. Test for jell point by dropping a little jam onto a cold saucer. It should be fairly thick and form a skin on the surface. If necessary, boil jam for a few minutes more, then retest.
6 Ladle jam into warmed jars. Cover, leaving ½ inch headroom, and process for 10 minutes in a boiling-water-bath.

cook's know-how

Squashy but not moldy blackberries, black currants and raspberries, can be made into misnamed fruit vinegars. In fact they are cordials, which when taken hot are a relief for sore throats, and when ice cold make a refreshing drink — add ice cubes, lemon pop or ginger ale, slices of fresh fruit, a sprig of borage or mint and you have a non-alcoholic Pimms! For every 1 pound of picked-over fruit, add 2½ cups of distilled white vinegar. Place in large china or glass bowl, cover and leave to stand 3–10 days (the longer the better), stirring the mixture occasionally. Strain (don't press the fruit or it will make a cloudy vinegar) and for every 2½ cups of liquid, add 2 cups of sugar. Boil for 10–15 minutes, cool, then bottle and seal securely. Store in a dark, dry place. To make a refreshing drink for a summer party, try this superb quick blender recipe.
Put the contents of a 16oz can of crushed pineapple, 6 tablespoons bottled lime juice, 2 ripe bananas, ½ teaspoon ground ginger and 5 cups of tonic water in a blender. Blend for 30 seconds until smooth. Pour over ice cubes in a jug and top up with chilled tonic. Serve immediately. The alcoholically inclined can add white rum to taste!

Autumn marmalade

This is an excellent mixed fruit marmalade which can be made in the autumn because it uses ordinary oranges, rather than the bitter Seville kind which are only available in late winter. Apples and pears are included and give a delectable mellow flavor

PRESERVE   Makes about 5lb

Overall timing $2\frac{1}{2}$ hours

Equipment Large kettle, cheesecloth bag, sterilized canning jars and lids, ladle

Freezing Not recommended

Storage Cool, dark place

Below: Autumn marmalade – delicious mix of fruit, cooked till thick then ladled into very clean, dry warm jars

INGREDIENTS

2lb	Mixed fruit (orange, grapefruit, lemon, apple, pear)
$7\frac{1}{2}$ cups	Water
6 cups	Sugar

METHOD

1 Squeeze juice and remove seeds from orange, grapefruit and lemon. Shred the rind and chop the flesh. Peel, core and chop apple and pear. Place seeds and cores in a cheesecloth bag.
2 Put the prepared fruit, shredded rind and cheesecloth bag in a kettle. Add the water and bring to a boil. Simmer until the volume is reduced by one-third.
3 Remove cheesecloth bag from kettle and discard. Add sugar and stir until it dissolves, then boil for 15 minutes.
4 Test jam for jell point by putting a little on a cold saucer. It should be fairly thick and form a skin on the surface which wrinkles when pressed lightly with fingertip. If necessary, boil for a few minutes longer, then retest.
5 Ladle jam into prepared jars. Cover, leaving $\frac{1}{2}$ inch headroom, and process for 10 minutes in a boiling-water-bath.

Spicy plum chutney

A chutney with fine sweet and sour flavors, spices and a good texture provided by chopped plums, apples, onions, dates and grated carrots. Resist the urge to taste the finished chutney for at least 6 weeks as it needs time to mature

PRESERVE   Makes about 4lb

Overall timing $1\frac{1}{4}$ hours

Equipment Bowl, large kettle, sterilized canning jars and lids, ladle

Freezing Not recommended

Storage Cool, dark place

INGREDIENTS

2lb	Plums
$\frac{3}{4}$ cup	Dates
2	Tart apples
2	Onions
3	Carrots
1 teaspoon	Ground cloves
1 teaspoon	Ground ginger
1 teaspoon	Ground allspice
1 tablespoon	Salt
$2\frac{1}{2}$ cups	Malt vinegar
$1\frac{1}{3}$ cups	Raw brown sugar

METHOD

1 Pit and chop plums and dates. Peel, core and chop apples. Peel and chop onions. Scrape and coarsely grate carrots.
2 Put the spices and salt into a bowl and mix with a little malt vinegar.
3 Put remaining vinegar and sugar in a kettle and heat slowly, stirring, till sugar is dissolved. At boiling point, stir in the prepared fruit, vegetables and spice mixture. Boil steadily for about 45 minutes till chutney is thick, then ladle into sterilized jars. Cover, leaving $\frac{1}{2}$ inch headroom, and process for 10 minutes in a boiling-water-bath.

VARIATION

To turn this into a chutney with a hotter flavor simply add from a pinch to 1 teaspoon cayenne with the other spices.

Blackberry and apple jelly

A glowing reddish-black jelly flavored with fresh fruit. If you like, you can make it just with blackberries, though the apples help to give a firmer set

PRESERVE Makes 4 jars

Overall timing 1 hour plus straining time

Equipment Large kettle, jelly bag, sterilized jelly glasses with lids, or liquid paraffin wax and lids

Freezing Not recommended

Storage Cool, dark place

Below: Blackberry and apple jelly — good with toast or hot croissants for breakfast

INGREDIENTS

4½lb	Blackberries
2	Tart apples
2½ cups	Water
	Sugar
2	Lemons

METHOD

1 Wash blackberries. Core and roughly chop apples. Place both in kettle with water and bring to a boil. Boil for 10 minutes over a moderate heat.

2 Remove pan from heat and squash fruit with a potato masher to press out as much juice as possible.

3 Strain through a scalded jelly bag overnight. Measure the juice and place in the clean kettle with 1½ cups of sugar to each 2½ cups of juice. Squeeze the lemons and add juice to the kettle.

4 Bring to a boil, stirring all the time. Cook for about 20 minutes, then test for jell point by placing a little jelly on a cold saucer. If it jells remove kettle from heat. It if doesn't, cook for a few minutes more, then test again.

5 Pour the jelly into heated, sterilized jelly glasses and seal at once. If using paraffin wax, leave ½ inch headroom and pour over a ⅛ inch layer of wax.

Green tomato chutney

If you grow your own tomatoes, this is a good way of using late ones which are often slow to ripen fully

PRESERVE   Makes about 5lb

Overall timing 2 hours

Equipment Cheesecloth bag, large kettle, sterilized canning jars and lids, ladle

Freezing Not recommended

Storage Cool, dry, dark place

INGREDIENTS

4lb	Green tomatoes
1lb	Onions
1lb	Tart apples
1oz	Pickling spices
2 inch	Piece of cinnamon stick
2 teaspoons	Salt
3 cups	Malt vinegar

METHOD

1 Wash and chop the tomatoes. Peel and finely chop the onions; core and chop the apples. Tie the pickling spices and cinnamon in a cheesecloth bag.
2 Put the tomatoes, onions, apples, salt and spices into a kettle with half the vinegar and bring to a boil. Simmer, uncovered, for 1 hour till pulpy.
3 Add sugar and remaining vinegar and stir till sugar dissolves. Bring to a boil and simmer for 10–15 minutes, stirring occasionally, till chutney is thick.
4 Discard the bag of spices. Ladle the chutney into warm sterilized jars, leaving ½ inch headroom. Cover and process in a boiling-water-bath for 10 minutes.

SQUASH CHUTNEY

Peel and seed 4lb large summer squash and chop. Sprinkle with salt and leave overnight. Next day, drain squash and place in saucepan with ⅔ cup chopped candied ginger, 4 garlic cloves, 2 cups raisins or chopped dates, ½ teaspoon cayenne and 2½ cups malt vinegar. Bring to a boil, cover and cook until squash is soft, then add 3 cups brown sugar. Return to a boil and cook over a moderate heat until consistency of jam. Ladle into sterilized jars, leaving ½ inch headroom, and cover. Process in a boiling-water-bath for 10 minutes.   **Makes about 3lb**

Apple chutney

A sharp, fruity chutney. Grinding the apples, onions and raisins produces a smooth texture

PRESERVE   Makes 8lb

Overall timing 1 hour

Equipment Grinder or food processor, large kettle, sterilized canning jars and lids, ladle

Freezing Not recommended

Storage Cool, dark place for 1 year

INGREDIENTS

4lb	Tart apples
1	Large onion
3 cups	Golden raisins
1 tablespoon	Mustard seed
	Grated rind of 1 lemon
2 tablespoons	Lemon juice
2 teaspoons	Ground ginger
3½ cups	Malt vinegar
5½ cups	Brown sugar

Below: Apple chutney – a sweet and savory mix to serve with cold cuts

METHOD

1 Peel and core apples. Peel and chop onion. Put apples, onion and raisins through a grinder or food processor, then place in a kettle.
2 Crush the mustard seed, and add to the kettle with the lemon rind and juice, ginger, and 2½ cups of the vinegar. Cover and simmer until soft.
3 Place the sugar in a pan with remaining vinegar and heat gently, stirring, till sugar has dissolved. Pour over the fruit mixture. Continue cooking, uncovered, until thick.
4 Ladle into jars, leaving ½ inch headroom. Cover and process in a boiling-water-bath for 10 minutes.

Grind peeled and cored apples with onions and raisins, then put in kettle

Add crushed mustard seed, rind and juice of lemon, and vinegar; simmer till soft

After vinegar syrup has been added, cook until thick, then ladle into hot jars

Chain-cooking techniques

Make the most of your freezer with these chain-cooking ideas. Start with a basic ingredient and make several dishes at once by dividing it up and using it with other ingredients. Begin with lean ground beef; you'll need 6 pounds of ground round, or less expensive ground beef, to make all four of the dishes suggested here.

Basic beef mixture

Melt 2 tablespoons butter or margarine in a large skillet. Add 1½lb of the ground beef and press into the hot fat with a spatula, but do not stir. When underside is brown, turn beef and cook till brown and crumbly. Remove from pan with slotted spoon and place in a large saucepan (or pressure cooker base). Pour away fat from skillet, add another 2 tablespoons butter or margarine and heat before adding a further 1½lb ground beef. Cook as before, then repeat process twice more till all 6lb beef is browned. Peel and chop 2lb onions. Heat 2 tablespoons butter or margarine in skillet, add onions and fry till golden, stirring occasionally. Add to beef with 3½ cups hot beef stock or broth, a bay leaf, salt and freshly-ground black pepper. Bring to a boil, cover and simmer for 20 minutes. Divide mixture between 4 mixing bowls.

Quick lasagne

Ingredients ¼lb bacon; ¼lb chicken livers; 2 tablespoons butter; 1 quantity basic beef mixture; 16oz can of tomatoes; 1 teaspoon dried oregano; ½lb cream cheese; 2 eggs; 1½ cups grated cheese; 6oz green lasagne pasta; 1 tablespoon soft breadcrumbs

Method Dice bacon; wipe and chop chicken livers. Heat butter in skillet, add bacon and fry till fat runs. Add chicken livers and fry quickly, stirring, till browned. Mix into beef with tomatoes and juice from can and oregano. Put cream cheese into bowl and beat till softened. Add eggs and all but ¼ cup of the grated cheese.

To freeze Spread one-third of the lasagne (no need to cook) in bottom of shallow foil or oven-to-freezer dish; cover with half the meat. Repeat, finishing with layer of pasta. Cover with cream cheese mixture and smooth top, Mix remaining grated cheese and breadcrumbs and sprinkle over cream cheese. Open freeze. Wrap in freezer wrap. Seal and label. Freezer life: 1 month.

To use: Unwrap, cover lightly with foil and bake in preheated 400° oven for 1¼ hours, removing foil for last 15 minutes to brown top. Serve with a tossed green salad. **Serves 4**

Beef stuffed loaf

Ingredients 1 small crusty loaf of bread; 1 tablespoon curry powder; 3 tablespoons chutney; 1 quantity basic beef mixture; $\frac{1}{4}$ cup butter

Method Slice off top third of loaf lengthwise and reserve. Carefully cut out center crumb* of base and lid to leave a crust about $\frac{3}{4}$ inch thick on the base, $\frac{1}{2}$ inch on the lid. Mix curry powder and chutney into beef mixture. Melt butter in small pan.

To freeze Spoon beef mixture into loaf and replace lid. Brush butter liberally over top and sides of loaf. Wrap in freezer wrap. Seal, label and freeze. Freezer life: 1 month.

To use Thaw overnight in refrigerator. Bake in foil in preheated 400° oven for 1 hour till crisp and golden, then slash top to reveal filling. Serve cut into thick slices with a cucumber, yogurt and mint salad. **Serves** 6

*Put crumbs in blender to make fine breadcrumbs. Pack in small freezer bag or rigid container. Seal, label and freezer. Freezer life: 3 months.

Fluffy-topped cottage pie

Ingredients 2lb potatoes; salt; $1\frac{1}{4}$ cups milk; 2 tablespoons butter; 2 eggs; $\frac{1}{4}$ cup grated Parmesan cheese; $\frac{1}{4}$ teaspoon freshly-grated nutmeg; $\frac{1}{2}$lb frozen mixed vegetables; 1 tablespoon Worcestershire sauce; 1 teaspoon prepared mustard; 1 quantity basic beef mixture

Method Peel and quarter potatoes. Bring to boil in lightly salted water, cover and simmer for 20 minutes till tender. Drain. Put milk and butter into the pan and melt butter. Return potatoes to pan and mash till smooth over gentle heat. Separate eggs. Add yolks to potatoes with cheese and nutmeg. Add vegetables, Worcestershire sauce and mustard to beef in bowl. Mix well. Beat egg whites till stiff; fold into potatoes.

To freeze Spread beef mixture in shallow foil dish. Spoon or pipe potato mixture over to cover beef completely. Open freeze, then overwrap with freezer wrap. Seal, label. Freezer life: 4 months.

To use Unwrap and thaw overnight in refrigerator. Bake in preheated 400° oven for 1 hour. **Serves 4**

Chili beef with beans

Ingredients $\frac{1}{4}$ teaspoon chili powder; 1 quantity basic beef mixture; 16oz can of red kidney beans; 16oz can of tomatoes; 2 tablespoons tomato paste; 1 teaspoon brown sugar; 1 red pepper

Method Stir chili powder into beef in bowl. Drain and rinse the beans, then add to beef with tomatoes and juice from can, tomato paste and sugar. Wash, halve, seed and slice pepper; blanch in boiling water for 3 minutes, then cool under cold running water. Drain well. Stir into beef mixture.

To freeze Place a freezer bag in a large saucepan, pour in beef mixture, exclude air and seal. Freeze in pan, then remove. Overwrap and label. Freezer life: 4 months.

To use Unwrap, place frozen block back in pan and cook over a low heat, stirring occasionally, till boiling. Taste and adjust seasoning, then thicken with 1 tablespoon cornstarch dissolved in a little water, if necessary. Cook till thickened. Serve with rice and salad. **Serves 4**

Chain-cooking chicken

The meat of chicken combines well with different ingredients, the bones give you a supply of chicken stock for soup or gravy, and the livers can be collected to be made into pâté at a later stage. The chickens should be fresh as frozen chicken cannot be thawed, then returned to the freezer uncooked. Four chickens plus a few vegetables and some pantry bits and pieces will give you six tasty dishes to store in the freezer to take out and serve over a period of 3 months, and stock to last for 6 months

Preparing the chickens

Remove the giblets. Separate livers, place in small rigid container, cover, label and freeze. Freezer life: 3 months.

Wash rest of giblets and reserve. Wipe chickens inside and out. Cut through skin between leg and carcass and push legs away from body to expose joint. Sever and remove the legs, then divide into drumsticks for Spicy broiled drumsticks, and thighs for Chicken and pineapple curry. Cut through skin and flesh along breastbone of each bird. Slip knife under flesh to one side of the bone and gradually detach breast from ribs and wings to give 8 boneless breasts — use 4 for Stuffed chicken breasts and 4 for Chicken and tarragon parcels.

Put remainder of chicken into large saucepan with giblets, peeled onion, scraped carrot, bay leaf and trimmed stalk of celery. Bring slowly to boil. Skim, then reduce heat and simmer for 45 minutes. Lift out carcasses, remove meat and reserve for Chicken and corn fricassée. Return bones to pan and simmer for 1 hour more. Strain stock, return to pan and boil till reduced to one-third. Cool quickly, pour into ice-cube trays and freeze. When frozen pack into freezer bag, seal and label. Freezer life: 6 months.

Stuffed chicken breasts

Ingredients 4 boneless chicken breasts; ¼lb Roquefort cheese; 2 tablespoons light cream; ¼ cup flour; 2 eggs; 3 cups fine soft breadcrumbs

Method Remove skin from chicken breasts (reserve to use in stock). Using a sharp knife, make deep horizontal cut along one side of each chicken breast to make a pocket. Beat Roquefort and cream till smooth and divide between each pocket. Close pockets with wooden toothpicks. Coat the chicken with flour. Beat eggs on a plate; spread breadcrumbs on waxed paper. Dip chicken into the egg to coat both sides, then press crumbs on firmly.

To freeze Place the coated chicken on a foil-lined baking sheet, cover lightly and open freeze. Wrap each in foil and pack into freezer bag. Seal and label. Freezer life: 1 month.

To use Unwrap, place on baking sheet and thaw in refrigerator for 4–6 hours. Heat oil in a deep-fat fryer to 320° and fry chicken breasts for about 10 minutes till golden. Drain on paper towels, remove toothpicks and serve. **Serves 4**

Chicken and corn fricassée

Ingredients 2–2½ cups cooked chicken meat; 1 large onion; 1 cup small mushrooms; ¼ cup butter; 3 tablespoons flour; 1¼ cups milk; ¾ cup strong chicken stock or broth; ½lb frozen whole kernel corn; salt; freshly-ground black pepper

Method Cut the chicken into neat pieces, removing any skin and bones (reserve them to use in stock). Peel and chop the onion; wipe, trim and slice the mushrooms. Heat the butter in a large saucepan and fry the onion gently till transparent. Add the mushrooms and fry for a further 3 minutes. Sprinkle the flour over and cook for 1 minute. Gradually add the milk and stock and bring to a boil, stirring. Add chicken and corn, mix well and season. Cool quickly.

To freeze Place a freezer bag inside a saucepan, pour the fricassée in, seal and freeze till hard. Remove, overwrap, label. Freezer life: 1 month.

To use Remove from bag, replace block in pan and heat gently, stirring occasionally. Stir in ¾ cup light cream and 1 tablespoon chopped parsley. Garnish with broiled bacon rolls and serve. **Serves 4**

Chicken and tarragon parcels

Ingredients 1 onion; $\frac{1}{4}$lb bacon; $\frac{1}{2}$ cup butter; 4 boneless chicken breasts; 1 tablespoon chopped fresh tarragon; salt; freshly-ground black pepper

Method Peel and chop the onion; dice the bacon. Heat 2 tablespoons of the butter in a skillet and fry the onion and bacon till golden. Cut four 10 inch squares of foil and sprinkle each with a quarter of onion and bacon. Arrange a chicken breast on top of each. Beat the remaining butter till soft, mix in the tarragon and seasoning, then spread over the chicken breasts. Bring two opposite sides of foil to center and roll edges together to seal well.

To freeze Place in freezer bag, seal, label and freeze. Freezer life: 2 months.

To use Remove parcels from bag, arrange on baking sheet and bake from frozen in preheated 375° oven for about 45 minutes till chicken is tender. Serve chicken in the parcels with creamed potatoes, broccoli spears and carrot sticks. **Serves 4**

Spicy broiled drumsticks

Ingredients 8 chicken drumsticks; $\frac{1}{2}$ teaspoon each of curry powder, ground cumin, ground coriander and turmeric; juice of 2 lemons; wine vinegar; $\frac{1}{4}$ cup oil

Method Prick each chicken drumstick several times with a fork. Mix spices together and rub into chicken. Place in a shallow rigid container. Measure lemon juice and add equal quantity of vinegar and the oil. Mix well, then pour over the chicken to cover it. (If it doesn't, make up more marinade.)

To freeze Cover container, seal and label. Freezer life: 1 month.

To use Thaw overnight in refrigerator, then pour off two-thirds of the marinade. Add $\frac{2}{3}$ cup plain yogurt and 1 teaspoon salt, turn chicken in it till coated, then leave for 20 minutes. Preheat broiler and line pan with foil. Arrange drumsticks on pan and broil for about 10 minutes, turning frequently till browned all over. Serve immediately with boiled rice and mango chutney. **Serves 4**

Chicken and pineapple curry

Ingredients $\frac{1}{4}$ cup butter; 2 tablespoons oil; 8 chicken thighs; 2 large onions; 1 tablespoon curry powder; 1 tablespoon flour; $1\frac{1}{2}$ cups chicken stock or broth; 8oz can of pineapple chunks; 2 tablespoons mango chutney

Method Heat the butter and oil in a large saucepan. Fry the chicken thighs, a few at a time, turning frequently till browned all over. Remove from pan and reserve. Peel and thinly slice the onions. Add to the pan and fry gently till transparent. Sprinkle the curry powder and flour over and fry for 1 minute. Gradually stir in the stock and bring to a boil, stirring. Return chicken to pan with the pineapple and juice and the chutney. Bring to a boil and simmer for 20 minutes.

To freeze Cool quickly. Line saucepan with freezer bag, pour curry in and push meat down into the sauce. Seal and freeze till hard. Remove from pan, label. Freezer life: 3 months.

To use Remove bag, replace block in pan and stir over low heat till boiling. Adjust seasoning and serve immediately with boiled rice. **Serves 4**

Chain-cooking pie pastry

This basic pastry is very easy to make, which might make you think it is not worth freezing. However, if you make a large batch of pastry, you can use it for a selection of sweet and savory pastries to keep on hand in the freezer for future needs — family meals or a party. It makes sense to set aside time in this way for it makes the freezer work for you

Basic pie pastry

Sift 5 cups of all-purpose flour and 1½ teaspoons salt into each of three bowls. Add 1¼ cups of fat (mixed butter, margarine or shortening) to each bowl and cut or rub in until resembling crumbs.

Batch 1: Add 6 tablespoons of sugar, 2 egg yolks and enough water to bind to a soft but not sticky dough. Foil-wrap and chill for 30 minutes. Roll out dough and use to line an 8 inch and a 9 inch tart or flan pan. Bake blind together in a preheated 375° oven for 15 minutes. Use for Rhubarb streusel tart and Almond cherry tart.

Batch 2: Stir in 2 cups of finely-grated cheese, ½ teaspoon powdered mustard and enough water to make smooth dough. Reserve half for Zucchini and bacon quiche; use rest for Cheese straws. Preheat oven to 400°. Roll out dough to ¼ inch thickness and cut into strips 3 inches long and ¼ inch wide. Glaze with egg yolk; sprinkle with mixed coarse sea-salt and poppy seeds. Arrange on baking sheets and bake for 10 minutes.

To freeze Cool quickly. Interleave layers in rigid container, cover, label and freeze. Freezer life: 3 months.

To use Refresh frozen straws for 10 minutes in preheated 425° oven.

Batch 3: Add enough water to make smooth dough. Use one-third for Rich beef and mushroom pie and the rest for Haddock and cheese braid.

Serves 6

Zucchini and bacon quiche

Ingredients ½ quantity cheese dough (Batch 2); 1 large onion; ½lb bacon; 2 tablespoons butter; ½lb zucchini; 3 eggs; ¾ cup light cream; 1 tablespoon chopped parsley; salt; freshly-ground black pepper

Method Roll out the dough and use to line a 9 inch quiche or flan pan. Bake blind in preheated 375° oven for 15 minutes. Peel and thinly slice the onion. Cut the bacon into large pieces with kitchen scissors. Heat the butter in a skillet and fry the bacon and onion till transparent. Wash, dry and thinly slice the zucchini. Add to the pan and fry over a high heat till golden. Spoon the mixture into the pastry case. Beat the eggs lightly with a fork, gradually adding the cream. Stir in parsley and seasoning. Pour into case.

To freeze Open freeze. Remove quiche, place in rigid container, cover and label. Freezer life: 2 months.

To use Remove from container, replace in pan and cover lightly with foil. Bake from frozen in preheated 375° oven for about 50 minutes. Remove the foil and bake for a further 10–15 minutes till golden. Serve hot with a tomato salad.   **Serves 4**

Haddock and cheese braid

Ingredients ¾lb smoked haddock fillets (finnan haddie); 2 cups milk; 6 tablespoons butter; 5 tablespoons flour; 1 cup shredded cheese; salt; freshly-ground black pepper; 1 cup frozen peas; ⅔ quantity basic dough (Batch 3); 1 beaten egg

Method Wipe haddock and place in large pan. Add milk and bring slowly to a boil. Reduce heat and poach for about 5 minutes till tender. Lift out fish and flake, discarding bones and skin. Strain the milk and reserve. Heat butter in a pan, add flour and cook for 1 minute. Gradually add milk and bring to a boil, stirring constantly. Simmer for 2 minutes, then remove from heat and stir in cheese and haddock. Season and add peas. Leave to cool completely. Roll out dough to a rectangle about 14 × 12 inches. With a short side nearest you, make 8 diagonal cuts in each long side, each cut being about 3 inches long. Brush edges of dough with egg, and spoon fish mixture along center. Fold short ends of dough in over filling, then bring strips alternately from left and right to form a braid.

To freeze Open freeze on foil-lined baking sheet. Wrap in freezer wrap, seal and label. Freezer life: 1 month.

To use Unwrap, place on baking sheet and bake from frozen in preheated 425° oven for about 45 minutes till crisp and golden.

Serves 6

Rich beef and mushroom pie

Ingredients 2lb beef for stew; $\frac{1}{4}$ cup margarine; 2 large onions; $\frac{1}{2}$lb mushrooms; 3 tablespoons flour; $\frac{1}{4}$ teaspoon ground allspice; $1\frac{1}{4}$ cups dark beer; 1 beef bouillon cube; salt; freshly-ground black pepper; $\frac{1}{3}$ quantity basic dough (Batch 3); beaten egg

Method Wipe, trim and cut meat into 1 inch cubes. Heat margarine in flameproof casserole and fry meat a few pieces at a time over high heat till browned. Remove. Preheat oven to 325°. Peel and slice onions; wipe and chop mushrooms. Fry onions in casserole till browned; add mushrooms and fry for 3 minutes. Add flour and allspice and fry for 1 minute. Gradually add beer and bring to a boil, stirring. Add bouillon cube and seasoning, cover and cook in oven for about $1\frac{1}{2}$ hours till meat is tender.

To freeze Cool quickly. Place in $1\frac{1}{2}$ quart foil container. Roll out dough and cover meat. Crimp edges; decorate with dough trimmings. Brush top with egg. Open freeze. Wrap in freezer wrap, seal and label. Freezer life: 3 months.

To use Unwrap and thaw overnight in refrigerator. Place on baking sheet and bake in preheated 400° oven for 20 minutes. Reduce temperature to 350° and bake for further 15–20 minutes till crisp. **Serves 6**

Almond cherry tart

Ingredients 1lb sweet cherries or 16oz can sweet cherries; 6 tablespoons sugar; 8 inch baked pie shell (Batch 1); 1 egg white; $\frac{1}{4}$ cup butter; 1 egg; $\frac{1}{2}$ teaspoon almond extract; $\frac{1}{2}$ cup ground almonds

Method Wash, dry and pit fresh cherries or drain and dry canned. Toss in 2 tablespoons of the sugar till lightly coated. Brush pie shell with egg white, then add cherries. Cream the butter and remaining sugar together till pale and fluffy. Beat in the egg, almond extract and almonds. Spread the mixture over the cherries and smooth the top.

To freeze Cover lightly and open freeze. Remove from pan, place in rigid container, cover and label. Freezer life: 3 months.

To use Remove from container, replace in pan and thaw for 2 hours at room temperature. Bake in preheated 350° oven for about 30 minutes till top is set and golden. Remove from the pan and place on a serving plate. Spread $\frac{3}{4}$ cup sour cream over the top of the tart and scatter $\frac{1}{4}$ cup toasted sliced almonds over. Serve warm. **Serves 6**

Rhubarb streusel tart

Ingredients 9 inch baked pie shell (Batch 1); 2lb rhubarb; 1 cup brown sugar; 6 tablespoons butter; 3 cups soft breacrumbs; grated rind of 1 orange

Method Wash and trim rhubarb and cut into 1 inch lengths. Put into a saucepan with half the sugar and stir over a low heat till sugar dissolves. Cover and simmer for 10 minutes till tender. Remove from heat and allow to cool slightly. Melt butter in a skillet, add remaining sugar, breadcrumbs and orange rind and stir till coated, being careful mixture doesn't burn. Spread rhubarb in pie shell. Sprinkle crumb mixture over and press down lightly with a fork.

To freeze Cover lightly with freezer wrap and open freeze. Remove from pan, overwrap, seal and label. Freezer life: 3 months.

To use Unwrap and replace in pan. Thaw at room temperature for 2 hours. Bake in preheated 400° oven for 30 minutes till topping is crisp and golden. Remove from pan and serve immediately with vanilla ice cream or whipped cream. Or, leave to cool and serve cold with warm custard sauce. **Serves 6**

Chain-cooking apples

When there is a glut of tart apples, make the most of them. Of course they could all be made into identical pies, but with 10 pounds, you can make five splendid desserts: Apple oat slice, Apple and lime whip, French apple tart, Quick apple brûlée and Nutty apple crumble, as well as apple purée to serve with roast pork, or, with dried fruits added, to use as a pie filling

Preparing the apples

Peel, quarter, core and thickly slice 10lb of tart apples, putting them immediately into water acidulated with lemon juice to prevent browning. Drain and place in a large saucepan with 1 cup sugar and $1\frac{1}{2}$ cups water. Mix gently and bring to a boil. Reduce heat and simmer gently for 15 minutes, till tender. Pour half the apples (about 2 quarts) into a large bowl. Use $2\frac{1}{2}$ cups to make Quick apple brûlée, $2\frac{1}{2}$ cups for Apple oat slice, and 3 cups for Nutty apple crumble.

Put the remaining half of the apples back on the heat and simmer for a further 10–15 minutes, stirring frequently till apples are pulpy. Purée in a blender or mash. Fill three 1-cup cartons or rigid containers, cover and label (apple sauce or pie filling). Freezer life: 6 months. To use: place block in pan and reheat gently.

Use 3 cups of remaining purée for Apple and lime whip, and remaining 2 cups for French apple tart.

Quick apple brûlée

Ingredients $2\frac{1}{2}$ cups stewed apples; $\frac{3}{4}$ cup heavy cream; 1 tablespoon sugar; $\frac{1}{2}$ cup brown sugar

Method Drain off any excess juice from apples and divide between four heat and freezerproof ramekins. Smooth tops. Whip cream till soft peaks form, then fold in sugar. Divide between ramekins, spreading it over the apples and smoothing the tops. Sprinkle brown sugar over in a thick, even layer to cover the cream completely.

To freeze Open freeze. Cover each dish with foil, then pack in a rigid container. Seal and label. Freezer life: 3 months.

To use Unwrap and thaw in refrigerator for 2 hours. Cook under preheated broiler for 2–3 minutes till sugar melts. Serve immediately with crisp ginger cookies. **Serves 4**

French apple tart

Ingredients 2 cups apple purée; grated rind of 1 lemon; 8 inch baked pie shell made with rich sweet pie dough

Method Stir the lemon rind into the apple purée. Leave the pie shell in its pan. Pour the purée into the case and smooth the top.

To freeze Open freeze. Wrap in freezer wrap, seal and label. Freezer life: 3 months.

To use Remove wrappings, place tart on serving plate and thaw at room temperature for 2–3 hours. Wash 2 red-skinned apples – do not peel. Cut into quarters and remove cores. Cut into very thin slices and toss in lemon juice to prevent browning. Arrange on top of tart in overlapping circles to cover the purée. Heat $\frac{1}{4}$ cup apricot jam with 1 tablespoon sugar. Rub through a sieve, then brush the glaze liberally over the sliced apples. Serve with cream. **Serves 6**

Nutty apple crumble

Ingredients 3 cups stewed apples; 1 cup chopped dates; grated rind of 1 orange; 1½ cups flour; 6 tablespoons butter or margarine; ½ cup brown sugar; ¼ cup chopped walnuts
Method Put apples in a bowl and stir in dates and orange rind. Pour into a 1½ quart foil or freezer-to-oven dish and smooth the top. Sift the flour into a bowl and rub in the fat till mixture resembles fine breadcrumbs. Stir in sugar and walnuts. Spread mixture over the fruit, pressing it down lightly with the back of a spoon.
To freeze Cover dish with freezer wrap. Seal, label and freeze. Freezer life: 3 months.
To use Remove wrappings and bake from frozen in preheated 400° oven for about 50 minutes till golden. Serve with custard sauce or unsweetened whipped cream. **Serves 6**

Apple and lime whip

Ingredients 3 cups apple purée; 1 package lime-flavored gelatin; ¾ cup whipping cream; 2 egg whites
Method Put the apple purée into a saucepan and heat till almost boiling. Gradually stir gelatin into purée and stir over a low heat till dissolved – do not boil. Remove from heat, pour into a large bowl and leave to cool, stirring occasionally. Whip cream till soft peaks form; beat egg whites till stiff but not dry. Fold the cream into the apple purée, then the egg whites. Pour into a rigid container and smooth top.
To freeze Cover with freezer wrap. Seal and label. Freezer life: 2 months.
To use Thaw for 3–4 hours at room temperature. Spoon into glasses and decorate with whipped cream and grated chocolate. **Serves 6**

Apple oat slice

Ingredients ½ cup butter or margarine; ¼ cup light corn syrup; 6 tablespoons brown sugar; 2 cups rolled oats; ½ teaspoon ground ginger; 2½ cups stewed apples
Method Grease and bottom-line an 8 inch square cake pan. Melt fat and syrup in a large saucepan. Remove from the heat and stir in the sugar, oats and ginger. Mix well and spread half over the bottom of the pan, pressing it down firmly with the back of a spoon. Cover with the apples, then carefully press remaining oat mixture on top.
To freeze Wrap in freezer wrap. Seal, label and freeze. Freezer life: 2 months.
To use Unwrap, thaw for 3 hours at room temperature, then bake in preheated 375° oven for about 45 minutes till crisp and golden. Run knife around sides of pan and unmold onto serving plate or board. Sift 2 tablespoons confectioners sugar over and serve immediately with cream or custard sauce.
Serves 6

Chain-cooking sponge cakes

Spend a morning making a range of cakes and puddings from the same basic mixture and you'll have goodies to rely on in the freezer. An all-in-one mix is simplest for chain cake making, and an electric mixer cuts down labor. Unlike other chains it's better to make the basic batter in small batches as a large amount is very difficult to divide accurately between pans

Basic cake batter

Sift 3 cups of self-rising flour and 1 tablespoon baking powder into a large bowl. Add $1\frac{1}{2}$ cups each of sugar and soft margarine, and 6 eggs. Beat for at least 4 minutes till smooth and fluffy.

Batch 1: Spread half the mixture into a deep 8 inch round cake pan (this is for Raspberry cream cake). Divide remaining batter between two 7 inch layer cake pans. Bake all the cakes together in a preheated 375° oven, placing larger pan on shelf just above center if necessary. Remove layer cakes after 20–25 minutes; cook larger cake for 10–15 minutes more.

Cool layer cakes, interleave, then wrap in freezer wrap. Seal, label and freeze. Freezer life: 4 months. To use: thaw in wrappings for 3–4 hours at room temperature, then sandwich with jam and sprinkle with sugar.

Batch 2: Use half to make Mincemeat cake; reserve the other half.

Batch 3: Make up basic batter, replacing $\frac{1}{4}$ cup of the flour with cocoa. Spread half the mixture into greased and bottom-lined $8\frac{1}{2} \times 12\frac{1}{2}$ inch jelly roll pan (this is for Coffee layer cake). Use two-thirds of remaining mixture to make Chocolate peach upside-down pudding. Bake both slab cake and pudding at 375°. Remove slab cake after 25–30 minutes; cook pudding for 10–15 minutes more. Use the reserved plain batter from Batch 2 and reserved chocolate batter from Batch 3 to make Marbled lamingtons.

Chocolate peach upside-down pudding

Ingredients 1lb 13oz can of peach halves; $\frac{1}{4}$ cup light corn or maple syrup; 9 glacé cherries; reserved quantity of chocolate cake batter (Batch 3)

Method Drain peaches thoroughly. Grease and bottom-line a deep 8 inch square cake pan and spoon the syrup over the bottom. Place a cherry in the cavity of each peach half and arrange, cut side down, in the pan. Carefully spread the cake batter over and smooth the top. Bake in a preheated 375° oven for 35–40 minutes till springy. Cool.

To freeze Cover with foil and overwrap. Seal, label and freeze. Freezer life: 3 months.

To use Remove wrapping but not foil. Reheat from frozen in preheated 375° oven for about 45 minutes. Unmold so peaches are on top and serve immediately with ice cream.

Serves 6–8

Coffee layer cake

Ingredients Cooked chocolate slab cake (Batch 3); $\frac{3}{4}$ cup unsalted butter; 3 cups confectioners sugar; 2 tablespoons instant coffee; 1–2 tablespoons boiling water

Method Cut the slab cake widthwise into 3 even-size pieces. Put the butter into a large bowl and beat till softened. Sift the sugar over and gradually mix into the fat. Dissolve the coffee in the water, add to the butter cream and beat till smooth. Spread half butter cream over the tops of the cakes. Assemble in layers with butter cream on top. Put the remaining butter cream into a pastry bag fitted with a star tube and pipe diagonal lines across the top, leaving a $\frac{1}{2}$ inch space between them.

To freeze Open freeze. Place in rigid container, cover, seal and label. Freezer life: 2 months.

To use Remove from container, place on serving plate and thaw for 2–3 hours at room temperature. Sprinkle $\frac{1}{4}$ cup finely chopped toasted hazelnuts into the spaces between the piped lines. Cut into thin slices to serve. **Serves 10**

Marbled lamingtons

Ingredients Reserved plain and chocolate batters (Batches 2 and 3); 2 tablespoons butter; ½ cup milk; 4 cups confectioners sugar; ¼ cup cocoa; 1½ cups shredded coconut

Method Grease and bottom-line an 8 inch square cake pan. Place spoonfuls of the chocolate batter at random in the pan and fill the spaces between them with plain batter. Stir lightly with a fine skewer to give a marbled appearance. Bake in a preheated 375° oven for 40–45 minutes till springy when pressed. Unmold and cool. Put butter and milk in large bowl over simmering water and stir till melted. Sift the sugar and cocoa into the milk and mix till smooth. Leave over hot water to keep it liquid. Cut the cake into 1¼ inch squares. Spear 1 on a skewer, dip in the frosting, then toss in coconut till evenly coated. Place on a wire rack to set. Repeat till all are coated.

To freeze Open freeze. Pack in rigid container. Freezer life: 3 months.

To use Unpack, arrange on serving plate and thaw for 1–2 hours at room temperature. **Makes 25**

Mincemeat cake

Ingredients ½ quantity basic plain cake batter (Batch 2); ¾ cup mincemeat; 2 tablespoons brown sugar

Method Grease and bottom-line a deep 8 inch round cake pan. Spread half the batter over the bottom of the pan. Spoon the mincemeat on top, then carefully cover with the remaining batter. Smooth the top and sprinkle the sugar over. Bake in a preheated 375° oven for 45–50 minutes, covering top if necessary, till springy when pressed. Allow to cool in pan for 10 minutes, then unmold and cool completely.

To freeze Place in freezer bag. Seal, label and freeze. Freezer life: 3 months.

To use Unwrap cake and replace in pan. Cover lightly with foil, reheat from frozen in preheated 375° oven for about 45 minutes. Serve hot with vanilla ice cream. **Serves 8**

Raspberry cream cake

Ingredients ½lb fresh raspberries; 1 tablespoon Kirsch; 3 tablespoons confectioners sugar; 2 cups heavy cream; baked deep 8 inch cake (Batch 1)

Method Hull the raspberries and put into a bowl with the Kirsch and 2 tablespoons of the confectioners sugar. Leave to macerate for 10 minutes. Whip ¾ cup of the cream till it forms soft peaks, then fold in the raspberry mix. Cut the cake in half and place the bottom on a baking sheet. Spread the raspberry cream over and cover with the top of the cake. Whip remaining cream and sugar till it forms stiff peaks. Spread half over top and sides of cake. Put rest into pastry bag and pipe 8 whirls around top.

To freeze Open freeze. Place in rigid container. Cover, seal and label. Freezer life: 3 months.

To use Remove from container, put on serving plate and thaw for about 3 hours at room temperature. Melt 2 squares (1oz each) semisweet chocolate and spread thickly on waxed paper. When set, cut into 8 triangles. Place one on each cream whirl. Grate remaining chocolate and press onto sides of cake. **Serves 8**

Kitchen cupboard techniques

Canned, bottled and dried foods, apart from being major standbys, are also an investment on which you expect to draw when needed. This is especially true if you buy in bulk and, having saved money, you don't want to make the mistake of leaving foods too long on the shelf so they have deteriorated by the time you use them.

Modern preserving methods, along with strict hygiene regulations, ensure that most foods have a long shelf life. The only real problems occur with foods that don't have a "best by" or "eat by" date because you can't be sure how long they've been on the store's shelves before you buy them. Dried legumes (beans, peas, lentils) age unnoticeably and if they have been around too long no amount of soaking and cooking is going to make them tender and tasty. Buying from stores with a quick turnover is a good rule for foods you intend to store. Label them immediately with date of purchase and, when you store them, bring existing stocks to the front.

Lengths of shelf life always vary and manufacturers err on the safe side because they cannot control storage conditions. Ideally cupboards should be cool (no warmer than 70°) without any damp or moisture to rust cans and lids or spoil ingredients in paper packs.

Removing foods from their wrappings can extend the shelf life — staples such as flour, salt and sugar are best stored in moistureproof containers. Herbs and spices, often bought in too great a quantity for quick use, keep their aromas and flavors better in dark glass screw-top jars. Air and light also have an adverse effect on oil which needs the protection of a metal airtight container. When buying cans to store, avoid any with dents or rust on top or bottom rims. A raised surface at either end can mean that the contents have started to ferment — watch for this when buying acidic foods.

FOOD	STORAGE TIME	IDEAL STORAGE	SIGNS OF DETERIORATION
baked beans/spaghetti	1 year	DCP	dents, rust on can
baking powder/cream of tartar/soda	1 year	CC, DCP	won't bubble when 1 teaspoon is mixed with $\frac{1}{3}$ cup hot water
bouillon cubes	6 months	AC, DCP	absorb moisture
bread mix	3 months	DCP	bag inflates
breadcrumbs	1 year	DCP, AC if opened	musty smell
cake mix	6 months	DCP	loss of flavor when cooked
chestnuts, purée	2 years	DCP	dents, rust on can
water, brined	1 year	DCP	lose crunchiness
chocolate, cooking	6 months	TW, DCP	bloom forms, becomes crumbly
powder	1 year	ST, DCP	dries out, loses flavor
cereals, breakfast	3 months	DCP, AC if opened	become soft, lose flavor
bran/wheatgerm	2–6 months	AC, DCP/R	rancid smell, weevils
rice/sago/semolina/ tapioca	1 year	CC, DCP	stale smell, taste
cocoa	indefinitely	ST, DCP	loses volatile oil, flavor
coconut, creamed	6 months	DCP	rancid smell
shredded	1 year	AC, DCP	becomes dry, tasteless
coffee, instant	2 years	AC, DCP	absorbs moisture
beans	6 months	AC, DCP	lose flavor
cookies	6 months	DCP	musty smell, become soft/crumbly
cream, sterilized	6 months	DCP	loses texture, becomes watery
desserts/topping, dried	6 months	TW, DCP	made-up dish not as intended
dried legumes (peas/ beans/lentils)	1 year	CC, DCP	won't soften when cooked
eggs	3–4 weeks	carton in R	become stale, bad
	2 weeks	room temperature	become stale, bad
pickled	indefinitely	DCP	liquid evaporates, changes color
fats, hydrogenated	1 year	DCP	surface cracks from drying
margarine, tubs	6 months	CC in R	surface cracks from drying
block	3 months	TW in R	becomes darker, can dry
butter, salted	1 month	TW in R	can become rancid
unsalted	3 months	TW in R	loses flavor
suet, packet	2 years	DCP, CC if opened	becomes very greasy
fish, pastes	1 year	DCP	become over salty
anchovies/sardines/ pilchards, in oil	indefinitely	DCP (turn over every so often	not noticeable
in tomato sauce	1 year	DCP	lose texture
herrings/mackerel/ salmon/tuna	2 years	DCP	lose texture, become over salty
flour, white	6–9 months	CC, DCP	musty smell
wholewheat	2 months	CC, DCP	rancid smell, weevils
	6 months	R	rancid smell
cornstarch/arrowroot	2 years	CC, DCP	musty smell
food colorings/extracts	indefinitely	ST, DCP	evaporate, lose flavor
fruit, canned/bottled in syrup	2 years	DCP	loses flavor, texture
prunes/rhubarb	1 year	DCP	high acid may affect can
berries, canned	6 months	DCP	lose flavor, texture
candied/glacé	indefinitely	DCP	hardness, stickiness (can be washed)
citrus segments/juice	1 year	DCP	high acid may affect can
dried	1 year	CC, DDCP	may dry out/ferment
in spirits	indefinitely	CC, DDCP	may lose texture
gelatin, unflavored	indefinitely	AC, DCP	absorb moisture; can absorb flavors from cupboard, other foods
flavored	indefinitely	AC, DCP	
aspic, sachet	6 months	DCP	loses quality
herbs	6 months	DGAC, DCP	musty smell, lose flavor
honey	indefinitely	AC, DCP	can crystallize, harden
horseradish, creamed	6 months	DCP	loses flavor
relish with vinegar	1 year	DCP	becomes sour tasting
ice cream mix, dried	6 months	DCP	absorbs moisture

FOOD	STORAGE TIME	IDEAL STORAGE	SIGNS OF DETERIORATION
jam/marmalade	2 years	ST, DCP	shrinks in jar
juices, concentrated	6 months	DCP	flavor alters, may change color
malt, powder	indefinitely	ST	dries out, becomes hard
marzipan (almond paste)	2 years	TW in AC	can become rancid
mayonnaise, bought	1 year	ST, DCP, in R if opened	dries out
meats, canned	18 months	DCP	dents, rust on can
ham	6 months	DCP	dents, rust on can
meringues, packet	6 months	CC, DCP	become crumbly, tasteless
milk, dried non-fat	1 year	ST, DCP	reconstitutes unevenly
condensed	6 months	DCP	loses texture
evaporated	6 months	DCP	darkens, becomes thick
sterilized	3 months	DCP	air causes souring
opened	3 days	R	air causes souring
mincemeat, bottled	indefinitely	DDCP	shrinks in jar
mushrooms, dried	6 months	DDCP	become smelly, absorb moisture
mustard, ready mixed	18 months	ST, DCP	dries out, loses flavor
nuts, in shells	1 year	DDCP	mold can form
canned	1 year	ST, DCP	become soft
chopped/ground	6 months	AC, DCP	become rancid
oils, cooking/salad	1 year	MC, DCP	air and light cause bad flavor
olives, canned	1 year	DCP	dents, rust on can
bottled	2 years	DDCP	evaporation of liquid
pasta	2 years	DCP	loses flavor
stuffed	1 year	AC, DCP	loses flavor
peanut butter	1 year	ST, DCP	develops bad flavor
peppercorns, whole	2 years	DGAC	lose pungency
brined	2 years	ST, DDCP	color bleaches out
pickles	indefinitely	ST, DDCP	liquid evaporates/contents shrink
popcorn	1 year	AC, DCP	won't pop, absorbs moisture
rennet, extract	4 months	ST, DCP	loses power
tablets	2 years	CC, DCP	lose power
salt	indefinitely	CC, DCP	absorbs moisture
sauces, bottled	1 year	DCP	lose flavor, thicken
shellfish, canned	1 year	DCP	rust on can
in oil/smoked	2 years	DCP	lose texture
in tomato sauce	1 year	DCP	lose texture
in vinegar, bottled	2 years	DCP	evaporation, cloudy liquid
soups, canned meat	6–9 months	DCP	lose flavor
canned vegetable	1 year	DCP	lose flavor
dried	18 months	DCP	lose flavor
spices	1 year	DGAC, DCP	lose effectiveness
stuffings, dry mixes	1 year	TW, DCP	lose flavor
sugar	2 years	CC, DCP	absorbs moisture/hardens
syrups, canned/bottled	indefinitely	ST, DDCP	changes in color, flavor
tea, boxes	2 years	DCP	loses flavor
open	1 year	AC, DCP	loses flavor, becomes musty
tomatoes, canned	1 year	DCP	high acid may affect can
paste	1 year	ST, DCP	thickens, changes color
vegetables, canned	2 years	DCP	loss of quality
bottled	3 years	DDCP	evaporation of liquid
dried, sachets	1 year	AC, DCP	loss of flavor
in brine	1 year	DDCP	loss of quality
vinegar	indefinitely	ST, DCP	sediment, strands in liquid (strain and rebottle)
yeast, active dry	6 months	CC, DCP	won't froth

cook's know-how

Foods from the kitchen cupboard can be used on their own for snacks, or combined with others to make meals. They also can be used with fresh foods (eg, canned soups as sauces for braised or steam roasted meat). When you're only cooking for yourself, or for two, smaller cans make more sense than larger, though larger ones can be used and half the dish saved for the next day. Canned vegetables bulk out leftover casseroles; drained and dressed with vinaigrette or mayonnaise (both kitchen cupboard ingredients) they become quick salads. In terms of nutrition, we all need fresh foods and cannot live by cans alone — the simple addition of grated cheese adds substance to dried or canned soup; an egg beaten into instant mashed potatoes instantly enriches as does milk in gelatins and soups. Fresh fruit mixed with canned makes an excellent fruit salad and you don't have to worry about making a syrup.

Abbreviations: R refrigerator; CC covered container; AC airtight container; ST sealed tightly; TW tightly wrapped; DCP dry cool place; DDCP dark dry cool place; DGAC dark glass airtight container; MC metal airtight container

233

Finishing touches

aspic

A fine, clear, savory gelatin, aspic is prized in cooking for its ability to glaze foods attractively (see page 236). Chopped into fine dice it enhances cold meats or stuffed eggs or tomatoes, and finely chopped it gives a sparkle to whatever it surrounds. Prettily cut vegetable shapes can be set in it to make an attractive topping for delicate savory mousses. Aspic can be made at home by clarifying stock with egg whites (a lengthy process), or aspic granules or powder can be bought in sachets to be made up with water. Canned broth or consommé can also be set with gelatin to make aspic. Anchovies, sliced hard-cooked egg, fruit and vegetable slices, truffles and mushrooms can all be set in an aspic topping – the vegetables can be stamped out into tiny shapes with aspic cutters (see page 239). The aspic should be almost syrupy before it's poured over or it will push your arrangement out of shape. Set aspic in a shallow pan for dicing, then unmold onto damp waxed paper and chop with a dry cook's knife. Don't touch the jelly or your fingers will cloud it. To make it a sparkly garnish, press through a wide-meshed strainer or chop finely.

branding

Gives meat and fish the look of having been cooked over bars on a charcoal fire. Press heated metal skewers flat onto skin or meat, criss-crossing to give a lattice effect (see also page 135).

cheese

Probably one of the most favored garnishes for it is easy to prepare, looks and tastes good and is nutritious into the bargain. Cheeses with distinctive colors make garnishing sense (choose hard ones for grating); Parmesan sprinkles finely; Gruyère, Emmenthal and Mozzarella have marvelous melting qualities. Vandyke an Edam cheese, then hollow out and use as a holder for dips. To garnish a cooked dish, use processed cheese stamped into a shape.

citrus fruit rind

The zest in the colored part of orange and lemon rinds adds a nice piquancy to soups, salads and sauces, particularly if the fruit is used in the dish (eg, duck with oranges). Using the finest side of the grater it can be grated over foods, but a finely cut julienne on soups should be blanched for 2 minutes.

coatings

Though part of a dish, these are considered garnishes for they create a texture contrast. Gratin dishes are topped with mixed cheese and breadcrumbs and can also have a saucy coat underneath. Fish and whole green beans are sprinkled with fried almonds (*amandine*). Fine-fleshed cutlets of veal, chicken or turkey are breaded (coated with egg and crumbs) to make a crispy outer layer. Tenderest lamb chops are dipped into a thick panade to give a fluffy coat after frying (*villeroi*), or wrapped in strips of pastry (*en croûte*) before being baked. The finest beef is protected by a pastry wrapping in the same way and this can be elaborately garnished with trimmings. Thin onion rings are coated with milk and seasoned flour before deep frying. All play a vital part in the final presentation.

cream and yogurt

Delicately piped rosettes or swirls of cream, yogurt, sour cream or smetana (stabilized buttermilk) are a Russian touch – and it was once said that no food could be complete without one of these being included. As garnishes they make a good contrast (the white of cream on the purple-red of beet soup) and also can "cool" a spicy taste. You have to take care when adding them to a bubbling-with-heat mixture for light cream and yogurt may separate, causing unsightly curdling. Have topping at room temperature and add from a spoon – create swirls with point of skewer or fork.

eggs

Hard-cooked eggs are used in many ways in garnishing, but they stand out most in the one called *polonaise* for both the whites and the yolks can be formed into artistic patterns. The yolks are sieved and the whites finely chopped and the two are sprinkled in alternate circles, bands or spirals, on top of cooked cauliflower, broccoli and fish dishes. To be successful, the colors must remain separate.

frosting glasses

A sort of icing on cocktail glasses. Salt or sugar can be used depending on the drink (Margarita is frosted with salt, Gin fizz with sugar). Lightly forked egg white or lemon juice can be used to hold the frost. Chill glass before filling.

Put lemon juice in a saucer, dip rim of cocktail glass in

Put wet rim into a thick layer of fine salt or sugar, then chill

glazes

Glazes aren't exactly garnishes but do make many foods look glossy and appetizing.

Aspic is used in a fine layer in *chaudfroid* (literally hot-cold) dishes — see right — and as a method of preventing other garnishes such as thin "scales" of cucumber on cold poached fish from drying out. The presence of the aspic is almost unnoticeable in taste terms, yet its role is valuable in giving a final set look to the dish. Cold roast duck, chicken or turkey can also be given an aspic glaze. After making up, the aspic should be left until syrupy before being ladled over the meat. This is especially important if a pattern is to be set in the aspic, for if it is too runny it will dislodge the arrangement. Place the meat on a wire rack over a shallow cake or roasting pan so that excess will fall into this and can be left to set, after which it can be finely chopped or pressed through a coarse sieve to make a sparkling jelly garnish. A galantine is stuffed and boned poultry, game, meat or fish, cooked in jellied stock and pressed under weights, then served cold with a surround of jelly. Pâtés can be treated in the same way.

Poach 6 boned, skinned chicken breasts in court-bouillon for 10 minutes till tender. Drain, cool on a wire rack over a tray. Make Béchamel sauce with $\frac{1}{4}$ cup butter, $\frac{1}{2}$ cup flour and $2\frac{1}{2}$ cups milk. Cool, spoon over chicken to coat evenly

Put 3 egg whites into a greased 7 inch layer cake pan. Place in a skillet containing $\frac{1}{2}$ inch water, cover and poach for 4–5 minutes till set. Unmold and cool. Cut petal shapes with a small cutter. Pit and halve 3 ripe olives

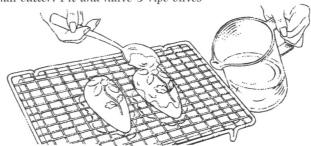

Make up 2 cups of aspic jelly, allow to set till syrupy. Arrange "petals" and olives to make flowers on chicken, using parsley for stalk and leaves. Spoon aspic over chicken to glaze. Set excess in tray, chop finely and use to garnish

Melted butter can be brushed on before cooking, used as a baste during cooking, or brushed on just before serving. If ham is brushed with melted butter, then sprinkled with brown sugar during baking, the glaze becomes crunchy. Bread brushed with melted butter before baking will have a soft crust. **Eggs** are used to give gloss to pastry and bread. Either the whole egg or just the yolk can be lightly beaten (with a pinch of salt for bread) and brushed over dough before baking. Egg glaze gives a professional crusty finish. On puff pastry don't brush it on the edges for it will prevent layers rising.

Below: Chicken breasts glazed with aspic — known also as chaudfroid de volaille — make an appetizing way of serving cold chicken for a summer lunch or formal buffet. The coating sauce keeps the chicken moist as well as adding flavor — the aspic keeps the sauce and garnish fresh-looking and glossy. Poached salmon steaks, coated with mayonnaise and garnished with cucumber and strips of red pepper can be glazed in the same way. Push the leftover aspic through a wide-meshed sieve to make the sparkling accompaniment

Half-and-Half can be used instead of egg to glaze bread, savory pastry and crackers. **Water** with a pinch of salt makes brown bread and rolls crusty. **Syrups**, included in barbecue sauces, or on their own give a sticky-topped finish to meats. Honey, maple syrup, marmalade and molasses are best with poultry and hams; red currant jelly or honey are good with lamb. They brush better if heated first, and marmalade can be strained to remove chunks of rind. Score the fat on hams, then create patterns by, for example, placing whole cloves at regular intervals to accentuate the diamond or lattice made by the knife. Canned fruit such as pineapple which has an affinity with ham makes a pretty contrast and the syrup can be used to glaze and flavor the meat. Sweet glazes need about 30 minutes in a hot oven — and frequent basting.

herbs and greenery

Bunches and sprigs of herbs are one of the easiest ways of garnishing, and they add a refreshing touch to platters containing a variety of goodies, and a welcome contrast with an array of one food such as cold cuts. Watercress has become the traditional end piece for roast turkey; winter lamb can be adorned with rosemary sprigs, summer lamb with mint. Borage with its pretty blue flower is also attractive and the classic addition to a Pimm's cocktail containing a mixture of fruits. Always use sprigs as fresh as possible and pick them over to remove any less than perfect parts. Herbs can be sprinkled over food before or after cooking as a garnish. Parsley is the all round favorite and to make it feathery squeeze it out in the corner of a dish towel or paper towel. Fresh basil leaves make a splendid garnish for tomatoes or poultry.

Score the fat on a ham into diamonds with sharp knife

Insert cloves into diamond points. Brush honey over, bake

Make paper frill to cover bone. Garnish with orange cartwheels

Wash parsley, put into cup. Scissor-snip into fine pieces

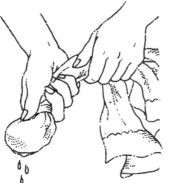

Squeeze chopped parsley in a cloth to dry for sprinkling

nuts

These can be chopped, flaked or sliced for sprinkling over food to give both a crunchy texture and to improve appearance. They are particularly suitable for making soft-textured mixtures more interesting. As garnishes are there to be eaten, nuts are often better if toasted for they have better color and taste. Use halved walnuts or pecans to garnish a cheeseboard, or pistachios which are an attractive golden color. Almonds are good with fresh vegetables, cashews, walnuts, macadamia nuts with salads.

oatmeal and grains

Marvelous finish for home-made wholewheat breads and rolls for they give a farmhouse look. Wholewheat grain is best but medium oatmeal can be used instead. The whole grains should be cracked in a blender before being sprinkled over dough that's been glazed with salted water. Coat filleted fish like mackerel with coarse oatmeal before frying to give a nutty flavor and a crisp brown crust.

pepper

Freshly-ground pepper is an instant garnish for most pasta dishes. Black has the advantage over white of being more visible, though a mixture of the two will give more piquancy. Pepper grinders or mills are a table garnish in themselves. Cracked pepper can be used to coat small homemade soft cheeses (called *fromage mystère*, because the origin of the cheese is a mystery) as can finely-chopped herbs, and sesame seeds.

peppercorns

The ones preserved in vinegar (as opposed to the dried ones for grinding) are pink or green and have a soft texture. They are drained and used whole as a garnish for steaks, fish, roast or broiled meat. Choose the color that gives most contrast to the food.

poppy seeds

These tiny purply black seeds are traditionally used on braided bread, and are equally good on white as they are on enriched, sweetish loaves. Sprinkle over top of dough after glazing with egg and before baking.

salt

Coarse sea-salt ground in a mill adds texture and interest to food. Added just before serving it helps bring out flavor. Black peppercorns and coarse salt can be mixed in a mill for added effect.

sesame seeds

Little whitish seeds that add crunch and look good on breads (add them in the same way as poppy seeds) and crackers. Sprinkle over hummus before serving to enhance the tahini flavor.

silver leaf

Available from Indian delicatessens (it is sometimes called *carak*) this is broken up and crumbled over curries just before serving. The garnish is also said to aid digestion!

spices

They have both color and aroma which is why they make such a good and easy garnish. A mere sprinkling of cayenne or paprika on mashed potatoes, creamy dips, white sauces with vegetables and cheesy-topped dishes adds cheerful color. Do use sparingly for their flavor can overwhelm more delicate ones. Sprinkle over in the same way as confectioners sugar — a small sifter is more controllable than finger and thumb. Whole spices in the form of seeds (cumin, fennel and dill) look splendid on crusty rolls; caraway enhances baked potatoes and buttered cabbage wedges. Cloves are used on hams; nutmeg can be ground directly over freshly-cooked spinach, and also goes well with cheese and egg.

Garnishing techniques

These are the little things that mean a lot when you present the food you have cooked. Garnishes are added to create an effect and it is important to choose complementary colors and textures to set off the food in the most appetizing way. As well as giving a fancy finishing touch, garnishes are there to be eaten and can give foods a lift by providing contrast — a swirl of sour cream with cucumber sticks and a fine julienne of orange peel raises tomato soup to gourmet class, and cold meats take on a new dimension if dressed with stamped-out vegetable shapes set in aspic. Time spent in garnishing is seldom wasted . . .

balling

With the help of a special tool called a baller, vegetable scoop or parisienne cutter, fruit and vegetables can be shaped into small balls. Melon, for example, not only looks better this way but is easier to eat. Cut the top off a small melon, or cut a larger one in half (by vandyking if wished), remove any seeds and scoop out flesh by pushing baller in and rotating until shapes form. Balls can be mixed with other ingredients or tossed in a dressing before being replaced in the shell for serving. Ballers come in several sizes and the smaller ones are used for carrots and turnips to garnish main course meat dishes or soups. Potatoes, too, are scooped into balls and sautéed to serve as *pommes parisienne* (see cooked garnishes, page 243). *Pommes château* to serve with Chateaubriand are made with an oval vegetable scoop when tiny new potatoes aren't available.

curls

Butter curls are made with a special curler which can be straight with a ridged end, or curled like a shepherd's crook, but both are used in the same way. You need a firm, cold block of butter, and the curler has to be gently scraped along the length towards you to create the shapes. Treat them gently and try not to touch them for hot hands will cause them to melt. Place immediately in ice-cold water or in bowl with ice cubes and chill for at least 1 hour before serving. Pile the curls in a glass dish to show them off, or use to garnish the tops of pâtés or terrines.

The influence of Chinese and other Far Eastern cuisines can be seen in the curling of various vegetables. They can be used to garnish any savory dish of any origin, but look particularly attractive as a finishing touch for stir-fried foods and soups.

Carrot curls are made by paring off fine slices along the length of a halved carrot with a vegetable peeler. Roll up the parings and secure each with a toothpick. Press on a tiny sprig of parsley and use as garnish for terrines, salads, platters of canapés or a cheese board.

Celery curls form better if the heart stalks are used. Wash, then cut into 2 inch lengths. With a sharp knife, make regular cuts about a third of the way into the length at one end, then the other, leaving a third uncut in the middle. The finer you can make the cuts, the more the celery will curl. Place in ice-cold water till curly. Thick stalks are tricky for you need to cut downwards across the width (difficult if the stalks are semi-circular) before cutting the fine strips in the length.

Scallions curl well. Wash, then cut off root end. Cut into the green lengthwise to make as many fine strips as possible. Place in ice-cold water till curly. Thin, young leeks can be curled in the same way.

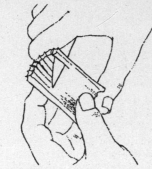

Cut fine strips at each end of celery. Don't cut center third

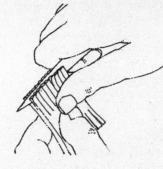

Thick stalks need to be cut across the width as well

Place celery lengths in ice cold water till ends curl up

flowers

Flowers made from vegetables in different shapes, sizes and colors are among the prettiest of all garnishes. A bouquet of them can make a spectacular centerpiece for a buffet table (splendid at any time but particularly when flowers are expensive or unavailable). Impale them on toothpicks and arrange on an upturned grapefruit half, a firm white or red cabbage, or in a basket.

Butter roses are not right for the centerpiece and are used to top terrines. Cream ½ cup of softened butter with a pinch of cream of tartar, then gradually beat in 1 teaspoon unflavored gelatin dissolved in 3 tablespoon hot water till mix looks like whipped cream. Place in pastry bag fitted with large potato tube and pipe rosettes onto terrine. Chill before serving.

Carrot flowers are formed from a number of curls (see left, and pictures right). Put

Below: simple twists and twirls create effective results. The equipment shown from left to right is: vegetable baller, vandyking knife, potato piping bag, vegetable peeler, cannelle knife, aspic cutters, olive pitter, vegetable knife, butter curler, egg wedger and slicer

curls on toothpicks and place in iced water for 1 hour before shaping into flowers.

Halve carrot and pare fine slices with a vegetable peeler

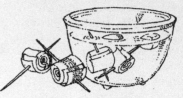

Roll up slices, secure with picks. Place in iced water

Pile curls at angles to form flower with cocktail onion in center. Impale on toothpicks

Onion chrysanthemums are made from pearl onions or bulbous scallions. Peel but leave root end on. Place root end down on flat surface and cut downwards into quarters, then eighths, sixteenths etc, until divisions are too thin to cut any more. Take care not to cut through root or your flower will fall apart. Gently prise the divisions apart, then place in iced water for 1 hour till petals open. Place in freezer bag in freezer for 30 minutes before using to lessen the onion's strong smell. Impale on toothpick for bouquet or arrange several around platter of cold cuts.

Radish waterlilies make a pretty garnish because of the contrast between red skin and white flesh. A special tool with blades like the spokes of a wheel will cut the central rose shape in one action. Otherwise, with sharp knife, cut slice off root end, then with tip cut petal shapes around radish almost to base. Cut second row inside first, cutting so petals are formed across the part where two outer petals meet. Place in ice-cold water till open. Arrange on fine radish slices to create waterlilies.

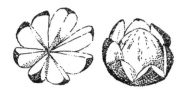

Radish roses are formed as center part of waterlilies. Or the radish can be cut downwards in tiny wedges as above left. Or cut around center to isolate it, then cut to halve or quarter, taking care not to cut through base.
Tomato roses can be made from one strip of peel, but two are easier to handle.

Cut a slice from the stalk end of firm tomato, but keep it attached so you can remove skin

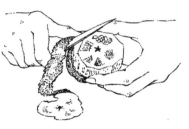

Using a sawing action remove skin with some flesh, working in a spiral around the tomato

Place slice on board and wind tomato skin around and around to form a flower shape on it

Second strip of skin can be used to make inner part of tomato rose more substantial

flutes

These give texture to the bland (mushroom caps), turn slices into cartwheels (oranges, lemons, limes) or highlight a skin color (cucumbers).
Citrus fruit cartwheels are easily made with a special knife called a cannelle (in French this means channel, which is exactly what you are making in the fruit) or the tip of a sharp vegetable peeler. Hold the fruit firmly and draw the knife or peeler through the skin from top to bottom removing a thin strip. Repeat at ⅛ inch intervals around the fruit till skin is well channelled (reserve strips for julienne, see below). Cut the fruit crosswise into thin slices and use to garnish drinks, savory mousses.
Cucumber stripes are made in the same way as the cartwheels but a quicker, though less dramatic, effect can be achieved by scoring with a fork.
Fluted mushrooms are popular as a garnish for fish in France. You need slightly larger mushrooms with a firm texture and uniformly rounded caps. Wipe over; trim stalks to cap level. Hold cap firmly between finger and thumb of one hand and, with tip of knife in the other, make shallow cuts, at the same time slightly rotating cap so channel is circular. Use strips in sauces, soups.

julienne

Fine, straw-like strips of citrus rind are used to garnish savory dishes that contain fruit (see also cooked garnishes). The strips left over from fluting make a julienne, or the colored part of the skin can be removed with a vegetable peeler, stacked and cut into fine strips. To remove toughness and any bitterness, blanch in boiling water for 2 minutes; rinse under cold running water. Leave to soak in cold water until required, but dry thoroughly before sprinkling on top of food.

Hold citrus fruit firmly, cut channels in skin with knife

A cucumber skin can be striped with a fork or cannelle knife

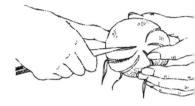

Hold mushroom firmly, but turn as shallow cuts are being made

Use tip of knife to make star shape on top where flutes meet

Pare off colored part of citrus rind with vegetable peeler

Stack parings, then use sharp knife to cut very fine strips

piping

Though usually associated with sweet decorations, piping is equally effective using savory ingredients. **Mayonnaise** has a golden sheen which looks attractive on savory dishes such as fish (salmon or trout) glazed in aspic. Add a pinch of cream of tartar to $\frac{3}{4}$ cup home-made mayonnaise and gradually beat in 1 teaspoon unflavored gelatin dissolved in 3 tablespoons hot water (this makes mixture firm). **Butter** can be mixed with gelatin in the same way as mayonnaise and piped into flowers (see page 239). **Cream cheese** makes an excellent "frosting" for a sandwich cake onto which can be piped a lattice or rosettes. Beat till smooth and fluffy, adding chopped herbs for color contrast, spices or sauces for flavor.

Pipe rosettes of mashed potatoes in rounds to make duchesse shape

Potato mashed to a purée over heat, then beaten till creamy with eggs and butter can be piped to make surrounds for scallop shells (see page 239), or to form rosettes or nests (*pommes duchesse*) to fill with mixed vegetables. A potato piping bag is larger than a pastry bag and the tube is wider to allow lots of swirling in the shaping. Piped potato on main course platters both garnishes and presents the food in an appetizing way. Nests and surrounds on scallop shells should be brushed with beaten egg and broiled until golden brown before serving.

rings and strips

Rings of raw vegetables (onions, red, green and yellow peppers) can be overlapped as a topping for fish dishes, savory mousses. **Strips** can be used to make vibrant patterns on tops of dishes. Anchovies (desalted by soaking in milk first) are excellent for making into a lattice on egg and cheese dishes, or pizzas. Choose your colors and you can create a rainbow of design — strips of tomato skin, slices of pepper, or pimiento, slices of olive (ripe, green and stuffed), egg white (poached in a layer cake pan, then cut), fine straws of carrot or parsnip (blanched for 2 minutes). Once arranged they can then be set in aspic (see page 235).

shredding

Shredded lettuce, sorrel and spinach used as a garnish on salads and soups is called a *chiffonade*. The vegetables need to be crisp and fresh. Wash and dry the outside leaves (not the heart), then stack and roll up. Use a sharp knife and even, fine cuts to make strips $\frac{1}{8}$ inch wide. Toss in colander to separate.

Shredded vegetables make an eye-catching garnish. Vary the colors as much as possible, avoiding beet as it bleeds color. Carrots, white and red cabbage, green, yellow and red peppers all look good when shredded. Cut the pepper into very fine strips and blanch before using. Carrots and cabbage can be shredded on a grater or food processor. This sort of garnish should look crisp so serve quickly. Tossing in a vinaigrette dressing (1 part vinegar to 3 parts oil) gives a good sheen.

vandyking

A culinary tribute to a painter (not his works of art, but his pointed beard), vandyking is a method of cutting edges of fruit and vegetables into V's or zigzags. If you have the time and temperament, you can use the method on stuffed olives and radishes, but generally it is most effective on tomatoes, hard-cooked eggs, melons, oranges, lemons, grapefruit.

With tip of a sharp knife, cut into fruit in zigzag fashion

When zigzags are complete the fruit comes apart garnished

To vandyke, cut a slice from top and bottom (or just one if a whole fruit or vegetable is being served). Using a sharp pointed vegetable knife (serrated for tomatoes to pierce the skin), make a cut at 45°, the next (joined to it) at 135° — this creates a V shape. Continue around the the food till it can be divided into halves, or the top lifted off — the cuts must go right through the center. The size of the zigzags can be varied according to the size of the fruit or vegetable. Special vandyking knives give a uniform, neat result — a melon baller can be used to give scalloped edges to melons. Vandyked oranges and lemons are used as garnishes for foods such as fish, duck, over which the juice is squeezed by the eater. Eggs cut this way can be topped with a mayonnaise swirl, tomatoes can be hollowed out to take a stuffing, either mixed vegetables in mayonnaise, or a savory

sherbet. Sweet sherbets can be set in vandyked oranges or lemons, or the vandyked shells can be used for individual soufflés. Grapefruit can be brûléed (see page 64) or served as is, as an appetizer or for breakfast. **Vandyked baskets** make a superb centerpiece or can be used to hold fruit salad or tiny scoops of ice cream. Melons such as honeydew, watermelon or canteloupe are most successful though the process can be applied to a firm lemon or orange for very special occasions. Cut a slice off the bottom so fruit will stand upright. Make two cuts on either side of a central strip (the handle) to come halfway down the fruit. Now vandyke around the center of the fruit so the two wdges beside the handle can be lifted out. Cut away the flesh inside the handle, and scoop out the flesh from the bottom half if the basket is to be filled. Fake baskets can be made with tomatoes — vandyke them, fill with piped cream cheese flavored with snipped chives or chopped onion and form handles from fine strips of blanched red pepper.

Make downward cuts in top half of melon to create a handle. Vandyke around middle of fruit

When top wedges are lifted off cut flesh from under handle and from the basket if filling

wedges and slices

The skilful use of a sharp vegetable knife can make various simple garnishes for many different dishes.

Orange, lemon, lime wedges are designed to be squeezed. Wipe skin, cut into halves, then quarters or eighths. Alternating orange and lemon wedges as a surround for a platter are most striking.

Hard-cooked eggs can be cut into wedges either with a warmed dry knife or an egg wedger. A most effective garnish can be made for a cold table by removing some wedges from a firm tomato and filling the spaces with egg wedges (see page 239). A beefsteak tomato (*marmande*) can be cut in slices, but not right through, and egg slices placed between (see page 239). Thinly sliced cheese can be used in the same way, as can slices of cucumber.

Citrus fruit slices are marvelously easy garnishes for drinks, savory mousses. They can be cut with or without their skin, or the skin can be fluted (see page 240). They can be made into a border for a platter – moisten every alternate edge and dip into feathery parsley for extra eye appeal.

Twists of citrus fruit are eye-catching garnishes for drinks, consommé and pâtés. Cut very thin slices of lemon,

Slice citrus fruit thinly. Make a cut from center to the edge

lime or orange (leave skin on and flute if liked), then place on a flat surface. With the tip of a sharp knife, cut from the center to the outer rind (the radius). Now lift the slice and hold each side of the cut between fingers and thumbs. Twist in opposite directions, place firmly on food. Two fine slices can be made into a double twist. Flatten first slice slightly and place cut part of second slice on top. Citrus twists can also be garnished with tiny parsley sprigs placed on either side where the rind twists.

Butterflies are made from fine citrus slices. Cut in half, then nick rind near a segment on the curve so that one quarter can be gently pulled away from the other to make wing shapes. The body of the butterfly can be formed with a slice of gherkin.

Citrus peel twists are the classic cocktail garnish for the zest adds the *je ne sais quoi* quality! They can

Hold fruit on each side of cut, twist in opposite directions

sometimes be impaled on a toothpick with or without a stuffed olive or maraschino cherry according to the drink. Use a vegetable peeler or sharp paring knife to remove the outer skin of a lemon or lime – work in a spiral from the pointed end, leaving behind every trace of pith. These long strips of colored zest can also be formed into roses as a garnish for cheese boards or salads.

Cucumber is malleable enough to make into twists and butterflies, and the rind can be pared in a spiral and used in summer punches and drinks such as Pimm's. The fine, almost transparent slices are also used as a garnish for cold poached salmon which, when glazed with aspic (to stop them curling), resemble fanciful scales.

Gherkins are one of the handiest garnishes for they happily stay in the cupboard until you need them. Finely chopped, they can be sprinkled over individual mousses, or

Make deep lengthwise cuts in gherkin, then fan out slices

cut into scale shapes to cover a fish mousse. Gherkin fans can adorn platters and open sandwiches. Choose gherkins about 2 inches long. Hold at the stalk end and make four cuts along most of the length, then spread the slices out carefully.

Olives are another standby to slice and pit for garnishes as needed. To prevent white mold forming in opened jar, add lemon slice to the brine.

Below: Gherkin scales enhance a fish-shaped mousse. Halve 8 large gherkins and slice lengthwise. Arrange slices in rows, starting at the tail end and overlapping the rows as you work towards the head. Place them skin side up in the last row and cover the edge with thin strips of gherkin to neaten. Use more strips to emphasize the shape of the head, mouth and tail. Coil a thin strip of canned pimiento for the eye.

Cooked garnishes

bacon rolls, crispy bits

A good use for bacon, but choose slices that aren't too fatty. Stretch them (see page 23), then roll up and secure with toothpicks. They can be broiled, fried or roasted alongside the poultry they'll be served with. Bacon can also be rolled around cocktail sausages, oysters and prunes.

Crispy bacon bits are also easy to make. Broil or fry till crisp, then drain on paper towels. Break up and scatter over dishes just before serving, or serve separately to add to soups, baked potatoes, pasta dishes.

carrot balls

Made with the smallest baller (see page 239), these are sometimes called "carrot peas". Peel or scrape a large carrot, scoop out balls and cook for 2 minutes in boiling salted water (as a soup garnish), or glaze as fruit slices (right) with butter and sugar (to garnish meat). White turnips can be made into balls or "peas". Balled vegetables used as a garnish should be carefully arranged around a roast like beads, with contrasting shapes arranged nearby (see celery bundles).

celery bundles

Scrub celery stalks and cut into julienne strips (see page 226). Form into bundles and secure each with a small ring of seeded pepper (green, yellow or red). While meat is "resting" before carving, arrange the bundles in a collapsible vegetable steamer and steam for 8–10 minutes. Carefully lift out and place around the meat with other garnishes.

croûtes and croûtons

Croûtes are large bread shapes, croûtons are small. Croûtes are cut round as a base for steaks and médaillons; are hollowed out to hold roast quail or *oeufs brouillés* (scrambled egg). Croûtons can be made heart or triangle shaped for bordering casseroles, dips, poultry and game dishes; or cut into dice to serve with soups, to add to salads (*chapons à l'ail* is French chicory salad with garlicky croûtons) or to sprinkle over omelettes. Crumbled bread, fried in butter, is a British garnish for roast game.

Frying makes croûtes and croûtons crisp. Use a mix of equal oil and butter and heat till very hot before adding the prepared bread. Fry quickly till golden, turning once. Drain on paper towels.

Deep frying is best for croûtes hollowed out to hold food. Heat oil to 360°, add croûtes and deep fry for 1–2 minutes.

Baking is a good method for round or heart shapes. Place on cookie sheet, brush generously with melted butter and bake in a preheated 400° oven for 20–25 minutes. Hollowed-out croûtes can also be baked.

Toasting gives dry croûtes, but they should be golden, not dark brown!

Below: Beads of carrot balls and celery bundles make a good garnish for hot or cold meats

To make croûtons, stack the bread slices, cut off crusts, cut into strips, then dice. Separate bread squares from crumbs, fry in oil and butter

Round croûtes which are used as a base for steaks, poached eggs, médaillons of lamb, can be cut with a 3 inch fluted cookie cutter or glass

To make a bread "basket" for roast quail, scrambled eggs, use a thick slice of bread, remove crusts after toasting, hollow out, then deep fry

To make triangular croûtes, remove crusts, then cut into quarters or halves. The large halves can also be made into pretty heart shapes

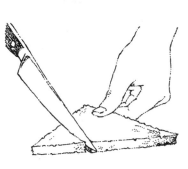

With tip of sharp knife, cut one pointed end of triangle to form a heart shape

As a final flourish, dip point of heart or triangle in oil, then chopped parsley

fruit

Orange, lemon and apple slices can be glazed to garnish meat and poultry dishes. Peel citrus fruit, but leave skin on apples (red ones are the prettiest) though remove core. Cut into $\frac{1}{4}$ inch slices and fry quickly on both sides in hot butter. Sprinkle with sugar and fry till glazed, shaking pan to prevent sticking – they should not break up. Serve very hot.

nests

Used to garnish edges of platters, usually with roast meats. Large cap mushrooms make good nests. Wipe, remove stalks, fry lightly in butter, then fill hollow with cooked peas, rice or mixed vegetables. Duchesse potatoes (see page 241) can be filled to garnish, as can peach halves, either fresh or canned. Warm through in oven, fill with rice, cream cheese, vegetables.

Frosting techniques

butter cream

Sweet and rich, with a texture that holds its shape and never sets hard, butter cream is easy to apply whether you spread or pipe it on. Use a flexible palette knife for spreading, press blade flat on to frosting, lift away sharply to form peaks. With a fork you can make wavy or straight lines, even a lattice in the frosting. The sides of cakes coated (and filled) with butter cream are often finished with chopped nuts or chocolate sprinkles. Butter cream made with $\frac{1}{2}$ cup softened unsalted butter, 2 cups confectioners sugar and 1–2 tablespoons warm water is easy to pipe and will remain in stiff stars or rosettes. If you make a mistake or change your mind about the design, the frosting can be lifted off and returned to the bag for repiping. Butter cream makes a delicious disguise for cakes that are of uneven shape for it can be used as thick as you like to cover joins, bumps or cracks, build up height. Butter cream is also good for indicating how many slices the cake is intended to be cut into. Mark the portions with a knife, then pipe between the markings so everyone gets a decorated wedge or square — in the case of mixed flavors, cut so the slice contains half of each. To pipe the topping for the cake below, mark the number of desired slices. Stand the pastry bag in a pitcher, fold back a cuff at the top, then fill with butter cream. Turn cuff up, twist bag and pipe same-size rosettes or stars in every second wedge. Change to second color and keeping the same rows, for a neat appearance pipe shapes in the remaining wedges.

Below: Different ways of decoration. From left to right: sponge cake with piped coffee and chocolate butter cream and a fence of chocolate finger cookies held in place with a brown ribbon; glacé feather icing on a cake; roses molded in fondant; jam tart with a pastry lattice; and a molded dessert with a decoration set in gelatin and piped whipped cream rosettes

cooked white frostings

These popular snow-white frostings set to a crisp finish and must be applied before they cool. Made with a syrup cooked to soft ball stage which is then gradually beaten into beaten egg whites along with any flavorings until thick, these frostings are never piped. Spread quickly with a palette knife, using the flat of the blade to form peaks. You can give a glossy flat surface, by pouring it over the cake on a wire rack. Rap rack on the table several times till frosting runs over sides.

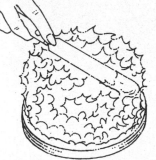

Press flat of blade on frosting then pull away to form peaks

glacé icing

This glass-like icing gives a simple smooth coat to cakes, breads and rolls. It is made by adding hot water slowly to confectioners sugar

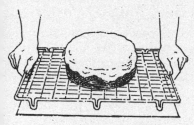

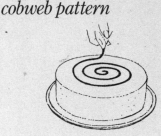

till the icing coats the knife blade thickly. It is usually applied by pouring onto the cake on a wire rack, spreading it out a little with a palette knife, then lifting the rack and tapping it sharply several times on the work surface so the icing flows over the sides. If you only want to ice the top of the cake, tie a paper collar around the cake, pour in icing and tip cake till icing covers top. Remove collar after icing sets.

Candied fruits make an attractive finish (for ginger cakes in particular) when covered with glacé icing. Arrange halved glacé cherries and chunks of preserved stem ginger on top, then pour over the icing so it covers the fruits and trickles down the sides.

The colors show through the glassy icing while the cake top is given an interesting uneven surface.

Small candies can be used as a topping under glacé icing, or over (but don't add till icing has set or the colors might run). Crystallized flowers, chocolates, halved or chopped walnuts are also good decorations on glacé icing.

Piped patterns are not done in the usual manner, but achieve much on glacé icing. Make the icing, then set aside a little and add a few drops of contrasting color. Ice the top of the cake in the usual way, and while it is still wet, put the colored icing into a pastry bag fitted with a small plain tube.

Feather icing is done by piping straight lines at regular intervals across the cake. Turn the cake so lines are horizontal and draw a skewer through the icing at intervals towards you. Now draw the skewer in the opposite direction between the first lines. All the lines going one way give a different result again.

Cobweb pattern is done by piping circles on top of the cake, then drawing the skewer from the center to the outside edge.

Lattices, words, etc are piped onto set glacé icing, using a plain tube. Flowers can be made in outline only, for glacé icing will not give you decorations with depth. Small squares of cake can be dipped in warm glacé icing (keep it runny in a bowl over hot water), then when set piped with different colored straight or lacy squiggles, or names if being made for a children's party.

feather pattern

Pipe contrasting colored icing lines on still-wet cake icing

Draw fine skewer across lines at intervals, in one direction

Draw skewer between V-shaped lines, in opposite direction

cobweb pattern

Pipe icing onto still-wet cake in spiralling line, from center

Draw skewer from center to edge of cake at regular intervals

Draw skewer from edge to center of cake between V-shaped lines

pastry bags

Paper pastry bags are easily made and are useful when you are piping several colors or patterns. They are used with metal or plastic tubes. Both waxed and parchment paper are suitable.

The right grip makes icing simple. If using a paper pastry bag, fold the corners into the center, then roll or pleat top down to force icing into tube. Grip bag in palm of hand with fingertips under rolled top, thumb over. By increasing pressure of fingers and rolling top of bag as icing is used, piping can be done with one hand and the other can steady the tube.

If using a nylon bag, twist top several times above level of icing to force it into the tube. Twist bag top around the thumb. Now turn the bag like a screw inside the hand which will force the icing out. As piping progresses, keep tightening bag into palm of hand.

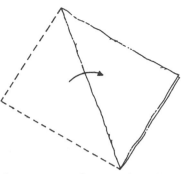

Cut a square of appropriate size from waxed or parchment paper. Fold diagonally in half

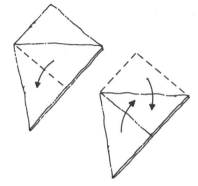

Fold one of the corners out again. Continue folding other down till it lies on top of it

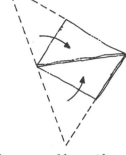

Fold corners of long side up to the 90° angle so they lie flat on top, making a square

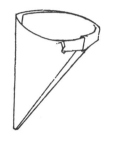

Open out to cone shape, fold corners over several times, pinch to fasten bag together

royal icing

Matt and white, with a consistency that can be piped, royal icing is the one most used for celebration cakes. A plan of operation is necessary, though. Royal icing is used on cakes which have been flat iced (with royal or soft fondant); when this is set make a paper template of the design you wish to create. Place on the cake and prick through the paper and into the icing with a pin. The overall effect is achieved by combining simple lines, stars or other shapes.

To pipe lines, the icing needs to be slightly slacker than that used for roses, stars etc. Hold bag at 45° angle about 1 inch above cake. Squeeze bag so icing appears and once the end is in the right position on the cake move the bag slowly so the line falls onto the cake following your design. A trellis or lattice uses two sets of lines at right angles to each other.

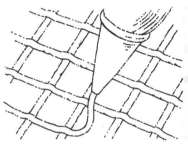

Pipe series of lines, pipe more lines across them to make lattice

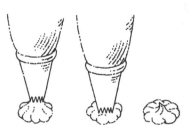

Push tube down slightly, into piped star, before pulling away

Roses and stars are piped with icing that stands in stiff peaks. Hold the bag so tube is at right angles to the surface you are piping on (top or sides). Squeeze bag till shape is right size. Pull tube away quickly to give a peaked star. Or press tube into the star, then pull away. Flowers can be piped on waxed paper and used when set.

Left: Gingerbread house — make 2 rectangles of gingerbread, about 16 × 10 inches. Cut 1 into 4 rectangles for the 2 sides and roof. Cut a 10 inch square from other cake, cut it in half. Trim off top corners of oblongs to make ends with triangular gables. Cut last strip lengthwise into 4 for chimney. Divide a batch of royal or glacé icing, color small portions red, yellow and green. Using a pastry bag with a small plain tube, pipe a line of white icing around edge of each slab, pipe outlines of windows, a door, rows of deeply scalloped lines on roof slabs and trellis on chimney. Leave to set. Thin colored icings till just-coating consistency. Using paper pastry bags, pipe colors inside outlines (see picture), to fill them. Allow to set flat before assembling. Pipe icing onto back edges of slabs. Join walls, pipe behind joins to hold in position. Pipe a thick line of icing on top edge of walls and gables. Fix roof slabs in place. Attach 1 chimney strip to the end of the house, attach others to it with icing. Leave to set

Cake and dessert techniques

chocolate

Used on cakes and cold desserts, the best chocolate for forming into shapes is the dark and glossy semisweet type which has a bitter/sweet flavor. For many decorations it has to be melted. If it becomes too hot it will become granular and lose gloss. Break it into pieces and put in a double boiler. The water must not touch the top pan or get into the chocolate (too much humidity in the air will also affect it). Stir till melted but don't boil.

Chocolate curls are made by pouring the melted chocolate onto a cold smooth surface (marble is ideal for it is heavy and won't slide about during the curling process). Spread it out with a palette knife till $\frac{1}{8}$ inch thick and leave to set. The consistency is crucial — if too hard it will flake, too soft and it will squash. Using a long-bladed knife at 45° angle and, working away from you, cut through the chocolate slowly and evenly so it rolls up. Collect any trimmings or rejected curls, melt and repeat. Store curls in an airtight container in cool place (not the refrigerator: they will become dull).

Chocolate squares and triangles are made by setting melted chocolate on waxed paper or foil. Cut into required shapes with a sharp knife, or use aspic cutters for fancy shapes. Peel paper away carefully.

Chocolate can be piped into letters, outlines of flowers, leaves, numbers or other shapes. Place melted chocolate in paper pastry bag, cut off tip and pipe onto waxed paper or foil. Pipe so they have no spindly stalks or thin lines which will snap when the paper is peeled away when they're set.

Chocolate coffee beans are bean-shaped dots with a coffee flavor and are usually bought at specialist candy stores.

Chocolate morsels can be bought or piped as above. They are mostly used to decorate butter cream cakes, and are effective when used to represent tiles on house-shaped novelty cakes.

Chocolate leaves are casts of rose leaves. Choose leaves of the appropriate size, with no blemish, wash and dry well. Spread melted chocolate over backs of leaves and leave to set, chocolate side up. When peeling off, avoid touching the chocolate. Place on cold desserts after chilling or the leaves will lose their gloss.

coatings

Royal icing or soft fondant, melted chocolate and whipped cream all make an impressive coating for the top and sides of a cake and at the same time add flavor, texture and color. Interest can be added with silver balls and whole nuts or crystallized flowers. For special occasion cakes (birthdays, weddings) paper frills and ribbon can be used as a surround but must be removed before the cake is cut.

Nuts or chocolate or colored sprinkles make a simple side decoration. Coat the sides with butter cream, sieved jam or whipped cream (don't cover the top yet). Spread nuts, grated chocolate or sprinkles on a sheet of waxed paper. Hold the cake so your palms are flat on the top and bottom of the cake. Dip an arc of the side into mixture, lift, rotate cake slightly, then press into mixture again. Repeat till side is completely covered. Place cake on plate or board and complete top. Cup cakes can be dipped into thin icing or warmed jam and rolled in nuts or shredded coconut till covered, Unbaked mixtures such as truffles are coated with chocolate sprinkles or cocoa before they set.

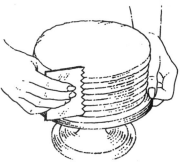

Press serrated comb firmly on side of cake, while turning

A serrated comb can be bought at specialist kitchen stores and is used to give flat iced cakes interesting texture contrast. It is easier to use if the cake is on a turntable. Hold the comb against the side and turn the cake smoothly and slowly so the teeth score even lines all the way around. You can also move the comb up and down to make undulating lines. The comb can be used on simple whipped cream or more elaborate cakes. For a two-tone effect on royal iced cakes, flat ice with colored icing, and when set spread a thin layer of white over. Use the comb as above, making straight or wavy lines around the cake - the colored icing shows through the lines.

Cookie edging makes an easy but effective surround for cakes coated in butter cream or whipped cream. The cookies can be chocolate coated, meringue or plain. Trim off one end if necessary so they are the same height as the sides plus any piping on top. Tie a ribbon around to hold them in place and fasten with a bow. Chocolate sticks or flakes can be used in the same way. Or try surrounding a cake with brandy snaps, piping a rosette of whipped cream in the open top so they resemble candles. Gelatin-set desserts can be set in a charlotte mold lined on the bottom and sides with ladyfinger cookies moistened with liqueur or syrup and placed flat side in. Chill till filling is set. Stand mold in very hot water for 30 seconds, then unmold. The cookies conceal the filling till the dessert is served.

Scrape curls from back of bar of chocolate with potato peeler

Melt chocolate in a double boiler. Spread over backs of prepared leaves, leave to set. Peel away and discard leaves

fruits and flowers

Candied decorations are made by preserving fresh flowers and leaves with a sugary coating that makes them sparkle as well as stiffening them into their characteristic shapes. Violets, primroses and rose petals are most often candied, but any small flattish flower or sprigs of fresh mint or borage (the flowers can also be sugared) are suitable. Pick unblemished flowers or leaves after any dew has dried. Put an egg white into a small bowl and beat lightly with a fork to break it up slightly. Spread sugar on a plate. Using a small paintbrush paint petals or leaves with egg white (don't dip them in; this will make them into an unrecognizable shape). Now dip the painted flowers or leaves into sugar to coat them. Shake off excess, repaint any uncoated parts and dip in sugar again. Leave to dry completely, then store in an airtight container (for up to 2 months). Arrange on large or small cakes, or desserts. Fresh fruit can be treated to this technique of candying. They don't last, however, and should be prepared and coated not long before use. Small clusters of seedless grapes or red currants make pretty finishing touches for cold desserts like soufflés or ice cream cakes. Julienne strips of citrus rind (see page 240) can be simmered in water or syrup for 5 minutes till soft, then drained and tossed in egg white and sugar for decorating syllabubs and individual cold soufflés. Glasses used for cold drinks or desserts can be frosted for a sparkling finish. Dip the dried rims into lightly forked egg white, then into a $\frac{1}{4}$ inch thick layer of sugar. Leave to dry and set before filling carefully.

Candied fruit is often chopped for use in decoration. Angelica is very useful for creating leaves and stalks to accompany flowers (see crystallized decorations, above). It is easier to cut if first soaked for a few minutes in boiling water. Cut into long strips for stalks, into diamond shapes for leaves. Candied peel, cut into strips or chopped, is best mixed with candied fruits to make a tutti-frutti decoration for ice cream or cakes. Candied fruit to be used as decorations on desserts served in individual dishes or glasses should be small and delicate. Cherries are probably the most popular glacé fruit. They are available in red, green and yellow and, whole or halved, add a splash of color to tops of cakes or desserts. They can be arranged on iced cakes (see glacé icing, page 244) or incorporated into another decoration or design. Candied pineapple makes an attractive top for rich fruit cakes in conjunction with other fruits and nuts or can be used to top swirls of cream on cold desserts.

molded decorations

Either almond paste (marzipan) or plastic icing can be shaped by hand to create decorations for all sorts of cakes. Plastic icing will eventually set hard; almond paste won't set but will gradually become crusty. Color the paste if you like — the least messy way is to place the paste in a small plastic bag with a few drops of the desired color. Close bag and knead through the plastic till paste take up color.

To make flowers, roll small pieces of paste into balls. Dip fingers and thumbs into confectioners sugar and squeeze each ball into flat pieces of the required petal shape. You now need something central to shape the petals around. With a rose you need a cone shape so the petals can curl up around it; a Christmas rose is more open so a blob will do, into which can be pressed the petal ends, and the joins covered with bought "stamens". A daisy can have its petals formed in a different way. Roll out a small strip of paste, then fringe it with a sharp knife. Now trim the strips to form petal shapes.

The strip can be rolled around a central ball of paste attached to a piece of fine wire. **Novelty shapes** (eg, Santa, Easter chicks, etc) can be made in several ways. **Dimensional** shapes should be formed from squares or rounds of paste so they can be modeled easily and colored, then assembled by pinching the pieces together. Fill in details with piped icing. **Rolled-out shapes** can be made with cutters or a template of your own design or cut from a magazine. Roll out paste or icing between sheets of waxed paper dredged with confectioners sugar. Either stamp out with cutters or cut around template with sharp knife. Place on cake with royal or glacé icing. **Molded desserts** look extra special when a decoration is set in the base so that when turned out it has a prettily patterned top. Spoon about $\frac{1}{4}$ inch syrupy fruit gelatin into mold and leave to set. Arrange small pieces of fresh or candied fruit, tiny angelica leaves on the gelatin — remember to place them upside down — then top with a little syrupy gelatin and leave to set before adding the dessert. Layered gelatins are made in much the same way and each layer has to set firm before the next is added. The mold can be tilted to one side during the setting so diagonal layers are formed. Layers of fruit set in gelatin look good as stripes in milky gelatin, and the fruit should have set gelatin above and below it so it creates a distinctive layer. **Meringue molds** are made by piping *meringue cuite* (a sort of Swiss meringue which is cooked over hot water before being baked) into basket or shell shapes.

nuts

All types of nuts can be used in different forms to decorate cakes and desserts. **Halved or whole,** they can be arranged with fruit in patterns on top of a cake after it's cooled. A glaze gives them a shine as well as keeping them in place. Sometimes nuts are placed in a cake mixture before it is cooked — Scottish Dundee cake is traditionally decorated with split almonds which become embedded in the cooked cake. **Chopped or sliced** nuts can be used to coat the sides of cakes (see page 247) as well as the top edges of a cold soufflé. To make a sticky nut topping, cream equal amounts of butter and sugar, then beat in a quarter of the combined amount in nuts chopped and toasted. Spread mix in bottom of greased cake pan, then add cake batter carefully. After baking, invert cake onto serving plate and serve nut-side up. **Slivered** nuts are often used to spike fruit. Press in firmly so they remain in place during cooking. Almonds can be arranged in peeled pears in a spiraling pattern before being poached in red wine, in apples before baking. Spikes of nuts pressed into small cakes coated with chocolate butter cream take on a "hedgehog" look.

Christmas rose

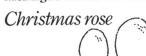

Shape curved oval petals, leave to dry. Pipe blob of royal icing on waxed paper. Insert petals at an angle, add stamens

daisy

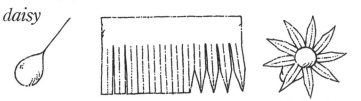

Make a yellow center on fine wire. Roll out strips of white icing, cut a fringe in each. Fold around center, curling petals

pastry

Sweet pastry dishes, especially tarts, are made in fluted pans to improve their appearance. **A lattice** of pastry strips cut from rolled-out trimmings shows off a pretty filling, and provides contrast. Use a serrated pastry wheel to cut frilly strips.

Decorated edges are usual on tarts and covered pies. First light horizontal cuts are made in the thickness of the dough to make it look thicker, neater and to establish layers (particularly in puffed pastries). The simplest method of decorating the edge is to press a fork onto the pastry rim all the way around. This also helps seal pastry to the pan and to keep lattice strips in place. To flute the edge, press a thumb onto the pastry and indent the pastry behind it with the back of a knife. Repeat till scalloped all around. A starry edge is made by making a $\frac{3}{4}$ inch cut in the pastry every $\frac{3}{4}$ inch around the top. Lift left corner of each square and fold diagonally.

Pastry trimmings can be cut into leaves to arrange on top: mark veins using tip of knife. To make roses, cut a narrow strip of pastry and roll up loosely. Arrange roses with surrounding leaves in clusters on the pie – dipping them in beaten egg first will make them secure. Brushing the whole top (avoiding the design so it doesn't become dislodged) will give the pie a good gloss after baking. Forked egg whites can also be brushed on pastry and sprinkled liberally with sugar before baking.

Right: Wispy golden strands of caramel, and flakes of almond make a pretty topping for ge)atin-set stewed apples. Spike the dessert with nuts. Make the caramel (see page 49), and while it's still hot, let it fall from a spoon held about 12 inches above the dessert, onto the top. Move the spoon from side to side, so the caramel forms a fine web, linking the almond flakes

sugar and caramel

A light dredging of fine sugar is often the only finish a simple cake needs. Jam-filled layer cakes can be sprinkled with either granulated or confectioners sugar.

To add interest to a sugared cake, arrange strips of waxed paper in a pattern on the top of the cake (or use a paper doily). Sift sugar over, then remove paper (lifting it up, not drawing it across the design).

Coarse sugar crystals are used as a decorative topping for several types of cake. Bath buns are sprinkled with coarse white sugar crystals before baking, and the same can be done to ginger cakes and baked sponge puddings. A sticky finish is given to sweet rolls by brushing them with sugar dissolved in milk when they come out of the oven.

Caramel is sugar boiled till it forms a golden syrup, and it is used in many cakes and desserts – in crème caramel as the sweet sauce revealed when the custard is un-molded, on the Hungarian Dobos torta it sets to a hard glaze on top of sponge cake. Fresh fruits such as strawberries and grapes can be dipped in caramel, then left till set. The carameled fruits won't dry out when arranged on cakes or cold desserts – but don't add them too soon before serving as the fruit's juice will eventually dissolve the caramel.

Spun sugar or caramel strands make a sparkling cobwebby topping for special desserts. Choux pastry balls are stuck together with caramel in Gâteau St Honoré, and piled with caramel to form a pyramid for Croquembouche. Both can be finished with spun strands if the caramel is warm and not set. Lift it with a knife point and stretch it across top till the fine strands form a pattern.

After the caramel stage is reached, the caramel can be carefully poured from a height onto a greased baking sheet where it will set in fine golden threads. They can be lifted onto a cream-smothered cake or cold desserts (not hot, the heat will melt the caramel). If poured onto an oiled baking sheet it will set as a thin sheet which can be shattered with a rolling pin and the fragments scattered over cold desserts and coffee cakes.

Praline made by adding un-blanched almonds and a pinch of cream of tartar (to prevent crystallization during stirring) to caramel, can be set on a greased baking sheet in same way. It is smashed to a powder or broken up to sprinkle over cakes and cold desserts, or to fold through ice cream.

A-Z food preparation

abalone Thinly slice muscle across grain, then pound to tenderize.

almonds Crack to remove shells; can be sliced, crushed, ground and chopped; toast or fry to bring out flavor.

anchovies Desalt if preferred; fresh can be filleted under running water; pat dry.

apples Peel and slice for fillings; core and score for stuffing. Grate for mincemeat and stuffings; core and cut into rings for fritters, drying.

apricots Blanch to remove skins, halve to remove pits.

asparagus Woody ends are trimmed off; stalks scraped with vegetable peeler to cook at same speed as delicate tips.

avocados Halve lengthwise to remove seed; flesh can be cut into chunks, slices, or mashed.

bacon Slices are chopped, sliced, diced; can be stretched.

bamboo shoots (fresh) Parboil 10–15 minutes before using.

bananas Peel and mash for cakes; peel and slice diagonally for frying; halve lengthwise for fritters.

barley Soak, rinse and drain.

bass Scale, clean along belly. Cut across width into steaks or leave whole. Can also be filleted.

beans (dried) Short or long soak, drain, then rinse and drain again before cooking.

beans (green and wax) Trim ends and remove tough strings if necessary. Slice diagonally or cut into pieces.

bean sprouts Rinse and drain.

beef Trim and wipe, never wash. Bone and roll rump and rib; corn rolled brisket. Trim, then grind chuck, tip sirloin or top round; trim fat from rump or blade braising steaks.

beets Scrub lightly to remove dirt. Cut off tops before cooking, and pull off roots and peel away skin after.

blackberries Pick over, rinse gently in colander, drain. Can be puréed; strain to remove seeds.

blackcurrants See currants.

blueberries Wash and remove stalks.

bok choy (Chinese cabbage) Remove wilted leaves, wash, drain.

boysenberries As blackberries. Wash just before using.

brains Wash, remove membrane (or do after blanching), then blanch for 20 minutes in boiling acidulated water.

Brazil nuts Crack to remove shells; can be chopped, ground, halved or left whole.

bread Remove crusts for croûtons, croûtes, for soaking in milk; make breadcrumbs by grating or blending, dry them by broiling, baking.

brill Large flat fish can be filleted; cut off head, fins if cooking whole. Rinse, pat dry.

broccoli Remove wilted outer leaves; trim and scrape bottom ends of stalks. Rinse, drain. Can be divided into smaller pieces (spears).

brussels sprouts Remove wilted or discolored outer leaves, score stalk end with a cross, wash, drain. If using raw, shred finely.

cabbage Cut away core and thick ribs; shred for salads, cut into wedges for boiling, steaming. To stuff whole, remove most of central core; to stuff leaves, remove ribs, blanch to soften.

capers Drain, chop or leave whole.

cardoon Strip strings from outer ribs, wash, drain. If not cooking immediately, soak in acidulated water to prevent discoloration.

carp Scale, remove head; clean along belly discarding bitter gall sac, reserving roe. Wash, drain, soak in vinegared water. Stuff or chop into steaks.

carrots Trim; scrape young carrots, peel older ones. To use raw, slice lengthwise, cut into matchsticks, or grate coarsely. Fine strips or diagonal slices can be blanched for stir-frying, dips.

cashews Raw ones should be lightly roasted or toasted before eating; chop, grind or use whole.

cauliflower Remove tough outer leaves, trim and score stalk, rinse and drain. Curds can be broken into florets or left whole; can be blanched for stir-frying, dips.

celeriac Scrub, cut into thick slices, then peel; or peel whole root and hollow out for stuffing; or grate or dice, blanch and dress, particularly with mayonnaise, for salads.

celery Trim base of bunch to loosen outer stalks and release inner heart. Leave leaves on stalks, or trim, remove strings, chop or cut into straight or diagonal slices.

cheese Hard cheese: grate for melting, slice for pizzas, dice and crumble for sauces, salads. Cottage cheese: rub through strainer for cheesecakes, dressings. Cream cheese: mash. Rinded cheese: derind for grating, slicing.

cherries Wash, dry, halve to remove pits or use cherry pitter and leave whole.

chestnuts Score from base to pointed end, blanch for 5 minutes, cool in water, then remove outer and inner skins. Chop, purée after boiling, leave whole for marrons glacés, stews.

chicken If feathered, pluck and dress; reserve giblets. Thaw frozen chicken. Truss after stuffing. Can be boned, or cut into pieces, quarters, halves.

chickpeas (garbanzo beans) Long or short soak, drain, rinse before cooking.

chicory Cut off stalk end to separate leaves. Trim. Dip leaves in water to clean, shake to remove excess water, pat dry with paper towels or leave to drain.

chili peppers Cut off tops, seed; leave whole, slice or dice; can be pounded or blended to a paste. The volatile oil can burn skin, so careful preparation is essential.

chocolate Break up to melt over hot water; can be grated, or melted chocolate can be set on a baking sheet and scraped with a knife held at 45° angle, to make curls.

chops Trim fat, scrape and trim bones; pound; cut pocket and stuff then sew or skewer.

clams Scrub, then pry open or steam or bake to open shells; cut through muscle to remove flesh, reserving clam liquor.

cocoa Blend with water to mix with liquids, or sift with other dry ingredients.

coconut Pierce "eyes" of fresh coconut to make pouring holes for coconut "milk"; hit shell with hammer to break into pieces. Flesh can be scraped from shell leaving behind brown inner rind, grate and infuse in water to make coconut milk, blend to make into a paste for curries, cocktails.

cod Fresh: scale, clean along belly, remove head, tail, cut into steaks or fillets. Dried and salted: soak overnight to reconstitute and to remove excess salt; pound.

coffee Grind whole roasted beans.

collard greens Remove discolored leaves, wash, cook in water that clings to leaves.

confectioners sugar Sift to remove lumps.

corn Trim stalk end, then husk: peel back leaves and pull off with silky strands. To remove kernels, hold ear upright and scrape downwards with the back of knife.

Cornish game hens As chicken.

cornstarch Dissolve to paste in water; sift with other dry ingredients.

crab Boil, then crack legs, claws to remove white meat, discarding cartilage.

cranberries Remove stalks, wash and drain.

crayfish (crawfish) Cook whole in their shells; cut in half lengthwise and remove green thread running length of tail.

cream Chill heavy cream before whipping; can be increased in volume by adding half the amount of light cream or quarter the amount of cold milk.

cucumbers Remove skin or leave on, scoop out seeds if being stuffed. Skin can be scored lengthwise with a fork; can be thinly sliced off. Slices or cubes can be salted and drained. Can also be cut into wedges, sticks, chunks, wafer-thin slices or dice.

currants String fresh fruit and pick over. Rinse and dry in colander. Pick over dried currants; can be plumped by soaking.

dab As flounder.

dasheen As potatoes.

dates Wash fresh dates, pat dry, halve to remove pits or use pitting gadget. Chop and pit semi-dried dates, chop dried and pressed dates. If using sugared dried chopped dates in cake mixture reduce quantity of sugar a little or proportions will be wrong.

dried legumes Long or short soak, drain, rinse before boiling. Before pressure cooking, soak for 1 hour.

duck Thaw frozen duck. Wipe over, dry, stuff with whole apple or onion. Prick skin before roasting. Can be boned as chicken; cut with poultry shears into portions to serve.

eel Cut off head and narrow tail; remove skin, cut into large pieces.

eggs Must be at room temperature to beat whites. Bowl and beater must be grease-free. Whites can be forked for glazing, Chinese batter; whole eggs are forked for scrambling, beaten lightly for breading. Egg shells are crushed for clarifying stocks, aspic.

eggplant Skin rarely removed but green stalky cap is. Can either be cut into halves, chunks or slices. Can be dégorged – that is, salted to draw out bitterness and prevent too much oil absorption. Rinse and drain before cooking.

elderberries String to remove berries, pick over, wash, drain.

escarole Wash in several changes of cold water, drain.

fennel Chop foliage and use as herb. Trim and chop bulb if using raw, trim top and base of whole bulb if steaming or braising.

field salad (corn salad) Wash, pick over, use whole as a salad vegetable or cook like spinach.

figs Blanch fresh figs to remove skins. Dried figs can be chopped or left whole, are reconstituted by soaking.

flounder Scale, cut off head to clean, wash, pat dry. Can be filleted – 2 fillets with skin or 4

skinless fillets; can be cut into strips to make goujonettes or pounded. Also called fluke or plaice.

French or Belgian endive Remove wilted outer leaves, cut out bitter core with non-carbon steel knife; blanch whole endive for baking; chop or slice for soups, salads.

frogs' legs Thaw if frozen, drain if canned.

garlic Divide whole bulb into cloves; trim and pull papery skin from cloves. Crush or chop finely, or cut into slivers.

gelatin Dissolve in boiling water. It should be syrupy for glazing, cooled and thickened for soufflés and mousses (a spoon drawn across it leaves ripples), almost set (it will stick to back of spoon) for lining molds.

gherkins Drain, can be halved, chopped, or left whole.

ginger Bruise dried ginger root to release flavor in cooking. Diagonally slice fresh ginger root, finely chop slices. Fresh is washed, dried but not usually peeled.

globe artichokes To wash, plunge upside-down in and out of cold water. Cut stem level with base and trim off tops of leaves. Drop into acidulated water to prevent discoloration. Remove hairy choke after cooking.

goose As duck. Carve to serve.

gooseberries Trim, pick over, wash, dry.

grapefruit Cut in half crosswise, remove membrane to release segments.

grapes Blanch quickly to remove skins. Halve or leave whole, seed using end of bobby pin.

grouse Hang, pluck and draw. Clean, wash and pat dry. Stuff for roasting. Can be "spatchcocked" or flattened for broiling.

guava Peel, cut into wedges or halves, remove seeds.

guinea fowl Hang, pluck and draw. Stuff and truss (as chicken); cut into portions with poultry shears.

haddock Wipe over fillets, unsmoked pieces and cutlets. Desalt smoked fish in milk.

halibut As flounder.

ham Soak country hams to remove excess saltiness. After boiling or baking remove rind – insert sharp knife between rind and fat, lift rind, cut into fat with short sharp strokes till rind comes off in one piece.

hare Hang head downwards for 7–10 days, eviscerate and skin. Divide into saddle (for roasting), use legs for pies, casseroles; cut up whole hare for jugging.

hazelnuts/filberts Crack to remove shells. To skin kernels, blanch and peel or broil and rub off. Leave whole, chop or grind.

herbs Remove stalks if fresh; chop finely or snip; tie into bouquet garni leaving string long enough to lift it out at end of cooking. Can be lightly bruised (eg, mint for drinks), or infused. Dry or freeze in water for long storage.

herrings (fresh) Scale, clean, bone whole fish; to fillet, remove head, bones, cut flesh into two fillets, skin.

hominy (dried) Reconstitute in water overnight; cook in liquid for several hours.

horseradish Peel, trim and grate just before using.

ice Crush for drinks; add cube to cream when whipping to make *crème chantilly.*

jerusalem artichokes Scrub, cut away roots and dark tips. Leave skin on and use whole, sliced; can be peeled after boiling. If peeled before boiling, place in acidulated water to prevent browning.

jicama Peel and thinly slice or cut into julienne strips. Serve raw or cook.

kale Wash, remove tough ribs and coarse stems. Break up into smaller florets or spears.

kidneys Soak beef and pork kidneys in vinegared water to remove odor. Wash veal and lamb kidneys under running water. Cut out central core and pull away outer membrane of lamb kidneys; cut out gristly core of beef and veal kidneys. Halve or chop.

kippers Can be marinated for 24 hours to soften flesh instead of cooking. Can be cut into strips, mashed or blended.

kiwifruit (Chinese gooseberry) Slice in half, scoop out flesh. Or, pare off skin and slice.

kohlrabi Trim base, cut off leaves and stalks; leave skin on young small ones, remove skins of large ones before or after boiling. Can be chopped, diced, sliced, hollowed out for stuffing.

kumquats Remove stalk ends. Wipe, halve or slice (skin is eatable).

lamb Bone loin, breast, leg and shoulder to stuff. Trim and chop shoulder for stew. Chine rib roast, divide into chops, flatten each with cleaver to make breading easier. Trim and wipe chops.

lampreys Soak in vinegared water, or marinade, to improve taste. Cut off head just below the gills, peel off skin (as eel). Slit, clean out innards, wash, cut into steaks.

leeks Cut off coarse top of leaves, roots, peel away outer layer. Place upright in jug of water for 1 hour so dirt can fall out; or slice lengthwise and wash out particles of grit between layers; or slice into rings and wash in a colander.

lemons Rind can be finely grated to obtain zest, or zest can be rubbed off with sugar cube. Rind can also be finely pared for flavoring stews, drinks. Warm in oven or hot water or roll under hand pressure on work surface before juicing.

lentils Wash, pick over. Some can be cooked without pre-soaking.

lettuce Dip leaves in and out of cold water to wash and crisp at same time. Shake to remove excess water, or dry in colander, or pat dry with paper towels. Leaves can be torn into pieces, or shredded to make a *chiffonade.* Whole lettuce can be blanched, hearts removed, then stuffed. Leaves can be blanched quickly to wrap around other foods.

lima beans Dried: long or short soak, drain, rinse before boiling. Shell fresh beans before cooking.

limes As lemons.

ling-fish As cod.

liver Wipe, remove outer membrane, veins. Soak beef, lamb and pork liver in milk for 30 minutes before cooking to remove odor. Darin, wipe dry.

lobster Pierce nerve cord of freshly caught lobster where head meets the body to sever. After boiling, remove stomach and intestinal vein and flesh (reserve coral colored roe and khaki liver for flavorings). Break off claws and antennae and crack so flesh can be removed.

loganberries Wipe, hull, pick over.

loquats Wash, dry, halve and remove pits. Can be peeled.

lychees (or litchi) Squeeze till shell cracks; peel off in bits, squeeze out pit.

macadamia nuts Crack to shell; roast whole nuts; chop and pound to paste with garlic, shallots, spices.

mackerel Clean, wash off scales under running water. Can be filleted, smoked. Backbone can be removed to cook *en colère*.

mandarins Peel, pull away net-like strands to remove pith. Divide into segments, chop or purée.

mangoes Score skin several times lengthwise, strip off. Slice flesh away from seed, cut into dice, cubes, or purée.

mangosteens Cut in half, remove rind, scoop out flesh with a spoon.

marrow bones Split with cleaver and scoop out marrow, slice or dice with knife dipped in hot water.

melon Halve, remove seeds, cut into wedges or cube or ball.

molasses Measure in spoon or cup dipped in hot water.

mulberries Dip in bowl of water, shake to dry, pick over and hull.

mullet Scale, then clean through the gills; cook whole. Mullet roe is considered a delicacy.

mushrooms Wipe over and trim stalk end. Use whole or cut into straight slices. Dried mushrooms: reconstitute in warmed water. Use whole or sliced.

mussels Soak, scrape shells, then scrub with a stiff brush. Bring to the boil in ½ inch water, cover, steam 5–10 minutes till shells open. Discard closed ones.

mustard Grind seeds, make mustard powder into a paste with cold water or vinegar.

navy beans Long or short soak. Drain and rinse before boiling.

nectarines Do not need to be peeled; wipe over, halve to remove pit; slice or chop.

octopus Remove stomach, eyes, mouth and ink sac. Wash thoroughly, pound with pestle or rolling pin to tenderize.

okra Soak in vinegared water, drain, rinse, cut off tops.

olives Brined olives should be rinsed before serving. Pit with an olive pitter, or halve and pit.

onions Blanch pearl onions for 5–10 minutes in boiling water to loosen skins, peel. Large and medium-sized onions can be peeled and cooked whole, or hollowed out for stuffings. Can also be sliced through the root into wedges, sliced into rings, diced or chopped; grated or minced.

oranges As lemons.

oysters Scrub shells under running water. Open through "eye" with oyster knife (called shucking).

palm hearts Wash, trim and tie in bundles like asparagus for steaming, or chop for salads.

papaya Cut in half and scoop out black inedible seeds. Cut into wedges and loosen flesh from skin, or remove skin and cube flesh.

parsley Rinse to remove grit, gently squeeze dry in paper towel. Cut off stalks, divide into small sprigs or finely chop.

parsnips Trim any roots. Thinly peel or scrub and cook in skins. Can be grated, straight or diagonally sliced or cut into vertical wedges.

passionfruit Cut in half and scoop out pulp.

peaches Skins of clingstone ones can be removed by blanching for 1 minute, then peeling. Halve freestone peaches to remove pit; crack to remove kernel. Flesh can be sliced, cubed.

peanuts Leave whole, or grind or chop finely.

pears Peel, halve and core. Can be cut into slices, wedges or chunks. Brush with lemon juice to prevent discoloration.

peas Press fresh pods to open, slide peas out with thumb. Dried peas: long or short soak.

pecans Crack to remove shells. Can be halved or chopped.

pepper Grind black, white, red or green peppercorns. Drain brined green or pink ones.

peppers Cut off tops to stuff, seed, blanch. Seed and cut into rings, halves or chunks. Halves can be broiled to char outer skin for easy peeling.

perch As mackerel.

persimmons Rub all over with back of knife to loosen skin, then peel. Slice into rings, cut into wedges. Sharon fruit are persimmons with eatable skins.

pheasant Hang by neck for 7–14 days. Pluck, draw. Bard, cut up.

pigeon Hang head down for 1 hour, pluck and draw, leaving in liver. Wipe, stuff to roast. Flatten to broil, cut up to braise or serve.

pike Soak overnight in salted water with extra salt packed into mouth. Wash salt off, scale and clean, wash, wipe dry. Can be stuffed and baked or braised; can be cut into steaks or filleted for frying or broiling. Pound flesh for quenelles.

pilchards As sardines.

pineapple Cut off leafy top and hollow out for stuffing; cut off rind in downward strips; or slice, cut off rind, remove central core. Flesh can be chopped, crushed.

pine nuts Remove from cone with point of knife, crack shell to remove kernels, broil or blanch to remove brown coat. Chop, pound or use whole.

pinto beans Long or short soak, drain, rinse before boiling.

pistachio nuts Break shells to remove raw kernels, blanch to remove skins. Can be left whole, halved, sliced or chopped.

plantain Bake unpeeled, or peel and slice to fry, broil, stew.

plums Wash, pat dry, halve and remove pits (can be left in if boiling for jam, then skimmed off). Can be quartered, sliced, chopped or puréed.

pomegranates Halve and scoop out seeds to eat raw or use as a flavoring. Press through sieve to remove juice from seeds.

porgy Soak in vinegared water to remove muddy flavor. Scale and clean along belly; fillet or leave whole, wash, drain, pat dry.

pork Shank end of fresh leg can be boned, stuffed. Slice tenderloin. Chine loin, leave whole or cut into chops. Trim spareribs.

potatoes New potatoes (waxy): scrub, pat dry, boil in skins; peel, soak and dry for sautéing. Can be cut into balls for shallow frying. General purpose and baking: peel, halve or quarter for boiling, stewing, roasting. Prick whole potatoes to be baked in skins, or skewer. Peel and slice for scalloping; peel and hollow out for stuffing. Dried potatoes: reconstitute with water or milk.

prairie chicken As grouse.

prawns As shrimp.

prickly or cactus pears Wear gloves to peel, cut into chunks or slices.

prunes Soak to plump. Slit to remove pits.

pumpkin Cut into wedges, scrape out fibrous center and seeds, bake. Peel, cut into chunks to braise, stew, fry.

quail Pluck, singe but do not draw. Bard or wrap to roast.

quinces Peel, core, cut into chunks, macerate. Quarter but don't peel or core for jelly — bits are strained out.

rabbit No hanging needed. Skin, eviscerate and cut up. Bard saddle with stretched bacon for roasting.

radishes Trim, wash, drain, slice or halve.

raisins Wash, drain and thoroughly dry loose fruit (not necessary with packet fruit). Plump by soaking.

rambutans Cut through middle to halve, peel and prise seed out.

raspberries Hull and pick over, dip quickly in water if necessary but don't wash. Dry on paper towels. Purée or leave whole.

red currants See currants.

red gurnard (or gurnet) Clean along belly, leave head on for baking. Can be filleted (use trimmings for stock).

red snapper As bass.

rhubarb Remove all leaves and trim stalk base. Cut into 1 inch lengths. Can be puréed.

rice Indian: soak for 1 hour before rinsing, boiling. Parboiled or pre-precooked rice: no preparation needed. Brown rice: rinse before cooking by absorption method. Wild rice: wash well in several changes of cold water.

roes Soft: wash, pat dry. Hard or smoked: remove skin, pound or blend.

rutabaga Peel thickly and slice or dice. Wash, drain.

saffron Crush strands and infuse in warm water or milk.

salmon Cut off fins, slit along belly to clean. Wash in cold running water and pat dry. Can be cut into steaks; flesh can be pounded. Very popular smoked.

salsify (oyster plant) Scrub and boil unpeeled, or peel, cut into 2 inch lengths and place in acidulated water to prevent discoloration. Drain, dry and coat with light flour paste before frying; boil in lightly acidulated water.

sardines Clean and fillet as anchovies; heads can be left on or removed for broiling, frying, baking. Canned: drain, mash or pound.

sauerkraut (fresh or in cans or jars) Rinse and drain.

sausages Fresh: blanch to remove excess fat before frying, broiling. Or prick, but only if placing in hot pan. Cooked: remove skin.

scallions Trim roots and tops of green leaves; peel off thin membrane, wash, drain.

scallops Scrub well, place round-side down in preheated 300° oven till shells open. Cut through muscle to remove flesh from shell. Flesh can be sliced across grain or used whole.

sesame seeds Roast or fry to bring out flavor; pound, grind or use whole.

shad Cut off head, scale and clean along belly. Wash, dry. If cut into steaks, remove small bones with tweezers before cooking. Shad roe is a great delicacy.

shallots As onions.

shrimp Pinch off heads and claws, and tail if not required. Peel off shells of cooked shrimp, then remove black intestinal vein that runs down center of back. Rinse and pat dry.

skate Skin, poach to remove cartilage; flake or pound.

smelts Wash, dry thoroughly.

snails Soak snails in several changes of salted, vinegared water. Rinse. Cook in salted water.

snipe No hanging needed. Cut off wings and pluck gently. Leave head on but remove eyes. Remove skin, wipe with a damp cloth. Fold legs crosswise, twist head at an angle then pass long beak through legs and into body.

snow peas Trim and string. Wash, drain and pat dry.

sole As flounder.

sorrel Cut away stalks and blemished leaves, wash under running water. Chop or shred leaves.

soybeans Wash, pick over, soak overnight, drain, rinse before boiling.

speck Dice or cut into strips.

spices Crush whole seeds or sticks lightly or grind. Fry ground spices to release flavors. Crush lightly for infusions.

spinach Remove stalks, wash and cook in water that clings to leaves. Shred or tear to eat raw.

spirits Warm in metal ladle before igniting for flambé.

sprats Fresh: clean through gills. Rinse and drain, pat dry.

squash, large summer Cut off the ends and peel completely or leave peel on. Halve, hollow out inside for stuffing, or cut into slices or chunks, remove seeds for boiling or steaming.

squash, winter Peel, scoop out seeds to stuff, or cut into chunks or wedges leaving seeds in.

squid Wash, grip head and tentacles and pull away bone and entrails. Discard head, ink sac, suckers. Stuff or cut into rings.

steak Remove any gristle, wipe and pat dry. Pound thin steaks; enclose small filets mignons with string so they keep their shape during cooking. Can be finely chopped for Steak tartare.

stockfish Pound thoroughly, reconstitute by soaking in cold water for 3–5 days, changing water twice a day.

strawberries Pick over and hull. Dip quickly in water to remove grit if necessary but don't wash. Pat dry. Purée or leave whole.

sturgeon Sold in fillets, slices or steaks. Wipe, pat dry, slit flesh of large pieces to interlard.

suet Grate or shred to use in mincemeat, pastry. Render to use for frying, roasting.

sugar Pound sugar cubes to use as decorative coarse sugar crystals.

sweetbreads As brains.

sweet potatoes Wash, dry, prick and bake in skins; or peel and slice or cut into cubes.

swiss chard Trim leaves from stalk, wash to remove grit, cook as spinach. Trim, wipe and cut stalks into lengths.

swordfish Sold in steaks; wipe and trim.

syrup, maple and corn As molasses.

tamarind Soak piece in warm water till soft, press to squeeze out juice (water is used as flavoring).

tomatillos As tomatoes. Use to make jam or sauce to serve with meat.

tomatoes Can be halved by vandyking. Blanch to remove skins. Flesh can be chopped, sliced, diced, cubed, seeded. Leave skins on if stuffing, but dégorge by salting.

tongue Boil to skin and bone.

tripe Usually bought blanched and parboiled. Cut into strips, squares.

trout To cook whole or stuff, scale and clean through belly; or slit along back, remove backbone and

clean. Can also be cut into chunks; whole trout or fillets can be smoked.

truffles Slice very thinly.

tuna Wipe bought steaks; can be marinated. Drain canned tuna, chop or flake.

turbot Clean, remove only tail fin before cooking whole. Or cut into steaks or fillet.

turkey As chicken.

turnips, white Peel, cut into slices, strips, cube or chunks. Grate very young turnips, or wash and cook whole in skin. Peel, halve and hollow out to stuff.

ugli fruit Peel, then divide into segments or slice.

vanilla Break beans into lengths, infuse, rinse, dry, store for re-use. Grind to flavor sugar.

veal Bone breast, shoulder, loin and rump. Chop shoulder meat. Pound cutlets between waxed paper sheets. Trim veal for stew. Chine loin and rib, and divide into chops. Saw shank into pieces.

venison Hang for 2–3 weeks. Bard or interlard and marinate roasts for braising, roasting.

vine leaves Blanch fresh leaves in boiling water to soften. Drain vacuum-packed and canned leaves, blanch several times to remove salt.

walnuts Crack to remove shells, blanch if necessary to peel off skin. Crush, pound, chop, halve.

water chestnuts (fresh) Peel, then slice, chop, sliver.

watercress Wash, dry, chop. Soak leaves-down in cold water to revive, crisp.

watermelon Cut into thick wedges, flick seeds out with knife tip.

whiting (or silver hake) As cod.

yams Peel, cut into chunks, slices or cubes. Small ones can be pricked and baked whole.

yeast Active dry: sprinkle over hand-hot water in which sugar has been dissolved, stir, leave till frothy. Compressed: mix with hand-hot water and use when dissolved.

Index